Governing for the Long Term
Democracy and the Politics of Investment

While political analysis has commonly focused on the distributive problem of who gets what, many of the hardest choices facing modern
societies are dilemmas of timing. If governments want to reduce public
debt, slow climate change, or shore up pension systems, they must
typically inflict immediate pain on citizens for gains that will only arrive
over the long run. In *Governing for the Long Term*, Alan M. Jacobs
investigates the conditions under which elected governments invest in
long-term social benefits at short-term social cost. Jacobs contends that,
along the path to adoption, investment-oriented policies must surmount
three distinct hurdles to future-oriented state action: a problem of electoral risk, rooted in the scarcity of voter attention; a problem of prediction, deriving from the complexity of long-term policy effects; and a
problem of institutional capacity, arising from interest groups' preferences for distributive gains over intertemporal bargains. Testing this
argument through a four-country historical analysis of pension policymaking, the book illuminates crucial differences between the causal
logics of distributive and intertemporal politics and makes a case for
bringing trade-offs over time to the center of the study of policymaking.

Alan M. Jacobs is Assistant Professor of Political Science at the University
of British Columbia. The recipient of the 2009 Mary Parker Follett Award
of the American Political Science Association and the 2005 John Heinz
Dissertation Award of the National Academy of Social Insurance, Jacobs
is the author of several articles and book chapters on comparative public
policy.

D1237215

Advance Praise for *Governing for the Long Term*

"If you care about the future, read this book. Anyone who worries about receiving a pension check when they retire, hopes for investment in education for their children or grandchildren, or is concerned about the preservation of our environment has to wonder why some elected governments impose short-term costs on their constituents to secure long-term social benefits, while others do not. Alan Jacobs advances a theoretically rich argument about the circumstances under which governments make these kinds of policy investments for the future. This book is sophisticated, innovative, and insightful. It contributes to scholarly literatures on historical institutionalism, the politics of time, and the welfare state. But it also tells us something fundamentally important about the political world we inhabit."

–Erik Bleich, Middlebury College

Governing for the Long Term

Democracy and the Politics of Investment

ALAN M. JACOBS
University of British Columbia

CAMBRIDGE
UNIVERSITY PRESS

CAMBRIDGE UNIVERSITY PRESS
Cambridge, New York, Melbourne, Madrid, Cape Town,
Singapore, São Paulo, Delhi, Tokyo, Mexico City

Cambridge University Press
32 Avenue of the Americas, New York, NY 10013-2473, USA

www.cambridge.org
Information on this title: www.cambridge.org/9780521171779

First published 2011

Printed in the United States of America

A catalog record for this publication is available from the British Library.

Library of Congress Cataloging in Publication Data
Jacobs, Alan M.
Governing for the long term: democracy and the politics of
investment / Alan M. Jacobs.
  p. cm.
ISBN 978-0-521-19585-0 (hardback)
1. Social policy. 2. Social choice. 3. Political planning. 4. Welfare economics.
5. Externalities (Economics) – Political aspects. 6. Pensions – Government
policy – Case studies. I. Title.
HN28.J29 2011
331.25′2–dc22   2010033557

ISBN 978-0-521-19585-0 Hardback
ISBN 978-0-521-17177-9 Paperback

For Ruby

Contents

Figures and Tables

Acknowledgments

Two things can be said of most scholarly books. They take a long time to write. And, even when sole-authored, they are implicitly collaborative endeavors. This book is an exemplar on both counts. In the dozen years since the project's inception, my work has benefited enormously from the insights, practical assistance, and material support of a vast number of individuals and institutions. On one level, it is a relief finally to have a bound sheaf of pages to show those who have aided and advised me along the way. And it is a delight finally to be able to name and thank them in print.

This book began life as a doctoral thesis, and the project took shape under the guidance of an exceptional committee of graduate supervisors: Peter Hall, Torben Iversen, Paul Pierson, and Theda Skocpol. In its framing of the intellectual problem, its analytical approach, and its empirical strategy, this study has profited immeasurably from their counsel – as well as from the examples of their scholarship. In their dedication to graduate training and their wisdom about the enterprise of social scientific research, these four people are models of mentorship.

To acknowledge the particular debts I owe to Peter Hall and Paul Pierson, however, I must say a bit more. As anyone who has worked with him knows, Peter Hall has an astonishing depth of commitment to the social sciences as a collegial enterprise. He is extraordinarily generous with his time and is the most thoughtful reader and critic I have ever known. He has a rare ability to place himself in your intellectual shoes, to tease out what's interesting about your arguments, and to help you unravel the analytical knots you've tied yourself into. As I can also attest, he does not shy away from remarking when he sees an argument or a project going badly astray. I will always be grateful to him for noting – upon my return from three months in the field – that my initial dissertation topic was intractable and best discarded. In countless ways, this is a better book because of Peter's input.

Of Paul Pierson I am by no means the first person to say that he got me thinking seriously about the importance of time in politics. But beyond substantive particulars, Paul's guidance has shaped my sense of the purposes of political analysis. Some of this impact can be summed up in the distinction that he drew for me between nice data and good questions. In a class my first semester of graduate school, Paul told the old joke about the drunken man who misplaces his keys one night and goes looking for them under a lamppost – not because that's where he thinks he lost them, but because that's where the light is better. Over the years to come, Paul would consistently urge me to follow the trail of important but hard problems. If I occasionally took a turn down a blind alley, I am grateful to him for encouraging me to search where the light isn't as good and for persuading me that there can be value in a less precise answer to a better question. I also thank him for assuring me that it is okay, as he memorably put it, "to care about your dependent variable."

As I undertook field research for this project, I took advantage of the excellent advice and assistance of a great many scholars who had traveled stretches of the book's empirical terrain before me. In Germany, Florian Tennstedt, Ulrike Haerendel, and Heidi Winter allowed me access to copies and transcripts of archival documents that they had collected for their project, based at the University of Kassel, documenting the foundations of the German welfare state (*Quellensammlung zur Geschichte der deutschen Sozialpolitik*). Along with Ben Hett and Christina von Hodenberg, these scholars also provided me with invaluable guidance on the use of the German Bundesarchiv. Similarly, Penny Bryden helped me chart a path through the National Archives of Canada; Jacob Hacker and Ed Berkowitz advised me on the use of the Social Security Administration History Archive and the U.S. National Archives; and John Macnicol provided tips on navigating Britain's Public Record Office. I am further indebted to Keith Banting, Giuliano Bonoli, John Myles, Martin Schludi, Steven Teles, and Kent Weaver for assistance in identifying potential interview subjects in the four countries.

As I worked my way through primary sources in the four countries, I was fortunate to have the assistance of many skilled and patient archivists and librarians. Among those who went well out of their way to help were Lillian Liu and Larry DeWitt at the Social Security Administration History Archive; Sandra Ferguson at the National Archives of Canada; Nora Cote at the library of the Canadian Labour Congress; Jill Spellman at the British Conservative Party Archive; and Paul Griffiths at the National Archive of the UK (then, the Public Record Office).

In each country to which I traveled, scholars and policy analysts from a range of disciplines took time for substantive conversations about the contours and historical development of national welfare-state politics. I wish to thank Wolfgang Ayaß, Christoph Conrad, Martin Geyer, Karl Hinrichs, Hans Günter Hockerts, Sven Jochem, Winfried Schmähl, and Manfred Schmidt in Germany; Perri 6, Phil Agulnik, Nicholas Barr, Andrew Dilnot, Howard Glennerster, Paul Johnson, and Peter Townsend in Britain; and Keith Banting, Ken Battle, Peter Hicks, Harvey Lazar, John Myles, and William Robson in Canada. These individuals corrected naïve misconceptions, brought key texts to my attention, introduced me to knowledgeable colleagues, helped fill gaps in case narratives, and proposed useful lines of explanation. I am particularly grateful, in this respect, to Phillip Manow. It was an early conversation about his innovative work on the history of German pensions that persuaded me of the fruitfulness of studying intertemporal trade-offs within this policy field.

I am greatly indebted to the scores of interview subjects in Germany, Britain, Canada, and the United States – mostly, direct participants in or close observers of recent processes of pension reform – who gave hours of their time to answer my questions. Those names not provided in the footnotes have been withheld at the subjects' request, but these individuals all know who they are. Without their willingness to help, much of this research would simply have been impossible. And I am grateful to friends and relatives around the world – Nabil Badr, Tim Lee, Kathryn Linehan, Marci Rosenthal, Oren Rosenthal, David Siu, Scott Thomas, and the Hacker and Entwistle families – who opened their homes to me as I undertook archival work and interviews in London and Washington, D.C.

As the thesis and book evolved, many colleagues offered careful feedback on chapter drafts and article-length segments of the book's argument and evidence. The final product is immeasurably better for their insights. In their efforts to "get inside" and wrestle with the project, Robert Fannion, Macartan Humphreys, Orit Kedar, J. Scott Matthews, Benjamin Nyblade, Angel O'Mahony, Benjamin Read, and Jonathan Wand went well beyond the call of collegial duty. Stephen Hanson, Philip Keefer, James Mahoney, Yves Tiberghien, Carolyn Tuohy, and Kent Weaver offered sharp and constructive comments on portions of the work presented at conferences and workshops. For thoughtful feedback on various parts of the text, I also wish to thank Gerard Alexander, Christopher Allen, Fiona Barker, Eva Bellin, Maxwell Cameron, John Gerring, Kathryn Harrison, Martin Hering, Andrew Karch, Philip Keefer, Patricia Keenan, Ted Marmor, Robert Mickey, Bruno Palier, Eric Patashnik, Naunihal Singh, Jeremy Weinstein, Martin West, and members of the American Politics Research Workshop at Harvard, the Sawyer Seminar on the Performance of Democracies at Harvard, and the Comparative and Canadian Politics Research Workshop at the University of British Columbia. The arguments in this book have additionally profited from the responses of audiences at the UCLA School of Public Policy and Social Research, the University of Oregon, McMaster University, Columbia University, the University of Iowa, the Northwestern University Workshop on Explaining Institutional Change, and the Colloquium for the Comparative Analysis of Political Systems at the Humboldt University in Berlin. A particularly perceptive comment by Matthias Orlowski at the Humboldt helped me to frame a central argument in the book.

At various stages of the project, a range of scholars allowed me to pick their brains (and, often, their bookshelves) for insights on specific policy issues, historical periods, literatures, and methodological dilemmas about which they knew more than I. Many thanks to Frank Alcock, Jim Alt, Gerald Baier, Theo Balderston, Chris Clark, William Clark, Fred Cutler, Martin Hering, Caroline Hoxby, Sheila Jasanoff, Richard Johnston, Christopher Kam, Nathaniel Keohane, Cathie Jo Martin, Robert Palacios, Paul Pennings, Hillel Soifer, Maiken Umbach,

Leeat Yariv, and Nicholas Ziegler. Equally invaluable was the advice of Peter Dauvergne, Tulia Falleti, Anna Grzymala-Busse, Eric Patashnik, Sven Steinmo, Allan Tupper, and Mark Warren as I navigated the world of book publishing. Samuel Dewey, Nicolas Dragojlovic, Frank Hangler, Steven Klein, Bruce Lyth, Beth Schwartz, Dennis Wells, and Danica Wong provided superb research assistance, and many thanks to Dianne Tiefensee for her work on the book's index.

It has been my good fortune to find myself working in a series of highly supportive institutional settings over the last decade. During visits abroad, gracious hosts supplied me with computer equipment, library access, and office space. In Germany, I owe special thanks to Thomas Cusack and David Soskice at the Wissenschaftszentrum Berlin für Sozialforschung; in Britain, to Elias Mossialos and LSE Health and Social Care; and in Canada, to Keith Banting and the School of Policy Studies at Queen's University. Back in Cambridge, Harvard's Minda de Gunzburg Center for European Studies provided an exceptionally congenial and supportive setting for writing up my results.

In going from thesis to book over the last few years, I have been surrounded by a community of smart and supportive colleagues at UBC, many of whom (mentioned individually above) engaged deeply with the project. As heads of my department, Richard Johnston and Allan Tupper have invested heavily in the careers of their junior colleagues. And I am grateful to our department's terrific administrative manager, Dory Urbano, for saving me untold hours and aggravation on a range of organizational matters. While making final revisions to the manuscript, I also had the privilege of spending a productive year in Ellen Immergut's unit at the Institut für Sozialwissenschaften and the Berlin Graduate School of the Social Sciences at the Humboldt University, a visit also facilitated by Martin Nagelschmidt and Bernd Wegener.

For funding the field research, I thank the Minda de Gunzburg Center for European Studies at Harvard, the Institute for the Study of World Politics, the German Marshall Fund of the United States, the Center for American Political Studies at Harvard, and the Canadian Embassy in the United States. Additional research and writing were generously supported by the UBC Department of Political Science, the UBC Hampton Fund, and the Social Sciences and Humanities Research Council of Canada (Standard Research Grant #410-2006-1174).

At Cambridge, I am grateful to Lew Bateman for his confidence in the manuscript, his prompt responses to countless queries, and his sage counsel throughout the publication process. It has also been a pleasure working with Anne Lovering Rounds, Emily Spangler, and Amanda Zagnoli during production. I would like to thank the Press's two anonymous reviewers for giving a long manuscript an extraordinarily careful read. Their astute suggestions have made the book's arguments substantially better and clearer.

Finally, I wish to thank a few people who began nurturing this project long before I had conceived of it. Harry Warren taught me and inspired me to read and to write. Ted Marmor, Rudolf Klein, and Graham Room introduced me to the theoretically informed study of public policy and helped me find my intellectual and professional bearings. My parents, Judy and Stanley Jacobs, and my sister, Amy Lippmann, have encouraged me and cheered me on for as long as I can remember. In recent years, I have appreciated how often they have displayed sincere interest in this book, and how rarely they have asked me when it would be finished.

My wife, Antje Ellermann, has been my closest partner: my most constructive critic, my emotional anchor, my traveling companion, my soul mate. For much more than I can express here, I thank her.

*　　　*　　　*

Permission to use the following materials from previously published articles and chapters is gratefully acknowledged:

Parts of Chapters 2, 7, and 8 draw on Alan M. Jacobs, 2008, "The Politics of When: Redistribution, Investment, and Policymaking for the Long Term," *British Journal of Political Science* 38 (2):193–220.

Parts of Chapters 2, 3, and 10 draw on Alan M. Jacobs 2009, "How Do Ideas Matter? Mental Models and Attention in German Pension Politics," *Comparative Political Studies* 42 (2), 2009:252–79.

Parts of Chapter 4 draw on Alan M. Jacobs, 2009, "Policymaking as Political Constraint: Institutional Development in the U.S. Social Security Program," in *Explaining Institutional Change: Ambiguity, Agency, and Power*, eds. James Mahoney and Kathleen Thelen, New York: Cambridge University Press, 94–131.

Part of Chapter 8 is based on Alan M. Jacobs and Steven Teles, 2007, "The Perils of Market-Making: The Case of British Pensions," in *Creating Competitive Markets: The Politics of Regulatory Reform*, eds. Marc K. Landy, Martin A. Levin, and Martin Shapiro, Washington, D.C.: Brookings Institution Press, 157–83.

PART I

PROBLEM AND THEORY

CHAPTER I

The Politics of When

Over seven decades ago, Harold Lasswell (1936) defined politics as "who gets what, when, how." Lasswell's now-classic formulation is an invitation to study political life as a fundamental process of distribution, a struggle over the production and allocation of valued goods. It is striking how much of political analysis, especially of public policymaking, has centered on conflicts over who will gain – or lose – what, and by what means. Why and through what processes, political scientists have so often inquired, do governments take actions that benefit some groups in society while disadvantaging others? The problem of policy choice has, in large part, been understood as a problem of distribution.

This massive and varied research agenda, however, has almost completely ignored a critical part of Lasswell's oft-cited definition. The matter of *when* – when the costs and benefits of public policies arrive – has been the focus of remarkably little systematic inquiry. Just as distributive choice is an unavoidable challenge of governing, politicians also routinely confront *intertemporal* dilemmas in making policy choices – trade-offs between the short-term impact and the long-run consequences of state action. Indeed, for elected governments the problem of timing may be among the thorniest of policy predicaments: while the electoral calendar forces politicians to court voters in the near term, many of the most important social problems and policy ramifications lie in the distant future. Students of the politics of public policy, however, have seldom conceptualized policymaking as a choice about timing. While we have developed an array of tools for explaining how governments distribute across groups, we have devoted little attention to illuminating how they allocate benefits and burdens between present and future.

This book brings trade-offs over time to the center of the study of public policymaking. The study seeks to understand how governments in the democratic world choose between the short run and the long run in their policy choices. In empirical terms, the book examines how elected politicians in industrialized societies have made intertemporal trade-offs in a policy sphere with massive consequences for the welfare of citizens: the field of public pensions. In both the short term and the long, governments' choices about pension policies have far-reaching social and economic effects – on the retirement incomes of the elderly, on the financial burdens borne by younger generations, on the availability of jobs, and on levels of savings and investment in the economy. Pension programs also routinely confront governments with a basic dilemma of timing: a choice between minimizing tax burdens and maximizing payouts in the short run, on the one hand, and enhancing long-run fiscal sustainability, social protection, and economic growth, on the other. Beyond its inherent importance, pension politics serves this book as a laboratory for investigating the politics of intertemporal choice. The study's core aim is to understand in general terms how elected politicians choose between maximizing social welfare today and investing for tomorrow. In particular, the book asks: *Under what conditions do democratic governments enact policies that impose costs on constituents in the short run in order to produce long-run social gains?*

In answering this question, the study seeks to illuminate how politicians manage a central challenge of democratic governance: promoting society's long-run welfare in the face of short-run political imperatives. The book also seeks to demonstrate the enormous analytical advantages of studying politics as a battle over timing as well as over distribution. When we view policymaking through a temporal lens, previously obscured features of the political world snap into focus: puzzling differences in the intertemporal choices that elected governments make, powerful effects of time on policymaking, and the profound consequences of timing for the lives of citizens.

Indeed – to take up this last point first – to those living with governments' policy choices, the timing of policy outcomes may matter just as much as their cross-sectional incidence. Today's citizens will often care as much about *when* costs and benefits will arrive as about *where* they will fall. Consider, for instance, a foundational moment in the development of the modern American welfare state: the creation of the United States' largest social program, Social Security, in 1935. As has been widely recognized, President Franklin Roosevelt and Congress's decision to establish a contributory public pension program was of enormous *distributive* significance – setting in motion a substantial reallocation of resources from America's active producers to those of retirement age, with especially important consequences for less-affluent seniors. To older Americans living in 1935, however, the construction of this massive engine of redistribution was a material nonevent. It mattered little to Depression-era seniors that the government was undertaking to insure people like them against poverty. A far more important fact was a matter of timing: although the collection of payroll taxes began in 1937, the program would closely tie individuals' benefits to their contribution records and would thus take decades to begin paying full pensions. Enacted amidst economic crisis and widespread poverty, public retirement insurance would do nothing for the needy elderly at the moment of its creation. To examine Social Security's origins in purely distributive terms would thus be to overlook what is probably the most normatively striking and intellectually perplexing feature of the program's design.

Time is also of the essence because many valued policy outcomes depend on it. There is a vast range of social goods that governments simply cannot provide without getting the timing of costs and benefits right. The very *slowness* of many social, economic, and physical processes imposes a temporal stricture on the logic of government action. Some policy goods can arrive swiftly: modern administrative states can boost subsidies to farmers or cut taxes virtually at the stroke of a pen. But no government can produce a skilled workforce quickly; the sluggish pace of human development and learning forbid it. Similarly, the slowness of large-scale economic processes places an effective speed limit on governments' efforts to undertake tasks such as promoting industrial development or paying down public debt. And physical and biological chains of cause and effect impose their own temporal constraints on states' attempts to clean the air and water, to slow climate change, or to replenish stocks of natural resources. In these spheres of activity, if governments want to produce goods widely valued by citizens, they will usually have to arrange policy consequences in a particular temporal order – starting to pay costs today for benefits that may not arrive for years or decades.

Beyond these social implications, few features of a policy can have such profound *political* consequences as the timing of its effects. As scholarship on the politics of policymaking has made clear, a policy's distribution of costs and benefits across groups will fundamentally shape the politics that surround it. At the same time, to a politician on an electoral schedule, little could be more important than *when* these losses and gains will emerge. A policy might promise to deliver large gains to important constituencies: reducing taxes on business, providing cleaner air to city residents, or expanding public transit to suburban voters. If the policy's costs must be imposed long before those benefits will arrive, however, then the politician faces a dilemma of timing just as brutal as any distributive trade-off. If she chooses to invest in valued social outcomes, the costs that she must impose today may be more salient to voters at the next election than payoffs that still lie in the temporal distance. But if she seeks solely to maximize net gains for her constituents today, she will do little to enhance – indeed, will likely diminish – their welfare over the long run.

A PUZZLE: VARIATION IN GOVERNMENTS' WILLINGNESS
TO INVEST

Most political analysts (and most citizens, for that matter) probably have a strong intuition about how the typical elected official responds to such dilemmas. Democratic politics, characterized by regular elections at short intervals, is usually thought to suffer from a bad case of policy myopia: determined to remain in office, incumbents routinely bribe shortsighted voters with immediate benefits, ignore the future consequences, and put off any sacrifice for as long as possible. While the myopic pressures of electoral politics are indeed formidable, the actual record of policymaking in the democratic world suggests a far more complicated pattern. Even a casual glance at the cross-national policy landscape suggests that democratic governments have, in a range of spheres, made widely differing intertemporal policy choices.

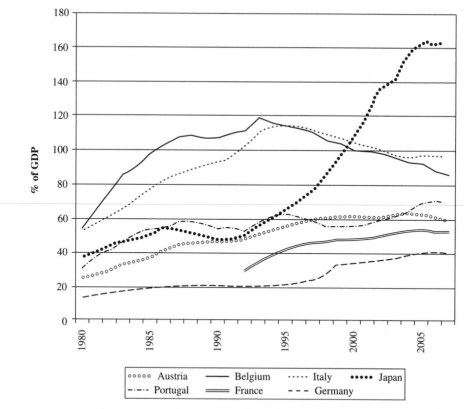

FIGURE I.I Debt-to-GDP Ratios in Seven Worst-Performing Advanced Industrialized Democracies, 1980–2007. Country performance defined as difference between debt-to-GDP ratio at beginning of period and debt-to-GDP ratio at end of period for which comparable data are available.

Consider, for instance, how governments have made broad trade-offs over time in state fiscal capacities. One measure of intertemporal choice in fiscal policy is the rate at which governments accumulate or pay down levels of public debt. Although the net macroeconomic effects of public debt are disputed, levels of debt have rather clear intertemporal implications for the public budget. All else equal, governments that reduce public debt levels are imposing higher burdens of taxation or distributing fewer programmatic goods *today* than they otherwise could, while reducing the interest payments that will have to be carved out of *future* budgets, whether through higher tax burdens or lower program expenditures tomorrow.

As Figures 1.1 and 1.2 demonstrate, advanced industrialized countries displayed impressive variation in debt trends from 1980 to 2007. At the extremes, as Japan's debt-to-GDP ratio skyrocketed from 37 percent to 164 percent, Ireland's fell from a peak of 107 percent to less than 20 percent. Statistical analyses suggest that only a fraction of such variation is the result of

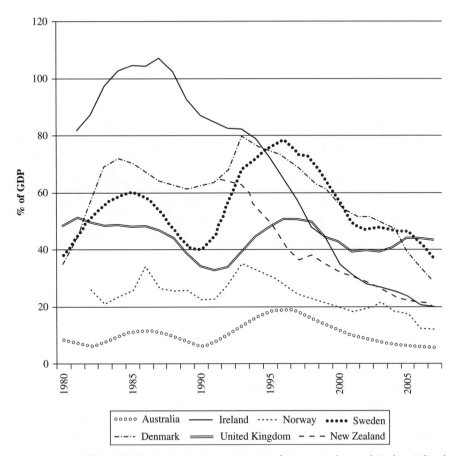

FIGURE 1.2 Debt-to-GDP Ratios in Seven Best-Performing Advanced Industrialized Democracies, 1980–2007. Country performance defined as difference between debt-to-GDP ratio at beginning of period and debt-to-GDP ratio at end of period for which comparable data are available.

economic forces beyond governments' control, such as rates of economic growth or unemployment (Franzese 2002): a great deal of the spread in debt trends represents politicians' own choices about levels of taxation and public expenditure. These divergent fiscal trajectories thus represent widely differing policy trade-offs between today's tax burdens and spending capacities and tomorrow's.

Governments have made similarly divergent intertemporal choices in specific spheres of government activity. In the field of education, for instance, spending on school construction and teachers' salaries diverts resources away from production for current consumption in order to invest in a long-term expansion of social and economic capacities. As Figure 1.3 suggests, democratic governments' willingness to invest currently available resources in the skills of future workforces varies tremendously. If we take public spending alone as a measure

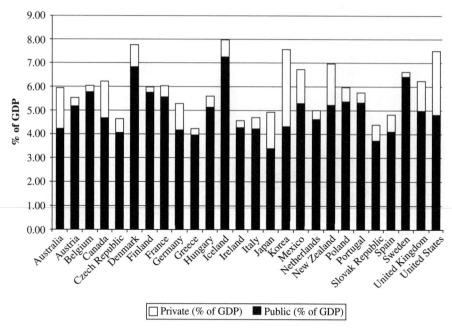

FIGURE 1.3 Expenditures on Educational Institutions in OECD Countries as a Percentage of GDP (2008)

of policy choice, OECD governments' allocation of national income to schooling at the end of the last decade ranged from Japan's 3.4 percent of GDP to Iceland's 7.2 percent; total (public plus private) and per-student spending levels vary nearly as widely. These resource allocations, moreover, are not a simple function of countries' levels of economic development, as comparisons of similar spenders – the United States and Hungary, New Zealand and Poland, Germany and Greece – make clear.

Elected governments also make widely varying intertemporal trade-offs when managing scarce natural resources. To illustrate, Figure 1.4 presents a cross-national portrait of forest conservation. At odds with common intuitions, all rich democracies effectively invested in future forest resources during the late 2000s by letting forests grow more quickly than they harvested them. The sizes of their investments, however, varied enormously. Whereas South Korea harvested less than 10 percent of its forest growth, Belgium and Switzerland consumed more than three-quarters of what they planted. In many cases, these figures also represent a dramatic shift over time. While Denmark, Finland, Belgium, Switzerland, and Portugal were depleting their timber resources in the 1970s and 1980s, all had shifted into conservation mode by the 1990s.

As we will observe in the course of the present study, a similar range of intertemporal variation marks governments' choices in the field of pensions. In developed democracies, few public policies shape society's use of resources as dramatically as do state retirement programs, which are typically the single

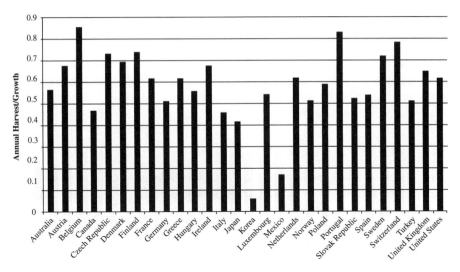

FIGURE 1.4 Intensity of Forest Use in OECD Countries (2008)

largest spending category in public budgets.[1] Over the last century, demographic change and the logic of contributory programs have typically confronted industrialized societies with a profile of rising expenditures. When such schemes were first established, the early cohorts of retirees would have accumulated short contribution records and earned a right to only modest benefits. Quite predictably, however, financial pressures have mounted over time as workers have accumulated larger entitlements to benefits and populations have grown older.

In both designing and maintaining public pension schemes, politicians have thus faced a choice about long-run financing. On the one hand, they could choose to minimize short-term costs by taxing workers and employers only as much as necessary to pay each year's pensions (pay-as-you-go, or PAYGO, financing), leaving higher future costs for tomorrow's taxpayers to bear. On the other hand, they could operate their pension programs on a "funded" basis by taxing *more* in the near term than was required to pay current benefits. A funded scheme would accumulate reserves that would help pay future pensions, thus moderating the burden on future workers and employers. As we will see, governments in Europe and North America have, over the course of the last century, made a wide range of intertemporal choices in this field. Whereas some have opted to hold down costs in the near term, running their retirement schemes on a PAYGO basis, others have chosen to impose far higher short-run contribution burdens in order to amass funds that would not be spent on tangible social benefits for many decades.

---

[1] OECD member governments spend on average 6.4 percent of GDP on old-age cash benefits compared to 5.9 percent on health – by far the two largest items of social expenditure (OECD 2007).

Looking across arenas of state activity, the governance record of advanced democracies appears to be characterized not by constant short-run maximization but by substantial intertemporal variance. While politicians have often chosen to boost constituency benefits and limit social costs in the short run, they have at other times opted to restrain spending, raise taxes, or slow economic activity today in order to enhance social welfare tomorrow. This is the basic empirical puzzle that motivates this book.

INTERTEMPORAL VERSUS DISTRIBUTIVE POLITICS

That governments respond to similar policy problems in different ways is a commonplace observation in the study of comparative politics. As political analysts, we have developed an increasingly nuanced understanding of the causal forces – institutional, organizational, economic, ideological – that give rise to this kind of variation. As this book argues, however, conventional approaches to explaining policy choices – tailored to illuminating the volume and cross-sectional distribution of policy benefits and costs – tend to be poorly suited to explaining the allocation of a policy's benefits and burdens over time.

There are three related reasons why we cannot simply import arguments about the politics of distribution into explanations of intertemporal choices. First, the very puzzles to be explained depend on the analytical question asked. Consider again the choices that governments have made within the field of public pensions. In recent years, a substantial literature has sought to explain why some governments have moved more aggressively than others to reform their pension systems over the last three decades (Hacker 2004; Swank 2002; Huber and Stephens 2001a; Bonoli 2000; Pierson 1994). This literature has framed the policy choice that governments confront as a decision about who gets – or, in this case, *loses* – what. In comparing and ranking outcomes across cases, analysts have typically focused on the scale of *benefit retrenchment* that governments have undertaken: those reforms that produce deeper benefit cuts are coded as cases of more radical change, whereas instances of benefit maintenance are considered cases of relative stasis. In the standard view, for instance, Margaret Thatcher's reforms of the British state pension system in the 1980s are considered among the most radical cases of policy change because she deeply slashed benefit levels in the flat-rate and earnings-related retirement schemes. By contrast, reforms in the United States (1977 and 1983) and Canada (1998), where benefit levels were adjusted only modestly, are considered cases of more incremental reform that kept the status quo largely intact (Béland and Myles 2005; Huber and Stephens 2001a; Pierson 1994). From a purely distributive perspective, the question is why the British government was able to impose far greater losses on pensioners than were U.S. and Canadian governments.

Viewed along the temporal axis, however, the cross-national comparison is actually *reversed*. While the British reforms reallocated future financial burdens from one social group (taxpayers) to another (pensioners), they changed little in intertemporal terms. It was, rather, U.S. and Canadian politicians who enacted the far more dramatic trade-offs over time. Largely by raising payroll taxes, these governments imposed major losses on constituents in the *near term* and, in doing so, enhanced the *long-run* financial sustainability of their pension programs. From an intertemporal perspective, the puzzle is thus a very different one: Why did the British government choose to reduce long-run tax burdens by imposing deferred losses on future pensioners, while politicians in Canada and the United States chose to impose massive short-term losses on constituents and to relieve financial pressures on workers, employers, and retirees decades hence? As this contrast of comparisons suggests, taking timing into account can fundamentally reorient the explanatory task itself.

Second, choices over time – as compared with choices across groups – often confront governments and their constituents with distinctively structured trade-offs. In particular, intertemporal choices may entail the prospect of *positive-sum* rather than merely *zero-sum* outcomes (King 1993). A central theme of much recent work on public policy (e.g., Weaver and Pal 2003; Pierson 1994; Weaver 1986) is that the politics of policy change tends to be dominated by the problem of imposing losses – of avoiding blame and circumventing opposition by those who would bear the new policy's costs. Investments in the long term will frequently inflict substantial pain on important constituencies, and their politics will be partly governed by the logics of loss imposition that have been elucidated elsewhere. Unlike a distributive trade-off between groups, however, a policy of investment may provide those who bear costs today with *a stream of even greater benefits over the long run.* For reasons to be explored later in this chapter, policy action over long periods of time is often conducive to the production of net aggregate benefits, rather than a mere reallocation of resources. The prospects for long-term investment should thus depend not only on the politics of inflicting pain but also on the politics of promising and delivering benefits – in particular, benefits that are substantially delayed in time. Put differently, the outcome of governments' intertemporal choices should hinge critically on the form that policy trade-offs take: in particular, on whether or not investment-oriented policies credibly promise influential actors long-run gains that outweigh their own short-run losses.

We thus need to *temporally disaggregate* our theories of the politics of imposing policy losses. There are critical differences between the politics of transferring resources between groups at a given point in time and the politics of imposing costs today to invest in gains tomorrow. In fact, the conditions that allow governments to make intertemporal transfers will sometimes be the mirror image of those that enable redistribution across groups. As I argue in the next chapter, it is precisely when actors face *obstacles* to expanding their resource share – i.e., when redistribution is most difficult – that they will be most willing to invest in increasing aggregate social welfare. Hence, those situations most conducive to imposing losses to redistribute will often be those least permissive of imposing losses to invest, and vice versa. In short, we cannot explain *who loses what* without also asking *who stands to gain what and when.*

Third, the politics of the long term presents actors with a distinctive problem of preference-formation. Most distributive theories of politics take actors' policy preferences as given, derivable from objective features of the choice situation and the expected material consequences of available policy options. Typically, students of distributive politics focus their analytical efforts on understanding how actors pursue these "given" preferences within institutional and organizational constraints. This common analytical strategy is tenable when we can safely assume that actors know and consider the major effects of the options before them. These core informational and cognitive assumptions, however, become harder to sustain as valued policy outcomes recede into the temporal distance. For reasons elaborated in Chapter 2, actors choosing over longer time horizons are likely to face far greater causal and informational complexity in predicting the consequences of their choices. As complexity increases and potential outcomes multiply, the analyst cannot take for granted that decision makers know or are even *paying attention* to all objectively important policy ramifications over the long run. If a rational-actor assumption is serviceable for many analyses of short-run distributive struggle, I will contend that a theory of long-term policy choice must identify the processes through which actors manage causal and informational complexity under cognitive constraints – how, in the face of this complexity, they come to understand the very trade-offs that they confront.

TIME IN CURRENT APPROACHES TO PUBLIC POLICY

Time and timing already play an important role in much political analysis. We have, in fact, recently witnessed a remarkable surge of attention by political scientists to issues of temporality. Time is central, for instance, to large and growing literatures on problems of political uncertainty, time inconsistency, and credible commitment. In models of these phenomena, the passage of time represents a key strategic challenge – a threat to existing preferences, allocations of power, and policy choices that makes bargains more difficult to achieve (McNollgast 1999; Horn 1995; North and Weingast 1989). In very different ways, historical institutionalists have developed increasingly elaborate arguments about social developments that unfold in patterned ways over time, such as those characterized by path dependence or sequencing effects (Pierson 2004; Buthe 2002). Historical institutionalist approaches to temporality reflect a concern with time, timing, and sequence as properties both of causal *processes* in the political world and of our causal *explanations*.[2]

Amongst these diverse treatments of time, however, an important gap stands out: the analysis of timing as a dimension of policy choice. Political scientists, that is, have rarely sought to systematically explain how governments allocate

---

[2] In yet another, different type of temporally sensitive analysis, Hanson (1997) examines the conceptions of time embedded in Marxist ideology and the ways in which political leaders construct social understandings of time in order to promote their political goals.

social costs and benefits over time. In this section, I seek to defend this characterization of the literature – and to more precisely define the subject matter of this book – by outlining the orientations toward time and timing that dominate the existing literatures on the politics of public policy. I focus here on the two most common approaches to the timing of policy consequences. In one category are analyses that *ignore the timing of policy effects,* both in characterizing variation in governments' choices and in explaining that variation. In the second and much smaller group are works that address the timing of policy outcomes but *consider long-term consequences to be uniformly politically irrelevant.* For the moment, I set aside works that explicitly model policymaking in intertemporal terms,[3] drawing on them in Chapter 2 as I construct a theory of intertemporal policy choice.

Policy Effects as Timeless

The most common tendency in the study of policymaking is to ignore the timing of policies' consequences. Most analyses of distributive politics do not make a meaningful conceptual or causal distinction between consequences that will occur shortly after policy enactment and those that will occur much further down the road. Rather, they compare policy options and governments' policy choices according to the volume of social costs and benefits that they generate and the distribution of those costs and benefits across groups. The variation to be explained is then defined by differences in who gets what and how under the policy arrangements being compared.

The distributive view marks a wide range of public policy and political-economy research, from analyses of how governments choose to spend to studies of how they tax, regulate, and manage the economy. The large body of research on the comparative politics of welfare-state origins and development perhaps displays most clearly this distributive orientation. For instance, Esping-Andersen's (1990) highly influential taxonomy of welfare states is tightly focused on cross-national differences in who gets what and how. The three worlds of welfare capitalism are demarcated by the degree to which they decommodify labor, detaching individuals' survival prospects from participation in the labor market, and the degree to which they reinforce or counteract the social stratification engendered by markets – all matters of how resources are allocated cross-sectionally. Critics have challenged Esping-Andersen's categorization of welfare states but have substituted alternative criteria equally focused on patterns of cross-sectional distribution, such as the gendered effects of social policies (Orloff 1993a; Skocpol 1992) or their balance between poverty alleviation and income

[3] The existing book-length study that most directly analyzes the politics of policy choice in intertemporal terms, and to which I refer at points throughout this study, is King (1993). And, though examining a different phenomenon from that treated here, I would draw attention to Teles's (2009) work on "political investment" – investments in long-run political outcomes, such as a coalition's support structure.

maintenance (Bonoli 1997). Other scholars have conceptualized welfare states primarily as mechanisms for pooling risk across individuals rather than redistribution (Baldwin 1990; Flora and Heidenheimer 1981). Yet the concept of risk pooling, like that of redistribution, refers to a transfer of resources between members of the pool (from those contributing to those experiencing the insured risk) at a given moment in time, rather than a choice about the allocation of social resources *over* time.

From a certain perspective, of course, conceptualizing welfare states in purely distributive terms seems only natural. After all, aren't social programs all about the distribution and redistribution of resources? Yet cross-sectional distribution has monopolized the attention even of students of a social policy field with a dramatic intertemporal component: public pensions. Economists and policy analysts commonly analyze pensions and savings instruments as engines of capital accumulation – as mechanisms for effecting a social tradeoff between present consumption and future production – and routinely inquire what governments can do today to enhance the long-run sustainability of their schemes in the face of aging populations (e.g., International Monetary Fund 1996; World Bank 1994). Yet, *political* analysts of the welfare state have almost always conceptualized pension policy design as a choice about the redistribution of resources from producers and taxpayers to retirees – and almost never as a choice about the allocation of resources or consumption possibilities over time (Lynch 2006; Bonoli 2000; Huber and Stephens 2001a; Pierson 1994; Orloff 1993b). To be clear, it is not that analysts have ignored *long-term* policy consequences. Scholars have indeed paid close attention to the temporally distant effects of pension policy choices, such as delayed or phased-in cuts in retirement benefits. But they have continued to characterize the key outcomes in *distributive* terms – as allocations of resources between groups at a given moment in time. To identify a delayed benefit cut is to take a distributive snapshot at a future point in time – to describe a redistribution from *tomorrow's* beneficiaries to *tomorrow's* taxpayers, rather than an allocation of consumption possibilities between today and tomorrow.

If welfare-state scholars have focused primarily on explaining how states allocate shares of the economic pie, much work in comparative political economy has additionally attended to forces that affect aggregate welfare, including the employment, inflation, and efficiency effects of trade rules (e.g., Frieden 1991; Rogowski 1987), patterns of labor organization and wage bargaining (e.g., Calmfors and Driffill 1988; Lange and Garrett 1985; Cameron 1984), tax policies (for a review, see King 1993), and broad production regimes (Hall and Soskice 2001b; Esping-Andersen 1999). Policies that affect the size of the economic pie will frequently involve intertemporal tradeoffs: consider, for instance, the investments required to enhance future skill levels, or strategies of economic reform that inflict pain in the short run but boost growth over the long run. Seldom, however, have political economists explicitly conceptualized their outcomes of interest or choices among policies and institutions in intertemporal terms.[4] There are important exceptions, considered in Chapter 2, and comparative political economists have probably been more sensitive to the temporal features of policy than scholars of most other areas of government activity. By and large, however, the field has been slow to analyze production regimes, economic institutions, and economic policies as tradeoffs in social welfare over time.

Equally surprising is the near-absence of intertemporal analysis in research on the politics of regulation. Regulatory decision making often involves the management of threats that are expected to emerge over long time horizons, such as long-range harms to human health or to the environment. Regulatory solutions, in turn, often involve clear intertemporal tradeoffs: the imposition of costly burdens now to avoid these temporally distant dangers. Yet dominant approaches to explaining regulatory choices hinge mostly on their distributive features. In seminal work on the subject, Wilson (1980) distinguished among policies according to the incidence of their costs and benefits. Patterns of political conflict, in this widely employed model, turn on whether a policy's costs and benefits are, respectively, concentrated on a relatively small segment of society or dispersed widely.

Whether or not they adopt Wilson's particular formulation, analyses of regulatory politics rarely take into systematic account the timing of policy consequences. The temporal profile of costs and benefits, for instance, plays little role in studies of environmental protection (see, e.g., Schreurs 2002; Scruggs 1999; Hoberg 1997; Harrison 1996; Macdonald 1991; Vogel 1986), even those that examine very long-term problems like climate change (Bailey and Rupp 2004; Skolnikoff 1999). Virtually across the board, intertemporal considerations are absent from analyses of regulations designed to manage long-term problems, from deforestation (e.g., Hoberg 2000; Kamieniecki 2000; Salazar and Alper 2000; Hessing and Howlett 1997; Weeks and Packard 1997) to natural disasters (e.g., Olson 2003; Twigg 2001; Platt and Rubin 1999; Burby, May 1997) to hazardous substances in the workplace (Moe 1989; Wilson 1985; Kelman 1981).[5]

The Long Term as Politically Irrelevant

A smaller strand of literature has attended more systematically to the timing of policy consequences. Significant scholarship on social and economic policy

---

[4] As just suggested, political economists have often analyzed intertemporal problems of credible commitment, but this is a different task from explaining why policies or institutions make differing tradeoffs over time in social welfare. Relatedly, studies of wage bargaining often seek to explain the varied willingness of economic actors to forego current consumption in favor of future income or investment in future productivity (e.g., Eichengreen and Iversen 1999; Przeworski and Wallerstein 1982). Typically, these studies seek to explain the intertemporal tradeoffs that economic actors make in the private sphere rather than the intertemporal tradeoffs that governments make in choosing public policies.

[5] A recent special issue of *Global Environmental Politics* includes important exceptions (Stone 2009; Sprinz 2009; Hovi, Sprinz, and Underdal 2009)

reform in the last two decades has made analytical distinctions between immediate policy outcomes and those expected to occur after a long stretch of time. And, by and large, this literature has theorized constituents' attitudes and choices as though they were driven far more by policies' near-term consequences than by their long-term effects; elected officials, in turn, are understood to face constant pressures to delay policy costs and frontload benefits.

This temporal logic, for instance, commonly informs studies of welfare-state retrenchment. Drawing on Weaver's (1986) pioneering formulation, analysts have often conceived of retrenchment as a process governed by politicians' need to avoid blame for the costs that they impose. Among the more commonly noted strategies of blame-avoidance in this literature is *delay*: the postponement of the pain of reform through, for instance, gradually phased-in benefit cuts (e.g., Weaver 2003; Huber and Stephens 2001a; Bonoli 2000; Pierson 1994). The assumption underlying this tactic is that voters, at election time, either substantially discount or do not even perceive those negative policy consequences that have not yet emerged.

Similarly, analysts of economic reform have often conceived of its consequences in intertemporal terms. The standard account of economic liberalization posits a J-shaped aggregate welfare effect over time: reform will make things worse before it makes things better. Scholars have sometimes, in turn, explained the modest scope and sluggish pace of structural reform as a product of this temporal sequence. Even if citizens will benefit from reform over the long term, they will vote at the next election based mostly on the painful sacrifices that reformist governments have imposed in the short run. Reelection-seeking incumbents thus face strong incentives to soften or delay liberalizing measures (Przeworski 1991; see also the review in Stokes 1996). Models of political business cycles similarly assume that voters – and thus governments – care only about the immediate gains from manipulation of the economy while ignoring its longer-term costs (e.g., Alesina and Roubini 1992; Nordhaus 1975).

Two important temporal propositions inform this class of explanations: (1) the timing of a policy's consequences shapes its politics, and (2) short-term outcomes dominate long-term outcomes in voters' – and, therefore, in politicians' – calculations. These claims undoubtedly capture a powerful set of forces tending to bias policymaking in democracies toward the present. At the same time, such arguments can offer only a limited account of the politics of intertemporal choice. To put the problem simply, it is difficult to explain a variable with a constant. An undifferentiated view of long-term consequences as politically irrelevant cannot account for the wide *variation* that we observe in elected governments' intertemporal policy tradeoffs. As I will argue in the next chapter, arguments suggesting constant policy myopia take too narrow a view of the temporal character of voter reasoning. It is, moreover, a significant mistake to assume that governments' policy choices are driven solely by the preferences of the mass electorate. Under certain competitive or informational conditions, politicians can enjoy substantial room for maneuver – a band of intertemporal choice within which they can safely act on motives other than winning votes.

A systematic inquiry into the politics of intertemporal policy choice needs to treat the political relevance of the long term as a *variable* rather than a constant. Instead of treating distant consequences as uniformly immaterial, a framework for explaining diverse intertemporal outcomes needs to ask *under what conditions* influential political actors are willing to engage in *tradeoffs* over time, paying short-term costs to achieve greater long-term benefits. In answering this question, we will need to consider particular features of the long run that shape its politics – asking what, from the perspective of politicians and their constituents, makes long-term different from short-term policy consequences.

THE OUTCOME OF INTEREST: POLICY INVESTMENT

The central question motivating this book is under what conditions elected governments will impose short-term costs on society in order to invest in long-term social benefits. Before proceeding to answer this question, we need to carefully define the outcome of interest: a particular intertemporal policy choice that I term a *policy investment*. I define a policy investment as a policy choice with two key structural features: (1) the *extraction of resources in the short term* and (2) the dedication of those resources to *a mechanism of intertemporal transfer*:

1. **Short-term aggregate resource extraction:** A policy investment imposes a cost in the short term by restricting the current aggregate consumption opportunities of a society. This short-run cost can take the form of the direct extraction of resources from individuals or organizations (e.g., an increase in taxes) or of a restriction of their consumption of a resource. For instance, a government might levy higher pension contribution rates on workers and employers today than are required to pay out current annual benefits. Similarly, in the field of forestry, a government might impose a short-term cost on logging companies and consumers of lumber by restricting current rates of harvest.

2. **A mechanism of intertemporal transfer toward the future:** Those resources extracted from society in the short run must be directed to (or subject to) an identifiable mechanism for increasing long-term consumption possibilities. There are three primary forms of intertemporal transfer toward the future: accumulation, the creation of capital goods, and the production of slowly emerging consumption goods. While these mechanisms are defined by their capacity to transfer consumption possibilities from present to future, each also represents an opportunity to generate a net long-term social enhancement – to convert a given amount of current welfare into a *greater* amount of future welfare.

   a. *Accumulation.* Setting aside the extracted resources for future consumption represents the simplest and most direct form of intertemporal transfer. Accumulation processes typically apply to goods that are scarce and expendable but that can be feasibly preserved over time, such as many natural resources. For instance, a tax or regulation that reduces the use of oil today will preserve this finite resource for future consumption. Logically equivalent to the accumulation of such goods is the *slowed* accumulation or reduction of a durable social "bad" – a good with a negative value.

Stockpiling a resource over time can enhance long-term social welfare if it helps to *smooth consumption* of that resource over time. Accumulation will typically smooth consumption whenever the flow or availability of that resource is expected to be lower in the future than in the present. Smoothing consumption, in turn, enhances social utility as long as the marginal returns to the resource are diminishing – that is, as long as an increment of the resource is worth more in welfare terms, the less of it one has. Diminishing marginal returns (or utilities) are a common microeconomic assumption and are likely to apply to a wide range of physical and natural resources.

b. *Creation of capital goods.* In a process of accumulation, a given good is saved over time in its original form. Alternatively, resources extracted from current consumption may be employed in the creation of some *other* good with long-term value. One possibility is the use of current resources to create *capital goods* – i.e., durable inputs into the production of other valued goods. Capital goods may include physical equipment and infrastructure, human resources (e.g., skills), knowledge, social structures and relationships, or environmental conditions that enable productive activities. The creation of capital typically requires a short-term shift in resources away from producing goods for current consumption. Meanwhile, the creation of capital usually takes time: consider the years required to complete a transit system or to educate a workforce. Since capital is durable, moreover, its payoffs typically flow over a period of time as a stream of enhancements in productivity, rather than a single instantaneous payoff.

Capital creation can enhance future consumption possibilities by raising productivity, allowing societies to produce more of a valued good with a given increment of labor or material. For example, financial resources extracted from taxpayers may be used to finance the construction of physical infrastructure, such as roads and bridges, that will make future economic and social activity possible. Taxes collected by government may be spent on education, thus generating forms of human capital that in future will yield more productive social and economic activity. In the field of pensions, excess revenues collected from workers at one point in time can be accumulated and invested in a portfolio of stocks and bonds. The investment of this fund, in effect, provides a new source of financing for the capital-creation activities of private firms (which commonly sell equity or issue debt to invest in physical or human capital or research-and-development) or public agencies (which frequently borrow to build infrastructure, such as schools and roads). Capital creation will generate a *net* improvement in social welfare, relative to pure consumption, as long as the consumption cost of an increment of capital is lower than the long-run value of the marginal enhancement in productivity that it generates.

As with accumulation, there is also an equivalent, inverse method of intertemporal transfer toward the future: slowing or stopping processes that *destroy* capital. A policy that directs current resources to lead-abatement in paint and pipes, for instance, may reduce the future losses to human capital resulting from developmental harms to children.

c. *Production of slowly emerging consumption goods.* Beyond the creation of productive capital, state action may also effect an intertemporal transfer by converting current resources into certain kinds of consumption goods. We can consider consumption goods, in the broadest sense, to be any material good (e.g., food, television sets), service (e.g., cleaning, medical care), or nonmaterial condition (e.g., personal health, the beauty of a natural environment) that directly generates welfare for members of society, as opposed to serving merely as an input into a process of production. Many goods with a direct consumption value are generated via intertemporal transfer *because of the slow-moving nature of the causal processes that generate them.*

On the one hand, policies may be designed to promote *positive* slow-moving processes. A classic instance is the biological process through which living natural resources reproduce themselves. If they are conserved rather than consumed, fish will multiply and timber will grow, generating a larger stock of resources for future consumption. Since this process of compound growth takes time to unfold, it represents a socially profitable tradeoff that can *only* be obtained intertemporally.

Alternatively, public policies can be designed to intervene early in the slow-moving processes that generate social "bads," such as illness or crime. Thus, for instance, costly action taken today to minimize exposure to a known carcinogen, like asbestos, will yield improved health only decades from now because of the slow pace of the process that turns exposure into illness (Magnani et al. 2008). Early education and family support policies directed at underprivileged children have been found to reduce rates of criminality; but the pace of children's cognitive and social development means that the costs of these interventions must be paid long before the gains will emerge (Yoshikawa 1994). Similarly, given the slow-moving effects of greenhouse-gas emissions on the climate, environmental benefits of a carbon tax will take decades to emerge (Nicholls and Lowe 2004). Early intervention in negative slow-moving processes will tend to trade short-run cost for greater long-run benefit whenever those processes have a structure that makes them easier or less costly to manipulate *further back* in the causal chain. Public health measures, for instance, are likely to have positive social returns whenever it is less costly or more effective to *prevent* illness than to treat it after it has emerged.

My definition of policy investment – as a policy that combines short-term resource-extraction with a mechanism of intertemporal transfer – allows us observationally to distinguish a policy investment from alternative policy trade-offs that governments might make. We can consider these alternatives as lying within a two-dimensional space, as depicted in Figure 1.5. In the figure, the status quo pattern of resource allocation – defined as the expected distribution of resources both across groups and over time under current policy – lies at the origin, and points off of the origin represent policy alternatives that would change that pattern of allocation. Policies above or below the x-axis shift aggregate consumption possibilities from present to future or from future to present, respectively; policies on either side of the y-axis change group shares of those aggregate resources. In this figure, Option 1 – as with any point lying directly along the y-axis and above the origin – represents a pure policy investment: an intertemporal tradeoff in favor of the future that does not disturb the current cross-sectional balance of resources across groups.

Option 2, in contrast, represents the intertemporal inverse of investment: a policy of long-term *depletion,* or disinvestment. Rather than raising taxes to pay down public debt, a government might borrow more heavily in order to reduce current taxes; instead of restricting fishing quotas to enable marine populations to rebound, policymakers might relax current rules and allow the seas to be plundered. Policies of depletion *add* resources to current consumption and, in doing so, withdraw them from processes that would otherwise be expected to generate future welfare.

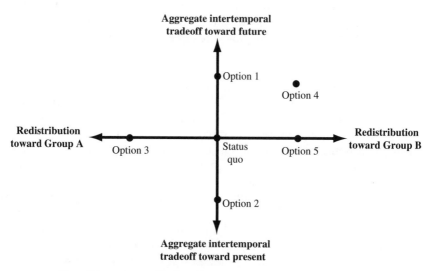

FIGURE 1.5 Two Dimensions of Policy Choice

Meanwhile, options directly on the right and left segments of the x-axis are policies of pure *cross-sectional redistribution.* A purely redistributive policy change might, like a policy investment, extract resources from some segment of society in the short run. But it would then, more or less simultaneously, make those same resources available to another segment of society for current consumption. Option 3, for instance, might be a decision to scale back social welfare benefits and use the savings to reduce tax rates. There would be no *aggregate* extraction of resources from current consumption and no direction of resources toward a mechanism of production of future social benefits. Purely redistributive policies are, in the aggregate, intertemporally neutral.

Finally, many policies will effect *both* an intertemporal *and* a cross-sectional shift in resources. Whereas the pure options lie directly on the two axes, the spaces within the four quadrants contain intertemporal and redistributive policy mixes. Option 4, for example, would both enhance aggregate future consumption possibilities and shift group shares of those aggregate resources in favor of Group B. An increase in top income tax rates to pay for the construction of social housing for the poor would yield this particular intertemporal-redistributive profile.

The book's theoretical framework and its empirical analyses pay close attention to the ways in which these two main dimensions of policy decision interact. As I will argue, in fact, the two axes of choice are not independent of one another: politicians often face a choice between redistributive and intertemporal responses to long-run policy problems. While the politics of cross-sectional distribution plays an important role in the analysis, however, the study's primary *object of explanation* is the intertemporal character of policies. To place the book's aims within the policy space in Figure 1.5: it seeks to identify the conditions under which elected governments will choose policies in the top half of the space (policy investments) rather than policies on or below the x-axis (policies of pure redistribution or depletion).

A number of further conceptual distinctions bear emphasis. First, I intentionally define the outcome of interest in terms of *policy structure,* rather than *policy outcomes* or *policymakers' motives.* Defining a policy investment in terms of its outcomes would create serious analytical problems because of the difficulty of observing an investment's long-term consequences. As I will argue, a common feature of investment-oriented policies – central, in fact, to their politics – is that their future payoffs are often not known with certainty in advance. For most policy investments, we can describe a logic through which their mechanisms of intertemporal transfer could *potentially* generate net long-term enhancements in social welfare. But all policy investments also carry a risk of failure – a risk that their transfer mechanisms will break down and that their future payoffs will not emerge. Even in hindsight, it will often be difficult for analysts to reliably attribute a given set of social conditions to the policies that generated them, especially if the two are separated by a substantial stretch of time.

This book's definition thus seeks to identify the intertemporal profile of a policy choice independently of its consequences (whether its true consequences or those inferred by the analyst). We are interested in *structural* features of a policy that observationally distinguish policies of investment from policies of depletion or of mere redistribution. An important implication of this definition is that a policy investment is not necessarily a state activity that *in actual fact* makes society better off over the long run (consider the tragic outcome of China's investment in a Great Leap Forward). Rather than this ultimate, hard-to-observe consequence, what constitutes a policy investment is an observable policy structure: the imposition of aggregate short-term social costs and the dedication of extracted resources to an identifiable mechanism of intertemporal transfer.

Similarly, this definition sets a policy's intertemporal structure apart from the *motives, intentions,* or *beliefs* of those who have chosen it. This separation avoids confusing explanation with explanandum. In accounting for a government's decision to invest, we do not want to *assume* that such a choice is motivated by any particular set of goals or beliefs. Instead, we want to allow a claim about decision-makers' intentions to be part of the theory or explanation being tested.

The analysis to come also rests on a related distinction between the *intertemporal structure* of a policy and the *time horizons* of those who enact it. An actor's time horizon is the length of time over which she considers the potential consequences of her choices. Policymakers may choose myopically, weighing only the immediate effects of the options before them, or they may act with foresight, seeking to shape outcomes years or decades hence. These differences in actors' time horizons, however, must not be conflated with the intertemporal structure of their choices.

A key reason is that policymakers may act with foresight *without* investing. Consider a long-run social development that is expected to harm a specific sector of society in coming decades. Government ministers might choose to respond to this problem not by investing in a reduction in the overall, long-term impact of the problem but by *redistributing* the future costs of the problem to another sector of society. Pension reformers, for instance, may respond to projected long-run cost increases resulting from an aging population by scaling back future benefit levels. In doing so, they are not reducing the aggregate costs of demographic change but shifting its impact from future taxpayers to future retirees: a purely redistributive move that nonetheless reflects substantial foresight and an effort to shape temporally distant social conditions. Policy investment, in other words, is just one option available to governments seeking to generate long-run outcomes. But it is a policy strategy with a distinct intertemporal structure from other types of long-term state action – and, as we shall see, with distinct political implications.

SUMMARY AND PLAN OF THE BOOK

The remainder of the book proceeds as follows. In Chapter 2, I propose a theoretical framework for explaining elected governments' intertemporal policy choices. The framework's organizing principle is that governments wishing to invest in the long term face three potential obstacles. Each of these three hurdles, in turn, implies a *necessary condition* for investment. Perhaps most obvious is the threat of electoral punishment for imposing short-term costs on voters in exchange for temporally distant benefits. I propose, first, that governments will only invest to the extent that it is electorally safe to do so. Yet intertemporal policy choice is only partly an electoral dilemma. An equally profound challenge is that of uncertainty: long-term policy consequences typically depend on highly complex causal processes that can be exceedingly difficult for decision makers to forecast. Even where they enjoy electoral room for maneuver, policymakers will only want to impose the costs of investment on constituents if the policy appears relatively certain to deliver positive long-run social returns. Third, governments that believe policy investment to be electorally safe and socially beneficial must have the institutional capacity to enact their preferred policy into law. A key challenge to this capacity is potential resistance from those groups – above all, *organized* groups – that would pay the costs of investment. In short, expected social returns, institutional capacity, and electoral safety represent the motive, means, and opportunity that make policy investment possible.

Having identified these necessary conditions in general terms, Chapter 2 then asks what observable causal factors should generate or inhibit their emergence. While the theorization yields a diverse set of causal variables, a common logic – a logic of *choice-definition* – runs through the analysis. I contend that the three conditions depend heavily on the policy preferences of three classes of powerful political actor: politicians (expected social returns), organized interests (institutional capacity), and voters (electoral safety). To each of these actors, I argue, there will be something inherently appealing about the intertemporal proposition that policy investment entails: converting some quantity of present welfare into a greater quantity of future welfare. The central problem of governance for the long term, I contend, is that *political actors do not always confront choices about policy investment structured in these terms*. The problem of choice-definition has both a cognitive and a strategic component. First, the sheer complexity of long-run causal processes, combined with the limitations of human cognition, mean that there are always *multiple* potential ways for a choice about investment to be defined. Second, political actors have strong incentives to seek redistributive *rather* than intertemporal trade-offs: to reallocate burdens and benefits cross-sectionally in their favor *instead* of making costly investments in long-term policy solutions.

The overarching claim of Chapter 2 – and of the book as a whole – is that the prospects for investment greatly depend on *whether influential political actors confront the choice as an unavoidable tradeoff between short-term loss and greater long-term gain*: on the extent, that is, to which actors *perceive* such an intertemporal dilemma and are *constrained* in their strategic efforts to escape it. In unpacking each of the three necessary conditions, Chapter 2 thus seeks to identify the variables and processes that exert an important structuring effect – on both a cognitive and strategic level – on voters', politicians', and organized interests' choices over the long run. Although politics is replete with choice-structuring forces, I lay emphasis on three: the varying salience of policy information; the simplifying effect of ideas; and the menu-shaping effects of political institutions. Chapter 2, in other words, hypothesizes the informational and ideational circumstances under which influential actors are most likely to *understand* policy investment as a profitable intertemporal exchange, and on the institutional conditions under which they are *compelled* to address policy choices in intertemporal terms.

The succeeding eight chapters then test this framework empirically by examining how elected governments in different national contexts and different time periods have responded to similar intertemporal dilemmas. To maximize parallelism in the structure of the policy problem, I have held constant across the cases the basic choice that governments confront: how to finance a contributory pension program. The policy field of contributory pensions offers a number of advantages as an object of investigation. First, choices made in this policy arena are of undeniable social importance. As pensions represent the largest item of public expenditure in most advanced democracies, choices about their design represent one of the chief mechanisms at governments' disposal for shaping the flow of resources within the domestic economy.

Second, pension policy is a field in which the option of policy investment can be crisply operationalized. As discussed earlier in this chapter, policymakers face a choice about how to manage the costs of state retirement schemes over time. On the one hand, they can finance their programs on a PAYGO basis, taking in each year only what they need to spend on annual benefits. At any given moment, PAYGO financing simply redistributes resources between groups, from current producers to current retirees. Where pension outlays are expected to rise over time – for instance, because of population aging – PAYGO financing is cheaper in the short run but subject to a rising contribution burden as expenditures mount. Alternatively, governments can choose a policy investment in funding. In a funded plan, contribution rates are set higher than needed to pay current benefits, thus accumulating surpluses that are invested in interest-bearing assets.[6]

Depending on its design, funding can activate two distinct mechanisms of intertemporal transfer. The most straightforward is accumulation: setting aside a portion of today's revenues allows future contribution burdens to rise more slowly than they would under PAYGO. Somewhat more indirectly, funding may also set in motion processes of capital creation: all else equal, the accumulation and investment of a pension fund in interest-bearing assets (e.g., bonds or stocks) raises the volume of national savings, enlarging the pool of capital available for private or public investments that can potentially boost future levels of economic productivity. These long-term payoffs are not a sure thing; as chapters to come will demonstrate, critics of funding have often argued that its purported benefits

---

[6] Note that governments can either make this investment in a public program or can require and/or subsidize contributions to private retirement vehicles financed on a funded basis.

TABLE 1.1 *Cases and Outcomes*

Case	Degree of policy investment in pension financing
Pension program creation	
Germany (1889)	High
Britain (1925)	None
United States (1935)	High
Canada (1965)	Moderate
Pension program reform	
United States (1977)	High
United States (1983)	High
Britain (1986)	Low
Canada (1998)	High
Germany (1989)	None
Germany (2001)	Low

are illusory. Whether it succeeds or fails, however, funding is a financing method with an observably distinct intertemporal structure from PAYGO financing: it involves the extraction of resources from constituents in the near term and a channeling of those resources toward financial and economic processes that will yield most of their social benefits only over the long run.

The empirical chapters analyze the intertemporal financing choices made by governments in four countries: Germany, Britain, the United States, and Canada. Each was an electoral democracy during the period under analysis (with the partial and illuminating exception of Wilhelmine Germany),[7] and each has established a contributory public pension scheme at some point over the last 120 years. Thus, elected officials in all four jurisdictions have at multiple points in time confronted similar intertemporal dilemmas of pension financing. Across these jurisdictions and over time within them, politicians have also made widely differing choices about whether to enact a policy investment in the financing of their state pension programs. As summarized in Table 1.1, these choices range from the adoption of full actuarial funding (a high degree of policy investment) to the financing of benefits on a strict PAYGO basis (no policy investment), providing plentiful variance in outcomes to be explained. Chapters 3 through 6 examine each government's choice about whether to build a policy investment into the initial design of its contributory public pension system. These four chapters ask: why did Germany (in 1889) and the United States (1935) create massive policy investments in its new retirement schemes,

---

[7] As will become clear in Chapter 2, Germany in 1889 will be an analytically useful case for testing implications of the theory precisely because of its unelected executive alongside an elected but relatively weak lower house of parliament.

while Canada (1965) adopted a modest investment and Britain (1925) rejected investment entirely?

Chapters 7 through 10 turn to periods of reform within the last 30 years, when each country considered reworking its pension system in the face of oncoming demographic change. These chapters seek to explain wide variation in governments' decisions about whether to invest in long-run fiscal sustainability through a transition to funded financing, whether within the public program or in private retirement-savings vehicles. Why did Canada (1998) and the United States (1977 and 1983) respond with massive new policy investments in their public pension programs, while Britain (1986) and Germany (1989 and 2001) made modest investments in private funded pensions but relied mostly on redistributive solutions that would reduce future tax burdens by cutting the benefit entitlements of tomorrow's pensioners?

In concluding the analysis, Chapter 11 summarizes the key findings from the case studies in light of the book's theoretical predictions. The chapter then draws out a set of larger implications of the study's findings for the analysis of both intertemporal politics and the politics of public policy more broadly. In considering these general insights, the chapter also speculates about how the politics of intertemporal choice will vary across policy fields. How might the political dynamics shaping investment in pensions examined in this book's empirical chapters differ from those shaping investment in education, environmental protection, public infrastructure, or protection against natural hazards?

The Strategy of Evidence and Inference

The book seeks to test the theoretical framework presented in Chapter 2 through two distinct strategies of causal inference. On one level, I analyze the cases *comparatively*, asking whether explanatory factors and outcomes are correlated across episodes in ways consistent with the theory (Skocpol and Somers 1980; Przeworski and Teune 1970; Mill 1868). Since the theory is one of necessary conditions, it implies that all of the conditions hypothesized to be necessary should have been *present* in those cases in which policy investment occurred. It further implies that policy investment should have *failed* to occur in any case in which any of its causal requirements was absent (Goertz and Starr 2003). One purpose of the empirical chapters, therefore, is to present evidence relevant to these predicted associations: to characterize the policy choice in each case and to investigate the degree to which the hypothesized necessary conditions were present.

At the same time, the careful analysis of causal processes *within* each of the ten cases provides an equally critical test of the theory. As qualitative methodologists have emphasized in recent years, a correlation between an independent and a dependent variable is only one potential indicator of a causal relationship between them (George and Bennett 2005; Collier, Brady, and Seawright 2004; Hall 2003). A clearly articulated causal theory also implies a set of specific causal processes for which we can look – observable features of a mediating mechanism that, according to the theory, turns cause into effect. The second aim of the case chapters is to examine whether the mechanisms and causal sequences playing out *within* each case are consistent with the proposed theory.

The theoretical claims forwarded in Chapter 2 have implications for a wide range of observable features of the policymaking and political processes from which intertemporal choices emerge. The hypotheses have implications, for instance, for the arguments and lines of reasoning that participants marshal in deliberative and decision-making settings; the models and metaphors they employ in reasoning about policy choices; the kinds of information upon which they draw; the presence or absence of actors within particular bargaining or deliberative settings; the power resources and institutional opportunities available to these actors; and the sequences in which events unfold. Each empirical chapter seeks evidence of these theoretically relevant elements of the processes from which policy choice emerged, and assesses whether these obser-vations are consistent with the causal logic advanced in Chapter 2.

In conducting this process analysis, the study draws on a wide range of primary and secondary sources. I focus especially on sources that illuminate the considerations, information, and lines of reasoning that shaped influential actors' beliefs, policy preferences, and choices. The analysis of decision making at moments of program creation, in Chapters 3 through 6, thus draws heavily on archival records of deliberative processes within governments, of deliber-ations within interest groups, and of consultations between interest-group leaders and government officials. To a large extent, the evidence is derived from documents that record the considerations that actors raised in *private* settings, enhancing the likelihood of capturing sincere reasoning prior to policy choice, rather than rhetoric crafted for public consumption and the *post hoc* legitimation of decisions. These documents include memoranda among minis-ters and senior civil servants, correspondence between government officials and outside groups, minutes of meetings among state actors or between state actors and interest-group leaders, and reports produced for internal consump-tion by bureaucratic actors. For the more recent episodes of reform, archival documents had for the most part not yet been made publicly accessible at the time of research. Thus, in Chapters 7 through 10, I draw substantially on interviews with direct participants in and close observers of the policymaking processes for accounts of the decision-making episode. My interview subjects in the four countries include senior civil servants (current and former), employer and trade union representatives, financial sector representatives, political party officials, and country pension experts. The study also makes use of publicly available primary sources, including newspaper reports, mem-oirs, and survey data contemporaneous with the decision-making episodes under examination. Finally, across all of the cases, I draw on secondary accounts both of specific decision-making episodes and of the background institutional, political, economic, and ideational conditions under which those decisions were made.

CHAPTER 2

Theorizing Intertemporal Policy Choice

One common view of democratic politics suggests both a clear prediction of policy myopia and a clear explanation of it. Office-seeking politicians, in this view, must regularly appeal to short-sighted voters and thus face strong incentives to mortgage the future for near-term benefits and to leave long-term problems to their successors. Indeed, a bias toward the present seems built into the temporal rhythm of democracy, an unhappy side effect of the frequent and competitive elections that lie at the core of popular rule.

At the same time, elected governments sometimes *do* choose to invest in the world beyond the next election. Politicians in advanced democracies at times enact costly regulations to mitigate long-term environmental harm, raise taxes to shrink budget deficits and debt, and take steps to limit the extraction of natural resources. Common approaches to the politics of public policy have a harder time explaining this fact – why elected officials would ever impose short-term costs on constituents for distant gain. More precisely, existing theories are not well suited to explaining *variation* in governments' intertemporal policy choices: why they sometimes maximize near-term benefits but at other times impose short-run pain for long-run gain.

The aim of this chapter is to develop a set of theoretical insights that can help us explain variation in elected governments' intertemporal policy choices. What factors, we will ask, affect the likelihood that an elected government will make a policy investment? The framework that I develop here is built around the chief political obstacles to enacting future-oriented intertemporal trade-offs in a democracy. As I will argue, electoral myopia represents one – but only one – impediment to the adoption of policy investment. In more general terms, the problem of policy investment is that it requires imposing definite and short-term losses on constituents – including, frequently, well-organized constituencies – in exchange for gains that, by virtue of their temporal distance, are often much less certain and much less salient. This troublesome trade-off presents governments not only with serious *electoral* risks but also with major *informational* challenges and *institutional* hurdles. Policy investment may indeed be punished by shortsighted voters at the polls; yet it may also be rejected by politicians who are uncertain about its long-term benefits; or it may be fought at key institutional decision points by well-organized groups who would have to pay its short-term costs.

Based on the identification of these obstacles, the chapter advances a theory of *necessary conditions* for the adoption of policy investment in a democracy. I hypothesize that the emergence of policy investment depends on the presence of the following three conditions:

1. **Electoral safety:** Elected officials must face a relatively low risk of losing office as a consequence of imposing investment's short-term costs on voters.
2. **Expected long-term social returns:** Influential elites must believe that policy investment will deliver long-run social benefits that exceed its costs.
3. **Institutional capacity:** Political institutions must lend proponents within the state the capacity to enact policy investment.

Having identified these prerequisites in general terms, the chapter then derives testable claims by theorizing a set of specific observable determinants of each condition. What specific causal variables, we will ask, should influence governments' electoral scope for investment, their expectations about investment's long-term outcomes, and their institutional capacity to enact intertemporal trade-offs?

In identifying these determinants, the chapter seeks particularly to focus our attention on the *distinctive* features of intertemporal policy choice and of decision making for the long term. It acknowledges, but dwells less upon, more generic influences on policymaking that have been well established in the standard literatures on distributive politics. As we will see, theorizing the politics of policy investment means considering many of the same explanatory factors that are staples of comparative politics and the study of policymaking, including institutional veto points, the organization of social interests, and the information available to voters. I argue, however, that understanding intertemporal politics requires us to reassess or reconfigure common theoretical building blocks, adapting their causal logics to the distinctive problem of choice over time. Explaining intertemporal policymaking also requires us to closely examine – and, in some cases, to revise – the basic assumptions about mass and elite political behavior that underpin (sometimes only implicitly) most studies of distributive politics.

Three distinctive features of the theoretical framework bear emphasis at the outset. First, unlike most theories of distributive choice, the framework presented here rests on an explicit assumption about political actors' time preferences. Specifically – and departing from common notions of radical myopia – the model assumes that citizens, officeholders, and interest groups place *modestly* less weight on long-term than on short-term outcomes. On the one hand, this assumption goes some way toward explaining how policy investment *can* emerge in democratic politics. Equally important, it implies that the *challenge* of long-term investment is not primarily a problem of impatience. Where investment is rejected, in this framework, it is not because actors do not *value* the future but because they fail to attend to temporally distant payoffs, are unable to predict them with confidence, or prefer to achieve them by alternative means.

Second, the analysis draws out important cognitive implications of the high causal complexity and uncertainty of long-term policy effects. In much of the politics of distribution, actors can be assumed to know fairly well the costs and benefits of policy options, and their preferences can be straightforwardly derived from objective features of the alternatives and of the choice environment. The analysis can thus focus largely on how the balance of power resources or structure of the playing field affects actors' capacities to achieve their preferred policies. Decision making for the long term, however, confronts boundedly rational individuals with an imposing set of informational and cognitive challenges in merely *figuring out* which policy alternatives they prefer. The argument below thus *lays a cognitive foundation for strategic action*. It first theorizes how political actors reason about long-term outcomes and form preferences over policy choices with long-range implications, and then examines how actors pursue those preferences within institutional constraints.

Third, the framework below departs in an important respect from recent analyses of the politics of costly policy reform. As discussed in Chapter 1, dominant approaches – especially in the field of welfare-state retrenchment – have understood the costs of policy change to be far more salient to actors than its benefits, in turn explaining the extent of reform mostly in terms of politicians' capacity and willingness to impose losses. While policy investments are by definition costly policy changes, I argue that their politics are not simply defined by a government's ability and inclination to inflict pain. The key reason is that voters, organized interests, and politicians themselves will sometimes view investment as a *trade-off* of current pain for future gain – and policy investment is far more likely to emerge when they do.

The central logic running through the chapter is that governments' intertemporal policy choices depend on *how those choices are structured* for influential actors. Political life is replete with processes – institutional, informational, and ideational – that shape choices by structuring them in particular ways. As positive political theorists have emphasized, for instance, political institutions impose structure on collective decision making by, among other things, shaping the menu of alternatives from which actors select and thus the trade-offs that they confront (Hall and Taylor 1996; Hammond 1996; Riker 1986; Shepsle 1979). Exploring choice as a cognitive process at the individual level, students of framing have demonstrated that people's preferences can be highly sensitive to the way in which information about an issue is presented to them, including the subset of potentially relevant considerations that are emphasized (Chong and Druckman 2007a; Sniderman and Bullock 2004; Druckman 2001; Sniderman 2000; Iyengar and Simon 1993; Kahneman and Tversky 1984). And analysts of ideational factors in politics have elucidated the role of conceptual frameworks, metaphors, and models in defining problems for decision makers and bounding the range of appropriate solutions (Jacobs 2009a; Jones and Baumgartner 2005; Bleich 2003).

Most policy choices are open to more than one possible definition and can be structured for actors in a range of potential ways. The heightened informational and causal complexity of *long-term* decision making, however, multiplies the interpretive possibilities and broadens the range of conceivable trade-offs. Critically, moreover, some choice definitions are far more favorable to policy investment than others. Specifically, I argue, policy investment will be most compelling to political actors when the choice assumes a specific intertemporal structure: when it is defined as a trade-off between a given amount of near-term welfare and the relatively certain prospect of a greater amount of long-term welfare. For politicians, organized interests, and voters to favor policy investment, they must *conceive* of the policy dilemma in these terms, and they must be *constrained* in their ability to escape this dilemma – that is, to enhance their future welfare *without* current sacrifice. To put this point another way, I propose that the chief obstacle to policy investment in a democracy is not that actors are inherently impatient or care insufficiently about longer-term policy outcomes. It is, rather, that policy trade-offs are often structured or understood in ways that militate against investment. As I will contend, the prospects for policy investment thus depend to a large degree on a set of informational, ideational, and institutional conditions that make a particular choice-definition more likely than the alternatives – forcing influential actors to choose between the avoidance of short-run pain and the pursuit of greater long-term gain.

BEHAVIORAL ASSUMPTIONS

Theorizing intertemporal politics requires us to make explicit a few basic assumptions about the nature of political decision making. Many parameters of political behavior – including actors' time horizons, actors' cognitive capacities, and politicians' basic goals – have drawn limited attention in the literature on policymaking to date, in part because they are of limited import for most short-term or distributive policy issues. These motivational and cognitive foundations of choice, however, are of major consequence for the ways in which politicians and their constituents weigh intertemporal trade-offs over long time horizons.

I concentrate here on the three classes of actor that typically wield the greatest influence over policy decisions: elected officials, organized interests, and voters. Across all three groups I assume instrumental behavior: that these actors form policy preferences, make choices, and dispose of political resources in ways that they believe will maximize a set of goals. For each class of actor, however, I make a more specific set of assumptions about both the nature of those *goals* and the *cognitive resources* that it brings to bear in maximizing those ends. What do politicians, voters, and interest groups want, and how do they figure out how to get it?

Goals

Elected officials' goals. I assume that elected officials are, first and foremost, motivated by policy goals: by a desire to achieve the social outcomes that public policies can generate. Politicians pursue and cling to public office, in turn, for the unparalleled opportunity that officeholding provides to shape society via state action. In most well-institutionalized democracies, the personal benefits of public office are relatively modest as compared to those of private-sector career alternatives. Indeed, one of the few unique advantages of holding public office is the power to pursue one's conception of the good society through the use of state authority (Quirk 1990). Professional politicians are thus, on average, likely to be a group self-selected for a strong interest in the use of public policy to achieve social conditions that they value.

Obtaining their preferred policy outcomes, however, requires politicians to achieve the intermediate objective of electoral success. And where electoral competition is stiff, the demands of vote-seeking will sometimes impose a strong constraint on an incumbent's policy choices. In addition to heeding the preferences of ordinary citizens, office-seeking politicians must also frequently attend to the demands of *organized groups*. Organization is a powerful force-multiplier, allowing social groups to generate coordinated action that can weigh heavily on an incumbent's reelection prospects: by shaping public attitudes, mobilizing voters on election day, financing election campaigns, and disrupting policy implementation or economic activity. In some party organizations, groups such as trade unions are also granted a direct role in candidate or leadership selection. Politicians who wish to retain *future* policy influence thus face strong incentives to take into account the preferences both of the electorate at large and of interest-group leaders in crafting public policies *today* (Bawn 1998).

I assume, in sum, that politicians must make enough voter- and group-pleasing policy to create a comfortable expected margin of victory over likely challengers, and will reject policy options with a substantial risk of costing them the next election. Yet these requirements still leave ample scope for the intrusion of non-electoral considerations into policymaking. In many choice situations, for instance, there will exist *more than one* policy option that could be pursued without serious detriment to an officeholder's reelection prospects: in such cases, she will bring her own policy preferences to bear on the decision. Moreover, if holding office is a means to policy ends, then the rational incumbent should *optimize* between electoral and policy considerations, rather than simply maximizing votes or reelection prospects. She should be willing, for instance, to accept a small vote loss in order to win a large policy achievement.

The assumption that politicians are primarily policy-seekers – and only secondarily office-seekers – has important consequences for the theory that follows. If we assumed that politicians were purely office- or vote-seekers, we would need to explain intertemporal policy choices solely as a function of the preferences of voters and interest groups, and we would predict investment to emerge when and only when the mass public or organized interests positively demanded it. In contrast, if politicians optimize between policy and electoral goals, then officeholders' *own* policy views will be a key determinant of intertemporal policy outputs. We will, in turn, need to theorize the sources of politicians' own long-run policy preferences.

Voters' goals. I assume that voters evaluate incumbents in substantial part based on the social outcomes of the policies that they enact. These judgments may in principle be either egocentric (based on the costs and benefits of policy to themselves) or sociotropic (based on costs and benefits to others). The core motivational premise here is that – alongside other potential influences on vote choice (e.g., party identification, candidate likeability, etc.) – policy outcomes play a significant role in citizens' judgments.

Organized interests' goals. Organized interests also judge politicians based on the consequences of the policies for which they are responsible. More narrowly than for voters, however, I posit that the leaders of interest organizations seek primarily to maximize material benefits for their members, not for society as a whole.[1] There do, of course, exist organized political groups – such as human-rights or environmental lobbies – that seek nonmaterial or other-regarding benefits. In general, however, groups built around the material interests of their members – such as business and labor organizations – have tended to have greater success overcoming the obstacles to collective action than have nonmaterial or postmaterial interests (Olson 1971). Thus, while the analysis to come will not capture the motives of all pressure groups, it is intended to characterize the behavior of the largest and most influential organizations.

Time preferences. How much do participants in politics care about the future? This is a fundamental question about the structure of preferences, with far-reaching implications for the explanation of political choice. So far, however, we do not have much of a theoretical or empirical basis for answering it. While observing that officeholders may have policy goals (e.g., Müller and Strøm 1999; Pierson 1994), analysts have not systematically examined the time horizons over which those goals extend. While studying the efforts of interest organizations to win policy gains, scholars have rarely asked how far into the future those groups seek to maximize their welfare. Even students of voting behavior and mass opinion – who have paid particular attention to the underlying structure of

---

[1] This formulation, of course, simplifies away possible conflicts of interest between group leaders and rank-and-file. For the sake of analytical tractability, the study brackets the potential effect of intraorganizational politics on interest-groups' intertemporal strategies.

preferences – have said little about the time horizons over which citizens care about and consider future policy outcomes.[2]

When discussing "time preferences," we are referring to differences in the relative value that a decision maker places on welfare effects at different points in the future. Typically, individuals are assumed to display a *positive* time preference, also known as impatience: to place greater value on temporally proximate utility than on temporally distant utility. It is crucial to maintain a sharp analytical distinction between time preferences and *other* potential reasons why decision makers might underweight future outcomes relative to current ones. These other reasons include uncertainty about the future; the opportunity costs (i.e., lost investment opportunities) associated with delay in the delivery of payoffs; and the potentially lower cognitive salience of and attention to events that are distant in time. Importantly, each of these factors can lead actors who greatly *value* future welfare to nonetheless discount future outcomes and make choices with a bias toward the present. Time preferences, however, refer strictly to the degree to which decision makers *value* more or less temporally distant utilities. Likewise, I will use the term *time-preference discount rate* to refer to the rate of time-discounting that derives *solely* from an actor's time preferences.[3]

As we theorize intertemporal policy choices, a key analytical decision is whether to assume that political actors' time-preference discount rates are generally *higher* than or *lower* than the expected rate of return to many plausible policy investments. If actors are so impatient that they discount the future at a steeper rate than potential policy investments can pay off, then they will never view the long-run benefits of investment as being worth its short-run costs. Future investment gains will be uniformly discounted away. In such a world, we would not expect anything about those payoffs – their incidence, their degree of certainty, the salience of information about them – to make any difference to actors' choices. Their choices, instead, would be driven solely by short-term considerations. Indeed, we would not want to model such radically impatient actors as making *intertemporal* policy trade-offs at all, but rather as maximizing present payoffs.

---

[2] Debates over retrospective and prospective voting, it should be noted, take temporality into account, but in a manner unrelated to the matter of time preferences. The controversy concerns not how voters *value* the future but how they *form expectations* about it: whether by extrapolating from past experience (e.g., Fiorina 1978; Kramer 1971) or by incorporating distinct predictive information (e.g., Erikson, MacKuen, and Stimson 2000). With rare exception, public opinion researchers have also left unexplored how voters value future long-term as compared to future short-term gains and losses.

[3] A discount rate represents the risk-free rate of return at which an individual is indifferent between the immediate consumption of some value and investment of that same value for future consumption. An actor with a higher discount rate is thus more impatient: she demands a higher rate of return to be willing to trade current for future consumption.

On the other hand, if politicians, interest groups, and voters place only modestly less value on future outcomes than on present ones – if they generally discount at a rate *lower* than the rate of return to feasible policy investments – then tomorrow's investment gains can potentially weigh on their decisions. Such actors will *in principle* be willing to make intertemporal policy trade-offs in favor of the future. And their evaluation of specific investment options will depend on both the nature of the long-run trade-offs that they confront and the constraints under which they confront them. In this world, actors' preferences over policy investment should hinge, for instance, on the character of the net long-term benefits that they expect investment to deliver; on how those payoffs compare to the benefits of policy alternatives; and on how political institutions limit the menu of feasible options. It is only under an assumption of modest time-preference discounting that such factors can influence intertemporal policy preferences. Moreover, it is only if actors care sufficiently about future outcomes that *other* reasons for time-discounting – such as the uncertainty of the long term – can shape their preferences over investment.

In short, it matters greatly how impatient we assume political actors to be relative to the steepness of the intertemporal trade-offs that they face. In the absence of explicit guidance on this point from the literature, I make an assumption that I believe to be reasonably consistent with other things we know about intertemporal decision making and about public policy. I posit relatively *modest* impatience: policy time-preference discount rates that, generally and for the most part, are lower than the returns to many feasible policy investments.[4]

Given the dearth of prior evidence on political time horizons, the justification of this assumption must in part have a "show me" logic, resting on the empirical strength of the theory that flows from it. If this assumption is wrong, then many of the hypotheses built on this basis will be falsified in the empirical chapters. Equally important, our observations of private, internal policymaking processes will yield indications of whether and how actors weighed short- against long-term potential consequences of their choices.

I want to suggest, however, that this assumption is broadly compatible with empirical evidence about individuals' time preferences, on the one hand, and about the consequences of investment-oriented public policies, on the other. Individuals' time preferences are notoriously difficult to isolate and measure (Frederick, Loewenstein, and O'Donoghue 2002), and the returns to potential policy investments are uncertain and highly variable. But a rough comparison between the two suggests that there exists quite a range of feasible investments that will pay off at higher rates than those at which most decision makers will plausibly discount the future.

---

[4] For a similar claim about political actors' time preferences, see Teles (2009) on political investment.

In a broad survey of the intertemporal-choice literatures in economics and psychology, Frederick et al. (2002) find that the majority of studies of individuals' discount rates estimate a rate of 0.25 or below. These estimates can be understood as an upper bound on the discount rate attributable to pure time preference because, as Frederick et al. point out, most measures also pick up additional sources of discounting, such as uncertainty and the opportunity costs of delay.

Moreover, aggregate measures of economic behavior outside the laboratory in advanced industrialized societies suggest a substantially lower time-preference discount rate. Real returns to virtually risk-free investments, such as U.S. Treasury bills, provide a rough indicator of the value that individuals place on future consumption because they represent the nearly certain rate of return in exchange for which individuals are willing to defer consumption into the future. The real annual return to relatively riskless securities has historically averaged a mere 1.0 percent in the United States, 1.1 percent in Britain, and 3.2 percent in Germany (Mehra 2003), with somewhat riskier long-term real bond yields at 2.5 percent in the U.S. (*Stocks, Bonds, Bills and Inflation* 2000).[5] Even on risky investments like common stocks, investors in the U.S., Germany, and Britain have historically demanded an average real annual return of only 7.9, 5.7, and 9.8 percent, respectively (Mehra 2003). All of these pretax figures overstate true returns and the implied degree of discounting wherever capital gains, dividend, or interest income is taxed. In short, aggregate measures of observed economic behavior would suggest a discount rate somewhere in the range of 0 to 0.11, and likely below 0.04.[6]

In the first direct examination of citizens' time preferences over policy, Jacobs and Matthews (2008) observe little indication of strong impatience. Drawing on a survey experiment administered to a nationally representative sample of the U.S. voting-age population, Jacobs and Matthews find that the timing of policy benefits in itself has no detectable impact on citizens' willingness to pay policy costs today when the benefits are made salient and are perceived to be relatively certain. While subjects displayed sensitivity to the practical implications of the timing of policy benefits – particularly to the effects of timing on the uncertainty of those benefits – the analysis uncovered little evidence that citizens overlook or greatly undervalue potential policy benefits *merely* because they are distant in time.

---

[5] For short-term bonds, the period for the U.S. figure is 1889–2000; for Britain 1947–99; for Germany 1978–97. For long-term U.S. bonds, the period is 1926–99.

[6] It could be countered that these interest rates are unlikely to represent the time preferences of the population at large since not all individuals save and invest. Rates of return on risk-free savings might underestimate discount rates if those who save tend to be more patient than those who do not. Empirical evidence from the United States, however, indicates that savings rates are highly correlated with income. This suggests that nonsaving is a stronger indication of a high marginal utility for expenditure – that is, of how much people need to spend today in order to subsist – than of impatience (Dynan, Skinner, and Zeldes 2000).

Turning now to the rates of return to policy investment, a review of the policy-analytic literatures across diverse domains suggests that a wide range of potential investments can be expected to yield social returns far in excess of time-preference discount rates. Consider, for instance, the following cost-benefit estimates, drawn from a broad spectrum of policy settings (all monetary figures in constant dollars):

- *Education.* Studying the effects of secondary education on crime rates, Lochner and Moretti (2004) estimate that a policy that would keep potential male high-school dropouts in school for an additional year would initially cost $6000 per student but would generate $1170 to $2100 per year thereafter in social benefits from reduced crime, an annual yield of 19.5 percent or more. Similarly, Nores et al. (2005), analyzing the effects of early education for at-risk children, find that spending $1 on preschool delivers $5.67 in long-term social gains, after discounting those gains at 7 percent per annum.
- *Self-reproducing natural resources.* Studies of fisheries frequently find that restricting the harvest of depleted populations boosts species biomass at rates that greatly exceed plausible discount rates. A study of 17 overfished U.S. stocks, for instance, found that a policy of tight harvest restrictions would yield a long-term catch with a net present value *triple* that deriving from the status quo policy of lax regulation, *after* discounting these future benefits at 7 percent per annum (Sumaila and Suatoni 2005). And in a historical study of policies to rebuild the Norwegian spring-spawning herring population, Ainsworth and Sumaila (2007) find that the regulations generated biomass annual returns of approximately 35 percent throughout the 1980s and 1990s.
- *Disaster preparedness.* Analyzing data from the United States, Healy and Malhotra (2009) estimate the benefits of investment in natural-disaster-preparedness measures, such as flood-control infrastructure and first-responder equipment and training. They find that an additional $1 spent on preparedness within a given 8-year period yields damage savings of $7.37 over the following 4 years, representing a real compound annual rate of return of at least 18, and likely closer to 40, percent.[7]
- *Public health.* According to two recent analyses of tobacco control, a national antismoking media campaign combined with a $1-per-pack increase in cigarette taxes would save 108,466 lives and 1.6 million years of potential life in the cohort of current 18-year-olds in the United States over a 67-year period, followed by the same payoffs for each successive cohort. Over the range of discount rates commonly employed in public-health

---

[7] The lowest rate of return occurs if the $1 is fully invested in Year 1 of the first two election cycles and the damage savings do not accrue until Year 4 of the third cycle. Assuming that the investment and savings occur in the middle of each period yields a real annual rate of return of 39.5 percent.

evaluation (3 to 7 percent, see Drummond et al. 1997; Gold 1996), these figures imply fiscal outlays of a mere $2,000 to $9,000, respectively, per life-year saved. These initial fiscal outlays, moreover, are offset by between $622 and $2353 per life year saved (at 3- to 7-percent discount rates, respectively) in medical-care cost-savings arising from long-term health improvements (Fishman et al. 2005; Rivara et al. 2004).

- *The environment.* Employing his widely cited model of climate-change mitigation, Nordhaus (2008) estimates that the immediate imposition of a carbon tax of $27 per ton, rising to $90 per ton by 2050, would pay for itself over the long run in avoided losses to global GDP, if those benefits are discounted at a 4-percent annual rate. Hope (2006) and Mityakov and Rühl (2009) report roughly similar results.

This is, of course, just an illustrative collection of findings. Importantly – and for reasons to be elaborated later – any forecast of long-run policy returns will also have considerable uncertainty attached to it. Given the additional imprecision in measuring time preferences, we can engage only in a ballpark comparison of the two. Such a comparison, however, broadly suggests that there are many technically feasible policy investments that could be expected to produce social returns substantially greater than the time-preference discount rates that political actors are likely to employ. In other words, while the returns to any investment are always uncertain, decision makers in many policy spheres are likely to confront investment options with plausible payoffs high enough that impatience *alone* is unlikely to lead to their rejection.

Another way of thinking about this assumption is as a delimitation of the scope of the study. The study's aim is not to try to explain how governments make decisions about intertemporal policy trade-offs with little or no social profit. Rather, the question of interest is under what conditions governments adopt policies that, while costly in the short run, could plausibly deliver substantial net long-term social gains. And by "substantial," I mean gains large enough that they will not be discounted away by decision makers on the grounds of mere impatience. The foregoing discussion is meant to suggest that, across a wide range of policy domains, such options will frequently feature on the policy menu.

Cognitive Capacities

If politicians, interest groups, and citizens view public policy as a tool for producing valued social outcomes over substantial time horizons, then they confront a task of causal inference: they must form beliefs about the outcomes that alternative policy options will generate over those horizons, if enacted. How do political actors form these long-range causal beliefs?

The simplest assumption that we could make is one of full rationality paired with full information about payoffs. If we adopt this frequent premise of choice- and game-theoretic models, then the problem of causal inference goes away.

Actors derive their policy preferences from a comparison of the objectively known consequences of the available options, and we as analysts can explain their choices by doing the same. If outcomes are uncertain, we need only attach the additional assumption that actors seek to maximize *expected* utility (Savage 1954). The rational decision maker will represent each policy option as a lottery over possible outcomes and weight the utility of each outcome by its likelihood of occurring. She will then rank options based on their probability-adjusted payoffs.

As students of decision-making behavior have long argued, however, the spare assumptions of microeconomic theory are at variance with much of what we know about the structure of human cognition. Psychologists and behavioral economists have pointed to a panoply of empirical departures from rationalist tenets (e.g., Thaler 1991; Kahneman and Tversky 1984). My focus here is on those departures that limit decision-makers' capacity *to assess the consequences of their choices.* Importantly, behavioral research does not portray the human agent as a random chooser. Rather, according to a wealth of evidence, human decision makers behave as "cognitive misers," economizing in systematic ways on the use of scarce mental resources as they interpret the world around them (Fiske and Taylor 1991).

One of the most consistently observed constraints on human cognition is the scarcity of attention. As Herbert Simon famously formulated the problem, humans make decisions in an "information-rich world" in which the mass of signals overwhelms their capacity for processing: agents forming beliefs and making choices simply cannot attend to all available and potentially relevant information (Simon 1971). The main bottleneck is the restricted capacity of "working memory," a cognitive process in which information is temporarily represented and made accessible for evaluation and detailed analysis (Knudsen 2007; Jones and Baumgartner 2005). The boundedness of working memory creates, on one level, a constraint on the number of environmental stimuli or object attributes that individuals can take into account at a given time (Knudsen 2007; Jones 2001; Simon 1971; Miller 1956).

Relatedly, there are important limitations on the conceptual complexity that individuals can manage. In conceiving of objects and relationships, people tend to rely on simplified mental representations – such as schemata (Fiske and Taylor 1991) or associations of attributes (Smith 1998) – that abstract from the full detail of empirical instances. In forming attitudes and making trade-offs, moreover, individuals do not reason about and weigh all potentially relevant dimensions of the issue at hand. Rather, as studies of priming and framing have made clear, they focus their attention on a *subset* of the potentially relevant considerations, implications, or consequences (Druckman 2004; Nelson and Oxley 1997; Iyengar 1991; see also Zaller 1992).

If real human decision making falls short of a rationalist ideal, psychological and behavioral economic studies indicate that it does so in *patterned* ways. As information competes for access to working memory, the allocation of attention is shaped both by features of the information itself ("bottom-up" processes) and by characteristics of the recipient ("top-down" processes). In terms of the bottom-up influences, information that is more salient – standing out as especially vivid, dramatic, or threatening – is more likely to draw attention (Knudsen 2007; Fiske and Taylor 1991; Lau 1985). So too are considerations and issue dimensions that are primed by repeated mention or highlighted by a prominent frame (e.g., Zaller 1992; Iyengar 1991). The constraints on time and processing capacity also mean that relatively simple cues and easy-to-process signals are likely to have a disproportionate impact on agents' inferences (e.g., Lupia and McCubbins 1998; Sniderman, Brody, and Tetlock 1991). Among the most important top-down factors, agents' prior beliefs and mental representations of the world make them more likely to attend to and place weight on confirmatory information than on discrepant information (Smith 1998; Fiske and Taylor 1991; March and Olsen 1989; Higgins and Bargh 1987).

Notably, none of these cognitive influences on the weighting of information bear a necessary relation to the objective probability or value of outcomes, the criteria foreseen by expected-utility theory. This divergence has especially important consequences for the study of long-term policy choice. An assumption of expected-utility maximization may be workable for certain kinds of policy choices – where valued outcomes can be predicted by simple causal models; where the number of issue dimensions is low; and where diagnostic information is limited in volume, salient, and easy to process. For reasons to be elaborated later in this chapter, however, these conditions do not describe most decision making over the long term. As actors seek to assess consequences over longer time horizons, the complexity of the relevant causal processes tends to go up; the range of potential outcomes grows; the volume of information to be processed expands; and the salience and the interpretability of that information falls. In other words, boundedly rational decision makers facing long-term policy trade-offs will generally be able to take into account only a *subset* of the information and considerations relevant to their choice. A crucial influence on political actors' intertemporal policy preferences will thus be how they allocate finite cognitive resources – in particular, *which causal possibilities and data they attend to and which they ignore.*

At the same time, it is likely that the cognitive dynamics shaping *elite* decision-making will differ in key respects from those shaping the preferences of the *mass electorate.* In thinking about this difference, we can draw upon the distinction between two modes of information-processing commonly theorized by cognitive and social psychologists (for a review, see Smith and DeCoster 2000). Most of the time, individuals are understood to engage in a relatively low-effort mode of reasoning, sometimes called heuristic (Chaiken 1980) or peripheral (Petty and Cacioppo 1981) processing. When processing heuristically, individuals judge messages based on salient cues, attend to broad and superficial similarities between objects, apply simple decision rules, and draw inferences based on associations learned from past experience. A second, less common mode of reasoning – often termed systematic (Chaiken 1980) or central processing

(Petty and Cacioppo 1981) – requires a higher level of cognitive commitment. When systematically processing, people tend to seek out and consider a wide range of relevant information, focus on message content rather than surface attributes, disaggregate objects into analytically relevant components, reason according to abstract logical rules, and reflect on scenarios that have not yet occurred.[8] Systematic processing is constrained by the fundamental bounds of human attention just described and may be subject to its own sources of bias; as compared to heuristic reasoning, however, it draws on a greater *share* of an individual's cognitive resources.

How individuals process a problem hinges on their motivation to arrive at an accurate judgment and on the time and cognitive capacities that they are able to devote to the task (Druckman 2004; Denzau and North 1994; Petty and Cacioppo 1986). Elites and ordinary citizens weighing public policy issues are likely to be quite different in these two respects. As political actors by profession, officeholders and interest-group leaders typically have considerable policy influence, a substantial stake in the character of state action, and significant cognitive and organizational resources (e.g., expert staff) to invest in the assessment of policy options. Further, political professionals frequently operate with background knowledge of and well-developed ideas about politics and policy – such as ideologies and causal theories – that help guide and structure their processing of information.

The average citizen, in contrast, has little influence over policy and is only diffusely and imperceptibly affected by much state action. Decades of public-opinion research have yielded overwhelming evidence that most voters possess little political knowledge and lack well-developed ideational frameworks for interpreting policy issues (e.g., Kuklinski and Quirk 2001; Kuklinski et al. 2000; Delli Carpini and Keeter 1997; Zaller 1992; Luskin 1987; Converse 1964). Though there is considerable debate about how effectively voters can exercise electoral judgment, even the more optimistic accounts reveal an electorate that pays modest attention to public affairs and economizes on information and cognitive effort (e.g., Lupia and McCubbins 1998; Sniderman et al. 1991; Iyengar 1990). Among the potential objects of citizens' finite stock of time and attention, politics and public policy appear to rank rather low.

In short, the *context* of policy choice will tend to activate higher-effort reasoning among those who engage professionally in political decision making than among the broad electorate. In theorizing preference-formation, I thus posit two different patterns of information-processing and attention-allocation. As heuristic decision makers, voters are likely to be especially sensitive to the particular *form* that information takes. Whether they attend to policy-relevant evidence – whether they take a "cue" from a given signal – will depend heavily

---

[8] Summarize here common elements of a set of theories that are often termed "dual process models." While not all such models share these characteristics, an important subset of them – found especially in studies of persuasion and attitude change – do. See also Brewer (1988).

on *bottom-up* features of the information itself: on the strength and salience of the signal and the ease of processing it. By contrast, politicians and interest-group leaders will make substantial efforts to seek and assess information that is analytically relevant to the choices that they want to get right. In elites' more systematic mode of processing, attention to information will depend less on how dramatic a form it takes and more on its diagnostic value. Even elites, however, face cognitive limits: confronted with complex decisions they will be unable to take into account all relevant data and considerations. In complex choice situations, elites' cognitive resources are likely to be channeled by *top-down* processes of selection, in which their preexisting knowledge and mental representations of policy issues structure their search for information and their reasoning about policy consequences.

In sum, the remainder of this chapter will advance a theory of policy investment based on four sets of assumptions about the goals and decision-making capabilities of influential political actors:

1. **Policy-seeking politicians:** Politicians' ultimate goal is to use public policy to achieve their preferred social outcomes. They will thus reject policy options that pose a substantial risk of losing reelection (which would eliminate future policy influence) but, when it is electorally safe to do so, will choose policies that they believe will generate their preferred social outcomes.

2. **Policy-seeking constituents:** Voters and interest groups choose between candidates/parties in part based on policy outcomes, with groups focused on material effects on their members.

3. **Future-orientedness:** Actors apply a modest time-preference discount to future social outcomes, relative to the plausible returns to feasible policy investments.

4. **Cognitive constraint:** All actors face limits on the range of relevant information and considerations to which they can attend in forming policy preferences, though these limits are tighter for voters than for elites. While the attention of voters is guided (bottom-up) by the character of available information, the attention of elites is directed (top-down) by their preexisting ideational representations of policy issues.

EXPLAINING VARIATION IN POLICY INVESTMENT: THREE
NECESSARY CONDITIONS

With these behavioral premises in place, we are now in a position to theorize the sources of variation in the degree to which governments enact policy investments. The theory is constructed according to a logic of *necessary conditions*. At the broadest level, the framework holds that policy investment requires motive, means, and opportunity: ministers considering a long-term problem must *expect* the investment to generate valued social outcomes; they must be *institutionally capable* of enacting it; and they must see an *opportunity* to do so without substantial risk of losing office. As governments decide not just whether to make policy investments but also *how much* to invest, the outcome in the present study is fundamentally a continuous one. Equally, the necessary conditions – electoral safety, expected social returns, and institutional capacity – may be present to a greater or lesser degree in a given case. I thus conceptualize the relationship of necessity itself in continuous terms, with each condition serving as an independent limiting factor on the outcome: we should expect the degree of policy investment to be constrained by the strength of *the most weakly present* of the conditions.

After establishing the general importance of each necessary condition, the main task of each section is to identify these conditions' observable determinants – the specific independent variables that influence their strength. Since each condition can in principle be affected by a wide range of causal factors, I focus the discussion in a couple of ways. First, I pay more attention to causal propositions of which the book's empirical cases allow a good test. Historical case studies of policymaking are better suited to examining some kinds of hypotheses than others. In particular, I devote more attention to causal variables that are observable either at the aggregate level or in elite behavior – i.e., for which we are likely to have reliable historical evidence – than on factors that could only be observed in micro-level data on individual citizens, which is typically unavailable for historical cases.

To further delimit the analytic task, the discussion assumes a particular sequence to the policymaking process and cuts into that sequence at a specific point. I assume that elected officeholders within the executive (i.e., ministers) have already become aware of the long-term policy issue in question and are now weighing whether and how to respond.[9] Taking this state of affairs as our starting point concentrates the theory-building on explaining *the selection among intertemporal policy alternatives*. Notwithstanding the potential importance of prior processes of problem-recognition, this choice of focus rests on the expectation that a great deal of the intertemporal variation in public policies derives from processes that *follow* the identification of long-term challenges and potential solutions – that is, from the political and cognitive challenges of imposing short-term social costs to invest in distant social benefits.

Taking the presence of a long-term problem on the elite agenda as given, we will ask what factors determine whether governments respond with a policy investment, as opposed to intertemporal alternatives. To help structure the exposition, the discussion casts ministers in the role of policy protagonists, treating the policy output as emerging from their electorally and institutionally

---

[9] Policymaking may be shaped by two potential dynamics of attention. The dynamic that the present theory brackets is the allocation of elite attention across policy areas in which governments might take action (e.g., climate change, public debt, pensions, etc). A distinct problem, considered in detail in the following sections, is the allocation of attention *across potential considerations within a given decision-making process* – for instance, across alternative possible consequences of a given policy option. In discussing the cognitive challenges of uncertainty, my emphasis is on the latter problem of attention.

constrained choices among alternatives. As it represents the most familiar constraint on policymaking for the long term, we turn first to the electoral condition.

NECESSARY CONDITION I: ELECTORAL SAFETY

Our first claim of necessity is that governments will only invest within a zone of electoral safety – that is, to the extent that they are shielded from significant risk of voter retribution for this policy choice. Whatever the social merits of a policy investment, even policy-seeking ministers will reject it if it poses a substantial threat to reelection, since future influence over policy hinges on remaining in office.

Why exactly is policy investment electorally risky? One of the simplest and most widely employed models of electoral accountability – the theory of voter retrospection – suggests a compelling answer. In this model, voters make up their minds at election time by judging the past performance of the current government. In the most basic form of retrospection, voters form this judgment simply by comparing their economic circumstances today with those at the last election (Fiorina 1978; Kramer 1971). In some cases, analysts have made the somewhat stronger assumption that citizens credit or blame incumbents specifically for those past gains and losses that derived from the government's policy choices (Pierson 1994; Arnold 1990). Either way, if voters take into account only those consequences that have already emerged at election time, then incumbents confront a clear set of temporal electoral incentives to maximize policy benefits and minimize costs before the next election. As Nordhaus (1975) frames the basic prediction, "...[A] perfect democracy with retrospective evaluation of parties will make decisions biased against future generations" (187). This logic underpins arguments, for instance, in the literatures on political business and budgetary cycles (e.g., Alesina and Roubini 1992; Rogoff 1990; Alt and Chrystal 1983; Tufte 1978) and on strategies of blame-avoidance in welfare-state reform (e.g., Weaver 2003; Pierson 1994).

By itself, however, a retrospective-electoral model of policymaking is limited as an explanation of intertemporal policy choices. The theory implies that policy investment – at least if it takes more than one electoral cycle to pay off – will always pose an electoral risk and should, in turn, never be adopted by incumbents who want to remain in office. A standard retrospective model thus cannot account for the *variation* that we observe in governments' intertemporal policy decisions. Nor can we do better by simply assuming the opposite – that voters are farsighted or prospective judges of their governments (e.g., Erikson et al. 2000; Chappell and Keech 1985). If electorates routinely form realistic expectations about, and vote on the basis of, *post*-election consequences, then politicians should face constant electoral incentives to invest – an equally implausible prediction. Neither approach to voting behavior – at least in its standard formulation – can explain why elected governments sometimes maximize in the short run but at other times enact investments.

One possible solution to this problem is to posit that incumbents face varying degrees of electoral *pressure*. Analysts studying both democratic and authoritarian regimes have suggested that politicians' time horizons or willingness to impose short-run losses may vary with their degree of security in office (Wright 2008; King 1997; Geddes 1994; Williamson 1994; Garrett 1993; Evans 1992; Waterbury 1992; Levi 1988; on loss-imposition in pensions, see Immergut and Anderson 2006). We may thus be able to explain some of the variation in elected politicians' willingness to invest, within a retrospective model, by relaxing the assumption that elected governments always face capable rivals and a credible threat of losing office. If the opposition is weak or divided (in ways likely to be punished by electoral rules), then the government may have votes to spare, and it can impose some pre-election losses, even on retrospective voters, without significant risk of losing office. The degree of competitive threat posed by the opposition, then, is one independent variable that should influence the extent of investment that governments can undertake with electoral safety.

Substantial competitive slack, however, is likely to be relatively rare and fleeting. Under ordinary competitive circumstances, incumbent politicians will face a credible threat of electoral punishment and will therefore be constrained by voters' judgments. In the remainder of this section, I thus emphasize the sources of voters' attitudes toward intertemporal policy trade-offs.

A Cognitive Tilt Against Investment

It is useful to ponder the behavioral logic underlying the model of the retrospective voter. In its most common formulation, the model is in fact based on the same behavorial assumptions about the electorate – as prospectively oriented and boundedly rational – that I adopt here. In the standard retrospective setup, the voter is assumed to care about future policy consequences and to seek the candidate or party that, in office, would deliver the best outcomes. Making this assessment requires, at a minimum, forming a judgment about the likely future performance of the current incumbent. The voter makes this evaluation *retrospectively*, however, as a matter of cognitive simplicity: she ignores future consequences not because she is impatient, but because retrospection is an easy shortcut to judgments about the future. Rather than comprehensively assessing the (past and future) consequences of those policies for which the current government is specifically responsible, the voter economizes on information and cognitive effort by settling for a rough-and-ready approximation: a comparison of current conditions with those at the last election (Kramer 1971; Butler and Stokes 1969; Downs 1957).[10]

Critically, however, retrospective judgment is merely one of many possible decision rules consistent with these behavioral premises. What *generally* follows

---

[10] Key's (Key and Cummings 1966) earlier and simpler reward-and-punish logic does not assume prospective motives but is, in its pure form, applied less frequently in contemporary arguments about retrospection.

from these assumptions – and from a wealth of findings in social and political psychology – is that citizens' use of information about policy consequences should depend on the cognitive costs: on how readily accessible, salient, and easy to process the information is. Starting from this more fundamental logic, we can identify two distinct reasons why citizens' attitudes will, on average, be biased against policy investment.

First, information about more temporally distant dangers and consequences will tend to take less dramatic form than information about policy costs or social difficulties that have already taken effect. Second, for reasons elaborated later, predicting long-run policy consequences often requires confronting far greater informational and causal complexity than assessing current conditions. By comparison to weighing current costs against unrealized long-run benefits, a retrospective decision rule – "Am I better off today than I was four years ago?" – offers a cognitively simple path to judgment.

Policy investment may be additionally disadvantaged by a second cognitive pattern: a well-documented "negativity bias" in information processing. All else equal, negative or threatening information tends to be more salient to individuals than positive information (Vonk 1993; Lau 1985). Additionally, individuals are loss-averse, weighting potential losses relative to the status quo more heavily than prospective gains of equal size (Kahneman, Knetsch, and Thaler 1991). There is substantial evidence that negative information and loss play a greater role than positive considerations when citizens make political judgments – when forming impressions of candidates, assessing economic conditions, judging public policies, and making voting decisions (Soroka 2006; Weyland 1998; Klein 1991; Weaver 1986; Kernell 1977). Because policy investment seeks to trade pain for gain, this negativity bias will tilt citizen attitudes against the option: even if information about an investment's benefits is available and clear, voters may accord it less weight than information about the investment's costs.

These features of human cognition matter because they affect the ways in which citizens understand the *structure* of the policy-investment choice. To be more precise, the character of human information-processing will tend to bias voters against favorable *elite framings* of the investment decision. Inattentive voters will not generally form policy understandings unassisted; rather, motivated politicians will usually *supply* potential choice structures which voters may either accept or reject. To justify a costly policy investment to the electorate, governments will seek to frame the decision in favorable terms. Specifically, investment advocates will attempt to depict the measure in (a) intertemporal terms, as an exchange of some short-run pain for much larger long-run gain *rather* than (b) retrospective terms, as a policy that merely makes voters worse off than they were at the last election. Put another way, investing governments will seek to shift the electoral question from, "Are you better off today than you were four years ago?" to "Have we made you better off over the long run?"

Elites, however, are not unconstrained in their capacity to frame issues for voters. Rather, the effectiveness of frames – their credibility and perceived applicability – is known to depend on the broader informational context in which they are employed (see, e.g., Chong and Druckman 2007b). It will, therefore, be far harder for governments to effectively frame a policy as a favorable long-run trade-off if information about its *benefits* is much less cognitively accessible to citizens than information about its *costs*. The informational structure of an intertemporal choice, in other words, may conspire against politicians' best rhetorical efforts. While politicians attempt to portray investment as a profitable long-run exchange, citizens – focused more on current and vivid negative outcomes than on murky and prospective positive ones – may simply reject this frame and instead conceive of the policy as a simple act of loss-imposition.

The Intertemporal Balance of Information

Informational features of the typical policy investment will thus, on average, tend to interact with human cognition in ways that generate voter bias against investment. At the same time, a cognitive understanding of mass policy attitudes can help explain *variation* in the electoral risks of investment. As the informational character of an intertemporal trade-off varies – as information about long-term benefits or short-term costs becomes more or less salient or interpretable – so too should politicians' framing opportunities and, in turn, voters' understanding of the choice. Information about policy investment may vary in two principal ways.

First, information about the *costs* of policy investment may vary, often by intentional policy design. Analysts of the politics of loss-imposition have identified a range of strategies that politicians can employ to make it harder for boundedly rational voters to notice or interpret information about policy costs (Pierson 1994; Nelson 1992; Arnold 1990; Weaver 1986). Governments can disguise painful measures in ways that are difficult for voters to perceive as losses – by, for instance, holding social-welfare benefits constant in an inflationary context, postponing losses until after the next election, spreading losses thinly across large numbers of individuals, or pairing those costs with more visible compensatory benefits. Alternatively, they can obscure the link between losses and the policies that produce them by, for example, imposing costs on intermediaries, like service providers, rather than directly on individuals.[11] The very fact that voters are paying little attention can thus work in policy investment's favor, by allowing politicians to mislead the electorate about its painful consequences.

---

[11] The literature also points to a third general blame-avoidance strategy: politicians can occlude their own role in imposing costs by, for example, "passing the buck" to other actors or forging a broad, cross-party consensus in favor of costly initiatives. The electoral effect of this tactic follows a distinct logic: rather than shaping voter attitudes toward policy choices, it clouds *responsibility* for those choices. Separate from the framing logic emphasized above, we might further predict that politicians will enjoy electoral safety to invest to the extent that political institutions disperse authority, facilitating the delegation or cross-party negotiation of policy decisions (Pierson 1994; see also Whitten and Palmer 1999; Powell and Whitten 1993). Though I do not emphasize this dynamic here, it is to some degree in evidence in the case studies to come.

The blame-avoidance literature also suggests, however, that governments' capacities to obfuscate are bounded – constrained by the structure of existing programs, the availability of resources, and the character of the intended change. Attempts to reduce real benefits by holding them constant, for instance, will be much more visible when a scheme's payouts are automatically indexed to prices or wages. Likewise, it is harder to shift costs onto intermediaries in the domain of direct cash transfers than in the realm of service provision (Pierson 1994). Strategies of compensation typically require a degree of budgetary slack, and efforts to render costs imperceptible by spreading them thinly depend crucially on those costs being, on the whole, relatively low. Nonetheless, under the right structural and fiscal conditions, governments should sometimes be able to design policy investments in ways that limit the salience of their short-run costs, thus enhancing the persuasiveness of frames that emphasize their net long-run benefits.

Second, information about the long-term *benefits* of policy investment may vary in salience. In his seminal work on agenda-setting, Kingdon (1984) highlights the role of focusing events and crises – such as plane crashes, industrial accidents, or company bankruptcies – in turning the public's attention to social outcomes that would otherwise persist unnoticed. In basic perceptual terms, salient stimuli are those that stand out as unusual in their environment: "a sudden sound, a flash of light, or a red dot in a field of green dots" (Knudsen 2007, 64). Similarly, focusing events stand out against the background hum of social life, generating rare, dramatic, punctuated signals of trouble. They aggregate and concentrate outcomes that are otherwise highly diffused, and they provide vivid, emotionally interesting imagery with which voters can easily associate a policy problem. Moreover, as indicators of *negative* potential outcomes, focusing events are especially likely to be processed intensively by voters. A wealth of psychological research has also demonstrated that individuals judge the frequency or probability of an event in part by its cognitive "availability" – by the ease with which instances can be brought to mind (Vaughn and Weary 2002; Gersen 2001; Tversky and Kahneman 1973; Kates 1962). The recent and dramatic occurrence of an adverse event, by making the outcome easier for citizens to imagine, should thus substantially increase the perceived likelihood of similar harms emerging in the future.

Kingdon applies the concept of a focusing event to incidents that draw attention to *current* problems. Yet, this same informational logic can apply to long-term problems that have not yet fully emerged. Crises and disasters that take place today are sometimes the leading edge of causal processes that will gather intensity or speed over time, generating greater or more frequent calamity tomorrow. A train accident may draw attention to the mounting risks posed by an aging transport infrastructure; a nuclear plant accident may raise the salience of distant dangers of atomic-waste storage; and a rival state's satellite launch can draw attention to domestic underinvestment in scientific skills. Sometimes signals of long-term trouble can be generated by government programs themselves. Pierson (1994) and Patashnik (2000) have argued, for instance, that public programs financed out of a "trust fund" can distill complex information about distant fiscal outcomes into easily understood signals about future "bank-ruptcy," acting as alarm bells that raise the salience of a program's long-term financial troubles. And sometimes the true relationship between current event and future problem is rather tenuous, and the attentional effect purely fortu-itous, as when an unusually warm winter turns voters' attention to longer-term processes of climate change.

Focusing events can thus minimize the electoral risks of policy investment by drawing citizen attention to long-term problems and making a powerful set of rhetorical tools available to politicians. Specifically, they make it easier for governments to frame investment in terms that emphasize its long-run benefits as a key consideration. Moreover, by signaling the prospect of future harm, they allow politicians to credibly justify the costs of investment as necessary to avoid *even larger losses* – turning voters' negativity bias to their persuasive advantage (Weyland 1998).

In sum, the electoral risks of policy investment will hinge greatly on the locus of voter attention: whether the electorate judges investment solely based on its past costs or also by reference to its prospective benefits. On *average*, past policy losses should have the cognitive upper hand against future gains. But departing from standard models of constant voter retrospection, I have argued that the temporal focus of citizen attention on a given issue – and thus the framing opportunities available to politicians – should be highly *contingent* on informational context: dependent on the salience and interpret-ability of public information about investment's near-term effects as com-pared to information about its long-term consequences. Governments can invest with electoral safety to the extent that (a) politicians enjoy opportuni-ties – generated by the policy or fiscal context – to strategically obscure investment's short-term costs or (b) information about the long run is struc-tured in a way that vividly signals the prospect of future losses without investment (e.g., by a negative focusing event). The more heavily the informa-tional scales are tilted toward an investment's benefits, the easier it is for officeholders to effectively frame the policy as a favorable long-run tradeoff and the greater the scale of investment that incumbents can undertake without significant danger of losing office.[12]

---

[12] There are, of course, other plausible determinants of citizens' intertemporal policy attitudes and, hence, of electoral safety. Experimental work by Jacobs and Matthews (2008) indicates, for instance, that citizens' level of trust in government conditions their willingness to accept policy investments by moderating the relationship between a delay in benefits and uncertainty about those benefits. Stone (2009), in a related vein, points to a challenge that heterogeneous risk preferences in the electorate pose for investments that insure against long-run risks. As mentioned previously, I focus the theorization here on hypotheses that can be reliably tested using the present study's empirical material. Levels and effects of mass-level cognitive factors such as political trust or risk-preferences would be almost impossible to assess in historical case studies, given the lack of high-quality comparative-historical survey data.

NECESSARY CONDITION 2: EXPECTED LONG-TERM SOCIAL RETURNS

Let us assume that the government enjoys a measure of intertemporal electoral safety: ministers believe that they can make a given policy investment without significant risk of losing office. Protection from electoral retribution provides incumbents with room to maneuver when choosing among policy alternatives, but it falls well short of dictating the choice. It implies neither that ministers will *want* to use that latitude to invest nor that they would have the *institutional capacity* to do so. In this section, we turn to the problem of government officials' policy preferences, leaving institutional capacity to the next section.

As with voters, politicians' favorability toward policy investment should depend greatly on how the choice is defined. Recall two of our key assumptions about officeholders: that they seek to use public policy to achieve social outcomes that they value and that they discount the future modestly relative to the rate of return on feasible policy investments. On these premises, politicians should find investment attractive when the policy trade-off assumes the intertemporal structure of an exchange of current social welfare for the relatively certain prospect of substantially greater future social welfare. Where the social benefits in question are outcomes that she values, this is a bargain that a modestly impatient, outcome-oriented officeholder should in principle be interested in making.

I will argue, however, that there are fundamental reasons why politicians may *not* understand policy investment in these terms. In contrast to voters, politicians are much less likely to ignore longer-term outcomes merely because they are signaled less vividly and dramatically. As systematic processors of policy information, officeholders are more likely to be influenced by the content of information than by its form. Yet, the structure of a choice over long-term policy investment is especially open and indeterminate, even for attentive elites. The central problem is the unusual *uncertainty* of long-term policy outcomes. Of course, the consequences of all policies have *some* measure of uncertainty attached to them. For many policy choices – such as those involving a short-term redistribution of resources – this uncertainty will typically be low enough that it will have little effect on preferences or policy decisions.

The long term, however, poses a problem of prediction at an especially high order of complexity. Not only are the social effects of policy less predictable over the long run, but policy commitments themselves become less reliable over longer time horizons. In contrast, the costs of policy investment are usually much more immediate and, hence, much more certain. So, too, are the benefits of intertemporal alternatives that would maximize gains in the present. Government officials, however electorally insulated and forward-thinking they might be, have little reason to impose the social costs of a policy investment if its purported gains appear unlikely to emerge.

In this section, I first elaborate the nature of the uncertainty that is particularly likely to plague policymaking for the long run. I then argue that the causal complexity of the long run presents policy makers with a set of distinct and profound predictive challenges that cannot be reduced to a straightforward task of expected-utility maximization. As relatively sophisticated decision makers, officeholders will usually confront these challenges with powerful cognitive tools in hand: ideational models of important causal dynamics within the policy sphere. As simplified representations of the dynamics at work in a given domain, these cognitive structures help make judgment and decision possible in the face of massive complexity and uncertainty. In turn, processes of elite reasoning and preference-formation over long-run intertemporal choices are powerfully shaped by the content of the *particular* mental models that they bring to the task. Put differently, how policymakers perceive the structure of the trade-offs that they confront – whether they perceive investment as an exchange of short-term pain for greater long-term gain, a mere redistribution of resources, or a costly gamble – will depend greatly on the ideational lens through which they view the policy domain. Though the discussion in this section is framed in terms of the preferences of officeholders, the ideational processes described here are intended to apply generally to the intertemporal policy preferences of political elites – including, importantly, those of senior civil servants and of interest-group leaders weighing investment's long-term consequences for their members.[13]

The Uncertainty of the Long Run

There are at least two reasons why the long-term consequences of policy invest-ment may be uncertain. First, policies that pay off only in the long term often depend on mechanisms that involve especially extended causal chains. Consider, for instance, the long and complex chains of causation required to turn an energy-tax hike today into a stabilization of the climate 50 years hence, or the processes that must unfold to convert spending on early childhood education into enhanced economic productivity over a period of two decades. Because uncertainty about the final outcome is the product of the uncertainty of each link in the chain, what I will term *consequence uncertainty* mounts steeply as the required causal sequence lengthens. What is worse, steps in the process may depend on aspects of the current economic, social, or physical environment that become more likely to change as time elapses.

In addition to consequence uncertainty, policy investment is vulnerable to a second risk – a threat from politics. Not only may actors have difficulty deter-mining the long-term effects of a plan faithfully implemented, but they also face the risk that a policy adopted today will be overturned tomorrow (Hovi et al.

---

[13] Voters' policy opinions may also be affected by uncertainty, but the determinants of voter uncertainty are likely to be different from the determinants of elite uncertainty, given the much lower levels of cognitive investment in policy issues that ordinary citizens make. In particular, voters are less likely to be operating with clear mental models of specific policy fields of the kind that I argue shape elites' reasoning. On uncertainty and mass intertemporal policy attitudes, see Jacobs and Matthews (2008).

2009; North 1993; Moe 1990). In a democratic context, this *political uncertainty* plagues policy investment for two reasons. First, at least one election is likely to fall between a policy investment's up-front costs and its long-term benefits. Thus, the interests and policy preferences of those in government may well change midstream, producing a risk of policy reversal before the investment has paid off.

Second, policy investments often provide future governments not just with an *opportunity* to dismantle them: they may also provide a compelling *motive*. Many policy investments, by the nature of their mechanisms of intertemporal transfer, require the *accumulation* of fungible resources over long periods of time. This accumulation makes the investment an especially tempting target for future governments in need of resources for their own policy ventures. The fiscal surpluses amassed by today's incumbents through painful tax increases may look to tomorrow's officeholders like a convenient source of financing for new farm subsidies or fighter jets. If today's government creates a strategic petroleum reserve, tomorrow's may expend it opportunistically rather than saving it for the supply shock for which it was intended. Where the invested resources are fungible, today's officeholders (and, similarly, today's senior civil servants or organized interests) cannot know for sure that the policy arrangement will survive to produce its long-term benefits.

The Cognitive Challenge of Causal Complexity[14]

The problem is not just that the long-term benefits of policy investment are uncertain, but that the dynamics governing, and information about, those consequences are inordinately *complex*. To see why this complexity matters, consider again the standard rationalist treatment of uncertainty. From a rationalist perspective, uncertainty presents no fundamental challenge to choice. As discussed, rational actors choose under uncertainty by calculating and comparing the expected utilities of the alternatives. To do so, they assign probabilities and utilities to all possible outcomes of the available options and choose the option with the greatest probability-weighted utility (Savage 1954). This procedure requires individuals to consider all potential consequences of the alternatives and to use all relevant information to assess their probabilities and their payoffs (or otherwise to choose *as if* they had done so).[15]

Unlike the average voter, policy-seeking officeholders will typically be motivated and able to think quite hard about the potential consequences of their choices: as systematic processors of policy issues, they are likely to actively gather and carefully interpret information, to engage in comparisons across alternatives, to weigh positive against negative consequences, and to ponder more than one way in which things might turn out. Such

---

[14] Parts of the next two subsections are drawn from Jacobs (2009a).

[15] I discuss specific rationalist approaches to political uncertainty and commitment problems in Chapter 11.

processes of effortful search and analysis should substantially dampen the effects of superficial informational attributes – such as vividness – on elite judgments, making elites more responsive to informational content and objective circumstances. Indeed, for relatively simple choices, elites may well arrive at decisions that approximate a maximization of expected utility.

Judgments about long-term policy outcomes, however, will rarely be amenable to anything approaching comprehensively rational calculation, even for motivated elites. The difficulty derives from the inordinate conceptual and informational complexity of causal reasoning over long time horizons. Longer causal chains between policy choices and valued consequences generally require much more elaborate causal theories to model. Over longer stretches of time, a useful causal theory also has to capture both increasingly complex potential interactions between policy mechanisms and a changing social and political environment. In turn, as theories become more complex, they require more data and more complex analytical procedures to apply, test, and update. Making matters worse, the quality and clarity of these data will be especially low: the longer the time lag between a policy choice and the valued outcome, the less frequent and less interpretable will be the feedback from similar past decisions. As compared to state action over short time horizons, policymaking for the long term is hence far more likely to run up against the bounds of human rationality discussed earlier in this chapter.

We can therefore think of the difficulty of outcome-prediction over the long term as having two components: a problem of "unknowns" and a problem of attention. Given vast causal complexity and incomplete data, it will usually be impossible – even for motivated and sophisticated elites – to assign meaningful probabilities to all potential outcomes of policy investment, or even to identify all potential outcomes with a nontrivial probability of occurrence.[16] Even if actors took all available information into account, key parameters of an expected-utility calculation would remain unknown or known with little confidence. More than that, however, policy decisions over the long term will generally involve far more data and considerations than boundedly rational decision makers can comprehensively attend to. Even as they seek out and carefully reason about relevant information, the supply of data and logical possibilities will still far exceed their supply of cognitive resources.

Ideas, Causal Inference, and Attention

As we have noted, a key distinction between mass and elite modes of policy reasoning is that elites are more likely to process policy issues systematically.

[16] The distinction I am making – between the conditions under which expected-utility calculations are possible and those under which they are not – roughly corresponds to the distinction between "weak" uncertainty or "risk," on the one hand, and "strong" or Knightian uncertainty, on the other (Denzau and North 1994).

Central to elites' capacity for systematic processing is their possession of structured *prior knowledge* of public policy: relatively well-developed and coherent ideas about state action, ranging from general political worldviews to specific mental maps of a given policy field (Bleich 2003; Blyth 2002; Goldstein and Keohane 1993; Hall 1993). Of greatest relevance to the present discussion are the *causal* ideas that elites hold – those capturing relationships of cause and effect governing policy problems and policy mechanisms. Among the kinds of causal frameworks commonly employed by policy actors are the causal components of political ideologies (e.g., conservatism's teachings about the effects of state intervention on individual welfare), formal theories imported from academic research (e.g., Keynesian economics), and analogies between public policy and other domains (e.g., the understanding of public budgeting as akin to household budgeting; on analogical reasoning by political elites, see Khong (1992)). Moreover, given the importance of future *political* dynamics in shaping the resilience of policy investment, actors will often draw on mental models of politics itself – understandings of the interactions between politicians and their constituents, for instance – in judging the likelihood that an investment will survive and succeed.

Importantly, these causal mappings are always *models* of the real world – which is to say that they capture only a subset of the potentially relevant dynamics. A traditional Keynesian model of the economy, for instance, captures the effect of government spending, via levels of aggregate demand, on employment – but, in turn, is silent on the effect of government spending on workers' inflationary expectations and wage demands, and all that follows from them.

While the policy literature is replete with arguments about the role of ideas in decision making, there are good reasons to think that such causal frameworks play an especially critical role in policymaking over the long term. Cognitive research points to at least two important ways in which ideas can guide causal reasoning and influence policy preferences, particularly under conditions of ambiguity and complexity. On the one hand, students of mental representation have found that abstract knowledge structures, such as schemata and mental models, help agents draw inferences about unknowns. Confronted with incomplete information about a person, choice, or object, individuals employ mental mappings of the world to "fill in the missing data" (Lodge and McGraw 1991, 1362; see also Gentner 2002; Gentner and Collins 1987; Johnson-Laird 1983; Bruner 1973). Policy-relevant causal frameworks usually supply general propositions (e.g., "higher taxes lead to reduced employment") that actors can use to resolve ambiguity about the consequences of specific options. Often, mental models also contain linked "moving parts" that facilitate reasoning about cause and effect (Gentner 2002; Gentner and Collins 1987; Johnson-Laird 1983). Consider, for instance, the structured relationships among key macroeconomic variables in a Keynesian model of the economy, or the requisite balance between levels of spending and revenue implied by a "household" model of budgeting. Such frameworks allow actors to mentally simulate generalized relationships that can then fill in "unknowns" in particular choice situations. Mental models thus identify a limited set of manipulable elements of a system, the necessary relations among them, and the likely consequences of manipulation.

Political scientists have frequently pointed to ideational effects along these lines. Blyth (2002), for instance, in his study of comparative economic policy-making argues that economic ideas – such as *laissez-faire* liberalism or Keynesianism – "account[ed] for the workings of the economy" (37), helping actors determine the sources of problems and predict the consequences of alternative solutions when the data were ambiguous (see also Hall 1993; Weir 1989). Similar inferential effects – in which ideas resolve uncertainty or fill in "unknowns" – have been demonstrated for policies in a wide range of fields, including race relations (Bleich 2002), regulation (Derthick and Quirk 1985), and trade (Goldstein 1993).

Second – and much less explored in political analyses to date – mental representations are known to guide the allocation of individuals' cognitive resources, channeling their attention toward some pieces of available information and away from others (Jacobs 2009a). As Smith (1998) explains, what we see depends on what we *expect* to see:

One of the most fundamental insights of social psychology is that people do not approach situations as neutral observers or recording devices; instead, they bring their own wishes and expectations with them, potentially influencing what they notice and remember (394).

In particular, prior cognitive structures tend to direct information-processing in *self-reinforcing* ways. Indeed, one of the most robust findings in all of cognitive and social psychology is that individuals display a panoply of "confirmation biases" in the processing of information. When confronted with a new instance of a phenomenon, individuals' attention tends to be directed toward attributes that are consistent with or captured by their existing schema and away from features that are inconsistent with or irrelevant to it (Fiske and Taylor 1991). They also display powerful tendencies to more actively *seek out* data that confirm their current understandings, to *recall* such information later, and to *discount* or *reinterpret* evidence that challenges prior expectations (Nickerson 1998; Smith 1998; Fiske and Taylor 1991; Higgins and Bargh 1987). These confirmatory biases, moreover, have been found to persist even among expert decision makers (Einhorn and Hogarth 1988; Lodge and Hamill 1986).

The implications of these findings can be usefully contrasted with the predictions of a rationalist view. In both approaches, actors form expectations about the future utility that will be derived from a given option with multiple possible outcomes. In a rationalist framework, however, the influence of a potential payoff on preferences depends strictly on its objective magnitude and its probability of occurrence. In a cognitive view, by contrast, the impact of a potential policy outcome on an actor's calculations hinges in large part on the degree to which the relevant causal relationship is captured by her preexisting cognitive framework. While decision makers actively seek and reason through information about the size and likelihood of alternative consequences, their mental models of the domain *constrain* this analytic process. Actors will devote substantial attention to those lines of causal reasoning that are captured by their mental model and will interpret information in ways consistent with those causal logics. Equally important, they will invest fewer cognitive resources in arguments and data that happen to be inconsistent with or orthogonal to the model. By making some causal relationships appear more certain and more salient than others, cognitive frameworks thus shape decision makers' basic understandings of the consequences of action and, in turn, of the basic trade-offs that they confront.[17]

Plagued by especially high levels of causal ambiguity and complexity, intertemporal policy choices over long time horizons should be a prime site for the effect of ideas on both inferences and attention. To illustrate, consider a proposed policy investment that would boost public spending on transport infrastructure. The total long-term impact of this investment would be composed of a large number of fiscal, economic, and social processes – some countervailing or interacting with others, each dependent on background conditions that might shift in unforeseeable ways over time. Next, consider a "household budgeting" model of fiscal policy effects. This framework particularly facilitates reasoning about the kinds of financial trade-offs that private actors face – such as the trade-off between spending on some things and spending on others, the relationship between outlays and income (i.e., revenues), and the trade-off between spending restraint today and high debt and interest payments tomorrow. At the same time, as a simplification of the full range of fiscal-policy dynamics, the household analogy is less suited to reasoning about other relationships. In particular, this analogy will tend to deemphasize consequences that are unique to resource-allocations by *public* actors – such as the potential impact of public-infrastructure enhancements today on future productivity and growth in the macroeconomy.

Faced with empirical ambiguity about the policy's net long-term effects, an actor employing the household model will be more likely to fill this gap with inferences about the negative effects of higher transport spending on tax rates, on spending elsewhere, and on debt than about its positive effects on future economic productivity. Further, faced with an overwhelming supply of potentially relevant information and considerations, she will be more likely to look for, attend to, credit, and keep accessible for later recall those data and arguments that point to these particular outcomes than those suggestive of a salutary impact on growth. This ideationally guided process of information-gathering and analysis will, in turn, favor particular understandings of the very trade-off that higher infrastructure spending implies. The decision maker is likely to understand this project either as a redistribution of resources – more transport spending for higher taxes or less spending on other things – or as an

---

[17] See also the discussion of "policy characterizations" in Jones and Baumgartner (2005).

intertemporal trade-off toward the present, with higher spending today yielding higher debt-servicing costs tomorrow. These are choice-definitions substantially biased *against* the investment.

In contrast, a policymaker who applied an alternative mental model to public-expenditure decisions – an endogenous-growth framework, for instance[18] – would tend to fill empirical gaps and gather and interpret data in ways that generate a different set of beliefs about the effects of an investment in infrastructure. She is more likely to expect that same investment to yield a long-run boost in economic welfare that offsets, and possibly outweighs, its short-run costs. She is, in turn, more likely to define the investment as a net-beneficial intertemporal trade-off of fiscal burdens today for economic expansion tomorrow.

In sum, before politicians will support a costly policy investment, they must expect it to have positive long-run social returns. That is to say, officeholders must conceive of investment as a particular kind of trade-off: an exchange of short-run social losses for greater long-run social benefits. Yet because of uncertainty about their consequences, choices about investment are open to multiple potential understandings. Moreover, in the face of vast causal and informational complexity, boundedly rational decision makers are unable to attend to all potential causal considerations and diagnostically relevant information. Policymakers' preexisting mental models of a policy sphere – their simplified mappings of key causal relationships in the domain – allow them to draw inferences about many of the "unknowns," while directing their attention toward some causal possibilities and – equally importantly – *away* from others. The result is a set of causal beliefs about investment that includes only *some* of its conceivable consequences.

In winnowing lines of causal reasoning, ideational frameworks thus play a critical role in defining actors' long-term choices. By emphasizing a limited set of manipulable "moving parts" in a policy system, indicating the relations among them, and suggesting the social consequences of manipulation, mental models lend structure to the trade-offs that policy makers perceive. Whether a politician understands investment as a socially profitable long-run proposition – or as a risky gamble, a cross-sectional redistribution of resources, or the simple imposition of losses – will depend on *how* her cognitive mapping simplifies causal relationships in the policy field: the degree to which it *captures* causal dynamics through which the investment could generate positive social returns over time and *excludes* causal logics through which it might fail, disadvantage major sectors of society, or yield undesired aggregate long-run effects. While I have formulated this argument in terms of politicians' judgments, understandings of investment's consequences

---

[18] Endogenous-growth theory models the ways in which policy – especially investment in human and nonhuman capital – can affect rates of economic growth. For early statements, see Romer (1990) and Barro (1990).

by other political elites – in particular, interest-group leaders and senior state bureaucrats – should be subject to the same dynamic.

To be clear, the independent variable driving this process is an ideational framework to which policymakers subscribe *prior* to the specific intertemporal choice to be explained (or that, at a minimum, derives from a source exogenous to that choice). Mental models that only emerge *in the course* of a policymaking process are unlikely determinants of its outcome. Accordingly, in assessing the influence of policy ideas, the empirical analysis will pay special attention to those ideas' intellectual and historical origins. It is also worth noting that my argument implies that we should observe a good deal of ideational stability over time, even in the face of new information. Mental models' attentional effects should tend to be self-reinforcing as prior expectations lead to the selective collection, processing, and recall of corroborating over discrepant data. Within state bureaucracies, legislatures, and interest associations, these individual-level processes are also likely to be accompanied by collective processes through which cognitive maps become encoded, reproduced over time, and defended within organizations (see, e.g., DiMaggio 1997; Walsh and Ungson 1991; Boynton 1990; Levitt and March 1988; Gioia and Poole 1984). At the same time, the empirical analysis to follow provides evidence of infrequent but major ideational change in the field of pensions. I reflect on these dynamics in the book's concluding chapter and consider there the conditions under which dominant mental models are most likely to be replaced.

NECESSARY CONDITION 3: INSTITUTIONAL CAPACITY[19]

Let us suppose that our first two conditions for policy investment have been met. Government ministers enjoy an opportunity to pursue investment without substantial risk of electoral retribution, and they believe that the investment would generate substantial net long-term social benefits that they value. In most democracies, of course, significant policy change requires more than the agreement of a handful of government officials. Rather, institutional rules require the assent of a considerable range of actors before substantial changes can be made to the disposition of state power. In order to enact policy investment, ministers need not only a policy motive and an electoral opportunity to invest, but also the *institutional capacity* to do so. By institutional capacity, I mean quite simply the ability of ministers to enact their preferred policies into law.

The discussion that follows treats the matter of institutional capacity largely as a problem of overcoming potential challenge from *organized interests* – groups that seek to exploit institutional decision points to block policy investments that they oppose. This is, of course, not the only way in which one might think about the problem of institutional constraint; nor are interest groups the only actors who might take advantage of institutional "veto points" (Immergut 1992a). Comparative institutional analyses, however, have laid particular

---

[19] Parts of this section draw on Jacobs (2008).

emphasis on the effect of political structure on interest-group influence (e.g., Sheingate 2001; Steinmo 1993; Immergut 1992a), and this focus has two analytical advantages. First, among the social groups affected by a policy invest-ment, it is those that are *organized* that are most likely to possess the sophisti-cation, coordination capacity, and resources needed to exploit institutional openings – by lobbying officials, for instance, or forcing referenda. Second, policy investments – from pension reform to environmental regulation – will frequently impose their costs on relatively well-organized sectors of society, including business and unionized workers. Organized interests will thus often be among those actors with the greatest stake in intertemporal policy choices. Conceptualizing institutional capacity as the ability to resist organized opposi-tion directs our attention to those societal actors with the greatest means and, frequently, the greatest motive to take advantage of institutional opportunities.

The key independent variable on which this section focuses – as a concrete determinant of institutional capacity – is the structure of institutions themselves. Without explicitly conceptualizing policy choices in intertemporal terms, vast literatures on the politics of policy change suggest a basic intuition about the institutional conditions that should enhance ministers' capacity to enact policies with substantial costs. In this common logic, ministers' ability to enact their preferred policies, in the face of organized opposition from the cost-bearers, should be higher to the degree that the policymaking process is *insulated* from societal pressure – especially where institutional veto points are few (e.g., Pal and Weaver 2003; Swank 2002; Huber and Stephens 2001a; Bonoli 2000; Pierson 1994; Williamson 1994; Immergut 1992a; Waterbury 1992).

While this familiar line of argument illuminates certain aspects of the politics of investment, it is premised on an essentially distributive understanding of policy choice – in which those groups that would pay the costs of a policy change are assumed to *oppose* it. As I will argue, understanding the effect of institutions on intertemporal policy choice requires us to think carefully about interest groups' policy preferences with respect to the long run and how they choose, within constraints, between alternative means of promoting their members' long-term welfare. In analyzing interest groups' calculations and institutional effects, we shift from the realm of cognitively bounded belief- and preference-formation to the realm of strategic goal-maximization. We now assume that politicians' and interest-group leaders' beliefs about the long-term consequences of a given policy investment have been formed (through processes described under Necessary Condition 2) and that they agree that the investment would generate positive long-term social returns relative to the status quo. With the expected long-run payoff structure thus given, the issue now is how groups seek to maximize net gains within a given institutional setting – and how their strategies affect governments' capacity to invest.

As we shift from cognitive to strategic dynamics, however, we retain our focus on how intertemporal policy choices are *structured* for powerful actors. At the stages of belief- and preference-formation, the main work of choice-definition is performed by patterns of information-processing and ideational frameworks. As actors seek to achieve their preferred policies, however, it is institutional rules that impose a basic structure on their strategic dilemmas. As I will argue, institutions shape the politics of investment not only by governing the degree of *access* afforded to interest groups. They also delimit the *menu of feasible options* from which groups choose and, in turn, influence the intertemporal policy positions that groups take. Institutions, in other words, shape ministers' capacity to invest not only by determining the scope and distribution of interest-group influence but also by structuring the choices that powerful cost-bearing groups are forced to confront. As will be noted, this second effect depends in part on the exact character of the investment: in particular, it will be strongest for investments that confront organized groups themselves with trade-offs between their own short-run and long-run welfare.

Interest Groups' Preferences

We have assumed that interest-group leaders – like other political actors – are only modestly impatient with respect to policy effects (relative, that is, to the rate of return to common policy investment options). All else equal, then, interest group officials will prioritize immediate gains and losses, but will nonetheless value outcomes expected to affect their members years or decades in the future. Union officials, for instance, will worry not just about their members' wages but also about the security of their pension benefits. Industry groups will care not just about firms' current profits but also about the effects of slowly crumbling transport infrastructure on long-run productivity; of demographic change on future social-insurance tax burdens; and of failing schools on the capabilities of tomorrow's workforce. Moreover, their considerable informational capacities mean that interest groups not only care about but also are *aware of* and *attentive to* temporally distant but foreseeable consequences. Let us further assume that a group-centered version of Necessary Condition 2 has been met: like politicians, group leaders have formed causal beliefs that a given policy investment will generate positive long-run social returns.

If organized interests value and are alert to long-term policy benefits, then they should in principle be interested in – and willing to pay something for – policy investments that are expected to deliver substantial long-term payoffs. Indeed, as influential actors attentive to future social outcomes, interest groups potentially constitute a powerful political force *favoring* farsighted policy action. At the same time, two features of interest groups' calculations substantially limit their willingness to support – and, in particular, to accept the costs of – policy investment.

First, however farsighted they may be, most organized interests seek to maximize their *own members'* expected welfare over the long run, not society's as a whole. Depending on the size of the group and the scope of its organization, the two sets of interests may diverge widely (Olson 1982). This means that interest groups' positions on a policy investment will turn in part on its *distributive* qualities – on how the investment allocates its costs and its benefits cross-sectionally. Second, in pursuing long-term gains for their members, interest groups do not simply compare policy investment to the status quo: rather, they compare investment to the range of feasible alternatives that might enhance the group's future welfare. And for reasons elaborated later, even if its gains exceed its costs, policy investment will not always be the policy option that promises an organized group the greatest net long-term benefits.

Institutions and Governments' Capacities to Invest

Let us consider the implications of group capabilities and calculations for the effect of institutional structure on governments' capacities to invest. As I will argue, the effect of institutions on ministerial capacity depends on the cross-sectional distributive profile of the investment in question. We can begin by noting that, for those policy investments that do *not* impose significant costs on any organized interest – e.g., that diffuse their costs broadly across society – institutional capacity should be high and minimally affected by the structure of the institutions themselves (Pierson 1994; Weingast, Shepsle, and Johnsen 1981; Wilson 1980; Olson 1971). Because interest groups are the actors best-equipped to exploit institutional openings, the enactment of an investment that no organized group has reason to oppose should depend little on the availability of institutional veto opportunities.[20]

We can turn now to policy investments that do impose substantial costs on organized interests. It is analytically usefully to differentiate such investments according to their profiles of expected benefits: specifically, by whether the group(s) paying the short-term costs can also expect to capture positive long-term returns. The first type of trade-off – which I will term a *horizontal* investment – imposes its short-term costs on one group while directing its expected benefits to another. Most straightforwardly, an investment may be horizontal by virtue of its objective distributive profile. Environmental regulations, for instance, often concentrate their burden on industry, but disperse their future gains (e.g., clean air or water) widely across society (Harrison 1996). With similar effect, cost-paying groups – for reasons of long-term uncertainty explored in the last section – may not *believe* that an investment will deliver its promised gains to them. Governments may tell industry groups, for instance, that a new levy on their profits will be used to invest in the transport infrastructure on which manufacturing processes depend. But if business leaders do not find this promise credible – if they suspect that governments will end up spending the new revenues on other things – then business will perceive the investment as a simple transfer of resources away from them.

I address horizontal investments only briefly because they should be subject to institutional effects familiar from comparative studies of distributive politics.

---

[20] At most, systems with many veto points may make the enactment of such investments more difficult by empowering nonexecutive officeholders with the power to block policies that they *personally* oppose.

Cost-bearing groups should always oppose policy investments with uncaptured returns since such investments are, from their perspective, simply a losing proposition. Where the group is well organized, the standard logic of institutional insulation should then apply. Institutional capacity to enact such an investment should be highest where the policymaking process is most insulated from societal influence – for instance, where there are fewer institutional veto points for the plan's organized opponents to exploit.

The institutional logic of investment, however, departs markedly from that of distributive politics for policies that confront groups themselves with intertemporal trade-offs. What I term *vertical* investments are those that impose a substantial share of their short-run costs on *and* direct a substantial share of their long-term benefits to the *same* group, at a positive expected rate of return to that group. For instance, the state might raise consumption taxes paid predominantly by workers in order to finance investment tax credits for business that are expected to boost capital formation and, in turn, future productivity, wages, and job prospects. Alternatively, a levy might be imposed on industrial employers to pay for expanded job training that is expected to upgrade workforce skills and enhance firms' long-run competitiveness and profitability. Fiscal reform may impose higher income taxes on the affluent members of a taxpayers' association today in order to pay down public debt and minimize tax burdens tomorrow. Such investments are vertical as long as cost-paying groups expect to capture a sufficient share of their social payoffs such that the policy's long-term (time-preference-discounted) returns to the cost-bearers are positive.

The key difference between the politics of vertical investment and the politics of cross-sectional redistribution or horizontal investment is that vertical investment does not divide the political world into losers and winners: rather, *actors who pay costs today also stand to gain benefits tomorrow.* Because the trade-off is *intra*-group rather than just inter-group, cost-bearers are not necessarily opponents. If the expected rate of return to a vertical investment is sufficiently high, then it makes the group paying its costs better off than the status quo. As King (1993) demonstrates in his study of intertemporal choice in tax policy, for instance, labor unions will sometimes accept revenue policies that tax workers more heavily than capital in the near term in order to maximize wages and the availability of jobs over the long run (see also Przeworski and Wallerstein 1982).

Crucially, however, interest groups' choices about vertical investment need not be structured as simple trade-offs between short-term loss and greater long-term gain. This is because investment is not the only policy option that can enhance a group's long-term welfare. Imagine that an organized Group A faces a problem that will deliver its impact over the long term. Group A might, for instance, be a manufacturers' association facing crumbling transport infrastructure or a trade union facing declining earnings prospects over time. In principle, Group A should be willing to accept a vertical investment that imposes costs on it in the near term but substantially mitigates its problem – improves infrastructure, expands employment – over the long run. However, in many cases it will be possible for a group to achieve similar long-term gains through *purely* cross-sectional means, by arranging for future resources to be shifted in its favor. In a policy move that I will term *long-term redistribution,* one group benefits over the long run at the expense of others, rather than through an aggregate increase in social welfare. Trade unions, for instance, rather than sacrificing now for investments in future productivity, can seek an expansion of unemployment benefits or wage subsidies: without enhancing future economic efficiency, this policy would shield future workers from the long-term effects of stagnant productivity at the expense of other social groups, such as affluent taxpayers or employers. An industry organization facing a particular skill shortage can seek immigration laws that allow skilled foreign workers to enter the country – a move costly to domestic workers – rather than investment at home in training or education. A taxpayers' association could seek to protect its affluent members against the future impact of public debt through budgetary rules that make it difficult to raise taxes, forcing future cuts in spending enjoyed by other groups, rather than through painful near-term deficit-reduction measures. In each case, the group in question is extracting future resources from or shifting long-run burdens onto another sector of society; the response is purely redistributive and not at all intertemporal, as consumption possibilities are transferred cross-sectionally but not over time. In Figure 1.5, Option 3 (or any point along the x-axis to the left of the status quo) would represent a long-run redistributive policy in favor of Group A at the expense of Group B if it generates a relatively durable reallocation of resources between the two groups.

Thus, when assessing means of enhancing their members' long-term welfare, group leaders will *compare* intertemporal and redistributive alternatives. In general, they will have a quite straightforward preference-ordering between vertical policy investment and long-term redistribution. While a vertical investment with substantial positive returns may make the group better off than the status quo, long-term redistribution allows them to reap future policy benefits *without* having to pay the short-term costs of investment.[21] Thus, farsighted interest groups should not, in fact, be natural advocates of policy investment: long-term redistribution should be their first-choice solution.

We can now place these preferences in institutional context to hypothesize how they are likely to be expressed under different policymaking rules. When it

---

[21] This logic also implies elements of group preference-orderings that will not be explored here. For instance, a group should prefer a horizontal investment from which they reap the benefits but for which another group pays the costs over a vertical investment for which they themselves pay the costs. A group should also prefer a horizontal investment with a given cost basis over a long-term redistribution of those same resources since the investment (assuming a positive expected, discounted rate of return) will convert those costs into larger benefits.

comes to vertical investments, the degree of institutional insulation of executive actors from societal influence should have two *countervailing* effects on ministers' capacity to invest.

1. *Veto-opportunity effect.* This is the veto effect familiar from analyses of distributive politics and likewise applicable to horizontal investments. The greater the access of organized groups to the policymaking process, the more opportunity for those that would pay the costs of investment to block its adoption if that investment is not their preferred alternative. Via this mechanism, *greater* insulation from societal pressure via more centralized authority enhances ministers' institutional capacity to invest.

2. *Menu-shaping effect.* Via a second mechanism, however, *decentralized* institutional authority should enhance governments' capacities to invest. The dispersion of authority can make investment more feasible by *removing redistributive alternatives from the menu of options from which interest groups must choose.*

   Suppose that Group A and Group B – the potential winner and loser, respectively, from long-term redistribution – are both organized. Group B's leadership will be just as attentive as Group A's to policies' long-term consequences for its members. As a result, the political feasibility of long-run redistribution will depend on the *distribution of political influence* among those organized groups that have a stake in the outcome. Where Group A enjoys disproportionate sway over the policy process, it will find it relatively easy to achieve a future reallocation of resources in its favor. On the other hand, where the prospective losers can block policy change, long-term redistribution may be effectively removed from the policy menu. All else equal, the broader the coalition required for policy change in a given context, the harder it will be for one social group to extract future resources from another.

   Institutional settings that concentrate policymaking authority – e.g., in the hands of a single-party cabinet commanding a disciplined parliamentary majority – will tend to generate systematic asymmetries in influence among organized interests. As discussed previously, politicians and political parties fighting regular, competitive elections typically depend on a set of critical financial and organizational resources possessed by interest groups. We can think of this dependency as the fundamental basis of interest-group influence. Parties, moreover, tend to forge the strongest and most durable alliances and organizational linkages with those groups whose interests align well with the party's ideological orientation and programmatic commitments. While parties of the right, for instance, tend to form mutually beneficial ties to business organizations, parties of the left are often closely linked to trade union federations. In such relationships, political resources and support are exchanged (whether explicitly or implicitly) for policy influence and outputs.

The prevalence of strategic group-party ties in democratic politics has a powerful implication for the effects of institutional centralization on group influence. As long as parties require interest-group resources and support to win elections, a lack of veto points does not mean a lack of interest-group access: rather, it means an *asymmetry* in group influence and veto power. Where institutions concentrate authority in the hands of the executive, those groups that enjoy close linkages to the party in government will enjoy privileged access to top decision makers; meanwhile, opposing groups will likely be locked out of key venues of policy deliberation and choice. Centralized authority in a competitive electoral context, in other words, tends to generate winning policymaking coalitions that contain a Group A seeking distributive gains, but exclude a Group B from which resources can be extracted or onto which burdens can be shifted. In this way, democratic institutional settings with few veto points facilitate long-run redistribution in favor of those groups with strong ties to the most powerful officeholders.

Political institutions that widely disperse veto power, in contrast, tend on average to expand the range of social interests that must be accommodated to change policy. The greater the veto opportunities, in turn, the easier it is for a Group B to defend its long-run interests by appealing to its own allies in office. Where veto points are multiplied, then, Group B will have greater capacity to block Group A's efforts to redistribute long-term benefits and burdens at Group B's expense.

Group As thus confront the task of optimizing under institutional constraints. Where the government wields unfettered policymaking authority – i.e., the number of veto points is low – a Group A allied with the ruling party will have little reason to accept the costs of policy investment because of the high feasibility of achieving a preferable alternative: a long-run resource-grab from a relatively powerless Group B. Where authority is widely dispersed such that potential Group Bs enjoy veto opportunities, however, Group A's first choice of long-run redistribution is far less practicable. Group A now faces a reduced menu of options: vertical policy investment – for which it pays short-run costs but from which it expects to receive greater long-term benefits – or the status quo. Thus, if a vertical investment offers Group A positive expected returns relative to current policy, then the group is more likely to accept the costs of that investment to the extent that a dispersion of policymaking authority makes redistributive alternatives infeasible. This menu-shaping dynamic thus affects institutional capacity by driving powerful groups' strategic preferences. Through leverage over its allies in office, Group A has the *opportunity* to block investment whether veto points are many or few. But in a context of diffused authority, Group A will have less *interest* in doing so.

In its core logic, this menu-shaping effect is analogous to a dynamic of interest-group preferences identified by Mancur Olson (1982). Olson pointed out that a group's policy positions depend critically on the extent to which the group must *internalize the social consequences* of public policies, as opposed to shifting costs onto or extracting resources from other sectors of society. In Olson's argument, the key determinant of internalization is the encompassingness of group organization – the share of society represented by the interest group. In parallel, I am contending that political institutions also affect the degree to which organized interests must internalize social outcomes. Centralized authority makes benefit- and burden-shifting easier, allowing a Group A allied with the governing party to win future benefits at the expense of others. In effect, Group A in this setting can externalize the long-run social effects of public policy: it can escape the consequences of *not* investing – the long-run payoffs foregone – by extracting equivalent future gains from another segment of society. Decentralized authority, in contrast, forces groups to internalize more of the long-run social impact of state action by blocking redistributive escape routes: where redistribution is off the table, *not* investing implies foregoing net long-run gains that cannot be achieved by any other available means. Put differently, with limited scope for achieving an appealing *inter*-group trade-off, Group A is confronted with its own *intra*-group trade-off over time: a choice between inaction and profitable investment.

This argument underlines two reasons why standard veto-point theories of policy change cannot simply be applied "as is" to understanding intertemporal choice in electoral democracies. First, the common veto-point logic applies best to policies of redistribution because such measures have outright *losers*. With an intertemporal trade-off, however, today's losers may stand to gain in the long run: the cost-bearers of investment may not want to use available veto opportunities to block an investment that will serve their own long-term interests. Second, as analysts of distributive politics have commonly noted, concentrated power makes the cross-sectional redistribution of burdens easier. But it is precisely for this reason that it makes groups allied with the governing party less likely to accept short-term pain for long-term gain. For policy investment to occur, influential organized groups must be constrained from achieving their long-range goals through purely redistributive means. Only when they must internalize their long-run problems do they – and their allies in government – have reason to invest in a solution.

Predictions of Institutional Effects

We are now in a position to assess these two countervailing institutional effects – the veto-opportunity effect and the menu-shaping effect – alongside one another.

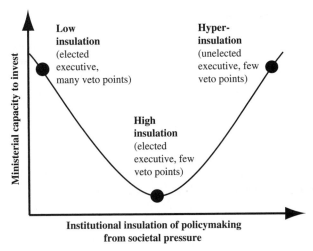

FIGURE 2.1 Predicted Effect of Institutional Structure on Ministers' Capacity to Enact Vertical Policy Investments

Which mechanism should dominate the effect of institutional insulation on ministers' capacity to enact vertical investments? Our predictions are summarized in Figure 2.1. First, compare the conditions of low and high insulation: a setting in which an elected government must overcome many institutional veto points to enact policy (e.g., the United States) versus a setting in which an elected government must overcome few (e.g., the United Kingdom). On the one hand, cost-bearing groups (Group As) in the more decentralized setting have more plentiful opportunities to block investments that they oppose (the veto-opportunity effect). However, as long as the potential losers from long-run redistribution (Group Bs) are organized, decentralized authority structures the choice in a way that makes Group A less interested in *using* available veto opportunities, by removing long-term redistribution from the menu of feasible alternatives (the menu-shaping effect). In this setting, a group offered a vertical intertemporal trade-off that makes it better off than the status quo should be more likely to accept it, even if they *can* reject it. The *supply* of veto points, that is, should not inhibit policy change without the *demand* for a veto. Likewise, where power is concentrated in the hands of an elected ruling party, a cost-bearing Group A allied with the governing party will have *both* the means *and* the motive to reject that same intertemporal trade-off: the means because of the governing party's dependence on the group's strategic resources and support to win elections; and the motive because its preferred redistributive alternative is institutionally feasible. Ministers in this setting will have less capacity to impose the costs of a vertical investment on the group.

Thus, in comparing elected governments in more or less centralized polities, the menu-shaping effect should dominate the veto-opportunity effect: greater centralization means greater capacity to redistribute but correspondingly *reduced* capacity to impose the costs of vertical investment on organized interests.[22] Yet the logic of group influence also implies that the effect of institutions on ministerial capacity to invest should become *curvilinear* at very high levels of institutional insulation. Now compare two political systems, *both* with authority concentrated in ministers' hands: one in which the executive is directly or indirectly elected (e.g., the United Kingdom) and one in which the executive is *un*elected. While policymaking can be considered highly insulated in the first, it is *hyper*-insulated in the second. The pre-1919 German Reich – with its strong and unelected government and its elected but relatively weak lower house of parliament – approximates a polity with hyper-insulation of policymaking. Policy decisions made by unelected bureaucrats, in otherwise electorally competitive democracies, should display similar qualities of hyper-insulation.

As we move from highly to hyper-insulated policymaking, it is now the veto-opportunity effect that should matter most. On the one hand, ministers in both settings dominate the policymaking process. But because ministers in hyper-insulated executives do not need to mobilize votes in the near term, they are less dependent on the political resources possessed by interest groups. Thus, not only does a government in this setting enjoy an institutionally assured form of electoral safety, but as a consequence, it is also far less entangled in support-for-policy exchanges with organized interests.[23] At this extreme of the insulation spectrum, greater executive autonomy should *enhance* ministerial capacity to invest by depriving cost-bearing groups – including those that might otherwise

---

[22] The above logic also implies an exception to this expectation: a vertical investment that imposes its costs on and delivers its benefits to organized groups *not* allied with the party in control of the executive. For an investment with this profile, ministerial capacity to invest should be relatively high and minimally affected by the degree of centralization of authority. In a decentralized setting, where major redistributive shifts are difficult, an outsider group faces the same incentives as an insider group: while veto opportunities are *available*, the group will prefer not to use them to block a vertical intertemporal trade-off that improves its long-run welfare over the only feasible alternative, the status quo. And in a centralized setting, the outsider group – without privileged access to ministers – lacks means as well as motive to reject a profitable vertical investment. To emphasize, this logic applies to vertical investments only – i.e., those that both impose their short-run costs and deliver their long-run benefits to the outsider group at a positive rate of return to that group. An investment that only imposes its costs on the outsider group but delivers its benefits elsewhere is a horizontal investment and should be subject to the standard, distributive institutional logic in which insulation straightforwardly enhances ministerial capacity to invest.

[23] To be clear, this claim is a *ceteris paribus* proposition comparing hyper-insulated to moderately insulated decision making. It is not meant to imply that unelected governments or bureaucrats do not form strategic alliances with organized interests. Bismarck's government, for instance, enjoyed well-known linkages to landowning and heavy-industrial interests (Blackbourn 1998), and bureaucrats in regulatory agencies may grant undue influence to the groups that they are intended to regulate (Stigler 1971). My claim is that, all else equal, the absence of electoral pressure – the lack of a direct short-run dependence on groups for the maintenance of office – greatly *reduces* the imperative for policymakers to tailor policy to organized interests' preferences.

be natural allies – of the leverage they would need to block investment or to demand a redistributive alternative.

It should further be noted that formal institutions are not the only factor that can set in motion these basic logics. At its core, this logic turns on the degree and balance of interest groups' effective veto power over policy change; and as theories of veto points and players recognize, capacities for obstruction depend on more than just formal institutional arrangements. Quasi-formal features of a political system – including the outcome of elections, the degree of party discipline in a legislature, and the degree of group organization – can affect groups' opportunities to influence or block policies that they oppose (Tsebelis 1995; Immergut 1992b). Material and ideational conditions – such as economic crisis or the wide acceptance of ideological doctrines – may also impinge on groups' effective veto power by shaping the credibility or the perceived legitimacy of their claims. Whatever the sources of groups' effective veto power, however, the basic causal logic remains the same: governments' investment capacity should be highest either when affected social groups lack veto opportunities altogether or when those opportunities are roughly balanced across groups; and lowest when veto power is substantially unbalanced, concentrated in the hands of just one set of affected interests.

KEY HYPOTHESES

We can now summarize the key theoretical propositions to be tested in the empirical chapters to come. When governments are considering potential responses to long-term policy problems, the enactment of policy investment should depend on the presence of three general necessary conditions: electoral safety, the expectation of long-term social returns, and institutional capacity. The strength of each general condition is, in turn, determined by a set of concrete observable variables. The main hypothesized relationships between observable determinants (emphasized in bold) and necessary conditions are as follows:

Necessary Condition 1: Electoral Safety

Ministers can invest with greater electoral safety where:

- **electoral competitiveness** is low;
- politicians enjoy **opportunities to minimize the relative salience of investment's short-run costs** through strategic policy design, opportunities that will be conditioned by features of the policy and fiscal context (e.g., inherited program structures, available budgetary slack, or the relative size of the costs); or
- the **occurrence of focusing events** draws voters' attention to long-term social problems and policy consequences.

Necessary Condition 2: Expected Long-Term Social Returns

Ministers will perceive a policy investment as yielding greater net long-term social benefits to the extent that:

- the **mental model** that they employ to conceptualize the policy sphere captures causal dynamics through which the investment could generate benefits and excludes causal dynamics through which the investment could generate costs or through which the production of benefits could fail.

Necessary Condition 3: Institutional Capacity

Ministers' capacity to enact a policy investment will depend on the degree of **institutional insulation of policymaking** from societal influence, as determined both by the number of institutional veto points outside the executive and by whether executive decision makers must win elections to remain in office. The nature of the effect is contingent on the cross-sectional distribution of the investment's costs and benefits.

For *horizontal* investments with significant costs for organized interests, institutional capacity will:

- be greater to the extent that policymaking is more insulated from societal influence (the number of veto points is low or the executive is unelected).

For *vertical* investments with costs for organized interests, institutional capacity will be:

- high under conditions of low institutional insulation, i.e., where an elected executive faces multiple veto points in enacting policy;
- low under conditions of high institutional insulation, i.e., where institutions centralize policymaking authority in the hands of an elected executive; and
- high under conditions of hyper-insulation, i.e., where institutions centralize policymaking authority in the hands of an *un*elected executive.[24]

For investments that do not impose significant costs on organized interests, institutional capacity will be:

- high and minimally dependent on the structure of political institutions.

While the framework identifies a considerable range of causal variables, a common logic of choice-structuring has run through the analysis. Instrumental, modestly impatient actors who care about social outcomes have reason to look favorably upon a policy trade-off that would exchange short-run

---

[24] As noted, however, capacity should be high and minimally affected by institutional structure for vertical investments that impose their costs only on those organized groups that are not allied with the party holding the executive. Because investments in pension financing typically have costs that cut across a wide swathe of society – usually falling on both labor and capital – this particular prediction cannot be tested in the present study.

pain for greater long-run gain. Major obstacles to policy investment thus derive from the fact that voters, organized interests, and politicians will not always confront intertemporal choices in these terms. The complexity of the long run, the bounds of human cognition, and the multiplicity of long-term policy options create opportunities for alternative choice-definitions to dominate actors' decisions. The above hypotheses, for the most part, seek to identify the circumstances under which long-term policy trade-offs will be structured in the terms that are most favorable to policy investment: the informational and ideational conditions under which actors will conceive of investment as a profitable intertemporal exchange, and the institutional conditions that will constrain their efforts to evade intertemporal dilemmas altogether.[25]

We turn now to testing the fruitfulness of this approach by empirically analyzing intertemporal decision making within a major field of state activity: public pensions. The case analyses are divided into two parts, each focusing on a distinct stage of policy development. In the four country chapters in Part II of the book, we consider the trade-offs over time that governments in Germany, Britain, the United States, and Canada made when they created their public contributory pension schemes. Part III then moves forward in time to consider how governments in these same countries have faced the intertemporal trade-offs posed by aging populations and fiscal constraint over the last 30 years. In all cases, governments faced a similarly structured dilemma of timing – pitting short-run benefits and burdens against long-run financial sustainability – but responded with widely differing intertemporal policy decisions.

As discussed in Chapter 1, we will derive leverage on the theory in two ways. As a matter of cross-case analysis, we will examine whether the outcomes align as predicted with the values of our independent variables. Second – and comprising the bulk of the empirical discussion – we will turn to detailed evidence about the processes of policymaking in each case to examine whether the causal processes that generate the outcomes are consistent with this chapter's theoretical logic. To help guide readers through this substantial body of empirical material, Tables 11.1 and 11.2 in the concluding chapter summarize the case studies' main findings.

---

[25] As the reader may have noted, this chapter's theoretical logic does not explicitly distinguish between *intra*generational and *inter*generational intertemporal trade-offs. It treats today's societal actors as though they are considering future benefits that they – the current cohort, rather than a future generation – will reap over the long run. Many policy investments will pay off over time horizons that make this a reasonable assumption for most voters and interest-group members. For very long-term investments (e.g., those that yield a social profit only after several decades), we could further allow for *dynastic* utility functions (Becker and Barro 1988), incorporating the utility that current individuals derive from the expected welfare of their descendants. We could also understand interest-group leaders as seeking to promote the long-run welfare of a *sector* of society (e.g., labor or capital), not just of current members of that sector. These are, of course, significant simplifying assumptions. This study leaves to future analysis, however, a direct examination of how the specifically intergenerational character of some intertemporal policy trade-offs might affect their politics.

PART II

PROGRAMMATIC ORIGINS:

INTERTEMPORAL CHOICE IN PENSION DESIGN

Introduction

What was at stake in social politics at the dawn of the welfare state? Most welfare-state scholars have described the birth of social programs as the development of a set of rules governing the redistribution of resources across individuals and groups. "...[W]hatever form it takes, the distinguishing mark of social policy seems to be its character as a unilateral transfer, in contrast to the bilateral exchange of the market," writes Hugh Heclo (1974, 2) in the opening chapter of his classic treatment of the early politics of social protection. Heclo characterizes the construction of the modern welfare state as a fundamental change in the conditions under which individuals could claim resources from governments, "an expansion of state transfer programs from the narrow and disqualifying relief of the poor law to a vast range of transfers by right" (2). Peter Baldwin (1990), in his masterful comparative study of the politics of social insurance, similarly identifies at the core of political conflict over social policy a redistributive tug of war. "...[A]pproached from the right angle," he writes, "the nuts and bolts of social policy testify to the heated struggles of classes and interests" (1). In Baldwin's view, battles among workers, employers, and early social policy makers over the structure of welfare state programs were primarily "disputes among groups for redistributive advantage, contests over solidarity..." (1).

Alongside pitched battles over redistributive advantage and solidarity, however, unfolded quieter but highly consequential struggles over the distribution of social policy's benefits and burdens *over time:* in the terms of the present study, struggles over whether to build policy investments into new social programs. In fact, the problem of *intertemporal* distribution was itself framed by the choices governments made with regard to cross-sectional distribution, especially about eligibility rules and the distribution of burdens across groups. Such ordinary distributive choices had major implications for the over-time trajectory of state commitments in succeeding decades.

One crucial distributive choice, for instance, was the decision by most advanced industrialized countries to establish major old-age security programs on a *contributory* basis: individuals would earn eligibility to pension benefits through a record of contributions, which, alongside matching employer premiums, would be the chief source of financing for the scheme. As other studies have detailed, the choice of a contributory structure had little to do with its intertemporal effects. By creating an earmarked tax on workers, in an era in which few workers paid income taxes, governments aimed to tap a new source of revenue to pay for this new spending commitment. And by basing eligibility for benefits on a contributory record rather than on need or citizenship, policy designers generated an earned entitlement that they believed distinguished social insurance arrangements from stigmatizing, dehumanizing social assistance. Yet, if contributory financing was usually chosen for its distributive, fiscal, and moral advantages, the contributory logic also set in motion a trend of *increasing* generosity and expenditure over time.

To simplify the dynamic slightly, contributory schemes that required that workers pay premiums in order to receive benefits started out as remarkably cheap propositions. While revenues poured in from current workers in the early years, few of the current elderly had yet paid premiums that entitled them to substantial benefits.[1] Gradually, however, as workers amassed contributory records, the burden of the state's pension promises would grow since the ranks of the elderly would be increasingly comprised of individuals with an earned right to a pension. Moreover, where the size of an individual's pension depended on how much he had paid in, the contributory logic would push up individual benefit levels for several decades as workers amassed longer contributory records and, in an earnings-related system, as wages increased. If in addition fertility rates were falling or lifespan was increasing, pension systems would also face mounting burdens as the contributing population shrunk and the beneficiary population grew.

This process of maturing state commitments – a side effect of distributive features of policy design – presented governments with a choice about how to distribute the cost of these outlays over time. On the one hand, policy makers could finance the system on a pay-as-you-go (PAYGO) basis: they could set contribution rates at a level sufficient to pay each year's actual pension costs, allowing contribution rates to rise with the mounting pension burden. Under a PAYGO system, the state would be engaging in a pure transfer of resources among groups, doling out to one what it extracted from another in a given year. Alternatively, governments could choose to adopt a *policy investment* by "funding" the new schemes: they could set initial contribution rates at a level *higher* than was required to meet current costs, building up a fund that would be invested in interest-bearing assets. The accumulated principal and the return on those assets would then help pay tomorrow's far larger pension bills.

What was at stake in this choice? Like most policy investments, the enterprise of pension funding confronted vast long-term causal complexity. While the funding of a pension scheme involves a clearly identifiable mechanism of

---

[1] In fact, for both social and political reasons, governments tended to grant some benefits to those already elderly at the time the program was set up.

intertemporal transfer (accumulation and, in some cases, capital-creation, as discussed in Chapter 1), its ultimate long-run social consequences are difficult to predict in advance. Decision makers weighing this option could potentially reason about a vast range of plausible causal sequences and possible long-term outcomes. On the one hand, the accumulation and investment of a large fund should allow the program to impose smaller long-term burdens on contributors while maintaining a given level of benefit-generosity, even as overall outlays increased. A large reserve buildup might also protect the state against the future risk of having to bail out a program that, for unforeseen reasons, could not meet its obligations to retirees. Depending on program design, the amassed funds could also provide a pool of financing for public and private capital investments that might enhance future economic productivity.

If policy investment promised long-term advantages, however, it also carried major potential risks. By imposing higher short-term costs than necessary to pay benefits, governments might increase opposition to the new social programs among both the workers and the employers who had to pay for them. Because a great deal of welfare-state development took place at moments of economic distress, politicians also had cause to worry that higher short-term contribution burdens risked impeding economic recovery by raising the costs of industrial production. Over the longer run, a large fund accumulated today might face both political and economic threats tomorrow. Future governments might choose to abandon the hard-won investment, liquidating the fund for other purposes. Alternatively, a fall in asset values or a rise in prices might wipe out the fund's real value before it could deliver its long-term social benefits. As we shall observe, this multiplicity of causal possibilities allowed for a vast range of potential definitions of the financing choice and of the trade-offs that policy investment entailed.

The focus of Part II of this book is the widely divergent choices that four governments made about whether and how much to invest in funded pensions. Germany in 1889 and the United States in 1935 chose to build major policy investments into their contributory pension systems, establishing them on a nearly fully funded basis. At the other extreme, Britain opted in 1925 for a purely PAYGO arrangement that strictly redistributed resources cross-sectionally across current generations. Canada, an intermediate case, chose in 1965 to make a moderately sized investment in a partially funded system. The next four chapters will examine why German, British, U.S., and Canadian governments made the intertemporal policy choices they did. In each case, we will investigate the importance of the three conditions theorized in the previous chapter to be necessary for investment – electoral safety, expected social returns, and institutional capacity – and the effects of the independent variables that we hypothesized to generate them.

CHAPTER 3

Investing in the State

The Origins of German Pensions, 1889[1]

On November 17, 1881, Emperor Wilhelm I of Germany announced – as would become clear in retrospect – the birth of the modern welfare state. In a Royal Proclamation, the emperor declared his government's intention to legislate the world's first comprehensive package of social insurance for manual workers. Covering the risks of accident, sickness, disability, and old age, this edifice of income and health security would be built, piece by piece, over the following eight years. In initiating this project of social protection, Germany's Chancellor, Otto von Bismarck, was not primarily motivated by a humanitarian desire to relieve the miserable social and economic conditions of the working class. As the preamble to the accident insurance bill made explicit, this endeavor did not just represent an "obligation of humanity and Christianity" to the propertyless classes: it was, the government explained, "a policy of state-preservation."[2]

The main threat to the state that Bismarck saw looming on the horizon was the rapid growth of the workers' movement and the Socialist Party. The socialists, in his view, threatened the unity of the German Reich, still a recent and fragile constitutional achievement. In 1878, Bismarck convinced a conservative-dominated parliament to pass a harshly repressive antisocialist law intended to debilitate the movement organizationally and electorally (Craig 1981). Yet this crackdown was only the first prong of the iron chancellor's defense of the social and political status quo. Bismarck aimed to complement the stick of suppression with the carrot of state beneficence. A measure of social protection, he thought, would immunize workers against socialist propaganda while driving a wedge between socialist leaders and their followers and binding the working class to the state. A worker with a pension awaiting him would be more conservative in outlook, less likely to be swept up by revolutionary sentiment, than a worker

---

[1] Parts of this chapter are drawn from Jacobs (2009a). Archival records cited are from the Bundesarchiv-Berlin (BArch). In some cases, I consulted transcriptions of original documents furnished by Florian Tennstedt and Ulrike Haerendel; all citations, however, are to the original archival locations. All translations are mine. Transcriptions of many of these documents can also be found in Haerendel (2004).

[2] The March 8, 1881, draft of the accident insurance bill is quoted in Ritter (1983, 28).

with no economic security and nothing to lose (Ritter 1983). While the anti-socialist laws would crush the workers' movement organizationally, social insurance would forge a political alliance between the Wilhelmine state and the working class.

With health and accident insurance in place by the mid-1880s, Bismarck's government turned to old-age and disability insurance toward the end of the decade. The Chancellor's broad vision of worker protection, however, left open fundamental issues of policy design. Among these was how the new pension scheme would be financed. For the senior civil servants who would craft the program, one of the chief challenges was that the costs of a contributory pension scheme would be unevenly distributed over time. While the program's payouts would start small – since few workers would have accumulated claims to benefits – they would rise steeply as successive generations of workers amassed larger contribution records and benefit entitlements.

The logic of contributory pensions thus presented policymakers with an intertemporal dilemma. On the one hand, the government could choose to put off most of the costs for decades by tying contribution rates to current expenditures: the contribution burden would start out exceedingly low but rise over time as pension outlays rose. On the other hand, by taxing ahead – matching *current* contribution rates to the value of *future* benefit entitlements – and investing the resulting surpluses, the government could keep the long-term costs of the system far lower and more stable over the long run. In the end, the Reich chose to maximize the program's long-term financial sustainability at great short-run expense. What conditions made this large policy investment possible?

THE LOGIC OF LONG-TERM INVESTMENT

Once Bismarck had decided upon the broad goals of his social insurance system, he largely delegated the tasks of policy design to his ministers and civil servants. The design process was centered primarily within the Reich's Interior Office, in consultation with the Treasury. In fact, officials quickly departed from one of Bismarck's initial principles for financing the scheme. The Chancellor's original plan was that the entire pension program would be financed directly by the state Treasury out of general tax revenues, without worker premiums. Given his goal of binding workers to the regime, the Chancellor preferred to have the state play the sole role of benefactor, avoiding that of tax-collector. Yet Interior Office officials judged this notion to be flatly impractical, noting that the Reich could never squeeze such a sum of money – amounting to a 20 percent increase in public spending – out of existing revenue sources. Tight constraints on the central state's taxing powers under the 1870 constitution further limited the Reich's options for general-revenue financing (Craig 1981). The Interior Office concluded that only a contributory arrangement – financed mostly by new, earmarked premiums paid by workers and their employers, topped up by a subsidy from the Reich treasury – was fiscally plausible (Haerendel 2000).

Once settled upon, the actuarial and moral logic of contributory financing forced policymakers to confront a further set of dilemmas. If workers were to be required to make contributions in exchange for rights to a pension, then benefit entitlements would in some measure need to reflect contribution records. This contributory principle meant that the scheme's ultimate costs would only be realized after a substantial stretch of time. Initially, the scheme would be collecting contributions from all blue-collar workers while few of the elderly or disabled would have earned a right to substantial benefits. With every year that passed, however, contributing workers would be accumulating rights to larger and larger pensions, mounting obligations that the state would have to meet at a future date (Sniegs 1996).

This rising trajectory of benefit obligations presented officials with an intertemporal choice. As explained in earlier chapters, two broad options were available. At one end of the spectrum, the Reich could defer the costs of those obligations until they came due. Financing the pension plan on a pay-as-you-go (PAYGO) basis would mean setting contribution levels each year so that the scheme's revenues just covered its benefit payments for that year. While the contribution burden of PAYGO financing (*Umlageverfahren*) would start out low, actuaries advised the Interior Office that its premium levels would rise more than *13*-fold over the next several decades (Rosenstock 1934). At the other extreme, the government could smooth the financing burden over time by imposing the costs of future benefit payments immediately. Under a pure system of funding (*Prämiendeckungsverfahren*), the state would levy premiums on each cohort of workers (and their employers) sufficient to cover the actuarial costs of that cohort's own future pensions, rather than the cost of current benefit outlays. At the outset, this would mean imposing a contribution burden more then 10 times as high as a PAYGO system and accumulating enormous surpluses. Because it would extract resources far earlier, however, a funded scheme would, in theory, end up much less expensive over the long term. Rather than rising with benefit outlays, the funded contribution rate could remain relatively stable over time, at a level 25 percent below the ultimate PAYGO rate. These different cost trajectories derived from the simple logics of accumulation and compound interest: the higher contribution rates collected earlier under a funded regime would produce annual surpluses which would be invested to generate interest income that would help pay future benefits (Rosenstock 1934).

Faced with this intertemporal trade-off, Interior officials strongly preferred the logic of investment over the logic of deferred pain. They believed that PAYGO financing – which revealed its true costs only after decades – was far less honest as a method of providing for a long-term risk like disability or old age: costs should be paid, they believed, when liabilities are incurred.[3] As one official argued in a memo to the Interior Secretary, "Pay-as-you-go financing shifts a part of the burden onto the future, and is therefore only useful when there

---

[3] On this point, and for a masterful discussion of the debate over funding and PAYGO financing in Germany from the 1880s onward, see Manow (2000). See also Rosenstock (1934).

are overwhelming practical reasons that justify this relief for the present." If there is reason to believe, he explained, that tomorrow's burdens will be lower than today's, then there may be a case for shifting some current costs onto the future. But with disability and old age insurance, he concluded, there was no reason to think that there will be any long-term fall in expenditures to counteract the natural cost explosion of a PAYGO mechanism.[4]

More concretely, policymakers believed that PAYGO's upward trend in contribution rates, and the much higher final rate that this financing method implied, would have long-term political costs for the Reich. As officials argued, PAYGO financing would burden future workers in "a prohibitively expensive and unjustified way for the sake of current workers."[5] This intergenerational injustice was not only of normative concern but also appeared to threaten the long-term political goal at the heart of Bismarck's social insurance project: forging a political alliance with workers that would protect the state against revolutionary threat. In order for social programs to have these state-preserving effects, workers would have to view them as a good financial bargain. If future workers facing exorbitant pension contribution rates found that they could get a better deal through private arrangements, then they were bound to resent paying these premiums to the state.[6] Even the simple fact of increases over time could be dangerous, as the Interior Secretary noted:

We can set to one side the question of whether the future will be in a position to carry the additional burden that pay-as-you-go financing would produce. At any rate, the annual increases in contribution rates that pay-as-you-go financing would require until maturity is objectionable if for no other reason than that the discord over the increasing burden of workers' insurance will be continually nourished and, unlike in the case of the accident insurance [where employers pay the entire contribution], will not be limited to the circle of employers.[7]

The steady increases in social insurance taxes that PAYGO financing would bring with it could, as time passed, become the focus of worker discontent – precisely the opposite of the policy's intended political effect (Bosse and Woedtke 1891, 288).

---

[4] Memo from Erich von Woedtke to Karl Heinrich von Boetticher on the disadvantages of PAYGO financing, [no title], December 4, 1888, R 1501/100024, BArch, pp. 227–229RS.

[5] "Denkschrift, betreffend Alters- und Invalidenversicherung," [no author], July 6, 1887, R43/565, BArch, pp. 87–98RS.

[6] A comparison of the "deal" future workers would get from the state pension system with that which they could get from private life insurers was an explicit part of Interior's evaluation of a parliamentary proposal (discussed later) to reduce the level of funding in the system. See Rechnungsgrundlagen: "Betrifft die Einführung des Kapitaldeckungsverfahrens an stelle des Prämienverfahrens bei der Alters- und Invaliditätsversicherung," [no author], R1501/100097, BArch, pp. 161 and 161RS.

[7] "Votum des Vize-Präsidenten des Staatsministeriums, Staatssekretär des Innern Dr. von Boetticher, betreffend die Revision des Invaliditäts- und Altersversicherungsgesetzes sowie die Vereinfachung und Zusammenlegung der Arbeiterversicherung," December 1, 1895, R2/41575, BArch, p. 326. Though writing in 1895, Von Boetticher was referring to choices made in the late 1880s. For reference to the government's argument on this point during the original pensions' debate in the late 1880s, see Preußischer Volkswirtschaftsrat (1887, 93).

Moreover, officials believed that funding would place the scheme on a more solid financial footing, better protecting the state's own long-term fiscal capacities. Because a funded scheme always had assets on hand to cover its accumulated liabilities, it would not be hostage to fluctuations in contribution revenues. A PAYGO plan, in contrast, would depend on each year's income to pay benefits; operating with little buffer, it would be far more vulnerable to unexpected contingencies or miscalculation. As the Treasury secretary wrote to the Interior minister, funding ensured "that the continuing financial capacity of the insurance institutions is as secure as possible."[8] For the state itself, much was at stake in the pension program's future financial solidity. As officials repeatedly pointed out, if the scheme were ever to run short of funds to pay benefits, it was highly likely that the state Treasury itself would have to step in to make up the difference.[9]

Ministers and senior civil servants thus placed a high value on funding's long-term social, fiscal, and political benefits. Nonetheless, this policy investment would have substantial short-run costs for important sectors of society. Could the government afford the political risk of imposing such a heavy burden on workers and industry in the near term? Would not organized producer interests – especially business – fight to block such a costly move? And given the novelty of the public-pension enterprise, why were officials willing to invest in such distant payoffs? How could policymakers be sure that an accumulated fund would not fall prey to political manipulation or unforeseen economic developments?

MAINTAINING OFFICE FOR THE LONG RUN

One striking feature of the policy choice that ministers made was the degree to which it exposed them to potential blame from voters unhappy with the short-run costs. The costs of the policy investment in funding were not to be embedded by stealth into a complex policy formula, and fiscal constraints precluded diluting them across the state budget. Indeed, a brand new tax was to be visibly imposed on all manual workers – a levy that would have to be more than 10 times higher if the government chose funding than if it opted for PAYGO financing. Moreover, the informational environment provided no vivid signals – no focusing event, in the language of Chapter 2 – that might turn voters' attention toward the long-term consequences of the financing choice. The very fact that the public pension system was being created *de novo* radically limited the supply of potential focusing signals, especially from public programs themselves. At the moment of program creation, there simply *was* no state pension scheme that could transmit dramatic information

---

[8] Jacobi to von Boetticher, July 20, 1887, R1501/100096, BArch, p. 158RS.
[9] Bosse to Jacobi [State Secretary of the Treasury], August, 5, 1887, R2/41569, BArch, p. 115; Jacobi to von Boetticher, July 20, 1887, R1501/100096, BArch, p. 158RS; Memo from Erich von Woedtke to Karl Heinrich von Boetticher on the disadvantages of PAYGO financing, December 4, 1888, R1501/100024, BArch, pp. 227–229RS.

about future program insolvency, rising contribution rates, or a threat to promised benefits. (By contrast, see the U.S. and Canadian reform episodes in Part III.) Informational conditions thus helped politicians neither to obscure the costs of investment nor to frame and justify the choice in terms of funding's long-run advantages. With the Reichstag elected via universal suffrage amidst vibrant multiparty competition, there was ample opportunity for policy investment to yield adverse electoral consequences.

Social policymaking in Wilhelmine Germany, however, presents a useful study in the effects of electoral safety on governments' intertemporal calculations. To the extent that Bismarck's ministers worried about maintaining office, such considerations actually made policy investment *more* rather than less attractive. To see why, we have to consider the specific structure of the political challenges that the government confronted.

Imperial officials were living in a political world in which threats to their grip on power were growing, but growing slowly. As historian Gordon Craig (1981) writes of the emerging socialist challenge, "If he had thought only in terms of present voting and parliamentary strength, Bismarck's concern would not have been great in 1878" (95). Indeed, the Social Democratic Party had won only 12 seats in the Reichstag (out of 401) in the previous election and a mere 500,000 votes. But, as Craig points out, Bismarck saw organizational developments – such as the concentrated strength of socialism in urbanized and industrial regions and the growing reach of socialist periodicals – that threatened the existing political and social order over the long term. The movement also had momentum: that half-a-million votes in 1878 represented a fivefold increase over worker-party support 7 years earlier. That same year, Bismarck began pushing through parliament a series of antisocialist laws that aimed to weaken party and trade-union organizations (Craig 1981). Despite a ban on official use of the party label, the Social Democrats' vote shares tripled over the decade (as members ran as independents) and union membership mounted rapidly (Berman 1998).

At the same time, the institutional position of Bismarck's ministers meant that this threat did not require an immediate policy response. Not responsible to Parliament, cabinet officials did not have to fight for their own political survival in regular elections. Crucially, this meant that short-term losses incurred in the electoral realm did not greatly loosen the government's grip on the reins of power. While electoral setbacks to government-friendly parties could make it harder to cobble together parliamentary majorities for passing legislation, they would not endanger the incumbency of executive officeholders, who served at the emperor's, rather than the legislature's, pleasure.

Given the structure and pace of the mounting socialist threat, what Reich officials needed most was not to maximize near-term vote tallies but to undermine the left's long-term organizational momentum. The government's time horizon for policy planning thus could be – in fact, *needed* to be – quite extended. Indeed, a review of Interior and Finance ministry correspondence and minutes of internal meetings, as well as of contemporary secondary accounts, uncovered no reference to the near-term implications of funding on public attitudes or electoral results. The only discussion of mass attitudes focused, as mentioned earlier, on the *long*-term effects of the financing choice on levels of worker discontent.[10] Ministers' preference for funding *was* thus in large part driven by a desire to retain public office, but it was office-seeking over the long run, not the short.

THE DOMINANCE OF THE INSURANCE MODEL

Though policy investment in principle offered substantial fiscal and political benefits, those benefits were potentially beclouded by enormous uncertainty. Planning a pension system required the calculation of consequences far beyond the usual time horizon of government activity. If a funded pension scheme were to stabilize contribution rates and protect the Treasury over the long run while providing appreciable improvements in workers' standard of living, several things would have to go right over the next 40 to 50 years. Interest rates on bonds and other safe investments, for instance, would have to remain near or above the actuaries' assumptions of 3.5 percent for several decades, or the accumulated fund would not grow sufficiently to meet future liabilities.[11] The policy investment also depended on stable monetary values: if there was significant inflation, then the nominal benefits written into the law – and against which contribution levels and funding requirements were calculated – would gradually lose their value to workers. Further, the investment would only work if future governments and Reichstags could be trusted to leave the accumulating pension funds – expected to reach almost 5 billion marks, or 20 percent of GDP in 1891 (Sniegs 1996) – untouched and dedicated to the program.

Indeed, in designing the world's first public contributory pension system, officials were aware that they faced substantial uncertainty about the true costs of their endeavor. In forecasting the system's future financial development, the government confronted substantial informational and theoretical blind-spots. Feedback from past experience was limited since compulsory social insurance was a largely untested financial and organizational concept, either within or outside of Germany. By 1887, when the Interior Office released an outline of the plan, the Reich had had just three years' experience with accident and health insurance. Even descriptive data on the current state of the world left much to be desired. Prior to the creation of a public program for invalidity and old age, the government had seen no compelling need to track disability or mortality rates on a national scale. As a result, the best available data on the incidence of the risks being insured came from a single industry, the railroads, and were 14 years out of date (Sniegs 1996).

[10] Files reviewed from the Bundesarchiv (Federal Archive) in Berlin include R2 41569; R1501 100024, 100027, 100096, 100097; R101 3138. For contemporary commentary, see Bosse and von Woedtke (1891) and Landmann and Ralp (1891).

[11] Actuarial assumptions in a memo from Adolf Heinrich Wilhelm von Scholz [Prussian Finance Minister] to Otto von Bismarck, August 21, 1887, R2/41569, BArch, p. 126.

Moreover, policymakers had poor technical tools at their disposal for predicting how a complex system like a pension insurance plan would evolve over time. Strikingly, the model that the Interior Office employed to chart cost developments over decades was almost completely static. While it predicted increasing costs as a result of the system's maturation – the expansion of benefits as workers amassed contribution records – it assumed no shifts in the age distribution of the population or in background factors that would influence disability rates, such as advancing industrialization or changes in workplace conditions (Sniegs 1996). Not only did the actuarial projections make no attempt to gauge the future effects of a changing wage structure, but policymakers lacked reliable data on the *current* age profile of each wage class – critical parameters in a wage-related insurance scheme (Sniegs 1996).

Correspondence among top officials betray an uneasiness with these difficulties of prediction,[12] and insurance experts working on the bill commonly referred to the entire venture as "a leap in the dark" (Rudloff 2000, 98–99). Furthermore, historical hindsight reveals in dramatic fashion that funding *was* a risky venture, courting objective dangers of investment failure. Within three decades of the pension scheme's establishment, political manipulation and inflation would completely void the intertemporal bargain of 1889. During World War I, the government would make the fateful decision to finance its military operations out of loans, rather than taxes. Meanwhile, the wartime Reichstag would suspend the usual rules tying the currency to the gold standard, literally granting a license to print money (Craig 1981). Indirectly, these choices would constitute a raid on all Reichmark-denominated savings to finance the war while, more directly, over half of the public pension funds were to be invested in Reich war bonds by 1918 (Manow 2000). Exacerbated by the terms of defeat, inflation was followed by a period of hyperinflation in which virtually the entire value of the pension scheme's assets – built up over 30 years – was wiped out. By 1924, the system's benefit payments, denominated in nominal terms, were to be worth almost nothing to contributors.

Given not only the forecasting challenges they faced but the objective risks attending the project, why did Bismarck's ministers view funding as a safe investment? Crucial for officials' reasoning about distant consequences were the ideational conditions under which they operated: in particular, the mental model that they used to conceptualize the policy field, and its apparent legitimation by cognitively available experience. Rather than weighing all potential risks of investment, and discounting those deemed less likely, ministers and civil servants – as well as parliamentarians and interest-group leaders – appear to have paid attention only to those consequences captured by the policy schema dominant within Reich policymaking circles.

---

[12] See, for instance, Jacobi [State Secretary of the Treasury] to von Boetticher [State Secretary of the Interior], July 20, 1887, R1501/100096, BArch, pp. 158RS-159; and Bosse to Jacobi, August 5, 1887, R2/41569, BArch, p. 115.

As they imagined potential outcomes of the two financing methods, policy-makers had available to them a limited range of plausible models from which to draw lessons. As welfare-state pioneers, they could not look to other public pension systems for insights, but they could evaluate two other analogous enter-prises: the widespread German miners' cooperatives (*Knappschaften*) and private life insurance. The miners' cooperatives, in operation since the Middle Ages, were a form of risk pooling for workers in a dangerous and demanding profession, protecting against sickness and old age. Much of the inspiration for social insurance in Germany, in fact, derived from this pioneering example. These cooperatives were also the most prominent example of a PAYGO-financed institution in the Reich policymakers' environment. For the most part, their financial situation in the 1880s was precarious. Because they carried no reserves to speak of, the cooperatives were highly vulnerable to macroeco-nomic or firm-level shocks or to changes in demographic conditions, and they made benefit payments dependent on each year's contribution revenues. Throughout the 1880s, with some high-profile collapses, their financial arrange-ments became a target of intense criticism in debates over social insurance. Indeed, these PAYGO arrangements became an illustration of all that could go wrong with financing worker protection (Tennstedt 2002; Geyer 1987).[13]

In contrast, private life insurance, operated on the actuarial principle of funding, seemed to offer a financially sound, prosperous alternative. Though life insurance was a relatively new form of risk-pooling, it had been growing rapidly since mid-century, and continued to flourish even through the deep depression of the 1870s. With assets rising fivefold between 1860 and 1880, faster than those of credit or savings banks, the private life insurance industry appeared a model of financial prudence and was a growing source of old-age security for an increasing number of Germans (Borscheid 1989).

This available experience, in turn, suggested and supported the mental model of pension policy dominant within the German bureaucracy. In reasoning through the system's design, Reich policymakers explicitly and repeatedly defined the new pension scheme as a system of "insurance" akin to private arrangements. Records of internal deliberations reveal that Reich officials did not interpret the insurance analogy loosely, as a convenient label, but saw the "insurance principle" as deeply embedded in the structure of their project.[14] In their minds, "insurance," as a scheme paid for by the beneficiaries themselves, was clearly distinct from public welfare (Geyer 1987). They even took pains to distinguish the pension scheme from other social programs – such as protection against accidents – that also happened to be tagged "insurance." As Interior officials made explicit, they saw the accident system as based on a principle of

---

[13] For contemporary examples of these critiques, see Karl Brämer's essay "Der finanzielle Zustand der preußischen Knappschaftswesen" (item 97) and "Sitzungsprotokoll der zweiten Kammer des sächsischen Landtags, November 27, 1879" (item 80) published in Tennstedt and Winter (2002).

[14] "Denkschrift, betreffend Alters- und Invalidenversicherung," [no author], July 6, 1887, R43/565, pp. 87–98RS.

state "provision" for those who suffered injury while the pension system would be based on a distinctive principle of "insurance." What made old-age and disability benefits a matter of insurance was the temporal separation between the payment of premiums and the receipt of benefits:

It involves the payment of contributions over many years so that, as a very likely event arises years later, the necessary resources for paying pensions are on hand: completely in contrast to the accident [system], where each period has its own discrete risks.[15]

The insurance analogy pervaded the design process and deliberations. Like private insurance – and unlike a system of redistribution or welfare – the new scheme was to pay benefits in proportion to a worker's past record of contributions, rather than according to need. Financing methods were judged in part based on how the "deal" future workers would get from the state pension system would compare with that they could get from a private life insurer.[16] Drafts of the legislation declared that the scheme would be run on "the insurance principle,"[17] and the entire repertoire of concepts and tools used to describe and analyze alternative financing arrangements – the notion of funding and the methods for calculating premiums – had themselves been borrowed directly from the actuarial practices of the private-insurance industry.

The mental model of public pensions as insurance had direct implications for how actors reasoned through the choice of financing methods. Those implications stemmed from the particular way in which the model simplified the causal dynamics of pension policy. Specifically, the insurance analogy conceived of a pension program as a closed, self-supporting arrangement, like a private insurance firm. In the world of private insurance, all benefits are paid for out of a combination of premium revenues and the returns on the scheme's accumulated assets. Should the plan fall out of actuarial balance, an insurance scheme faces the risk of insolvency. The key design challenge for such a plan is thus to choose contribution and benefit schedules that will balance future streams of income against long-run obligations.

While the insurance model captured a piece of the causal logic governing state pensions, it stripped away other causal dynamics. Most strikingly, the model simplified away the distinctive conditions governing a *public* program. While a private insurance firm relies on relations of voluntary exchange to extract

---

[15] Tonio Bödiker in minutes taken by Bödiker of meeting with Paul Eck [Under State Secretary of the Interior], Robert Bosse [Director of Economic Affairs in Interior Office], and Karl Heinrich von Boetticher [State Secretary of the Interior], July 7, 1884, R1501/100096, BArch.

[16] Rechnungsgrundlagen: "Betrifft die Einführung des Kapitaldeckungsverfahrens an stelle des Prämienverfahrens bei der Alters- und Invaliditätsversicherung," [no author], R1501/100097, BArch, pp. 161 and 161RS.

[17] "Denkschrift, betreffend Alters- und Invalidenversicherung," [no author], July 6, 1887, R43/565, BArch, pp. 87–98RS. Underlining in original. For very similar language see also the Begründung ("Justification") of the bill as introduced to the Reichstag, "Entwurf eines Gesetzes, betreffend die Alters- und Invaliditätsversicherung," in Deutscher Reichstag (1889b, Anlage 10, p. 59).

revenues, a state has recourse to unique powers of *coercion*. If a public pension scheme's income is insufficient to pay benefits, the state can always raise contribution rates or taxes to close the gap; "insolvency" *per se* is not a meaningful possibility (Manow 2000). Similarly, the private insurance model obscured the implications of inflation for pension financing. For a private life insurer, the distinction between nominal value (money) and real economic value is not an important one. The private insurer's financing problem is typically a nominal one: with insurance contracts expressed in nominal currency units, the task is to maintain sufficient nominal resources on hand to pay the promised nominal benefits. What happens to currency values or prices is of little concern. For a state policymaker, on the other hand, the underlying distribution of *real* economic resources to pensioners might in principle be of greater interest and will be captured only partially by the scheme's balance sheet.

Further, the insurance analogy failed to capture the uniquely political risks that could bedevil public-pension financing. In particular, the model simplified away the problem of property rights over state pension funds. In the well-ordered German *Rechtsstaat,* a private insurance firm could assume that it would retain property rights over any assets that it accumulated. In the world of politics, where dispositions of resources are subject to revision by the sovereign of the day, an additional problem of long-term commitment arises: funds accumulated today for one long-run end can be raided or redirected tomorrow for an entirely unrelated purpose (Moe 1990).

German policymakers invested attention disproportionately in those potential causal sequences captured by the insurance model, especially the dynamics of actuarial balance and solvency. As discussed earlier, officials deliberated repeatedly about how their choices would affect the scheme's financial stability over the long run. Similarly, conceiving of a pension scheme as a self-supporting actuarial arrangement, actors focused heavily on the contribution rates that each financing method would require in order to maintain actuarial balance.

Equally striking, however, are the causal dynamics to which decision makers did *not* attend. Most significantly in light of later events, decision makers paid virtually no attention to the causal dynamics of commitment failure – the possibility that accumulated funds might be subject to political manipulation or diversion. A thorough examination of detailed records of extensive written and oral deliberations within the executive yielded not a single mention of the possibility that accumulated pension funds might be raided by future governments for other purposes. Nor was any distinction made between the nominal and the real value of accumulated assets or any reference made to potential threats to their real value, such as inflation.[18]

---

[18] Ministry archival holdings consulted at the Bundesarchiv-Berlin and in Haerendel (2004) include: for the Reich Office of the Interior (lead department in pension-policy formulation), file groups R1501/100024, 100026, 100027, 100035, 100043, 100054 through 100059, 100096 through 100098, 100104, and 100105; for the Reich Treasury Office (secondary responsibility) file groups

With the insurance metaphor broadly accepted in elite political circles, the same allocation of attention prevailed in other deliberative venues. In parliament, in the internal deliberations of business associations, and on the business-dominated Prussian Economic Council, the pension scheme's proposed financing method was discussed in depth. From a rationalist perspective, the institutional context in which legislators and interest groups were operating ought to have raised especially strong concerns about funding's political vulnerabilities (e.g., North and Weingast 1989). Reich institutions offered actors outside the executive few tools for protecting pension funds against predation by a future government. Not only did the Reichstag have relatively weak veto powers, but producer interests were as yet weakly integrated into the policymaking process in ways that might help hold governments to their promises over time (Craig 1981).

Nevertheless, there is almost no evidence that legislators or business leaders attended to threats to the commitment of pension funds over time. A wide-ranging review of debates outside the executive – in closed Reichstag committee meetings, in Reichstag plenary sessions, and among business leaders (whose firms would be paying part of the scheme's costs) – uncovered only a single instance in which a participant raised the possibility that pension funds might be diverted or misappropriated. The comment elicited not a single response.[19] Perhaps most telling is that even actors, such as business leaders, who strongly *opposed* funding – and thus had strong incentives to consider its risks – did not refer to potential dangers that were outside the dominant model. Though funding's political and inflationary vulnerabilities would have constituted powerful lines of argument, opponents almost never raised them as possible disadvantages. It is not that actors *considered* these possibilities and dismissed them: rather, they appear not to have attended to them at all.

The record of available experience reinforced the cognitive effects of the insurance model in submerging these same risks of policy investment. With the welfare state a novel enterprise – and the accident and insurance programs run on a PAYGO basis – history offered no examples of the political manipulation of social insurance funds. Similarly, with inflation running at an average rate of

---

R2/41569 through 415172, 415175, 415176, 41599, 45800, 45801, 45803; and for the Reich Insurance Office, parts of R89 Teil 3.

[19] See legislator von Wendt's comments in minutes of the 14th and 15th closed-door meetings of the Sixth Reichstag Committee, 1st Reading, January 29–30, 1889, R101/3138, pp. 161RS and 173RS. The review of deliberation outside the executive included the full text of all plenary session debates on all sections of the bill relating to the financing of the scheme and administration of the funds from the Reichstag's 7th Legislative Period, Sessions II and IV (Deutscher Reichstag 1888, 1889a); complete minutes of closed sessions of the responsible parliamentary committee, the Sixth Reichstag Committee, cited above; the committee's report (VI. Kommission des Reichstages 1889); minutes of debate on the bill by the business-dominated Prussian Economic Council (Preußischer Volkswirtschaftsrat 1887); and debates on the bill by the largest industry group (Bueck 1887).

approximately zero over the previous 10 years,[20] and no historical experience with hyperinflation, the monetary disaster of the Weimar years would have been particularly difficult for actors in the 1880s to imagine, despite being a logically plausible outcome of their choice.

Thus, Bismarckian policymakers' uncertainty was confined to worries about the quality of existing data and whether the actuaries' calculations were sufficiently conservative.[21] Aside from these narrow concerns, Germany's ministers, civil servants, legislators, and businessmen accepted the actuaries' cost projections for PAYGO financing and funding at face value. Conflict and deliberation thus centered on whether funding's near-term costs were affordable and whether PAYGO's greater long-term costs were sustainable. German policy makers, in other words, understood the financing decision in terms of the intertemporal trade-off captured by the actuaries' trend lines: as a choice between minimizing costs in the present and avoiding far greater burdens in the future. For actors choosing over substantial time horizons, this was a choice-definition highly favorable to policy investment.

INVESTING AGAINST GROUP OPPOSITION

At the same time, funding would impose large short-run costs on concentrated interests in the industrial sector, specifically workers and their employers. The new law would also require the assent of the two chambers of parliament – the Bundesrat, representing the governments of the German states, and the directly elected Reichstag – each a potential veto opportunity for any organized opponents.

Indeed, organized business and labor groups were hostile to the policy investment. Labor groups had reason to oppose the entire social-insurance project as Bismarck had conceived it, quite aside from the particulars of the financing choice. In the context of state repression, the left viewed the government as competitor rather than benefactor and distrusted ministers' motives in creating workers' insurance programs. Moreover, the left considered the bill's proposed benefit levels meager and the eligibility requirements far too strict (Haerendel 2000; Mann 1968; Wolff 1933). Yet labor interests had few institutional opportunities to influence the policy choice. Trade unions, even those unaffiliated with the socialist movement, were completely shut out of the government's consultative and deliberative processes. Unions' other primary channel of potential influence would have been through its Social Democratic allies in parliament. With only 11 members in the Reichstag, however, the Social Democrats lacked status as an official parliamentary party and were excluded from the Reichstag committee that marked up the legislation (Hennock 2000). Their small seat

---

[20] Global Financial Database, http://www.globalfindata.com/ (Series: Inflation: Consumer Price Indices, Germany Consumer Prices (Inflation)).

[21] Bosse to Jacobi [State Secretary of the Treasury], August, 5, 1887, R2/41569, BArch, pp. 113, 114RS, 115, 115RS.

share and extreme relative ideological position limited their leverage over the policy outcome.

More serious potential opposition came from business interests. In stark contrast to its relationship with the labor movement, Bismarck's government viewed Germany's captains of heavy industry as important political allies and actively sought their comment on an early draft of the pensions bill (Ullmann 1979). The best-organized national umbrella group, the Central Association of German Industrialists (CAGI), and the consultative Prussian Economic Council (PEC) each debated the proposal at length during the late 1880s. While the business community was divided on the issue, large industrial employers in the Rhineland, Westphalia, the Saarland, and Upper Silesia – who tended to dominate the CAGI – were broadly supportive of the plan for a public pension scheme. Heavily dependent on a stable workforce for factory production processes, many industrialists shared Bismarck's hope that state beneficence would contribute to social peace and undercut the socialist movement. Indeed, some of the very first calls for state social protection had come from business quarters (Breger 1982; Ullmann 1979).

At the same time, employers were generally opposed to funding the new scheme. Though funding would have moderated employers' long-run contribution rates, a number of considerations seem to have spoken against policy investment in pensions for Germany's heavy manufacturers. First, at this economic moment, employers perceived the direct short-run costs of investment to be high. Not only had business just taken on the financial burdens of accident and health insurance, but German heavy industry was suffering through an extended period of falling prices and excess capacity and faced stiff foreign competition on world markets. In competitive terms, it did not help that – at the dawn of the modern welfare state – Germany was alone in imposing such burdens on its business sector (Feldenkirchen 1991; Ritter 1983; Breger 1982). An investment in distant cost-constraint would not have been appealing if it threatened firms' prospects of *survival* into the long term. Moreover, business leaders viewed the *opportunity* costs of funding to be substantial. In particular, they worried that the accumulation of a large fund in the pension system would dampen consumer demand for their output while extracting resources that could be used as productive capital (Breger 1994, 1982; Bueck 1887). To be clear, business leaders largely accepted the insurance model as a conceptualization of the financing choice and acknowledged the basic aggregate intertemporal trade-off that ministers perceived. Yet industrialists viewed the near-term costs of investment as punishingly high and believed that firms had more profitable private uses for the resources that funding would extract.

Furthermore, employers had little reason to *internalize* the full long-term costs of PAYGO financing in their calculations of their own interests. Businessmen did not have to worry to the same degree as public officials about the problem of fund solvency: if the pension fund should ever become unable to pay benefits, it would likely be the state itself, not firms, that would have to step into the breach. Moreover, the current political environment would have suggested to employers that they stood a good chance of winning future distributive battles over pension costs. Amidst Bismarck's repression and exclusion of the labor movement, the balance of political advantage among social groups was heavily tilted toward capital. If the system became unaffordable in the future, business could reasonably expect the resulting costs to be imposed on the politically hobbled working class, through either benefit cuts or an increase in workers' share of the contribution. From the perspective of employers, there would thus have been little reason to view the long-term trajectory of pension contribution rates under PAYGO as a cost that *they* would have to pay – and, thus, to conceptualize the financing choice as a vertical intertemporal trade-off for *themselves*. Instead, it made sense to try to minimize their own burdens in the short term, and to plan to continue minimizing those costs through future distributive burden-shifting over the long run.

If capital was largely opposed to investment, however, German policymaking institutions lent business limited opportunities to influence the final policy choice. Over the previous decade, heavy industry had developed a constructive working relationship with Bismarck, especially on the issue of tariffs, and the Chancellor nurtured consultative fora for business such as the PEC. Moreover, Bismarck and his officials viewed long-term industrial success as central to national prosperity. While these factors allowed industrialists to win some policy concessions, executive officials ultimately retained broad room for maneuver – a capacity to weigh long-run interests of state heavily against industrialists' myopic and particularist demands. This insulation had important institutional foundations: while ministers often found it useful to consult with industry, take its interests into account, and mobilize its backing for their initiatives, they did not need business support to fight and win elections. Although it sought to ensure the broad and long-run success of German industry, the government was not so dependent on the group's day-to-day support that it needed to regularly heed businessmen's detailed programmatic demands. Indeed, rather than acting as agents of capital, ministers tended more often to *instrumentalize* business as a convenient ally in the pursuit of their own policy goals; Bismarck in fact had created the PEC primarily to provide him with an institutional counterweight to parliament. To a large extent, it was businessmen who needed the government: employers adopted a conciliatory attitude toward Bismarck's social insurance project in large part to nurture good relations with the Chancellor and to attain at least some influence over the legislation's final form (Ullmann 1981).

After consultations with industry groups, ministers did adjust their initial proposal in a number of ways – most importantly, by eliminating the role of trade associations, an emerging organizational competitor to the CAGI, in the administration of the new pension funds. On core financial matters, however, the government refused to bend. The course of the PEC's deliberations on the pension proposal illustrates the level of government insulation from interest-group pressure – and, indeed, the influence that state officials could exert over social interests. Reflecting a widely held preference in the business community – almost all of Germany's industry associations, including the CAGI, had come out against funding (Breger 1982) – the PEC standing committee that reviewed the proposal voted against funding the new pension scheme (Preußischer Volkswirtschaftsrat 1887). Before the proposal came to a plenary vote, however, senior Interior official Erich von Woedtke made a floor speech to the Council, imploring members to support the government's position (Haerendel 2001).[22] Against the broad current of business opinion, the PEC plenary then voted in favor of a compromise position – partial funding of the new program (*Kapitaldeckungsverfahren* rather than *Prämiendeckungsverfahren*) – likely reflecting a strategic adjustment to the government's pleadings. Even after this major concession by business, however, the government's proposal for full funding went forward to parliament unchanged, the policy investment fully intact.

Though business interests failed to avert policy investment via the PEC, parliamentary deliberations offered another opportunity to influence the outcome. The Bundesrat, representing state governments, was an unlikely forum for success. Like the Reich government, state governments were invested with their authority by kings and princes, not by parliaments or elections, leaving them relatively insulated from short-term social pressures. Moreover, the states' interests were closely aligned with those of the Reich since, through their transfer grants, they played a large role in financing the Reich itself: any fiscal crisis for the Reich would thus mean fiscal trouble for the states. State governments also shared Reich officials' concern about the long-run threat to political stability if future workers grew unhappy with continually increasing contribution rates.[23] While we do not have evidence of business attempts to lobby state governments on the issue, the states would not have been favorably disposed toward a case for PAYGO financing, and they supported the central government's plans for funding.

The Reichstag, on the other hand, offered a more promising venue for winning amendments to the government's plans. Bismarck could usually depend on a coalition of parties in the lower house that shared his political outlook – typically the agrarian Conservative Party, the agrarian and industrialist Reichspartei, and the National Liberals. Unfortunately for the government in this case, all three parties were divided on the virtues of social insurance. Agrarian interests within the Conservative Party and the Reichspartei were flatly opposed to old-age and disability insurance because they feared it would weaken traditional, patriarchal ties between agricultural workers and their employers (Flemming 2000). The National Liberals were also split. While they generally opposed

---

[22] For the minutes of von Woedtke's speech, see (Preußischer Volkswirtschaftsrat 1887). See the 3rd Meeting [3. Sitzung] at pp. 96–97.

[23] See the comments of Württemberg's representative to the Reichstag committee that considered the bill. Drawing on experience with increasing contribution rates in the accident insurance system, he argues that increasing rates will lead to dissatisfaction among workers. Minutes of the meetings of the Sixth Reichstag Committee [VI. Reichstagskommission], 1st Reading [1. Lesung], 14th Meeting [14. Sitzung], January 29, 1889, R101/3138, BArch, p. 167. See also Bosse and von Woedtke (1891, 285).

state intervention in the economy and compulsion, since the 1870s some began to argue that policies based on pure "Manchester liberalism" might fail to provide sufficient security to the working class (Haerendel 2001). With party discipline weak in the German Reichstag, the government's initiative balanced on a razor's edge.

With some of its usual supporters backing away, the government needed to bargain with legislators in order to cobble together a majority. Along with the National Liberals, the Center Party – a cross-class grouping representing Catholics – was a particularly important source of swing votes. In the absence of significant Social Democratic representation in parliament, the Center Party – influenced both by its links to the Christian trade unions and by Catholic social thought – served as a crucial voice for workers' interests and demanded improvements in the benefit scale. The government sought to win these pivotal votes both by introducing a wage-related element to the benefits – thus enhancing their value to better-paid workers – and by setting the Treasury's top-up contribution as an equal amount in absolute terms for all pensioners, ensuring a certain progressivity in payouts (Haerendel 2001).[24]

This same dynamic of legislative bargaining also gave opponents of funding leverage. Particularly important negotiations took place within the Sixth Reichstag Committee, the panel that marked up the bill in closed sessions. While funding had defenders on the Committee, legislators from the Center and National Liberal parties representing a wide range of interests made common cause in opposing funding for the short-run sacrifices it would require. While a National Liberal mine manager and a landowner sought to avoid placing an unnecessary burden on struggling sectors of the economy,[25] a Centrist theologian pointed out that foregoing a large fund would free up resources to provide survivor benefits to orphans and widows.[26] Following its first reading, the Committee called for eliminating funding from the bill.

When both the Reich government and state governments balked, however, declaring PAYGO financing wholly unacceptable, legislators faced strong institutional incentives to compromise. While the Wilhelmine quasi-parliamentary system did not lend itself to modern forms of executive dominance, the 1871 constitution left the chamber with limited bargaining leverage against the government. If the lower house defeated a government bill, the body would be dissolved and new elections would be called – an outcome that would threaten legislators' hold on office but not the executive's. In the end, the Reichstag committee conceded far more than the government, agreeing to a

---

[24] See arguments of parliamentarians Hitze and Buhl in Minutes of the meetings of the Sixth Reichstag Committee [VI. Reichstagskommission], 1st Reading [1. Lesung], 14th Meeting [14. Sitzung], January 29, 1889, R101/3138, BArch, pp. 166–168.

[25] Kleine and Buhl in Minutes of the meetings of the Sixth Reichstag Committee [VI. Reichstagskommission], 1st Reading [1. Lesung], 14th Meeting [14. Sitzung], January 29, 1889, R101/3138, BArch, pp. 166–167Rs.

[26] Hitze in ibid, p. 166.

large degree of (but not full) funding.[27] Contribution rates would start out much higher than under PAYGO but lower than under full funding. While contribution rates would rise over time, the government decided that this relatively modest upward trajectory – with a long-run cost about a third higher than full funding – was acceptable.[28] The government had conceded just enough to ensure the bill's passage through the full chamber, and – on a vote of 185 to 165 – the eventual support of a large majority of National Liberals and a minority of Center Party legislators was crucial to its enactment (Haerendel 2001).

CONCLUSION

Policy investment in Germany's new pension scheme depended heavily on the advantages of electoral safety and executive insulation enjoyed by the Reich government. As guardians of the state's interests, German ministers and senior civil servants found the long-term logic of funding compelling. Shielded from immediate electoral pressures, policymakers did not feel bound to minimize the near-term costs of each policy decision, either for voters or for organized groups. At the same time, facing both emerging competition from radical political forces and institutionalized fiscal constraints, they needed to deeply entrench, not momentarily boost, the new German state's authority and capacities. Their time horizons institutionally and situationally extended, officials pursued policy gains that they believed were sustainable, seeking to maximize the scheme's political, social, and fiscal benefits *over the long term*. A policy investment in funding seemed to them to be the intertemporally optimal option – paying now for today's benefit promises, holding down the long-term tax burden on workers, and ensuring that the scheme would always have assets on hand to cover its liabilities.

However prudent from the perspective of state actors, this policy investment would impose a large share of its costs on a social group that did not see itself reaping a substantial share of its returns. At this early stage in the political organization of industry and in its integration into the policymaking process,

---

[27] Under the compromise arrangement, known as *Kapitaldeckungsverfahren*, the contribution rate would be set initially for a 10-year period, during which sufficient funds would be raised to cover both the pensions paid during that period and the present value of all pension payments due in the future to all individuals in receipt of benefits at the end of the decade. The rate would then increase to a level sufficient to meet the same demands for the next 10-year period, and so on. By contrast, full funding would have required a contribution rate sufficient, in any given period, to cover all benefits paid in a given period plus the present value of all future pension benefits for which liabilities had been generated during that period. The difference is that *Kapitaldeckung* required reserves to cover only the present value of the stream of liabilities for pensions *already* in payment at the end of the period. See Mörschel (1990).

[28] For Interior Office views on this arrangement, see Rechnungsgrundlagen: "Betrifft die Einführung des Kapitaldeckungsverfahrens an stelle des Prämienverfahrens bei der Alters- und Invaliditätsversicherung," [no author] R1501/100097, BArch.

however, business's influence with unelected ministers was modest. By contrast, the elected, fractious Reichstag offered a better opportunity for societal interests to influence policy outcomes, and it is in this forum that investment faced its most formidable challenge. While the lower chamber forced ministers to adjust their policy blueprint, however, the executive's strong constitutional position allowed the government to reject demands that endangered its core policy priorities, including the scheme's long-term financial integrity. Myopic effect thus mirrored institutional balance: organized opponents achieved a modest reduction in the scale of policy investment through a policymaking institution with modest effective veto power.

Nor were ministers deterred by the potential risks and uncertainty of their endeavor. In fact, the poor state of social statistics and incalculability of future social and economic developments made the financial buffer of an accumulated fund appear even more important. In forming expectations about the long-run social effects of funding as compared to PAYGO financing, policymakers drew their key concepts and analytical tools from the flourishing model of private insurance. As a mental map of pension policy, the insurance analogy drew special attention to the dynamics of actuarial balance – central to the operation of a self-supporting private plan – and emphasized the relationships among a small set of moving parts: current contribution rates, future contribution burdens, and the risk of insolvency. This model was made all the more compelling by cognitively available information drawn from recent and local experience with similar endeavors. The starkly contrasting performance of funded life insurance as compared to PAYGO miners' cooperatives highlighted the financial instability of the latter model relative to the former. While capturing causal logics through which funding could generate long-run social returns, the private-insurance model also obscured potential risks – especially misappropriation and inflation – that were particular threats to a *public* social program. In doing so, ministers' ideational map of pension policy framed the policy investment for them as a clear trade-off of short-term social pain for greater long-term gain – a framing highly favorable to investment. As we will see, it also systematically biased their attention away from precisely those dangers that would destroy the pension scheme 30 years later.

CHAPTER 4

The Politics of Mistrust

The Origins of British Pensions, 1925

In Britain's first major state effort to protect against poverty in old age, the country's Liberal government in 1908 created a means-tested, tax-financed pension scheme that began paying pensions at age 70.[1] Initially popular among beneficiaries, the scheme was soon strained politically by rapidly rising prices during World War I and mounting criticism of the inequities and indignities of the means test. The old-age pensioners' lobby became increasingly militant in its demands for more generous state benefits on a universal basis. Meanwhile, as trade unions gathered organizational strength and the right to vote was extended to the nonpropertied, the parliamentary Labour Party tremendously improved its electoral position. Though the government increased pension levels during and after the war as partial compensation for inflation, electoral and social pressures for more generous and widely available pensions grew. Postwar governments of all partisan stripes contemplated either supplementing or replacing the 1908 system. While organized labor and most of the Labour Party called for universal tax-financed pensions, the Conservative Party began in the early 1920s to investigate the possibility of a contributory pension scheme, free of a means test.

In the midst of these preparations came the watershed election of 1924. The vote that year marked the end of the Liberal Party as a serious contender for government office. With 48.3 percent of the vote in a three-way contest in a first-past-the-post electoral system, the Conservatives won 419 parliamentary seats to Labour's 151 and the Liberals' 40 – the largest Tory majority since 1832. With Liberal support plummeting to 17.6 percent of the electorate, it looked likely that electoral competition would once again become a two-party affair, with Labour as the chief opposition to the Conservatives (Self 2000; Ramsden 1998; Pugh 1982). In turning their strategic sights on the Labour Party, the Tories faced a critical choice. As Anthony Seldon (1994) has framed the Conservatives' dilemma:

---

[1] For accounts of the creation and structure of this scheme, see Williams (1970), Macnicol (1998), and Orloff (1993b).

Should [party leader Stanley] Baldwin now adopt the Peelite solution of an alliance between property and order to contain the working- (and middle-) class clamour with piecemeal, limited reform? Or should he adopt the more direct (if opportunistic) Disraelian response of appealing to the members of the working class with a programme of action to retain their loyalty, meeting their needs better than any rival party (32–33)?

Baldwin and his colleagues in Cabinet charted a course somewhere in between. Despite their impressive electoral performance in 1924, party leaders feared that they were programmatically ill-equipped for an age of mass democracy. Even before the election, senior party official Neville Chamberlain had proposed the outlines of a "New Conservatism" reflecting his belief that "unless we leave our mark as social reformers the country will take it out of us hereafter."[2] The New Conservative project was an attempt to strengthen the party's cross-class appeal through a blend of social protection, tax cuts, and orthodox fiscal policy. Rejecting the party's old, purist *laissez-faire* doctrine, the new 1924 Tory government adopted significant initiatives in the fields of housing, slum clearance, Poor Law reform, health care, and women's suffrage as well as contributory pensions.

In the field of pensions, Chancellor of the Exchequer Winston Churchill and Chamberlain, now Minister of Health, took the lead in policy design. As head of the Conservative Party's committee on pensions before the election, Chamberlain already had in hand a proposal for a contributory scheme designed by a Liverpool actuary: it would have operated on a strictly funded basis, with the first full benefits payable after 49 years. This funded plan, adopted as party policy before the election, would have represented an even greater policy investment than the German government's initial proposal. Once in government, however, Chamberlain and Churchill retreated from the prospect of funding, driving through parliament a bill for a largely PAYGO-financed pension scheme, with benefits available within a few years and large cost increases delayed for decades. Why did British politicians reject investment, opting instead for pure redistribution?

Ministers' rejection of policy investment was, in fact, overdetermined: none of our three hypothesized necessary conditions was present as the government weighed alternative financing methods for their new pension program. Put differently, three tremendous hurdles stood in policy investment's path. Analysis of the decision-making process and the context in which it unfolded, however, allows us to distinguish the relative contribution of each obstacle to this specific outcome. As I will argue, proposals for a funded scheme primarily fell prey to high levels of uncertainty, conditioned by dominant mental models, about the long-term social returns to policy investment. Yet process tracing also allows us to engage in counterfactual analysis of the likely effect of electoral risk and interest-group opposition – to ask how they *would* have shaped ministers' decisions if

---

[2] Quoted in Self (2000, 167).

other necessary conditions had been in place. We begin with this counter-factual analysis.

COMPETING FOR LABOUR VOTERS

In the rapidly changing electoral environment of the 1920s, the reformist faction ascendant within Baldwin's party perceived a strategic imperative in appealing to the working class. Competing for the allegiance of the proletariat was, in fact, a perfectly viable strategic option: confounding Marxist expectations, the Tories had always drawn substantial working-class support (Waller 1994). Labour's formidable electoral challenge was itself built on promises of improvement in workers' material and social conditions – a platform, in essence, addressed to a substantial segment of the Conservative base. The New Conservatives in turn saw social policy as a powerful and necessary tool for deepening and extending their own political alliance with Britain's workers.

Taken as a snapshot, the British Conservatives' competitive situation did not differ fundamentally from Bismarck's. A group of rightwing politicians was attempting, through ameliorative social-policy innovations, to slow the advance of a political party that was making explicit class appeals to workers. Yet, crucially, the threat to the British Conservatives was more advanced and much quicker in tempo. Not only had Labour already ruled Britain once – albeit fleetingly and as a minority government – but the Tories also had to fight regular electoral battles for control of the executive. And while the Conservatives enjoyed a towering parliamentary majority at the moment, Britain's first-past-the-post electoral rules could rapidly turn modest shifts in the popular vote into large seat swings. In fact, the Conservatives would lose office to Labour as soon as the next election, in 1929, even while maintaining a plurality of the vote.

Pension policy, with its direct material implications for millions of voters, was a crucial electoral battleground. Sharpening the Tories' dilemma in this field was the Labour Party's promise of universal pensions financed solely out of general taxation. With the general tax burden borne largely by the propertied classes, Labour's pensions would be free from the point of view of most workers and available immediately. While an attractive campaign pledge for an opposition party, a "free pension" was an exceedingly difficult offer for the incumbent government to match. With the Exchequer groaning under the strain of monumental war debt – debt servicing comprised fully 40 percent of public expenditure (Ponting 1994) – Treasury officials were scrambling to find economies in the budget. Even during Labour's short stint in office in 1924, the party's own Chancellor of the Exchequer, Philip Snowden, had argued against an expansion of the 1908 pension scheme on the grounds of fiscal constraint, and Labour failed to fulfill its own election vow on the issue (Macnicol 1998).

The Tories faced an additional electoral obstacle to financing pensions on the backs of affluent taxpayers: partly to achieve balance in a New Conservative platform that otherwise offered much to the working class, Churchill had during the 1924 campaign promised the party's base a *cut* in general taxation. In short,

Baldwin's ministers were both fiscally and electorally constrained in their choice of financing methods. Only a contributory scheme – financed by a new dedicated tax, paid by workers themselves and their employers – could generate the necessary stream of new resources without alienating the Tories' core supporters.

As chairman of the Conservative Party's "All-In Insurance Subcommittee" while in opposition in early 1924, Chamberlain asked actuary Duncan Fraser of the Royal Insurance Company of Liverpool to advise on the design of a compulsory contributory state pension plan. The resulting proposal would have vastly expanded the existing 10-shilling-a-week means-tested pension, payable at age 70, with a pension of 15 shillings starting at age 65 and available to all workers, without a means test. Among its most striking features, however, Fraser's blueprint called for financing on a fully funded basis, with benefits governed by exacting insurance principles. Since benefits would be based strictly on the actuarial value of a worker's past contributions, the full 15-shilling pension would not be paid out until those retiring had contributed to the system for their full working lives, starting at age 16 – that is, 49 years after the scheme's commencement. Because the program would start collecting full contributions of 7.5 pence per week long before it paid full benefits, it would accumulate a large capital fund, projected to reach £2 billion by 1991, representing an enormous policy investment in future retirement incomes and fiscal capacities (Macnicol 1998; Heclo 1974; Walley 1972).

This proposed policy investment was not, in the end, enacted. And as will be detailed in later sections, the plan was rejected on its merits as a policy, not for its electoral effects. It is nonetheless likely that – *had* they thought better of the policy – Conservative ministers would have seen stark electoral risks in adopting it. The record of ministerial deliberations over pension policy reflects a keen sensitivity to how a pension scheme's profile of costs and benefits for workers would influence the Conservatives' prospects of maintaining office. Even when considering PAYGO options that entailed much *lower* contribution rates, ministers worried that imposing any significant pension tax would place them at a serious disadvantage in the battle for workers' loyalties against Labour, with its competing promise of "free" retirement benefits. As Churchill wrote to Chamberlain in December of 1924, for instance, any contribution burden imposed on workers could end up neutralizing the program's political benefits. Referring to a PAYGO contributory plan much like that which was finally enacted, Churchill worried that workers would resent having to pay for their own pensions:

...[6 pence] a week per man from both employers and employed is a pretty stiff poll tax, having regard to their existing obligations. This is the part of the scheme which preoccupies me the most. To what extent, for instance, would the Labour Party use the argument, "You are only making us live on our own tails"? On facts and figures we have a smashing reply. But we do not want to take all this trouble and incur all this expense and have the scheme ungratefully received.[3]

If PAYGO contributory pensions were considered electorally risky, then *funded* contributory pensions would have been political poison: not only would Fraser's scheme have required a substantially higher 7.5 pence per week premium in the short run, but it would have delayed full pension payouts for decades. Meanwhile, the Chancellor saw no near-term electoral benefit in investing in distant fiscal outcomes. "I do not believe that any popular feeling will be excited about actuarial events to take place 30 years on," Churchill wrote to the Government Actuary. "The Parliaments of those days will be responsible...."[4] To put the problem in cognitive terms, the only available information about long-term outcomes – mathematical projections of the future financial parameters of a program that did not yet exist – was unlikely to make those distant consequences salient to the average citizen.

While crafting the pensions bill that would eventually become law, ministers also devoted special attention to the timing of its costs and benefits relative to upcoming elections. In a letter to Chamberlain the following April, for example, Churchill mulled carefully the electoral implications of delaying the payment of the first old-age benefits for a mere 3 years and making widows' benefits payable immediately, concluding that such a timetable would deliver its gains just in time. "Politically, I do not feel that there is any disadvantage," he wrote. "On the contrary there may be a gain of having two joy days instead of one, and the second of them" – the start of old-age pensions – "falling not very far off a General Election."[5] To ministers seeking temporal proximity between social payoffs and elections, the fully funded Fraser plan had little to offer.

The substantial costs of funding would fall immediately, directly, and visibly on a pivotal segment of the electorate; responsibility for them would be sharply focused on the sole party in government in a political system with relatively concentrated authority; and information about the offsetting benefits would be too abstract to draw public attention. Working-class voters, in other words, would be unlikely to perceive funding as an intertemporal trade-off between higher pension taxes today and lower tax burdens or better fiscal outcomes tomorrow; they would most likely view it as mere loss-imposition. To ministers seeking to face down a clear and present political threat, Fraser's large-scale policy investment would have appeared a recipe for electoral ruin.

BUSINESS HOSTILITY

Had the Fraser plan not been rejected for other reasons, its electoral risks would probably have been sufficient to kill it. To consider a second counterfactual,

---

[3] Churchill to Chamberlain, December 30, 1924, T171/247, The National Archives: Public Record Office (TNA: PRO) [third and fourth pages, letter not paginated].

[4] Churchill to Alfred Watson, April 17, [1925] PRO 171/247.

[5] Churchill to Chamberlain, April 3, 1925, PRO T171/247, p. 3.

however, a funded plan would *also* have faced formidable opposition from influential organized interests, weakening the government's capacity to enact it, had they wanted to. As we will see, many of the key decisions on program design were taken in closed-door deliberations by cabinet and civil service committees, without direct interest-group input (Walley 1972). Moreover, British political institutions – including electoral rules that tended to produce majority government and tight party discipline in the House of Commons – virtually eliminated veto opportunities outside the cabinet.[6] In this highly insulated policymaking context, organized interests' prospects of shaping policy were limited by their degree of access to the executive. Trade unions were particularly disadvantaged with the Baldwin government in office, as they lacked any direct conduit of influence to the Conservative leadership. Business, with important linkages to both the Tory Party and the bureaucracy, was thus left with disproportionate sway over the policy process. Capital's influence was somewhat constrained both by the fractious state of its organization – employers were represented by three different national associations with somewhat diverging outlooks – and by the Tories' electoral goal of courting working-class voters. It is nonetheless likely that employers' policy demands and perceived interests would have militated considerably against the enactment of a substantial policy investment.

Not only were employers directly and privately consulted by the Baldwin government, but their interests drew special attention even in fora in which they did not directly participate. Because the Fraser plan was quashed early and never publicly released, employer groups did not have to directly confront the choice between funding and PAYGO financing of the pension program, and analysis of their intertemporal preferences must remain somewhat speculative. However, from demands voiced on other issues and later in the pension policymaking process, it is clear that industry understood social policy in terms unfavorable to an investment in funding.

The 1920s were a decade of prolonged economic malaise, characterized by rising labor costs, falling international competitiveness, and widespread industrial contraction (Garside 1990; Aldcroft 1970). The most vocal of business groups on social-policy matters – the National Confederation of Employers Organizations (NCEO) – defined issues of economic management and social policy almost exclusively in terms of the minimization of labor costs (Rodgers 1988; see also Williams 1970). When consulted during the planning of the new pension scheme, the NCEO vigorously lobbied the Baldwin government to limit contribution costs (Addison 1992). Its strategy, moreover, was not to invest at short-run expense in a moderation of *long-term* contribution burdens by accumulating a fund. To the contrary, the Confederation urged the Chancellor to *draw down* existing social-insurance funds – specifically, to dissipate unforeseen

---

[6] Not only were laws immune from judicial review by the courts, but since the Parliament Act of 1911, even the House of Lords had lost the power to permanently veto legislation.

surpluses in the health sector – in order to cross-subsidize and mitigate the short-term costs of the new pension scheme.[7] Rather than pushing the government to invest in stabilizing social-policy costs over time, in other words, business pressed ministers to limit burdens in the present.

Even working in private, moreover, government officials carefully considered the effect of program design on British capital in ways that undermined the case for investment. A key civil service committee weighing financing options argued against funding in part by warning of insurmountable business opposition to any plan that imposed a higher current contribution burden than was required to meet current benefits.[8] A top Treasury official similarly counseled Churchill that pension taxes would "certainly not be a tonic, or assist industry to face competitive prices in the world markets."[9] Aside from their raw political leverage, employers benefited from the compatibility of their demands with orthodox-economic prescriptions widely credited within Whitehall, including the view that a resumption of economic growth hinged on a reduction of the costs of production.

Employers' preferences and their considerable sway within the ruling party and bureaucracy would likely have limited ministers' capacity to invest in a funded pension scheme. But from what sources did business opposition to investment stem? In part, employers' position was a function of the dire economic conditions of the 1920s – a crisis that likely foreshortened capitalists' time horizons. Projected long-range contribution burdens were of limited concern to a firm or industry facing the threat of imminent collapse. Of more direct relevance to the hypotheses in Chapter 2, business's strategy also seems to have derived from the asymmetrical distribution of group influence in this highly insulated institutional context. Given labor's limited influence over policy to date, British business in the 1920s had good reason to use its privileged position to pursue its interests through distributive, rather than intertemporal means. It was logical, that is, for capitalists to seek to minimize long-run costs by pushing friendly governments and ministries to *limit the generosity* of the welfare state, rather than by investing in the welfare state's long-run sustainability. Finally, and of greater importance, business leaders – like senior policymakers inside the state – did not find policy investment credible as an intertemporal trade-off: they did not believe that surpluses accumulated today would *in fact* be used to minimize contribution burdens tomorrow. It is to this perceived uncertainty of the long term that we now turn.

---

[7] "Extract from Minutes of Meeting of Executive Committee of the Federation of British Industries, on 13 May, 1925," MSS.200/B/3/2/C645 pt. 1, British Employers' Confederation Papers, Modern Records Centre (MRC).

[8] "Committee on Insurance and Other Social Services. Third Interim Report," [1925], PIN 1/3.

[9] Otto Niemeyer [Financial Controller of the Treasury] to Chancellor of the Exchequer, March 28, 1925, T171/247, TNA: PRO [first page, memo not paginated].

THE POLITICAL VULNERABILITY OF INVESTMENT

While both electoral and interest-group pressures would have made policy investment difficult, Fraser and Chamberlain's planned investment was in fact rejected largely because of its expected *long-term* consequences – in particular, its exposure to the political uncertainty of the long run. In designing their new pension scheme, British politicians in the 1920s enjoyed important informational advantages as compared with their German predecessors 45 years earlier. Most importantly, what was *terra nova* for German policymakers was now well-charted territory. By 1925, 25 countries had already adopted some form of national compulsory pension program, 16 of them contributory (Social Security Board 1937). This international experience – while not studied in great detail by British policymakers – at least set upper bounds on how badly things could go for a contributory public pension program.[10] Closer to home, domestic experience with national health and unemployment insurance and means-tested pensions likely gave policymakers further confidence about their ability to design social programs with roughly predictable outcomes. More concretely, because the eligible population for contributory pensions would be the same as that covered by national health insurance, actuaries could use health insurance data to help calculate revenues and costs. The British endeavor further benefited from the far more developed informational infrastructure of the inter-war British state, which provided rich decennial census data on mortality, family structure, and occupation for the entire population.[11] While any cost estimates were still subject to uncertainty, the risks of miscalculation were perceived to be modest. As Chancellor, for instance, Churchill expressed a level of confidence in financial projections that would have been unthinkable for his German counterpart, assuring Chamberlain that "everything will work out according to the actuaries."[12]

This far lower level of *consequence* uncertainty meant that Treasury officials and ministers did not need to build vast margins for error into the program's financing. Moreover, they needed to rely far less than their German counterparts on analogical reasoning from a loosely related field of economic activity in order to understand their policy project. While British officials saw some parallel between contributory state schemes and private insurance (and applied the

---

[10] The influence of foreign models on policy design choices appears to have been modest, limited to creating a general sense of the plausibility of the project. Interestingly, I have uncovered no evidence that the British debate over funding was influenced by the recent devastation of the German pension funds through hyperinflation in the early 1920s. And for an excellent account of how poorly the Asquith government had used available information about the German scheme in designing its 1908 means-tested pensions, see Hennock (1987).

[11] See "Widows', Orphans' and Old Age Contributory Pensions Bill: Report by the Government Actuary on the Financial Provisions of the Bill" ("Widows', Orphans' and Old Age Contributory Pensions Bill: Report by the Government Actuary on the Financial Provisions of the Bill" 1925)

[12] Churchill to Chamberlain, December 30, 1924, T171/247, TNA: PRO [fourth page, letter not paginated].

"insurance" label to the former), they explicitly recognized fundamental differences between the two types of endeavor, including the distinctive distributive aims and political dynamics governing a public program.[13] In evaluating the new pension proposal, British policymakers drew less on the logic of private insurance and, as we shall see, more on a mental model drawn from past experience with financing *state* initiatives.

However sound its actuarial foundation, Fraser's policy investment – with its projected buildup of massive surpluses – ran up against a wall of bureaucratic suspicion of fund accumulation within the state. Official misgivings within Whitehall about allowing governments to amass and carry over large surpluses were longstanding. Over the preceding decades, government and independent experts had on numerous occasions proposed blueprints for possible systems of contributory old-age insurance to replace the 1908 scheme.[14] And as civil-service committees assessed the proposals, any element of funding in these plans was routinely and sharply criticized.[15]

The notion of building up surpluses today to spend on tomorrow's policy goals clashed directly with a fiscal doctrine deeply entrenched within the UK Treasury. Officials within this most powerful of government departments shared a relatively coherent and stable understanding of the principles of budgetary policy. At the center of the Treasury view lay a mental model of the political economy of public spending: a model in which the electoral incentives facing governments diverged widely from the dictates of sound financial and economic management. In this view of public finance, governments were understood to be maximizers of short-run vote tallies, with little regard for the long-run economic consequences of their choices. Elected officials could be counted on – if they were permitted – to spend all available resources for immediate political gain, to pay off narrow constituencies at the expense of economic efficiency, and to manipulate the currency for short-term advantage. By contrast, Treasury officials had long seen *themselves* – insulated from the vulgar demands of politics – as neutral guardians of the state's long-run financial and economic interests. To defend against government predation, the Treasury thus sought to organize budgeting processes and economic institutions so as to minimize politicians' day-to-day discretion over policy parameters: so, for instance, the currency should be pegged to the price of gold, trade should be free, and budgets should be balanced on an annual basis (Daunton 2002; Peden 2002).

Of most direct relevance to the problem of pensions was this last implication of the Treasury model. According to the principle of annualized budgeting,

---

[13] Williams (1970) points out that British governments had progressively moved "state insurance theory" farther away from "private insurance orthodoxy" since national insurance had been enacted.

[14] Notable among these are schemes proposed by Joseph Chamberlain, Canon Blackley, and Charles Booth. See Macnicol (1998). I refer the reader to Macnicol's book for the most thorough history of British pension politics prior to 1948.

[15] *Royal Commission on the Aged Poor*, 1895, C-7684, para. 334; *Report of the Commission on Old Age Pensions*, 1898, C. 8911.

which the Treasury had applied since 1829, any surpluses run in one year were to be used immediately to pay down the national debt (Peden 2000). This rule effectively blocked the accumulation of a large fund dedicated to a programmatic purpose. As Basil Blackett, an official in the Treasury's Finance Division explained in a 1910 memo, the doctrine was a hedge against the political risks of fund accumulation:

> ... [T]here is much objection to using the chance surplus of one year for the ordinary expenditure of the next – such a system would lead to much political jobbery, as a strong government would build up a surplus in its early years and use it to remit taxation when its popularity was waning and leave its successors of the opposite party with an empty Exchequer.[16]

Even if stockpiling resources might in theory make fiscal sense as a means of smoothing tax burdens over time, the Treasury saw little reason to believe that governments would *in practice* leave a fund untouched long enough for this future benefit to emerge. This causal belief was likely underwritten, in part, by the institutional context of high (but not hyper-) insulation within which British Treasury officials operated. Like most elected governments, Whitehall's political masters faced popular pressures to disburse resources to constituents in the short run. The lack of veto points within the British policymaking process, moreover, maximized opportunities for fiscal manipulation: with first-past-the-post elections, a fused legislature and executive, and a relatively weak upper house, Westminster institutions tended to vest enormous political authority in single-party majority cabinets (Wood 2001). Treasury officials also saw public pensions – an exceptionally popular form of state largesse – as posing a particularly vexing problem of political commitment: once established, they believed, a retirement program invited future governments to routinely seek public favor by expanding benefits (Macnicol 1998). Among the few hand-binding tools available to civil servants in a highly centralized polity was the institutionalization of fiscal rules that kept politicians on a short revenue leash.

The Treasury's understanding of fiscal policy was deeply embedded in policymaking routines across the bureaucracy, including at the lead department on pensions, the Ministry of Health.[17] British ministers, moreover, relied heavily on the expertise of senior bureaucrats in formulating and assessing policy proposals. Near the end of their last term in office in 1923, the Conservatives had in fact appointed an interdepartmental committee of top civil servants, chaired by the Permanent Secretary of the Home Office, John Anderson, to propose a design for a new contributory pension program. The Anderson Committee continued to consider policy options and outline a proposal during the Labour

---

[16] "Finance Bill 1911," Memorandum by Blackett, Nov. 22, [1910], T171/9, TNA: PRO, quoted in Peden (2000, 42).

[17] Despite having primary responsibility for social spending, officials at the Ministry of Health were known for their strong allegiance to the Exchequer's drive for efficiency, commonly displaying far greater concern for fiscal prudence than for the welfare of the poor (Savage 1996).

Party's brief stint in government in 1924. Chamberlain then submitted Fraser's blueprint to the Anderson Committee for vetting shortly after returning to office in late 1924 (Macnicol 1998).

It was in this influential panel's deliberations that the principles of actuarial planning, drawn from the world of private insurance, clashed most directly with the accumulated wisdom of Whitehall. In private advice to the government, the Anderson Committee pointed out that the Fraser proposal, by accumulating a colossal fund, "challenges the principle on which public finance is conducted, namely, that the amount raised in taxation in any year is equated as nearly as may be to the payments to be made in the year."[18] The Committee acknowledged that contributory pensions involved a trajectory of rising spending obligations and revenue requirements over time. Yet it contended that pensions were unexceptional in this respect: many state obligations are known to be increasing over time, the panel argued, but it has never been considered necessary to accumulate reserves to cover future expenses. The Committee also drew on a stock of readily available policy experience that appeared to support this principle and the underlying mental model of public finance. While German officials in the 1880s had had no track record of accumulating programmatic reserves within the state, British policymakers in the mid-1920s had been operating National Insurance programs for over a decade. And as the Anderson Committee pointed out, whenever surpluses happened to develop within the health and unemployment insurance schemes, the extra monies immediately became the subject of myopic political wrangling. Forces both within and outside of Parliament routinely pressed demands to use the excess cash immediately, either to reduce contribution rates or to increase benefits in the near term – not to enhance the programs' long-term fiscal position.[19] The Committee soundly rejected the Fraser plan on these grounds and forwarded to ministers an alternative proposal based on PAYGO financing rules. Churchill, meanwhile, received similar advice against funding from within his own department.[20]

While civil servants' views were most decisive, it is worth noting that their understanding of fiscal policy was widely shared across elite policymaking networks, both within and outside the state. In meetings with ministers, for instance, business leaders echoed top bureaucrats' concerns that excess social insurance funds simply constituted a temptation to spend, rather than a prudent buffer against future cost increases. Speaking of the surpluses in the health-insurance funds, the NCEO's vice president argued to Chamberlain:

---

[18] "Committee on Insurance and Other Social Services. Third Interim Report," [1925], p. 4, PIN 1/3.

[19] "Committee on Insurance and Other Social Services. Third Interim Report."

[20] "There is no real advantage in the State providing money now to meet future liabilities and allowing a fund to accumulate these monies against those liabilities," wrote financial controller Otto Niemeyer. "It is both simpler and better for the State to pay this liability as and when they mature without ear-marking in advance special funds for that purpose." Addressee and year missing from original document, Nov. 18, T171/247.

I think myself that these very large funds are to a very large extent a danger. You have seen the danger yourself.... Pressure might be brought to bear on you or one of your successors in Office later on which might be very strong, and I think it is a really serious danger to have very large funds which are very tempting in times of financial stress to be appropriated to purposes for which they were not intended.[21]

Business's own opposition to policy investment was thus in large part driven by the dominant elite understanding of the dynamics of social spending – a model that facilitated reasoning about the political threats to fund accumulation.

As senior officials thus framed the choice for ministers, a funded pension plan would not trade current pain for decades of budgetary gain: rather, in extracting resources from constituents today, funding would merely expand the next government's opportunities to curry favor with voters. Given the electoral perils that they confronted, Churchill and Chamberlain had little incentive to push back against the weight of official counsel – to pursue fund accumulation at great short-run political risk against the best available policy advice. With both electoral logic and dominant policy understandings speaking against policy investment, ministers decided to base their bill on an Anderson Committee proposal for purely PAYGO-financed pensions. Parliament, dominated by a disciplined Conservative majority, passed the government's Widows', Orphans', and Old Age Contributory Pensions Act in 1925 (Walley 1972). Imposing premiums of 4.5 pence per week on workers and employers (as compared with 7 pence under the Fraser plan), the plan would pay a flat-rate 10-shilling weekly pension to all members of the national-insurance program once they reached 65 (removing the means-test from the 1908 pension payable at 70). Not only were contributions kept low in the near term, but full benefits would be available starting in 1928, shortly before the next general election.

CONCLUSION

British politics in the mid-1920s presented highly unpromising conditions – particularly, ideational and electoral – for policy investment. Though consequence uncertainty was perceived to be low, policy investment presented both short-run and long-run political risks. Drawing on a deeply entrenched mental model of fiscal management and on salient policy experience, senior civil servants warned of the tremendous long-term dangers of accumulating funds within a state program – funds that future ministers could divert toward other policy purposes. Delegated the central tasks of program design, these officials' causal judgments framed investment as an unappealing trade-off and effectively removed funding from the active menu of policy options. Drawing on a similar causal understanding, business groups with influence within the Conservative Party also perceived funding as a noncredible intertemporal bargain – or, put differently, as mere

---

[21] Milne Watson is speaking. "Widows', Orphans', and Old Age Contributory Pensions Bill: Deputation to the Minister of Health on 17th July, 1925," MSS.200/B/3/2/C645 pt. 3, p. 3, British Employers' Confederation Papers, MRC.

redistribution: if resources for actuarial funding were extracted from employers today, they would be spent on something and someone else tomorrow, rather than being used to minimize employers' own long-run contribution costs. Thus, if German policymakers perceived funding as a profitable intertemporal exchange, British actors' perceived this trade-off as simply *unobtainable* via the accumulation of resources within the state. Meanwhile, competitive conditions in the electoral arena gave ministers little reason to override expert bureaucrats and force policy investment back onto the agenda. If a fund was unlikely to survive the long-term threat of misappropriation, then ministers had little reason to take short-term electoral risks – or impose current losses on their business allies – to bring about its enactment.

What is perhaps most striking about the British case of program creation is the prominent role of career civil servants in the rejection of policy investment. In conventional understandings of policymaking, insulated technocrats are often thought to be the actors most willing to see short-term pain imposed for long-term gain (Williamson 1994; Evans 1992; Waterbury 1992). After all, they are the decision makers who should be least responsive to short-run electoral pressures. The British case both partially supports and partially challenges the view of bureaucrats as natural advocates of investment. On the one hand, it is clear that civil servants' rejection of policy investment did not reflect foreshortened time horizons. To the contrary, career officials were exceedingly forward-looking in their view of fiscal and pension policy, placing a high value on long-term goals such as debt reduction and the constraint of future governments. On the other hand, as farsighted actors, British career officials also provide a useful limiting case, demonstrating that foresight does not necessarily imply a preference for investment. British bureaucrats' intertemporal preferences resulted from a combination of their extended time horizons and their deep-seated *causal understandings* of the long term. And their choices, interestingly, depended heavily on how they perceived *other* actors' time horizons: a policy investment that relied on government promise-keeping seemed a dubious prospect to officials who conceived of their political masters as short-term opportunists.

CHAPTER 5

Investment as Political Constraint

The Origins of U.S. Pensions, 1935[1]

"Grass would grow in the streets of a hundred cities," President Herbert Hoover predicted, if his Democratic opponent were permitted to carry out his plans for large-scale federal intervention (Siracusa and Coleman 2002, 19). But by the time of the 1932 election, three years of economic contraction had already wrought devastation on an unprecedented scale. National income had been cut in half and 5,000 banks had collapsed, wiping out 9 million savings accounts. Most disconcerting was the persistence of plenty amidst want: while industry functioned at a small fraction of capacity, a substantial share of the population went without basic necessities. With fully one quarter of the workforce unemployed, many began to question whether the capitalist system itself would survive the damage. Against this backdrop of economic wreckage, Franklin Roosevelt defeated the deeply unpopular Republican incumbent with a stunning 57.4 percent of the vote while sweeping his party to new and vastly expanded majorities in the Senate and House of Representatives, respectively (Kennedy 1999).

Having promised a "new deal" for the American people, Roosevelt moved fast to enact a flurry of novel policy responses to the deepening crisis. Within his first year in office, the president acted to shore up the financial system with an Emergency Banking Act, to relieve farmers with the Agricultural Adjustment Act, and to boost industrial prices and employment with the innovative National Industrial Recovery Act. He offered economic assistance and redevelopment aid through the Federal Emergency Relief Administration, the Tennessee Valley Authority, and a range of other welfare, loan, and public works programs. All of this activity was aimed at meeting people's immediate economic needs in crisis and reviving the economy. This bold activism, while of questionable economic impact, made Roosevelt immensely popular, even across class lines. So high was his standing that the 1934 midterm Congressional elections produced an anomalous *gain* in seats for the party in the White

[1] Parts of this chapter draw on Jacobs (2009b).

House. The Democrats now controlled the House of Representatives with 322 seats to the Republicans' 103 and held over two thirds of the Senate.[2] As historian William Leuchtenburg (1963) has written of 1934:

The elections almost erased the Republican Party as a national force. They left the G.O.P. with only seven governorships, less than a third of Congress, no program of any substance, no leader with a popular appeal and none on the horizon (117).[3]

Yet, if challenge from the right had temporarily retreated, unyielding economic misery gave impetus to political dangers on Roosevelt's left in the form of growing radical, populist movements. As 1934 and 1935 wore on, the Administration took these movements increasingly seriously as threats to reelection and a Democratic political majority (Kennedy 1999). One possible response would have been to undermine these groups' popular appeal by expanding relief and redistributive welfare measures. Yet such a strategy, by itself, would have clashed with Roosevelt's deeply held ideological convictions. While multibillion dollar relief expenditures had already yielded mounting deficits, the President and most of his advisors clung tightly to a pre-Keynesian belief in the economic virtues of balanced budgets (Brinkley 1995). Public assistance and the dole were, in their view, stopgap measures with grave fiscal and political risks.

On the other hand, the New Dealers believed, a comprehensive system of social insurance – financed by contributions from the insured and payable irrespective of need – could provide the nation with economic security on a solid moral and fiscal basis. In June of 1934, Roosevelt appointed a Cabinet-level Committee on Economic Security (CES), headed by Secretary of Labor Frances Perkins, to design a public system of "cradle-to-grave" insurance. After 6 months of work by the CES staff, the Administration sent to Congress its Economic Security Bill, with provisions for contributory old-age insurance along with unemployment insurance, an expansion of public health grants, and a series of means-tested welfare schemes for specific groups including the elderly, children, and the blind. As enacted by Congress, the old-age insurance program was striking both for its sole reliance on contributions from workers and their employers – with no subsidy from general revenues – and for its near-complete adherence to the principles of funding. While new payroll taxes would be imposed starting in 1937, the first benefits would not be payable until 1942, starting out small and gradually rising to their maximum level over a 45-year period. By imposing high contribution costs long before the payment of full benefits, the program would build up a massive reserve. Generating a hefty stream of interest income, this fund was then projected to allow the program's long-term contribution burden to stabilize at a lower level than

---

[2] The Progressives and Farmer-Labor Party together held 10 House seats.
[3] The classic general history of the New Deal's early policy and political achievements is, of course, Schlesinger (1958).

PAYGO financing would have ultimately required – about 25 percent lower by 1970 – even as benefit rates climbed and the population aged.[4]

This chapter examines why American politicians adopted such a large policy investment, even in the midst of deep economic crisis. In the chapter's concluding pages, I will also consider funding's fate immediately following Social Security's enactment. A rapid shift in economic, ideational, and political circumstances would lead to the investment's unraveling within a few short years. As I will argue, identifying the forces that drove politicians to dismantle this investment throws into even sharper relief the specific conditions that had allowed them to enact it.

"INSURANCE, NOT CHARITY"

The task of designing a comprehensive program of social security, including old-age pensions, fell largely to a group of economists, social insurance experts, and actuaries who formed the staff of the CES. While granting them wide latitude to work out policy details, Roosevelt explicitly instructed the program's framers to plan over extended time horizons. As the president told a gathering of the Advisory Council to the CES, his belief in insurance "must not be understood as implying that we should do nothing further for the people now on relief. On the contrary, they must be our first concern" (Roosevelt 1938, 453). Yet, he explained:

At this time, we are deciding on long-time objectives. We are developing a plan of administration into which can be fitted the various parts of the security program when it is timely to do so. We cannot work miracles or solve all our problems at once. What we can do is to lay a sound foundation on which we can build a structure to give a greater measure of safety and happiness to the individual than any we have ever known (454–5).

What did the President's experts see when they looked into the distant future? Their levels of consequence uncertainty were relatively low. By 1934, social insurance experts had a fairly good grasp of the financial dynamics of retirement security programs. Diminishing the complexity of their choice was the availability of a range of state-level and foreign models which suggested both a finite menu of policy options and a finite range of potential outcomes. The CES's Old Age Security staff, in the course of its work, carried out an extensive analysis of 20 foreign pension schemes currently in operation (Rodgers 1998; Committee on Economic Security 1937). Expressing far more informational confidence than had German policymakers half a century earlier, they reported to the President that "actuarial problems, although involving extensive calculations based on available population and economic data, can be resolved with relative accuracy on a national basis."[5]

---

[4] Calculation derived from Table IV in U.S. House of Representatives (1935b).

[5] Committee on Economic Security Executive Director and Staff, "Preliminary Recommendations on Old Age Security," November 27, 1934, CES – Reports, Drawer #2: CES Materials, Lateral File #3, Social Security Administration History Archive (SSAHA), p. 12.

Of greater concern to Social Security's architects were the political dynamics that they believed might follow the creation of a national pension program. The New Dealers' thinking about the politics of social protection was heavily shaped by a specific ideational heritage, partly inspired by past experiences of policy failure. Roosevelt, central figures in his administration, and many of the CES experts had emerged from a Progressive intellectual and political tradition, some as veteran reformers at the state level.

While they viewed government intervention as a potentially powerful tool for advancing social justice, Social Security's architects also believed that public programs – especially, poorly designed schemes of social spending – could pose a serious threat to sound public management, governmental efficiency, and democratic accountability. In the New Dealers' shared mental model of welfare politics, social spending and electoral politics tended to exert a mutually corrupting influence upon one another. Where public social programs were operating, politicians and party bosses would reliably seek to exploit them as easy sources of constituency handouts, generating an unrestrained expansionary dynamic while underwriting the unhealthy influence of patronage-oriented party machines (Orloff 1988; Ikenberry and Skocpol 1987).

This understanding of social politics was to a large extent a product of dramatic and local historical experience: the deep infiltration of earlier American social benefit programs by electoral and patronage politics. As has been well documented elsewhere (Orloff 1993b; Skocpol 1992; Ikenberry and Skocpol 1987), politicians had massively expanded the scope of the Civil War pensions system for electoral gain – by 1900, fully one in three native-born men in the North were receiving payouts – while using welfare programs to provide jobs for party activists or to help party machines distribute benefits to supporters.

While more recent experience with pensions for civil servants and World War I veterans had been more encouraging, the Progressive model shaped the New Dealers' interpretation of current political events, continually drawing their attention to the potential for dangerous interactions between social benefits and democratic politics. Populist movements led by Dr. Francis Townsend, Father Coughlin, and Huey Long were winning increasing support for radically redistributive proposals. As Long touted his plan for free pensions financed by a tax on millionaires, Townsend's organization was gathering momentum in its push for pensions of $200 a month financed from a tax on transactions and had significant backing in the House of Representatives. With organizations in almost every congressional district pressing for generous and immediate universal old-age pensions, the Townsendites alone had gathered over 10 million petition signatures. Meanwhile, popular demands for noncontributory pensions had already pushed 19 states to adopt old-age assistance laws between 1929 and 1933 (Kennedy 1999; Orloff 1993b; Graebner 1980; Leuchtenburg 1963; Witte 1962; Schlesinger 1958). Viewed through a Progressive lens, these events seemed to buttress the New Dealers' understanding of democratic politics as prone to dangerous expansionary forces. Most New Dealers were also uncomfortable with the fact that 22 percent of Americans were now dependent on one of the three major relief agencies that Roosevelt had established. In their model of social politics, the very popularity of the early New Deal further demonstrated the dangerous populist potential of tax-financed relief (Rodgers 1998).

Aside from a specific causal understanding of the relationship between welfare and politics, Roosevelt and his advisors brought two additional preoccupations to the design of America's fledgling welfare state. The first was fear of the fiscal impact of new social spending. Despite 1932 campaign pledges to cut government spending and deficits, Roosevelt had so far overseen an enormous rise in both as relief efforts proliferated. Ambitious in scope and scale, the new social programs could not be allowed to aggravate what most in the Administration saw as a gathering budgetary crisis. In addition, Roosevelt's moral map of social policy raised a second concern about unintended social-policy consequences. Despite having spent the first two-and-a-half years of his presidency alleviating economic pain through a series of emergency relief programs, Roosevelt abhorred the "dole" as a matter of principle (Perkins 1946). As a handout divorced from merit or effort, welfare was to him "a narcotic, a subtle destroyer of the human spirit."[6] While harboring vast ambitions for his state scheme of social protection, the president was insistent that the system not be designed in a way that might undermine individual initiative or the virtues of self-reliance.

These causal and moral understandings of welfare politics led Administration and CES officials to place an especially high premium on the choice of an appropriate *financing* mechanism for the new social programs. In weighing financing options, CES staff and administration actors drew many of their ideas from familiar and well-established financial practices in analogous spheres, including both private and social insurance. As historian Daniel Rodgers has written, "The logic of commercial insurance so pervaded the air in 1930s America...that the New Dealers could not escape it" (444).[7] As in Bismarck's Germany, private insurance seemed to offer a financially robust, morally appealing framework of protection that could be usefully adapted for social purposes. CES staff members were equally impressed by the example of European *social* insurance (Perkins 1946). Through the 1910s and 1920s, a prior generation of American labor economists, social workers, and social-policy advocates had traveled to Europe in search of models for social reform. This store of knowledge then became institutionalized in economics departments and policy institutes across the country. Now, as Perkins' staff worked quickly amidst crisis, they had readily at hand decades of research on the principles and practices of contributory social insurance abroad (Rodgers 1998).

To Administration officials and Committee planners, the principles and structure of contributory insurance seemed powerful protection against the

---

[6] Quoted in Berkowitz (1991, 14).

[7] See also Marion Folsom's comments on the centrality of the private insurance model in 1935 in his contribution to the New York Times Oral History Program, Columbia University Oral History Collection, Part III, No. 158, Social Security Administration Project.

financial, moral, and political risks that they perceived in public social provision. From a budgetary perspective, contributory financing offered the considerable advantage of fiscal neutrality over the long run. Financing social protection through a set of new, earmarked premiums could avoid the fiscal drain that ordinary welfare typically threatened. The president was also drawn to the concept of insurance as a moral proposition, a more rigorous alternative to welfare or relief financed out of general taxation. While welfare offered benefits without effort, insurance was an inherently reciprocal arrangement that rewarded past contributions and the virtue of work (Berkowitz 1991).

Further, Roosevelt and his advisors saw contributory financing as far superior in its long-run *political* effects: an essential tool for curbing the politics of welfare profligacy, placing a brake on heedless program expansion. Tying expenditures to a visible dedicated tax, contributory social insurance would force politicians to impose costs visibly on constituents every time they made benefits more generous. Only a program that firmly tied benefits to visible costs, they believed, could resist the tide of political pressure for reckless social spending. Moreover, by linking the receipt and level of benefits tightly to an individual's record of premium payments, contributory financing would constrain politicians' discretion in distributing benefits (Kennedy 1999; Rodgers 1998; Orloff 1993b; Berkowitz 1991; Ikenberry and Skocpol 1987). As CES staff executive Edwin Witte warned the President, without a contributory system, "...[W]e are in for free pensions for everybody with constant pressure for higher pensions, far exceeding anything that the veterans have ever been able to exert" (quoted in Kennedy 1999, 266). "Of course one thing that we had in mind all along with the contributory system," recalled one of Roosevelt's key business allies, "was that the [House of Representatives] Ways and Means Committee and the Senate Finance Committee would keep a very careful watch on it to keep it from getting out of line because they know if they raise benefits, they've got to raise taxes. They know there's a certain limit to what the taxes are going to be."[8]

On Roosevelt's instructions, the CES thus designed its schemes of old-age benefits and unemployment assistance on a contributory basis. While Roosevelt would accept some tax-financed provision for programs targeted at those currently elderly and needy, the Administration's long-term solution to the problems of economic security was to be grounded in the principles of contributory insurance (Witte 1962). Like Bismarck, Roosevelt was a policy generalist, not an insurance expert, and he left the details of program design to his staff specialists. Exactly how closely he wanted his new social programs to mimic the logic of private insurance in fact seems to have been unclear to members of the Committee on Economic Security. A simple and strict adherence to insurance doctrine – as instantiated in the private-insurance industry – would have required that the scheme be financed not just on a contributory basis but on a

---

[8] Marion Folsom, New York Times Oral History Program, Columbia University Oral History Collection, Part III, No. 158, Social Security Administration Project.

fully funded basis, with each worker (and his or her employer) paying the full actuarial costs of the benefits that he or she would receive. Assuming it worked as intended, a fully funded scheme would be a monument to fiscal conservatism, completely insulating the Treasury from new expenditure demands while ensuring that the program always had assets on hand to cover its liabilities.

Yet the Committee experts – in line with both European practice and conceptualizations in the academic literatures on social policy and labor economics – understood the analogy between social and private insurance to be a relatively loose one. A generation of scholarship on European welfare states, together with the CES's own comparative analyses, suggested to the Committee a broad spectrum of plausible methods of financing contributory social programs, adhering more or less closely to commercial actuarial principles (Rodgers 1998). As this large body of research made clear, contributory social insurance was in fact rarely designed to simply mirror its private counterpart. Most European social programs, even those that required contributions from the insured, received an infusion of general revenues to help moderate costs for current workers and cut against the regressivity of payroll taxes.[9] Moreover, few such programs were funded on a strict actuarial basis. As the staff experts knew, full funding and strict PAYGO financing represented the purist endpoints of a broad spectrum of financial practices, with the vast majority of social programs falling somewhere in between. While actuarial logic might dominate a private insurance company's calculations, many governments had departed from a rigid relationship between contributions and benefits in order to minimize their programs' economic impact, to pursue social goals like poverty relief, and to build bases of political support.[10] Indeed, social insurance was generally understood by academic specialists and European policymakers as a flexible device for balancing the rigors of self-help against welfare-oriented goals and political pragmatism.

This hybrid mental model of social-program finance, informed by the untidy world of policy practice, lent CES planners a rather elastic understanding of the insurance principle as applied to public programs. Operating with a relatively complex conceptual toolkit, Roosevelt's expert group did not see the decision about funding as a simple choice between foolhardy short-run maximization and long-run fiscal prudence. Rather, their quite nuanced mental map of the policy sphere led them to reason through a broad range of potential

[9] This point is made in Edwin Witte [Director of CES], "Suggestions for a Long-Time and an Immediate Program for Economic Security," [no date], CES – Committee Activities, Volume 8, Lateral File #3, CES Materials, SSAHA; and Committee on Economic Security Executive Director and Staff, "Preliminary Recommendations on Old Age Security," November 27, 1934, CES Reports, CES Materials, Lateral File #3, SSAHA p. 16

[10] See, for instance, the reference to Britain's PAYGO model in "Outline of Old Age Security Program Proposed by Staff," November 9, 1934, CES – Staff Papers, CES Materials, Lateral File #3, SSAHA, p. 7. See also the prominent reference to "experience abroad" in justifying the group's proposal for a government subsidy in "Old Age Security Staff Report: To Mr. Witte," [no date], CES – Reports (folder #2), Drawer #2: CES Materials, Lateral File #3, SSAHA.

consequences of policy investment – including economic and political processes that could both magnify the ultimate costs of investment and threaten its long-run returns.

A chief disadvantage of funding, in the Committee's view, was the near-term burden that it would place on industry. A strictly funded plan – with contribution rates held constant over decades – would have required an immediate contribution burden of 4 percent of wages, shared equally between workers and their employers.[11] Despite all of the Administration's efforts for economic recovery, industrial production was falling in the summer of 1934, the economic crisis proving more stubborn than expected. The CES experts believed that a fully funded plan would carry grave economic risks in this context. Looking further into the future, the Committee also saw it as undesirable to accumulate as large a reserve as full funding would yield. A fully funded scheme, Treasury officials advised, would ultimately amass greater assets than the government could invest without disrupting capital markets. Such a large volume of cash would force the Treasury into the uncomfortable position of searching private financial markets or other government bond markets for secure and politically acceptable investments.[12] Echoing the concerns of British officials, the Committee's actuaries further noted "the practical problem of protecting a reserve of such huge dimensions from diversion into other channels under the pressure of emergency."[13]

Moreover, the Committee staff believed that adherence to strict actuarial logic would leave the scheme politically vulnerable in the short run. If retirement pensions were calculated solely on the basis of past contributions, then today's older workers would receive "such small pensions as to subject [the scheme] to general disapproval." As the CES's Old Age Security working group reported to the Committee's executive director, "...[I]t was deemed that the pensioners would believe that they were not receiving a fair return for their contributions." More broadly, a plan that tied benefits too closely to contributions would be "condemned as not providing a substantial reduction of old age dependency for more than a generation."[14] If the new program were to be politically saleable in

[11] Witte, "Suggestions for a Long-Time and an Immediate Program for Economic Security," [no date], CES – Committee Activities, Volume 8, Drawer #2: CES Materials, Lateral File #3, SSAHA, pp. 11–12.

[12] "Old Age Security Staff Report: To Mr. Witte," [no date], CES – Reports (folder #2), Drawer #2: CES Materials, Lateral File #3, SSAHA; "Outline of Old Age Security Program Proposed by Staff," November 9, 1934, CES – Staff Papers, CES Materials, SSAHA Lateral File #3, p. 7; "Report of the Staff on Old Age Security to the Technical Board Executive Committee," November 16, 1934, CES – Reports (folder #2) SSAHA, CES Materials, Lateral File #3.

[13] Committee on Economic Security Actuarial Committee, "Comments on the Recommendations for Old Age Security," Volume II, *Old Age Security: Final Staff Report*, Unpublished CES Series, SSAHA.

[14] "Old Age Security Staff Report: To Mr. Witte," [no date], CES – Reports (folder #2), Drawer #2: CES Materials, Lateral File #3, SSAHA; see also Witte, "Suggestions for a Long-Time and an Immediate Program for Economic Security," [no date], CES – Committee Activities, Volume 8, Lateral File #3, CES Materials, SSAHA, pp. 11–12.

the near term – and, hence, to *survive* into the long term – the Committee believed that it had to deliver greater benefits right away, making some special provision for those workers now in middle age.

Balancing a range of rival considerations, the Committee members opted for a pragmatic blend of mechanisms – a mix of financing measures that would hedge against the gravest dangers of any pure financing type. To begin with, the CES proposed timing the trajectory of contribution rates so that the program would impose its burdens on industry very slowly (Witte 1962). In the CES plan, the payroll tax for old-age insurance would begin at a rate of 1 percent in 1936, shared equally between workers and employers, gradually increasing over the next 20 years to 5 percent – the heaviest burden the Committee thought could ever be imposed without serious harm to workers' living standards (Derthick 1979). Paying its first pensions in its sixth year of operation, the program would relate the size of benefits to the length of a worker's contribution record, but with a formula that somewhat favored older workers. Separately, and in line with presidential instructions, the Committee also proposed a measure for immediate relief: a much smaller scheme of tax-financed, means-tested old-age assistance that would start paying benefits right away to the indigent elderly.

At the same time, however, these provisions collectively required a compromise of the principle of self-support. Keeping the scheme's near-term costs modest while, at the same time, paying early beneficiaries pensions in excess of their actuarial entitlement would place the scheme on a largely PAYGO basis: these provisions meant that most of the contribution revenue in the early years would be spent on current pensions, rather than being saved to pay future benefits. The plan would accumulate only a modest reserve of $12 billion (in 1935 dollars), intended as a contingency fund rather than a significant source of interest income for the system. Then, as the scheme matured – with each successive cohort of workers entitled to progressively larger pensions – holding long-run contribution rates to 5 percent would ultimately leave the program with an operating deficit. While the scheme could run strictly on contributions for its first three decades, the federal government would have to direct a share of general revenues to the system starting in 1965.

The Committee believed that it had struck a careful balance among a complex set of competing policy objectives: safeguarding the government's fiscal position and imposing the political constraint of contributory financing for several decades, while obviating the need for an unwieldy fund and minimally impeding industrial recovery in the short run (Douglas 1939; Committee on Economic Security 1935). The Committee members would soon learn, however, that they had underestimated the President's and the Treasury's attachment to the pure "self-supporting" principle.

While they shared a broad orientation toward social reform, two important ideational differences separated Roosevelt and Treasury Secretary Henry Morgenthau, on the one hand, from the Committee's social-policy specialists, on the other. The first was the former's deep commitment to a set of orthodox fiscal beliefs. Though the president never managed to balance the federal budget, he and Morgenthau continually tried to do so, uneasily reconciling themselves to deficits only as a temporary emergency measure to finance desperately needed relief programs.[15] While the later dynamics of recovery often obscure the fact, Roosevelt and his top economic advisors in the mid-1930s still subscribed to a causal model of the economy in which government borrowing could only serve to undermine business confidence, drain resources from more productive uses, and forestall recovery. Economic orthodoxy, that is, captured a rather different set of potential consequences of financing choices from those emphasized by the social-insurance framework dominant among CES experts.

Second, as a policy generalist, Roosevelt could not devote the same stock of cognitive resources to the problem of pension design that his staff experts invested in the task. Though he had experience with unemployment insurance and social assistance policy at the state level, the president would not have had easy cognitive access to the conceptual tools or the details of foreign models on which his aids relied. Instead, Roosevelt seems to have leaned heavily on the more proximate domestic model of private insurance and on a more elementary shortcut to reasoning about program financing. Most striking are the absolute terms in which the president distinguished between contributory "insurance" on the one hand and "relief" or the "dole"– that is, tax-financed social benefits – on the other hand. It is not just that Roosevelt saw advantages in contributory financing: more than that, he stripped a complex set of policy trade-offs and a broad continuum of financing options down to a strict dichotomy. As he instructed the CES on the design of unemployment insurance, for instance, the scheme had to take pure contributory form; any element of tax financing would reduce the scheme to welfare. "We must not allow this type of insurance to become a dole through the mingling of insurance and relief," he declared. "It is not charity. It must be financed by contributions, not taxes" (Roosevelt 1938, 453).

As a comparatively "heuristic" processor of social-policy information (relative to expert advisors, that is, not to the average voter), the President was likely to draw on somewhat more superficial cues in his environment and to reason about them in less differentiated ways. The collapse of European social insurance systems under the weight of the global economic crisis seems to have particularly drawn his attention, and (in line with his pre-existing model) he attributed their troubles to faulty policy design – specifically, their departure from strict insurance principles. As he admonished the CES's Advisory Council, "Let us profit by the mistakes of foreign countries and keep out of unemployment insurance every element which is actuarially unsound" (Roosevelt 1938, 453). While Roosevelt's inference was not an unreasonable one, foreign programs' financial troubles had in fact resulted as much from a sharp rise in unemployment – which brought both falling revenues and exploding outlays – as from any

---

[15] Detailed support for this claim can be found in Brinkley (1995), Leuchtenburg (1963), Leff (1978), and Mitchell (1947). See also Weir (1989) or Orloff (1993b).

particular feature of policy design. In drawing lessons from the experience of other nations, however, the president focused most closely on apparent correlations that reinforced his existing conceptual dichotomy.

Roosevelt and Treasury officials' particular ideational orientations heavily influenced their responses to the CES proposal. When the Committee delivered its draft report to the White House, the Treasury's Director of Research, George Haas, pointed out to Morgenathau the intertemporal profile of the CES's fiscal plans. Haas explained in a memo that, although the CES scheme would collect more in contributions than were required to pay benefits in the early years, it was far from self-supporting in the long term:

In an attempt to minimize the problem of managing large reserves, the Committee has proposed actuarially inadequate rates during the early years, thereby adding commensurately to the burdens of future generations. More particularly, by applying these low rates to now middle-aged and older workers, it contracts to give them far more than they pay for, the Federal Government borrowing the difference, in effect, from the current contributions of younger workers. The result, after the passage of sufficient time, is a very large Federal outlay annually for the system.[16]

Haas then suggested that it "would be far sounder actuarially" to increase contribution rates more quickly: to 6 percent in 10 years, instead of only 5 percent in 20 years. This steeper rise would have the equity advantage of making older workers pay more for their own pensions. More importantly, if the reserves were invested in government securities, then the state would in the future pay a share of the interest on its debt to the fund rather than to private bondholders, thereby "reducing the net demands on the Treasury" in the long term.[17]

To the Treasury Secretary, the CES's proposal implied a short-sighted trade-off over time. In private conversation, Morgenthau told trusted Roosevelt advisor and work-relief administrator Harry Hopkins that he feared that the President was unaware of the fiscal implications of the pension proposal. Hopkins responded that, in the short run, the plan would only cost the Treasury $25 to $30 million per year in spending on means-tested old-age assistance. Morgenthau countered that the immediate expenditures were beside the point; he was worried about the long-term consequences. "... It's the things that it runs into," he said. "That's the thing. That's what scares me." He was resolved to draw the President's and the Labor Secretary's attention to the long-run trend lines. "I want to show them the bad curves," he said.[18]

---

[16] Mr. Haas to Secretary Morgenthau, Subject: Report of the Committee on Economic Security, January 5, 1935. Copy at ALJ-Morgenthau on Self-Supporting, Arthur Altmeyer Papers 2, Drawer #1, Lateral File #2, SSAHA. Originally from the Presidential Diaries of Henry Morgenthau, Jr. (1938–1945), Book 3, Franklin D. Roosevelt Library, pp. 37–47.

[17] Ibid.

[18] Transcript of conversation between "H.M.Jr" and Harry Hopkins, January 7, 1935." Copy at ALJ-Morgenthau on Self-Supporting, Arthur Altmeyer Papers 2, Drawer #1, Lateral File #2,

Once informed, Roosevelt was equally appalled by the plan's long-run fiscal consequences and its departure from pure insurance principles. Indeed, the temporal remoteness of the plan's fiscal costs seems to have been almost immaterial to him. "Ah," he remarked to the CES's chair, Labor Secretary Frances Perkins, "but this is the same old dole under a different name. It is almost dishonest to build up an accumulated deficit for the Congress of the United States to meet in 1980. We can't do that. We can't sell the United States short in 1980 any more than in 1935."[19] In a separate meeting with the CES's executive director Edwin Witte, he crossed out the word "subsidy" in the draft report, referring to the future contribution from general revenues, and wrote the word "deficit," ordering him to fix the long-run contribution shortfall.

The CES revised its proposal as instructed, with a new schedule of rates that brought the costs of the pension program substantially forward in time: contributions would start in 1937 at 2 percent instead of 1 percent and would rise much more quickly, at 3 year intervals. The maximum rate would be a full percentage point higher than in the original proposal and would be reached 7 years earlier, in 1949. The scheme would now rely purely on dedicated payroll contributions, with no planned subsidy from general revenues. As a result of this new contribution schedule, the program's reserve would approach the level of full actuarial funding – reaching $280 billion, 12 times the program's annual expenditures – by 1980.[20]

A WINDOW OF OPPORTUNITY

Embedded in a package of social measures, this plan for a massive policy investment in old-age security was sent to Congress in early 1935. But, of course, the enactment of the president's intertemporal preferences still depended on his capacity to overcome institutional hurdles to policy change. In the United States' highly decentralized policymaking process – characterized by constitutionally separated powers, relatively weak party discipline, and two decentralized legislative chambers – any policy proposal must typically run a gauntlet of potential veto points before becoming law. Moreover, the old-age insurance plan would impose near-term costs on well-organized groups who might be expected to exploit these multiple institutional opportunities to derail it.

As we will see, however, a set of rare electoral and political circumstances allowed for unusually insulated policymaking in this formally fragmented

SSAHA. Originally from the Presidential Diaries of Henry Morgenthau, Jr. (1938–1945), Book 3, Franklin D. Roosevelt Library, pp. 58–60.

[19] Quoted in Perkins (1946, 294).

[20] Figure in 1980 dollars. "Statement of the Secretary of the Treasury on the Economic Security Bill," File 011.01, "Legislative History and Analysis." Chairman's File, 1935–1942, Records of the Social Security Board/Records of the Office of the Commissioner, RG 47, NACP. Calculation of current value employed GDP deflator (Johnston and Williamson 2008).

institutional setting. To begin with, the CES itself had operated in private, well insulated from lobbying by organized interests. Organized groups representing the elderly – especially the Townsend movement – had, in an indirect sense, exercised influence over the Administration's plans by forcing some kind of action on old-age security (Amenta 1992). But with bold action legitimated by unprecedented crisis – and the President and his party in an unusually dominant electoral position – the Administration did not see a political imperative to consult closely with organized interests, including potential allies, on specific matters of program design. In selecting Committee staff, Roosevelt and top CES officials specifically steered clear of leftwing organizations, choosing moderate experts who took a cautious and scientific view of what the state could achieve. Better-known advocates for government largesse like Abraham Epstein, representatives of reformist popular groups (like the American Association for Labor Legislation or the Eagles), and more radical advocates of noncontributory pensions were excluded entirely (Orloff 1993b).

Organized labor, meanwhile, demonstrated little interest in the CES's work on old-age insurance. In 1934, the American Federation of Labor (AF of L) was still emerging from its "voluntarist" view that employment conditions should be settled primarily through collective bargaining, free of government intervention; it had yet to develop a robust agenda for expanded state social protection. Though favorably inclined toward old-age insurance, the AF of L kept at far remove from the Committee's deliberations (Quadagno 1984; Derthick 1979). While the CES had an Advisory Council that included representatives of the Commerce Department's Business Advisory Council (BAC), employer influence at this stage was also tightly limited. Not only did the CES Advisory Council fail to meet until shortly before the pension proposal was completed, but few of its proposals were adopted by the Committee. Even then, the liberal views of the industrial representatives on the BAC were far from representative of the climate of opinion in corporate America (Orloff 1993b; Skocpol and Amenta 1985). For this unusual period and in this specific realm of policy choice, the U.S. executive operated with a degree of insulation from group input comparable to that enjoyed by Bismarck's unelected government.

Business Opposition

While organized groups did not have much opportunity to shape expert deliberations inside the executive, Congress might have offered a more promising arena for policy influence. Organized labor remained relatively disengaged, however, displaying far more interest in the unemployment insurance provisions of the bill – with their direct, near-term implications for union members – than in old-age pensions. In his testimony before the House Ways and Means Committee, AF of L President William Green did not even mention the latter, focusing solely on unemployment compensation (U.S. House of Representatives 1935a). In briefly discussing the financing of contributory pensions in his remarks before the Senate Finance Committee, Green expressed support for a payroll tax shared between workers and employers as a "sound foundation" for a "self-liquidating" insurance system. He also called for "bringing the old-age insurance plan into operation in the shortest possible time" by accelerating the tax schedule in the bill by a few years (U.S. Senate 1935, 181). This was not a plea for even greater policy investment but for an acceleration of the scheme's benefits: a more rapid imposition of the payroll tax (half of which was to be paid by employers) would allow for a more rapid payout of the contribution-linked pensions.

Representing the largest organization lobbying on behalf of the elderly themselves, Townsend pushed Congress to reject the old-age insurance plan outright in favor of his own plan for much more generous universal pensions, of $200 a month, financed out of a 2-percent value-added tax (U.S. Senate 1935). In addition to promoting far more dramatic redistribution from young to old and rich to poor, Townsend also advocated a very different intertemporal choice from that embedded in the Administration's proposal. While the Economic Security Bill would collect full contributions long before it paid full benefits, the Townsend plan would introduce the new tax *and* full benefits immediately, operating on a PAYGO basis. However, pushing a radical substitute rather than amendments to the existing bill, Townsend's capacity to influence the legislative outcome was quite limited. His opposition siphoned off a natural source of support for the Administration proposal, from the elderly themselves. However, with the movement's core strength still limited to the West in 1935, it lacked sufficient support in Congress and – with both chambers led by Roosevelt loyalists – sufficient access to the legislative agenda to derail the Administration's plan. Most legislators viewed the Townsend plan itself as a highly impractical alternative; if anything, its gathering popularity heightened the imperative to act quickly, further enhancing the appeal of the Administration's more sober initiative (Amenta 1992; Witte 1962).

If labor was broadly supportive and pensioners' organizations marginalized, business groups represented a more formidable challenge to the president's policy investment in old-age security. The concept of social insurance received support from a handful of progressive business leaders in close contact with the Administration – such as Marion Folsom of Eastman Kodak and Gerald Swope of General Electric – but American capitalists were on the whole deeply hostile to the proposed expansion of government's role in the economy (Hacker and Pierson 2002; Skocpol and Amenta 1985). At the broadest level, employers were critical of an extension of the social safety net that would, in their view, sap individual initiative, reduce the supply of labor, and impose a heavy burden on industry. They were also particularly alarmed by the new payroll taxes envisioned for both unemployment and old-age insurance. Leaders of the National Association of Manufacturers, the U.S. Chamber of Commerce, and the National Retail Dry Goods Association urged legislators to avoid or minimize a levy on wages that would depress labor demand, squeeze profits, raise the price of consumer goods, and place domestic industry at a disadvantage relative to foreign competitors. While they were willing to countenance the modest means-tested old-age assistance provisions in the bill, most businessmen testifying before Congress sought to have the old-age insurance provisions struck from the legislation altogether.[21]

Recognizing that the bill had broad political support, however, employers also aimed to ward off what they saw as its most dangerous elements. On the matter of program design, Roosevelt's proposed policy investment in funding drew especially sharp criticism. In the language of Chapter 2, funding offered employers, in principle, a profitable vertical investment: while it would have imposed higher contribution costs on firms in the short run, it ought to have also delivered greater benefits to them via lower tax burdens over the long run. Yet business leaders saw little reason to believe that, in practice, they would reap these hypothetical long-term gains. Whatever the actuarial tables projected, employers viewed the plan's enormous fund as highly vulnerable to political abuse. As the BAC's committee on social insurance wrote in its report on the bill, such massive surpluses would simply provide a painless opportunity for vote-seeking politicians to enrich pension benefits, nullifying the advantages of investment:

It is very doubtful whether under our form of government we could actually accumulate this large reserve fund.... There would be a strong tendency either to increase the benefits or to reduce the tax rate, with the former being the probable course. If this were done a tremendous burden would be placed upon future generations.[22]

Even liberal executives who supported state-run old-age insurance viewed funding as a financing mechanism fraught with long-run political risk. As Marion Folsom of Eastman Kodak told the Senate Finance Committee during hearings on the bill, the buildup of billions of dollars in the pension account would encourage "a strong tendency either to enlarge the benefits or to reduce the contributions, with a resulting deficit to be met by the Government in later years."[23]

Capitalists also worried that Congress would raid the pension fund for other purposes, generating runaway public spending. Pointing to recent experience with civil service pensions, a representative of the National Association of Manufacturers laid out the logic of the problem before the Senate's Finance Committee:

It...encourages further Government borrowing and opens practically unlimited possibilities of reckless public financing, since there would be enormous pressure from without, and perhaps from within, upon Congress to authorize [expenditure of the] accumulated

---

[21] See testimony of James A. Emery (National Association of Manufacturers) and Albert D. Hutzler (National Retail Dry Goods Association) in U.S. House of Representatives (1935a) and testimony of Henry I. Harriman (U.S. Chamber of Commerce) in U.S. Senate (1935).

[22] Business Advisory Council, "Report of the Committee on Social Legislation regarding Old Age Security Sections of the Bill H.R. 7260," April 30, 1935, CES – Reports, Drawer #2: CES Materials, Lateral File #3, (SSAHA), p. 3.

[23] See testimony by James A. Emery in U.S. Senate (1935, 588).

reserves. It will be recalled, moreover, that comparatively recently when a reserve was accumulated under the Federal civil service retirement and disability fund, those who had paid into the fund clamored that the reserve was in fact a surplus and besieged Congress to use what was a trust fund for future payments to establish immediately increased benefits. How much greater will the pressure for distribution of reserves be in a system involving millions of persons instead of 400,000? With billions of dollars apparently in the Treasury how great will the pressure be for vast Government expenditures of all kinds from these funds? The gravity of this problem has been pointed out in these hearings by the distinguished chairman of the committee who called attention to the "political agitation" which would exist to "dissipate any reserve that had been built up".... If such a distribution or spending program should once be started it would grow like a snowball and would lead to practically uncontrolled Government spending and impaired Government credit.[24]

Interestingly, both business leaders and top Administration officials were worried about the political problem of welfare populism, alarmed by the decade's radical movements. But they framed this problem in starkly differing terms, defined by competing mental models of democratic politics. As veteran progressives, the New Dealers were fundamentally believers in the capacity of state action to improve social conditions. Their answers to the problem of political vice were sound programmatic design, scientific management, and democratic reform; they wanted a state that was capable and efficient. Strikingly, public and archival records provide no indication that Roosevelt or Morgenthau worried about the potential political risks to a large pension fund; to them, this fund was a requirement of fiscal responsibility and would reinforce the constraining logic of actuarial insurance. In sharp contrast, most members of the American business community viewed politics through the lens of what David Vogel (1981) has called "an underlying mistrust and suspicion of government" (45). Vogel in part attributes American business's striking anti-statism to the unusual conditions of industrial development in the United States: the emergence of the large, modern corporation well before the rise of the modern administrative state. Firm owners thus did not view industrial success as dependent on state action.

Yet U.S. capitalists came especially to distrust their government as that government became increasingly democratic and open to popular pressures that were often hostile to business interests. The fundamental problem of state activism, in business's view, was capital's incapacity to *control* government in the face of electoral forces. In contrast to their counterparts in Europe or Japan, American capitalists lacked the protection of a strong and independent bureaucracy that could serve as a counterweight within the state against short-run popular pressures (Vogel 1981). In American industrialists' mental model of the U.S. political economy, elected politicians had overwhelming incentives to

[24] See testimony in U.S. Senate (1935, 953). See also Henry Harriman's (Chamber of Commerce) argument before the Committee about the dangers of government investment of such a large fund (U.S. Senate 1935, 719).

seek votes through redistributive and regulatory measures that would raise production costs and squeeze profits, and there were few checks on their capacity to do so. Thus, a state that was both strong and democratic – capable, efficient, and hostage to public opinion – was bad for business. Viewed through the lens of democratic suspicion, the answer to the threat of populism was *less* government responsibility and state power, not more. What good was "sound" program design if today's blueprint could be redrawn by tomorrow's elected majority? If public contributory pensions could not be avoided, better that they be designed to constrain, rather than enhance, the state's long-run fiscal capacities and future politicians' room for maneuver.

To American businessmen, actuarial funding of Social Security appeared a losing proposition. Had they perceived funding as a credible vertical investment – with long-run benefits to them outweighing its short-run costs to them – they might have been willing to entertain the idea. Instead, they believed that any resources extracted from them in the short run would get spent on other things, rather than saved to hold down the program's contribution rates. From employers' perspective, funding promised not a profitable intertemporal trade-off but a horizontal redistribution of resources in the wrong direction.

The Limits of Business Power in the New Deal

American business leaders in 1935 were, however, strikingly poorly positioned to influence the legislative outcome. As most scholarship on the period has concluded, economic crisis and the liberal electoral tide made the mid-1930s a period of unusual weakness in the political power of American capitalists (Hacker and Pierson 2002; Hacker 2000; Orloff 1993b; Skocpol and Amenta 1985). With their Republican allies reduced to a modest minority in Congress and with the White House held by a popular Democratic president, employers' access to the main policymaking venues had sharply diminished. The Depression itself, moreover, shook the economic foundations on which much of capital's influence had rested. With private investment at a near standstill, business's "structural power" – its actual or implied threat of a "capital strike" – had ebbed, while the near-collapse of the market economy shook many of the intellectual assumptions underlying laissez-faire policies. Meanwhile, the heightened mobilization of popular movements and labor unions during the Depression years served as an important countervailing influence on politicians' calculations (Hacker and Pierson 2002).

At the same time, the American policy process itself in the mid-1930s underwent a brief and rare transformation that further diluted business power. Under normal circumstances, business would have enjoyed multiple opportunities in Congress to amend or kill a White House proposal: in either chamber, in committee or on the floor, opponents needed only a single victory to upend a president's legislative initiative. More specifically, the greatest threat to Roosevelt's contributory pension proposal was that it might become detached from the rest of the bill. The old-age insurance plan, with its long-delayed benefits, was far less popular and drew far less support in Congress than the fast-acting measures of old-age assistance and unemployment compensation to which it was tied. Indeed, just as business leaders were urging, several members of the House Ways and Means Committee sought to strike contributory pensions from the bill, and an amendment to this effect was proposed on the floor of the Senate (Hacker 2002). Had either effort been successful, the president's policy investment would most likely have failed. Also under business pressure, a separate amendment – initially approved in the Senate – would have undermined the program's financial basis by allowing firms with equivalent private plans to opt out of the system (Berkowitz 1991).

Despite a policy process riddled with formal veto points, however, Roosevelt's first term in office was a period of unusual presidential influence within Congress. Not only did the Democrats have a massive legislative majority, but many – especially in the House, where all members had stood for reelection in late 1934 – owed their seats to the President's towering popularity. This loyalty, extending even to the party's Southern wing, allowed Roosevelt to effect an exceptional degree of party discipline. In the face of hostile amendments, the President successfully commanded and cajoled Democrats located at key positions on the Ways and Means Committee and in the Senate to keep his policy investment tied to provisions with immediate payoffs and to strike the opt-out amendment from the bill (Berkowitz 1991; Witte 1962; Schlesinger 1958). Put another way, the political allegiance that Roosevelt commanded in Congress made a normally fragmented set of institutions behave, for a brief period, more like those of a majoritarian parliamentary system. A set of fleeting political and economic conditions yielded extraordinarily insulated policymaking processes in both the executive and the legislature, opening a rare window of institutional opportunity for imposing large short-term costs on some of the best-organized interests in American politics.

ENACTING THE UNPOPULAR

Even if the president favored policy investment himself and wielded the institutional leverage to force it through Congress, doing so might have courted severe electoral risk. In Senate testimony, a representative of the Illinois Manufacturers' Association nicely characterized the plan's chief temporal liability:

These taxes are not to be used to relieve the present unemployment situation. They are not to be used to relieve the present difficulties of those now unemployed. These taxes are to be used to build up funds in the public treasuries with which to pay annuities of doubtful value to the aged after 1942....[25]

From an electoral perspective, then, why was Roosevelt willing, as a matter of electoral calculation, to saddle millions of voters with new payroll taxes while

---

[25] John Harrington's testimony appears in U.S. Senate (1935, 685).

delaying the payment of substantial pensions? Why would Democrats in Congress, with electoral goals of their own, yield to this intertemporal proposition?

In part, favorable political conditions offered Roosevelt and his copartisans in Congress a substantial cushion against the danger of losing office. With the national Republican Party reeling from electoral disaster at the 1934 mid-term elections – they held less than a quarter of the House and under a third of the Senate – the Democratic Party was ascendant, and Roosevelt himself commanded staggering levels of public support from which both he and his party benefited. Having spent the first years of his administration enacting a raft of highly popular relief measures, Roosevelt had in a sense accumulated a stock of electoral capital that he could now expend on the pursuit of his own policy preferences.

This is not to say that the White House believed its prospects in 1936 were completely secure. With feeble opposition on the right, the threat that concerned the Administration came from the left – specifically from the prospect of a presidential run by Huey Long on a platform of radical redistribution. When Democratic operatives conducted polling to determine the strength of Long's support, they were horrified to learn that the Senator might draw as much as 10 percent of the presidential vote as a third-party candidate. Their fear was not that Long would win the White House but that he might steal a sufficient number of votes on the left to – in Roosevelt's words – "defeat the Democratic Party and put in a reactionary Republican" (Kennedy 1999, 241). Already, as one Democratic Senator put it, the New Dealers had had to "accept many things... that otherwise we would not because we must prevent a union of discontent around [Long]" (Kennedy 1999, 241).

Against the backdrop of potential challenge from the left, what made policy investment an electorally safe proposition were two critical strategies of policy design. First, as discussed earlier, the Economic Security Bill bundled a policy investment in old-age insurance with faster-acting measures. Old-age assistance, which received an especially warm welcome in Congress, would begin immediately making grants of $50 million a year to the states to finance means-tested benefits for the elderly. These payments would help redress the absence of pension arrangements in many states as well as the gross inadequacy of those state programs that were already in place (Schlesinger 1958; Berkowitz 1991). The quick and carefully targeted distribution of these noncontributory benefits would help blunt popular demands for pensions by alleviating the distress of those most in need. Second, the old-age insurance plan would not levy its first payroll taxes until 1937 – just *after* the next presidential and congressional elections. While challengers in 1936 might warn voters about costs to come, those costs would be far less salient than the immediate benefits that the Act as a whole would be delivering. Indeed, what is most striking about the debates over the Economic Security Bill is how little attention – positive or negative – the old-age insurance scheme attracted. With this provision buried in a flurry of welfare proposals and its costs delayed, few citizens would notice Roosevelt's policy investment in the near term. Put differently, the nature of the information available to voters would make it difficult for challengers to persuasively frame the legislation as a whole as an act of loss-imposition.

The president's intertemporal choice was not devoid of all electoral danger: his Republican challenger in 1936 would, predictably, seek to depict the Social Security program as a "cruel hoax," and the perfectly vote-maximizing choice would surely have been to pay benefits immediately on the basis of PAYGO financing. Together, however, Roosevelt's popularity and strategic legislative design kept the risk of losing office within tolerable limits: for Roosevelt, it was worth taking a modest electoral gamble to make a large stride toward a deeply held policy preference. Moreover, with party leaders and committee chairs committed to keeping the bill intact, members of Congress faced a lopsided electoral calculation: they would have faced far greater peril in voting against the bill, because of its less popular but less salient components, than they did in voting for it, with its promise of visible and rapid relief of widespread deprivation. So strong was public support for the bill that even a Republican Party deeply hostile to public old-age insurance feared opposing the legislation: the (renamed) Social Security Act was adopted over a mere 25 "no" votes in the House and 6 in the Senate.

CODA AND CONCLUSION: THE 1939 AMENDMENTS AND THE UNRAVELING OF INVESTMENT

We can usefully set our explanation of the U.S. outcome against the framework elaborated in Chapter 2. Consistent with our hypotheses about electoral safety, the state of national party competition in 1935 – together with a strategy of policy design that minimized the public salience of information about short-term costs – kept the electoral risks of policy investment low. The mental model employed by top Administration officials generated expectations of high social returns to funding, framing the financing decision for them as a relatively straightforward choice between short-run sacrifice and far greater long-term fiscal and political dangers. And an unusual constellation of political conditions generated the kind of hyper-insulated policy process that, we hypothesized, maximizes the executive's capacity to enact its preferred investment over the opposition of cost-paying groups.

As succeeding years would make evident, however, the intertemporal bargain of 1935 rested on unstable foundations. While the durability of investment is not the chief outcome that I seek to explain, we can gain additional leverage on the drivers of intertemporal policy choice by observing what happens when conditions antecedent to investment change. By the end of 1937, several years of economic recovery went into rapid reverse, as 2 million workers were laid off, corporate profits dropped almost 80 percent, and share prices fell by almost a third. Economic collapse, in turn, undermined both the electoral and intellectual foundations of policy investment. Against a backdrop of renewed economic misery, the 1938 midterm elections brought major gains for Republicans and anti-Roosevelt Southern Democrats, substantially enlarging and emboldening the conservative coalition in Congress. Despite a large Democratic majority, the regional and ideological fissures within the party had reopened. With increasingly combative Southern Democrats in command of key Congressional committees, Roosevelt would no longer wield the influence over legislative affairs that he had at the New Deal's peak.

A key goal of the New Deal's reinvigorated opponents was to restrain what they continued to see as a threatening accumulation of assets in Social Security's trust fund. As they had in 1935, conservatives in Congress and business leaders attacked the fund as an irresistible temptation to public profligacy, arguing that future Congresses would inevitably spend the money for purposes other than that for which it was nominally being saved. As Republican Senator Robert Taft put it, "We don't want to build a house that someone else is going to occupy."[26] While under assault from a newly influential right, the program simultaneously faced attack on the left. The delay in benefit payments allowed the Townsend movement to continue gathering steam after 1935 in its push for flat-rate pensions. At the same time, the left bemoaned the regressivity of Social Security's payroll taxes, set to climb steeply in years to come.

Alongside political demands for reversing Roosevelt's investment, a profound shift in the ideational environment drew new attention to the economic dangers of funding. While their influence had been muted during Roosevelt's first term, the sharp recession of 1937 strengthened the hand of Keynesians within and close to the Administration, such as Federal Reserve Chair Marriner Eccles and Harvard economist Alvin Hansen. Advocates of countercyclical fiscal policy considered Social Security – which had begun collecting taxes at the start of 1937 but would pay no benefits for several years – a chief cause of the economic reversal. If the program's temporal profile appeared prudent when viewed through the lens of insurance theory, a Keynesian macroeconomic model drew decision makers' attention instead to the procyclical dangers of funding. As this new macroeconomic frame gained prominence, it lent crucial intellectual credibility to proposals for drawing down the program's assets.

By 1938, legislative majorities were coalescing around a package of measures to speed the payment of benefits, expand their scope, and forestall rises in the payroll tax – moves that would, collectively, dismantle the policy investment of 1935. Meanwhile, with the program under assault from both left and right, the President and top administrators came to believe that the payment of quicker and more generous benefits was necessary to build support for the scheme and ensure its political survival. With the reserve buildup amidst economic hard times proving a particular political liability, Roosevelt and Morgenthau publicly backed away from the principle of funding.

In 1939, Congress passed and Roosevelt signed amendments to the Social Security Act that began the gradual unwinding of the planned policy investment.

---

[26] Quoted in Leff (1988).

Among the most significant changes were the creation of survivors' and dependents' benefits, the payout of the first pensions in 1940 instead of 1942, and the postponement of scheduled increases in the contribution rate. Congress would repeat this last measure several times during the 1940s, draining the Social Security trust fund as expenditures mounted.[27]

This rapid dismantling of Roosevelt's policy investment underlines the importance of a set of fleeting political and ideational conditions surrounding the 1935 law's enactment. The investment's political vulnerability suggests how dependent the 1935 outcome was on the capacity of a small number of well-insulated executive-branch actors to force their preferred policy option through legislative institutions over the opposition of short-term losers. There is no evidence that by 1939 Roosevelt had ceased to believe in the long-term political wisdom of his initial policy investment, or that Morgenthau had changed his mind about its fiscal virtues (Brinkley 1995). But the ideas of a few Administration officials could no longer shape policy as they had at the height of the New Deal. Shifts in the balances of institutional power and intellectual authority now forced the Administration to accommodate its positions to political forces that it had been able to safely ignore four years earlier. In the absence of a deep recession – and the partisan and ideational changes it generated – the policy investment of 1935 might have survived far longer, given the obstacles to legislative change in a fragmented political environment. But the coalition against investment had become so broadly based, and was so well placed within federal institutions, that even a multiplicity of veto points could not halt the drive to dismantle it.

The early politics of Social Security also throw into sharp relief how the causal understandings of powerful actors can shape their intertemporal policy preferences by framing choices in alternative ways. One striking feature of the politics of program creation is how similar some of the central *goals* of the chief antagonists were. For instance, Administration officials and the business community shared the objectives of minimizing populist influence over social welfare policy and shielding the Treasury from excessive spending demands. In advancing these goals, however, both sets of actors faced daunting causal complexity. The logic of investment balanced on a knife's edge between competing but equally plausible lines of causal reasoning: while a program more closely aligned with private insurance might protect the public purse by anchoring the scheme in actuarial principles, it might also hand dangerous new fiscal capacities to future legislators. And if PAYGO financing might help constrain reckless spending by tomorrow's politicians, it might also bequeath large unfunded liabilities to tomorrow's taxpayers.

Which of these causal logics actors weighed most heavily depended greatly on their preexisting understandings of social politics. Viewed through the lens of progressive reformism, the problem of political uncertainty was best addressed through robust, fiscally responsible program design. Viewed through the lens of

---

[27] The brief account here is based on Kennedy (1999), Tynes (1996), Brinkley (1995), Achenbaum (1986), Derthick (1979), and Schlabach (1969).

fundamental democratic mistrust, program design seemed a weak defense against populist pressures that were *inherent* in American institutional arrangements. Cleverly crafted programs would do little to constrain legislative majorities that could always rewrite the law to divert funds or raise benefits. The best protection against majority sentiment, then, was to maximally *limit* government's capacity to act by depriving it of the resources to do so. Different causal understandings, in turn, generated different framings of the policy trade-off. While Roosevelt understood funding as a virtuous exchange of near-term pain for long-term gain, employers perceived it as both burdensome in the short run and futile over the long.

It is also notable that, among state actors, intertemporal policy positions did not align closely with electoral incentives: the most influential opponents of policy investment were the experts on the CES, insulated from short-term political pressures, while its champion was an elected official, the president. Though their time horizons were long, the Committee staff understood social insurance policy as distinct from private insurance, embodying a complex balance among social and actuarial goals. In their judgment, a policy investment in funded pensions, though it might moderate the long-run tax burden, was not worth the near-term costs in higher contribution rates and delayed benefits. Roosevelt's choices were partly facilitated by the degree of electoral insulation that he enjoyed. It is nonetheless striking that he was willing to forego the vote-maximizing option – full and immediate pensions on a PAYGO basis – to act on his own policy preferences.

CHAPTER 6

Investing for the Short Term

The Origins of Canadian Pensions, 1965

After 22 years in office – and having dominated federal politics for six decades – Canada's Liberal Party found itself thrust into opposition at the election of 1957. Despite the Liberals' winning a plurality of the popular vote, Canada's first-past-the-post electoral system handed a larger seat share to John Diefenbaker's Progressive Conservatives (PCs), who went on to form a minority government. When Diefenbaker called a snap election the following year, the results were more devastating: the PC Party emerged with the largest parliamentary majority in Canadian history, reducing the Liberal caucus to 48 members in the 265-seat House of Commons.

Resounding defeat provoked a period of ideological conflict and soul-searching within the Liberal Party, prompting debate over the party's direction on a range of social and economic issues. On matters of social welfare, the Liberals had some rightful claim to a legacy of popular reform. Under the governments of William Lyon Mackenzie King, the party had laid the foundations of the modern Canadian welfare state, enacting means-tested old-age pensions in 1927, unemployment insurance in 1940, and family allowances in 1945. Under Mackenzie King's successor, Louis St. Laurent, universal pensions followed in 1951 and national hospital insurance in 1957. At the same time, over the course of the 1950s, St. Laurent's party had lost the initiative in the field of social policy, moving only slowly and grudgingly toward expansions of the welfare state and allowing itself to be outflanked by the opposition. In the 1957 campaign, both the PC on its right and the New Democratic Party (NDP) on its left assailed the government for its meanness in social affairs. Mocking St. Laurent's ministers as the "six-buck boys" for a modest increase in pension benefits enacted just before the election, both rivals promised voters far more generous public spending. More broadly, after more than two decades of electoral dominance, the Liberal Party had come to be viewed as disengaged from constituents, favoring the interests of big business over the needs of the common citizen (Bryden 1997; Bothwell, Drummond, and English 1989).

The crushing defeat of 1958 strengthened the hand of a new generation of thinkers and activists within the party who now proposed a more socially progressive policy trajectory and called for a more active federal presence in the welfare sphere. Among the policy ideas gradually gaining currency within the party were an expansion of public health insurance and contributory pensions. With the leadership victory of progressive Lester Pearson, the reformers gradually solidified their grip on the party's policy agenda over the next few years. When the Liberals returned to power as a minority government in 1963, their platform committed them to establishing a second-tier contributory retirement scheme with earnings-related benefits (Bryden 1997).

As we will see, Canadian federal ministers and senior bureaucrats in the mid-1960s operated with a distinctive mental model of public pension policy – a model within which a policy investment in funding appeared to offer little long-term advantage. The electoral challenge confronting the Liberal Party also spoke in favor of delivering quick benefits and moderating near-term costs. Yet when the Canada Pension Plan (CPP) and its sister scheme, the Quebec Pension Plan (QPP), were enacted, they contained a substantial policy investment in funding. Contribution rates would start out at almost double the level required for PAYGO financing, but this early investment would allow them to hold steady for 30 years. On one level, the Canadian decision-making process displays important elements of the electoral, ideational, and institutional mechanisms theorized in Chapter 2. Yet the case also serves an important inductive function in suggesting a causal logic of policy investment *not* foreseen by our theoretical framework and distinct from that observed in the other cases. If German and U.S. governments enacted funding for its expected long-run benefits, Canadian politicians instead invested for the *short term*. They chose funding because of the *immediate* benefits that resource-accumulation would yield for an institutionally privileged set of actors: the provincial governments on whose assent the creation of the new pension program depended.

PRESSURES FOR SHORT-RUN DISTRIBUTION

Though the 1963 election had finally returned the Liberals to office, the party appeared far from the dominant electoral position of the Mackenzie King and St. Laurent years. Winning only 42 percent of the vote, Pearson came to power as head of a minority government tolerated by the social-democratic NDP, until then a relatively unusual outcome under Canada's first-past-the-post electoral rules. Not only did the Liberals' vote share appear stuck at historically low levels, but the Canadian party system was becoming progressively more fragmented. With a third and fourth party – Social Credit as well as the NDP – now taking a quarter of the votes between them, election outcomes under Canada's plurality rules might become increasingly volatile and majorities more difficult to achieve.

More specifically, Pearson's government faced strong pressures to deliver rapid benefits in the field of social welfare. With broadly based pensioners' organizations exerting pressure on parliament, the bidding war for the votes of seniors continued, and all parties called for more generous old-age benefits. The Liberals, moreover, were still eager to shake off their reputation for parsimony on pensions. As senior Pearson advisor Tom Kent put it shortly before the 1963 election, "The 'six buck boys' is still a damaging label (especially in Ontario, where most of our marginal seats have to be won)."[1] Against this competitive backdrop, the Liberals had pledged major initiatives on pensions during their campaign – both an immediate boost in benefits under the existing flat-rate, tax-financed scheme (Old Age Security, or OAS) and the establishment of a new contributory program (Bryden 1974). Party strategists saw both policy and political imperatives in ensuring that even the contributory program delivered its benefits quite quickly. "... [I]f a contributory plan is to deal with the cases of real hardship," Kent reasoned, "it must provide for some minimum benefit and provide it soon. Otherwise, the plan is not good social policy and nor is it wise politics – it is asking for money now without sizeable benefits for anyone until much later."[2]

Once in government, Liberal leaders continued to see important political implications in the timing of benefits. At a Cabinet meeting in July 1963, for instance, ministers considered a $10 increase in the monthly OAS pension, scheduled to take effect the following April. The Minister of Labour argued that even this small postponement of the distribution of benefits might be risky. "...[P]ublic demand for an earlier increase...was strong," he contended, and delay would "give the Opposition a very strong issue which would be raised on a supply motion." The Minister of Revenue agreed that "public expectations of an early increase could not be ignored, whether it was justified or not,"[3] and Cabinet decided to move the benefit increase forward by several months.

The Liberals' initial blueprint for a contributory pension plan reflected this same concern with hastening the delivery of benefits. Unlike either the German pension scheme or Social Security in the United States, the new Canada Pension Plan would move toward full benefits on a steeply accelerated schedule. Rather than enforcing strict proportionality between contributions and benefits – which would have delayed full pensions for 40 years – the scheme would treat those retiring in the first few years far more generously than their contribution records warranted; by the end of the first 10 years, retirees would be rewarded as though they had paid a lifetime of premiums (Bryden 1997). Early generosity in the calculation of benefits, however, would make it especially expensive to set up the system on a funded basis. Current younger workers and their employers would have to be asked to pay twice: once to finance the current benefits of their elders, and again to accumulate assets to pay for their own future benefits.

[1] Tom W. Kent to J. F. O'Sullivan, January 5, 1962, File: Jan. 1962 (1), Box 1, Thomas Kent Papers, Location 1300, Queen's University Archives (QUA), p. 3.

[2] Ibid.

[3] Cabinet Minutes, July 16, 1963, File 1963 Cabinet Minutes vol. 3, Vol. 6253, RG 2, National Archives of Canada (NAC), p. 4.

Ministers faced not only the risk of broad public opposition to the imposition of such costs but also organized pressure from those interests with the most to lose from policy investment. As in other countries, senior citizens' groups expressed little interest in the creation of a new contributory pension program which, by definition, would neither tax nor disburse benefits to current retirees. The pensioners' lobby instead focused its fire on the existing noncontributory program, OAS, calling for an immediate boost in the program's flat-rate benefits. Both employer and trade-union organizations, however, paid much closer attention to the design of a program that would have massive effects on their members.

Canada's business organizations were fundamentally – in some cases, rabidly – opposed to the creation of a public earnings-related pensions scheme, regardless of its financing principles. To Ontario Chamber of Commerce President W. J. Adams, the notion of a state-run contributory, wage-related plan could "only be described as socialistic in principle."[4] The Halifax Board of Trade sounded an even more alarmist note about "this burgeoning giant," "the biggest fiscal venture ever contemplated by a Canadian Government (not excluding the conduct of a World War!)," a hastily devised plan "now being force fed ... to reach its increasingly giant proportions in the shortest possible time."[5] Among the "very serious disadvantages to all government-operated contributory plans" were their tendency to depress domestic savings and the accumulation of capital and their chronic vulnerability to political pressures for expansion.[6]

Importantly, opposition to government intervention in this sphere did *not* represent a general rejection of policy investment in pensions. The most powerful Canadian business groups in fact favored investment in funded pensions, but via a different mechanism of accumulation. In cross-national perspective, Canada was a relative latecomer to the decision to establish a public contributory pension program. And by the 1960s, large Canadian firms had already developed substantial private, employment-based forms of social protection for their workforces, including occupational pensions. Though occupational pension plans still covered fewer than 2 million workers by 1960, their membership rolls were growing rapidly, and many employers saw them as a useful tool for encouraging worker loyalty and generating domestic pools of capital

[4] W. J. Adams, Presidential Address to Annual Meeting of Ontario Chamber of Commerce, May 29, 1963, File 30-6-2 pt. 1, vol. 1278, RG 29, NAC, p. 7.

[5] Halifax Board of Trade, "Why Canadian Citizens Are Entitled to – and Should Demand Reconsideration of the Canada Pension Plan," October 1963, File 30-6-2 pt. 1, vol. 1278, RG 29, NAC.

[6] Adams, Presidential Address. For similar business critiques of the CPP proposal, see also British Columbia Chamber of Commerce, "General Policy Statements and Resolutions," File 30-6-2 pt. 1, vol. 1278, RG 29, NAC; Montreal Trust Company, "Government Pension Planning," File 30-6-2 pt. 1, vol. 1278, RG 29, NAC; Canadian Chamber of Commerce, "Presentation by a Delegation of the Canadian Chamber of Commerce, To the Prime Minister and Cabinet," May 31, 1963, File 5–4, vol. 5, Series B8, MG 32, NAC.

(Banting 1987). The government of Ontario – the province in which Canadian industry was most heavily concentrated and most politically influential – had in fact moved ahead of Ottawa in the pensions field, enacting a law in 1963 that would compel all employers of more than 15 workers to establish a funded occupational pension scheme and would enforce portability of pension rights across firms (Balcer and Sahin 1984).

Ontario's new law itself represented a massive policy investment. Under the law, all occupational plans had to be funded to ensure that the employer would always have sufficient assets on hand to cover past promises to workers, even if the firm itself failed. The Ontario government was thus inflicting short-run pain for long-run gain, compelling all medium-sized and large firms in the province to start making actuarially appropriate payments right away in order to finance benefits that would not be paid out for decades. Crucially, most of the same employer organizations that opposed a public pension scheme – even on a PAYGO basis – voiced clear support for compulsory, funded private pensions.[7]

In fact, in employers' view, yet another disadvantage of public pensions was that state provision specifically *precluded* policy investment. Canadian industrialists saw it as an obvious fact that "[a] government plan cannot accumulate funds as the private plans must."[8] For one thing, a funded state pension scheme would threaten the very foundations of the free-enterprise economy. Looking across his southern border, Ontario Chamber of Commerce president Adams pointed out that the American Social Security program had to be run on a PAYGO basis because funding would have generated assets of a size "which the government obviously couldn't invest without owning or controlling a major share of U.S. business."[9] Moreover, as past experience with fund accumulation in social programs seemed to demonstrate, the funds themselves would be targets of political predation by vote-seeking governments:

...[I]t is politically impractical for any democratic government to have a fund of great size without yielding to overwhelming pressures to disburse it, as happened here in Canada with our Unemployment Insurance Fund.[10]

In a private brief to parliament, the Canadian Chamber echoed the fear that the buildup of a fund in state hands would encourage a wide range of demands for higher spending; governments could not be trusted to commit such a fund to its intended long-run purpose.[11]

---

[7] See, for instance, British Columbia Chamber of Commerce, "General Policy Statements and Resolutions"; Adams of the Ontario Chamber, Presidential Address. See also Bryden (1974).

[8] Adams, Presidential Address, p. 10.   [9] Ibid, p. 11.   [10] Ibid, p. 11.

[11] J. Laskin, "Notes on the Pension Fund – Drawn from the Minutes of Proceedings and Evidence of the Special Joint Committee of the Senate and of the House of Commons, Appointed to Consider and Report Upon Bill C-136," File: Canada Pension Plan, Working Papers, UF11, RG 6–44, Archives of Ontario (AO). In its presentation to the prime minister, the Canadian Chamber also stated that public schemes must "of necessity" be run on a PAYGO basis: Canadian Chamber of Commerce, "Presentation," p. 4.

Thus, in employers' view, it was only feasible to run a public program on a PAYGO basis. And yet business worried that PAYGO financing would, over the long run, become far more expensive than the funded arrangements possible in a private plan (Bryden 1974). The long-term advantages of funding, as employers understood them, derived from the logic of compound interest. As Adams argued:

This is because the government plan has no, or at the best, very small investment earnings, while in an employer plan the investment earning can double the pension provided from contributions alone.[12]

In the absence of an actuarial fund to invest, contribution rates in a PAYGO plan had to rise over time, a fact also "shown forcefully by the history of the United States plan," in which premiums rose from 2 percent in 1937 to 9.25 percent 30 years later. "The inevitable increase in tax rates," Adams contended, "constitutes a heavy burden on future taxpayers."[13] The Canadian Chamber emphasized this intertemporal drawback in a private briefing for the prime minister, explaining that "in the long run the pensions provided [by a PAYGO scheme] will cost up to twice as much as those provided by a funded plan."[14]

In sum, Canadian capitalists were opposed to an investment in funding the CPP because of their causal understanding of the politics of fund accumulation. Much like their American counterparts, businessmen in the late-developing Canadian state subscribed to a mental model of democratic politics – reinforced by cognitively available experience with unemployment insurance and cross-party bidding wars over pension benefits – in which elected governments routinely favored short-run vote-seeking over long-run promise-keeping. To business leaders, the intertemporal trade-off implied by a policy investment in public pensions was simply not credible: after paying the higher near-term costs of funding a public plan, employers would see the fund raided for benefit increases or other programmatic purposes, dissipating the investment's long-term benefits. By contrast, a policy investment in private pensions would partake of a more reliable commitment mechanism and a tighter logic of internalized long-run benefits. Firms' claims on the assets held in their occupational pension schemes were protected by legally enforceable property rights. Moreover, with funds held at the company level rather than pooled across the economy, the long-run returns would accrue directly to the firm and the workers that had made the contributions. In other words, Canadian businessmen did not oppose policy investment in the CPP because they were short-sighted: to the contrary, they favored private over public pensions in large part because they believed that the former, though more costly in the near term, were a better long-run proposition.

Organized labor also opposed funding the CPP, but for a very different set of reasons. The main trade-union umbrella association – the Canadian Labour Congress (CLC) – strongly supported the principle of contributory public

---

[12] Adams, Presidential Address, p. 8.   [13] Ibid.
[14] Canadian Chamber of Commerce, "Presentation," p. 4, emphasis in original.

pensions. As Canada already operated a universal tax-financed pension program, labor saw contributory financing as the most plausible way to pay for a
major expansion of public provision. As compared with existing private occupational pensions, a national public plan would also have the benefit of full
portability across employers. In the late 1950s, the Canadian labor movement
had even expressed interest in building up a pool of public capital dedicated to
financing state investments (Bryden 1974). Indeed, labor's interest in using
publicly accumulated assets for social purposes was precisely what business
was worried about. Labor *opposed* funding the CPP, however, out of a calculation of workers' distributive interests: social-insurance payroll taxes would be
a relatively regressive means of financing public investments. As far as the CLC
was concerned, pension contribution burdens on workers should be kept as low
as possible by supplementing payroll taxes with subsidies from the general
treasury; financing for social investment should likewise come from revenues,
such as income tax, collected from more affluent quarters (Bryden 1974).[15]

Employers' position, then, was "yes" to investment through *private* means,
but "no" to investment through public mechanisms – because of the unreliability
of political commitments. Labor, meanwhile, said "yes" to public investment,
but "no" to public investment via a *pension program* – because of the unfavorable cross-sectional distribution of that investment's costs.

"A WELFARE MEASURE – NOT A FISCAL MEASURE"

Pay-as-you-go financing did not just appear politically expedient to Pearson's
ministers: it also looked like good policy. Within policy and academic communities around the industrialized world, both economic thought and social-
insurance theory had undergone a substantial transformation since the eras of
Bismarck and Roosevelt. By the mid-1960s, Keynesian economics was now well
entrenched within most finance ministries in Western democracies, and understandings of social policy had become increasingly and more widely divorced
from earlier private-insurance analogies. Both Keynesianism and newer conceptualizations of the welfare state represented mental models of the political
economy that highlighted the substantial risks of funding public pensions,
while calling its real social benefits into question.

Unlike policymakers in other countries in earlier periods, Canadian ministers
and civil servants in the 1960s understood a public pension system as fundamentally different in purpose and structure from a private pension or life
insurance. Where Roosevelt and Reich officials had leaned heavily on the
insurance parallel, Canada's pension architects drew on contemporary bodies
of policy knowledge that emphasized core *dissimilarities*. In assessing the
relative merits of funding and PAYGO financing, Canadian officials looked
both to international experience and to the teachings of international policy

---

[15] Laskin, "Notes on the Pension Fund," Proceedings of 6th Constitutional Convention of the
Canadian Labour Congress, Winnipeg Manitoba, April 25–29, 1966.

and professional organizations, including the International Labor Organization (ILO), the International Social Security Association (ISSA), and foreign actuaries. In internal documents and discussions with other officials, Minister of National Welfare Judy LaMarsh and her deputy J. W. Willard pointed repeatedly to the fact that few other countries currently ran their public pension programs on a fully funded basis.[16] They also quoted extensively from ILO and ISSA writings that drew a clear distinction between the financing of public and private schemes.[17] At a key meeting of federal and provincial officials, for instance, Willard – the lead civil servant in the CPP's design – drew on a landmark 1942 ILO report to expound "the basic differences between private and social insurance."[18] While private pension schemes covering only a portion of the population typically need to be funded, he explained:

[a]ll or nearly all these conditions are changed if not reversed, in insurance schemes which are national in scope or compulsorily cover all or the greater part of the wage-earning population, and in which the benefits paid are uniform or vary only within narrow limits with the amount of the contributions paid and the duration of the insurance.[19]

Such a plan did not have to accumulate assets because – unlike a private insurance or pension company – it could rely on a steady long-term source of compulsory contribution revenue to pay future benefits. As long as governments had the power to tax, a public program could never become insolvent and thus had no need to balance current capital against future benefit promises.

In Canadian policymakers' mental model of pension policy, the critical determinants of financial capacity were society's real economic resources rather than the assets and liabilities of the pension program itself. In a real-economic view, a public plan's "assets" did not in themselves necessarily reflect savings for the future. As one internal document pointed out, if the CPP's assets were invested in government securities, then the long-run social cost of a funded scheme would be much the same as that of a PAYGO program. Though a

[16] See, for instance, "Funding Under the Canada Pension Plan," [no author], File 5004-2-1 pt 1, vol. 2431, RG 29, NAC; "Statement by the Minister of National Health and Welfare, Honourable Judy LaMarsh Respecting the Canada Pension Plan March 1964," file 2, vol. 1619, RG 29, NAC; "Pay-As-You-Go Principle," [no author, dated "? Sept 63"], Box 7, Location 1300, Thomas Kent Papers, QUA. During the process of policy formulation, the prime minister seems to have been particularly concerned that the CPP's design reflect the social-insurance experiences of other countries. At the Prime Minister's request, Kent provided him, in writing, with Willard's "formal assurance" that "[t]he technical details of the pension plan as approved [at the Cabinet meeting] last night are all drawn from plans in operation in other countries; it puts together what seem to be the best ideas, for Canadian conditions, from those plans; nothing in it is untried; and the package as a whole is simpler than many plans are."

[17] See "Funding Under the Canada Pension Plan;" "Statement by the Minister of National Health and Welfare."

[18] "Minutes of the Federal-Provincial Conference on the Canada Pension Plan September 9 and 10, 1963," file 5004-2-1 pt. 1, vol. 2431, RG 29, NAC, p. 5.

[19] "Minutes of the Federal-Provincial Conference ... September 9 and 10, 1963," p. 6.

funded plan could draw on interest earnings to help defray expenditures, those interest payments themselves would likely be made at the expense of citizens:

A moment's reflection will reveal that with a government plan investing its funds in government bonds there will be no difference in the cost to the taxpayer. Whether payments are made directly from taxpayers to the plan on a pay-as-you-go basis, or indirectly from taxpayers to the plan in the form of annual interest payments, it will amount to the same thing. The taxpayers must provide the money in either case.[20]

If funding implied lower future contribution rates, it implied higher offsetting resource-transfers through other mechanisms. As Willard further argued – quoting the highly regarded Chief Actuary of the U.S. Social Security system, Robert J. Myers – the actuarial notion of a deficit is a quantity "'only of theoretical interest and not of true significance under a long-range social insurance program.'"[21] Moreover, as Willard explained, even if PAYGO contribution rates could be expected to rise over time, improving industrial productivity would generate the real economic resources needed to support them, making these costs easier for future generations to bear.

The CPP's framers also understood the very purposes of social insurance as distinct from that of private arrangements. They openly acknowledged that, as business leaders had pointed out, a PAYGO-financed public pension plan would do nothing to help increase the rate of national savings. In their understanding of the objectives of social policy, however, that was decidedly beside the point. As Judy LaMarsh pointed out to provincial officials, "[T]he Canada Pension Plan was designed as a *welfare* measure – not a fiscal measure, nor a means to control capital investment."[22] While accumulating domestic capital was important for generating jobs and investment, that was the job of private retirement schemes, she argued. Prime Minister Pearson echoed the point, explaining that the CPP, rather than mimicking market arrangements, was meant to perform a social function that the private economy simply could not. The vast majority of people in their 40s or 50s, who would be retiring within the next 10 to 20 years, had no access to private, employer-provided pensions. A public plan could fill this gap, allowing those currently middle-aged to retire with an "adequate minimum measure of security." Yet, this would require the plan to depart from actuarial principles by paying full benefits quickly, within about a decade. "To abandon this objective," Pearson argued, "would remove much of the point of a public plan."[23]

[20] See "Pay-As-You-Go Principle." Willard makes the same point in "Minutes of the Federal-Provincial Conference ... September 9 and 10, 1963."

[21] "Minutes of the Federal-Provincial Conference ... September 9 and 10, 1963," p. 7. Willard also quotes from Britain's Chief Actuary upon the adoption of PAYGO-oriented legislation there in 1959.

[22] "Minutes of the Federal-Provincial Conference ... September 9 and 10, 1963," p. 4. Emphasis mine. See also "Statement by the Minister of National Health and Welfare."

[23] "Draft Memorandum from the Prime Minister to Provincial Premiers," [no date – late 1963], file 23-3-5, vol. 2114, RG 29, NAC, pp. 17–18. For corroboration of Pearson's stated rationale, see Kent's (1988, 265) memoir.

This distinctly *redistributive*, real-resource view of the welfare state dove-tailed with a deeply institutionalized causal framework for understanding the workings of the economy as a whole. As the CPP was being designed, the Canadian economy was rebounding from a downturn that had begun in the late 1950s, and ministers were eager to avoid policy measures that might threaten the still-fragile recovery. In an earlier era, pre-Keynesian orthodox economics had taught policymakers to respond to economic difficulty by entering into a particular kind of intertemporal bargain: if governments balanced budgets today and allowed market forces to liquidate the excesses of past prosperity, then the economy would over time return to a full-employment equilibrium (Salant 1989). Trying to manage the economy in the short run was, in the view of most pre-Keynesian policymakers, both futile and counterproductive. Orthodox economics was, in this sense, a doctrine that prescribed short-term pain to achieve long-term gain. As we observed in the U.S. case of program creation, its fiscal prescriptions fit neatly with the view of public pensions as governed by the principles of actuarial balance.

By contrast, Keynesian economics, the dominant view within Canadian economic policy making circles since the Second World War, taught that it was possible to achieve favorable economic outcomes in the short term *without* necessary detriment to the long run. Keynesianism suggested a novel intertem-poral possibility: that the long term could be taken care of by a succession of appropriate (i.e., countercyclical) responses to short-run economic conditions. This framework taught officials to focus their attention not on budgetary rigor in itself but on managing parameters of the current macroeconomy, such as levels of aggregate demand, prices, and the balance of payments (Bothwell et al. 1989). A Keynesian model of the economy counseled further caution about creating a funded pension plan at a moment of economic vulnerability. As LaMarsh reminded provincial officials, an important disadvantage of funding was that it would represent forced savings. "We regarded it as undesirable in the present state of the economy," she explained, "to withdraw hundreds of millions of dollars in payroll taxes from the private sector of the economy in order to build up large reserves within the public sector"[24] – an unwelcome suppression of aggregate demand.[25] PAYGO financing, in contrast, would continue to support consumption by foregoing capital accumulation and raising the incomes of seniors, who had a high marginal propensity to spend (Kent 1988).

Thus, CPP planners' causal maps of the political economy framed the financing choice as primarily a distributive, rather than intertemporal, trade-off. In their understanding, the actuaries' projections of long-run contribution rates under alternative financing mechanisms did not represent the true long-run social costs of each alternative. A public pension program was, in essence, a mechanism for reallocating real resources from young to old at a given moment in time, not a mechanism of saving for the future. In this redistributive model, the central

---

[24] "Minutes of the Federal-Provincial Conference ... September 9 and 10, 1963," p. 4.
[25] See also "Pay-As-You-Go Principle."

long-term question was *not* whether the scheme's nominal assets would cover its future liabilities but whether future workers and employers could bear the burden of future pension spending – a burden that would fall on them in some form regardless of financing method. The dominant Keynesian view further defined asset-accumulation as a losing proposition in current circumstances: withdrawing funds from a fragile economy merely to hold them against future liabilities could only mean short-run pain for the actuarial illusion of long-run gain.

INVESTING FOR THE SHORT TERM

To federal policymakers, funding the new contributory pension scheme appeared to be not only bad politics, but bad policy. Yet the financing arrangement finally written into the 1965 CPP legislation would in fact be partial funding, a moderate-sized policy investment. To understand why, we have to examine the way in which policy investment could be designed to serve the short-term interests of powerful actors – specifically, provincial politicians.

While still in opposition, Pearson had asked a small committee of advisors to design the outlines of a plan for public contributory pensions, a blueprint that formed a central plank in the Liberals' 1963 election manifesto. The program would be financed on a PAYGO basis and would offer older workers a generous deal by ramping up quickly to full benefits over the course of a decade. Upon taking office, the Liberal government charged an interdepartmental committee on social security with the more detailed formulation of the scheme, which included a low initial contribution rate of just 2 percent of wages, shared equally between employer and employee.

In proposing a national earnings-related retirement scheme, however, the federal government was arriving late to the field of contributory pensions. By 1963, both Ontario and Quebec were already pushing forward with their own, quite divergent pension initiatives. As noted earlier, Ontario had just enacted a provincial plan for compulsory, private occupational pensions that would serve a similar function to a contributory public scheme. And Ontario's preemptive action represented a serious obstacle to federal goals. Because a chief aim of the CPP was to provide nationwide portability, a program that excluded the largest province would be relatively unattractive. At the same time, layering the CPP on top of compulsory private pensions would place an unaffordable burden on both employers and workers in Ontario.

Meanwhile, the Quebec government of Jean Lesage had launched a broad nationalist, modernizing agenda that came to be known as the "Quiet Revolution." An important element of Lesage's moderate brand of Quebecois assertiveness included building a larger and more activist provincial state, both to meet individuals' welfare needs and to develop francophone sectors of the economy (Renaud 1987). By the time the Pearson government was ready to submit a federal plan to Parliament, Quebec was in the advanced stages of designing its own contributory pension system, which differed from the CPP in important respects. Unlike the CPP, the QPP would be a partially funded plan that would adopt a much higher starting contribution rate of about 4 percent – a rate that would then remain sufficient for the next 40 years. The plan would quickly accumulate substantial reserves – about $1 billion, or 4 percent of 1968's gross provincial product, within the first 5 years alone.[26] To achieve this accumulation of capital, the QPP would have to pay a high short-term social cost, delaying payment of full retirement benefits for 20 years. Like Ontario's private arrangement, a substantially funded Quebec plan would detract substantially from the federal goal of nationwide portability and would be difficult to harmonize with Ottawa's PAYGO plan, since the latter would award full benefits a decade sooner while requiring far lower contributions in the early years. Additionally, the Pearson Liberals wished to avoid preempting Lesage for larger reasons of state. While assertive on Quebec's behalf, the premier was a federalist, and weakening him might only strengthen the hand of far more radical francophone nationalists.[27]

Ottawa could thus only achieve its policy goals, at acceptable constitutional cost, by negotiating the CPP's enactment with the provinces. Informally, Ontario's and Quebec's preemptive maneuvers gave each a potential veto over federal plans: if Ottawa wanted to move ahead with a fully portable public contributory pension scheme, it had to either persuade these provincial governments to change course or align its own plans with theirs.

For Quebec's statist government, what was most at stake in its own partially funded design was the multibillion dollar fund itself: a funded program would immediately generate a steady stream of capital for the government to spend on popular and socially productive projects in the public and private sectors. To Quebec officials, in fact, this near-term accumulation of capital was a more important motivation for creating a public pension scheme than were the retirement benefits themselves. As Pearson advisor Tom Kent later recalled of a meeting with the Quebec premier:

While [Lesage] was obviously going to make this, publicly, a matter of nationalist fervour, he made plain to us the motive that was decisive: money.... The large reserve of public savings thus accumulating could be used to finance the great requirements of the new Quebec for social infrastructure – schools, roads, and all the rest (Kent 1988, 260).[28]

---

[26] Calculated from figures provided in Fitzmaurice (1985).
[27] In his memoir, Kent discusses the "tiger" Lesage was riding as pro-Quebec feelings edged closer to anti-Canada sentiment (Kent 1988). And in August 1963, Kent wrote, "We would be unwise to attempt a showdown with Lesage .... It seems quite certain that Lesage would fight to the end. I can see no way of negotiating him out of this attitude. He knows his strength. Constitutionally, he is on strong ground. Politically, such a fight would do enormous damage to 'cooperative federalism,' however it came out in the end. We have nothing to gain that would be worth the price." Tom Kent, "Pensions After the Quebec Resolution," August 27, 1963, Government Briefs, Reports, Drafts, etc., 1964–64, Box 4, Series 3, Location 5123, Thomas Kent Papers, QUA, p. 2. Kent advises Pearson that such a showdown would probably result in Ontario going its own way as well. See Tom Kent to the Prime Minister, "The State of the Government after Quebec," April 7, 1964, File: March 16–30, 1964, Box 3, Location 1300, Thomas Kent Papers, QUA.
[28] See also Bryden (1997).

Quebec, in other words, wanted a policy investment in pensions not to stabilize contribution rates or enhance benefits decades hence, but to underwrite state activities that would begin generating social and political payoffs over a much shorter time horizon.

John Robarts' Progressive Conservative government in Ontario expressed its own (somewhat overlapping) concerns about Ottawa's proposed PAYGO program – concerns that partly reflected the industrial and financial interests heavily concentrated in the province. First, like Quebec, the Ontario government viewed funded pensions as a crucial source of capital for encouraging economic development, though through *private* financial markets rather than state investment. Ontario's new compulsory occupational pensions, governed by strict funding requirements, were expected to contribute substantially to this goal of capital accumulation. Not only would a PAYGO public program accumulate no savings but, by imposing its own contribution burden, might even displace private plans currently amassing investment funds. This effect would be amplified, moreover, by the much more generous transition terms and quicker payment of full benefits that PAYGO financing made possible.[29]

In addition, Ontario officials shared the business community's concerns about the future political dynamic that a new public pension program might unleash. George Gathercole, the province's lead civil servant on pensions, argued that it would be difficult for the current federal government to bind its successors to a fixed schedule of contribution and benefit rates for the next 40 or 50 years. Rather, "[i]n seeking new sweeteners to put in the showcase, most political parties are likely to find enhanced pension benefits irresistible."[30] Premier Robarts' delegation demanded from Ottawa some form of "'built-in fiscal discipline' to prevent frequent upward adjustments in benefits unaccompanied by increases in current contributions."[31]

Further complicating the picture was the interest that other provinces expressed in a Quebec-style funded plan. At a meeting of the heads of the provincial and federal governments, Lesage described Quebec's partially funded plan to his colleagues, and voiced his intention to have Quebec contract out of any federal program. Kent recalled, "One could almost see the other provincial

---

[29] Ontario expresses this concern in many venues, including direct correspondence between heads of government: John F. Robarts (Premier of Ontario) to Lester Pearson, August 22, 1963, file 5004-2-1 pt. 1, vol. 2431, RG 29, NAC; consultations between Ottawa and Toronto delegations: "Notes on Meeting of the Canada and Ontario Representatives to Discuss the Canada Pension Plan," October 31, 1963, File: October 1963, Box 3, Location 1300, Thomas Kent Papers, QUA; George Gathercole, "The LaMarsh Pension Plan," [memo sent to Premier John Robarts], August 7, 1963, F1017, MU 5333, File: Portable Pensions 1963 July – Dec., AO; and in questions raised at a federal-provincial conference on the CPP. "Questions Submitted for Discussion at Federal-Provincial Conference on Pensions, Ottawa, September 9–10, 1963," file 5004-2-1 pt. 1, vol. 2431, RG 29, NAC. See also Bryden (1997) and Bryden (1974).

[30] G[eorge] E. Gathercole to John W. H. Bassett, April 17, 1964, F1017, MU 5334, File" Pensions – 1964, OA.

[31] "Report on Meeting Between Federal and Ontario Officials Respecting Pensions," Box 7, Location 1300, Thomas Kent Papers, QUA. [no pagination].

premiers licking their lips" (Kent 1988, 274). As minutes of the meeting note, Newfoundland's premier asked – only half-joking – "if a province could join either the Canada Pension Plan or the Quebec plan."[32] What most appealed to the other provincial governments about the QPP's design was the mounting fund – the pool of cheap credit – that the scheme promised (Bryden 1997). As these governments had made clear on numerous occasions, they too were in desperate need of cash to finance spending in a range of policy fields that fell within provincial responsibility, including education, roads, housing, and hospital care. Pressures for a more expansive state role in these fields had far outstripped provincial fiscal capacities.[33]

When they learned of Quebec's blueprint, even Ontario officials eyed its projected capital fund with envy and competitive angst. As Gathercole wondered, "Will Quebec be able to accelerate its development by operating its own pension plan? Can it not use this fund to induce firms that might otherwise settle in Ontario to settle in Quebec?"[34] Even if Ontario were to accept the principle of public contributory pensions, he advised Robarts, the province should also contract out of the federal scheme to accumulate its own funds for investment in the provincial economy, "putting itself in the same position as the Province of Quebec."[35]

Determined to fulfill a core campaign pledge and programmatic goal – the creation of a nationally portable, earnings-related pension plan – the Pearson government was forced to bend to provincial demands. The result would be a policy investment in pensions undertaken largely for its *near*-term fiscal benefits. Pearson's first gambit was to propose a modest level of funding in the CPP by reducing planned benefits from 30 percent of earnings at age 70 to 20 percent at age 65. Half of the fund that accumulated – $2.5 billion at the end of 10 years[36] – would be lent to provincial governments. This offer, however, failed to persuade Quebec and Ontario, providing too little capital for either and, for Ontario, offering benefits still too generous relative to the actuarial principles on which private plans operated (Kent 1988; Bryden 1974).

---

[32] "Notes on Federal-Provincial Plenary Conference at Quebec City, March 31-April 2, 1964," file 6–13-Notes on Federal Provincial Conference, vol. 6, MG 32, NAC, p. 16.

[33] Alberta's premier pressed the point at the March federal-provincial conference. "Notes on Federal-Provincial Plenary Conference at Quebec City, March 31-April 2, 1964," file 6–13-Notes on Federal Provincial Conference, vol. 6, MG 32, NAC, p. 10. British Columbia called for a fund within the CPP, to be lent to the provinces, at a federal-provincial conference in September 1963. "Minutes of the Federal-Provincial Conference...September 9 and 10, 1963," p. 8. Manitoba's premier welcomed Ottawa's initial move in late 1963 to partial funding (as discussed later), which would lend half the money to the provinces, but urged that the entire fund be lent to them. Duff Roblin to Prime Minister, January 18, 1964, File: Jan. 1-20, 1964, Box 3, Location 1300, Thomas Kent Papers, QUA. See also Kent (1988, 263).

[34] Gathercole, "The LaMarsh Plan."

[35] G[eorge] E. Gathercole to John P. Robarts, March 19, 1964, F1017, MU 5334, File: Pensions – 1964, AO.

[36] About $400 million of this was a result of an unrelated change to the plan: a decision not to finance a planned $10/month increase in Old-Age Security benefits out of CPP contributions.

After further, secret negotiations with Quebec, Ottawa agreed to an even larger policy investment. Under an accord between the two governments, Quebec would get to keep its own plan (the QPP), while the provisions of the two programs would be made parallel. Ottawa took a critical step in Lesage's direction by nearly doubling the level of funding to accumulate a planned $4.5 billion in assets within the first decade. Moreover, *all* of this fund would be lent to the provinces at the interest rate for federal long-term bonds, a rate lower than the market yield on provincial debt. Benefit levels were increased to 25 percent of earnings to match Quebec's more generous plan. At the same time, Ottawa refused to yield to Quebec's less generous *timing* of benefits, holding the line at full pensions within 10 years (rather than Quebec's proposed 20 years).

Instead of achieving partial funding through a delay in benefits, the two programs would achieve it by immediately imposing a much higher contribution rate than the federal proposal had initially envisioned.[37] A purely PAYGO plan with the same benefit profile would have started out with a 2-percent contribution rate, which would have climbed to about 3.5 percent by 1980 and well over 5 percent by 1995. By contrast, the financing method agreed with Quebec would mean a much higher initial premium of 3.6 percent of wages. Although largely incidental to the motives of Quebec and federal officials, the fund buildup was projected to allow that initial 3.6 percent rate to remain constant through the late 1990s.[38]

The agreement with Quebec ultimately made it hard for Ontario to continue to obstruct. The substantial element of funding and generous terms for provincial borrowing helped assuage the Robarts government's concerns about both capital accumulation and the rising cost trajectory of PAYGO financing. Moreover, with Quebec on board, Ontario was in a much weaker position to object. The Robarts government was unwilling to continue to defend its own less-comprehensive and less-portable private arrangement to stand as the sole impediment to the creation of a highly popular national program (Kent 1988).[39] Moreover, the pension issue had become a matter not only of social policy but an instrument of statecraft: as Lesage's Liberals attempted to hold off a far more radical form of francophone nationalism, Robarts understood that agreement on a national plan parallel to Quebec's would help foster a cooperative form of federalism that might avert constitutional crisis.[40]

Before granting its assent, however, Toronto demanded and won two final concessions: the right to leave the plan later and highly restrictive amendment rules. Any changes to the pension law would require the agreement of two-thirds

[37] The CPP was also part of a larger cross-issue bargain that included Ottawa's granting additional tax room to the provinces, a crucial issue for Lesage.

[38] Department of National Health and Welfare, "The Canada Pension Plan: Actuarial Report," November 6, 1964, File 201-11-4, pt.1, Vol.1519, RG 29, NAC.

[39] See also Kent, "Pensions After the Quebec Resolution."

[40] See "Pensions: Ontario and 'Opting Out,'" May 24, 1964, File 6-17, Interim Box 20, Vol. 6, Series B8, MG 32, NAC.

of the provinces representing two-thirds of the population, granting Ontario itself (given its massive share of the Canadian population) an effective veto over policy change. Both demands reflected the Ontario government's – and business groups' – concern that CPP benefits might spiral upwards over time in a process of electoral outbidding. Ontario officials were further reassured by the fact that the plan's reserves would be lent to the provinces: as they saw it, this arrangement would give the provincial governments a vested interest in resisting demands to spend the reserve on benefit increases because any drawdown of the fund would require the provinces to repay their debts.[41] As the coming decades would prove, the amendment rules and lending arrangement were indeed robust commitment mechanisms, helping to keep benefit levels more or less frozen for 30 years (Banting 1987).

CONCLUSION

The story of the creation of the Canada and Quebec Pension Plans follows a logic of policy investment not fully captured by the framework presented in Chapter 2. At the same time, the pattern of decision making confirms the importance of the causal variables – particularly the ideational and institutional factors – central to that framework.

Had they been able to act unilaterally, Pearson's ministers and officials would almost certainly have foregone policy investment in contributory pensions, choosing to establish the program on a purely redistributive, PAYGO basis. This preference was strongly shaped by both the conceptual lenses through which they viewed the policy issue at hand and by the electoral constraints under which they operated. Under the influence of contemporary understandings of the political economy, LaMarsh, Willard, and Kent perceived only the loosest of analogies between public social protection and private insurance and conceived of the welfare state primarily as a mechanism for redistributing real resources across social groups. In their mental models of public finance and the macroeconomy, funding a public pension plan was a mere bookkeeping operation with no real long-run social payoff but significant economic risks in the near term – hardly an intertemporal *trade-off* at all. At the same time, policy investment had potential electoral risks. Clinging to minority government, the party faced strong pressures to deliver substantial and broadly based social benefits in the near term, which funding made more difficult.

Yet, the dispersion of policy authority to subnational units and the specific configuration of provincial preferences prevented federal officials from acting straightforwardly on their own policy and electoral motives. Because the provinces had the constitutional authority to make their own arrangements in the field of retirement security – and because national portability was central to the

---

[41] "Report on Meeting Between Federal and Ontario Officials Respecting Pensions."

Liberals' aims – provincial premiers held an effective veto over the federal government's policy agenda. The rise of Quebec nationalism further strengthened the hand of the moderate Lesage government in claiming a provincial prerogative. While subnational ministers shared Ottawa's interest in an expanded public retirement regime, they valued contributory pensions as much for the pool of cheap capital they might yield as for their direct benefits to seniors.

The enormous bargaining leverage wielded by the provinces thus turned the Pearson government's policy and electoral motives upside down. The Liberals' chief policy goal was a cross-sectional allocation of resources: the provision of greater income security to retirees. That goal was also central to the pledges that the party had made to voters at the last election. But if Pearson wanted to enact this distributive electoral pledge, then he had to placate the provincial premiers. Policy investment was critical to meeting provincial demands *not* because of its ultimate long-term effects on the sustainability of the program or the trajectory of contribution rates, but because of the *intermediate* mechanism of accumulation through which it would operate. Because it involved the buildup of assets, the funding of a pension plan happened to lend itself to the distribution of short- to medium-term side payments. By setting premiums sufficiently high in the early years, Ottawa could extract surplus resources from constituents that it could then use to purchase provincial agreement.

From Ottawa's point of view, then, partial funding paved the path to a major distributive achievement. From the provinces' perspective, new taxes imposed under the politically convenient cover of a popular welfare-state program would allow them to spend on other popular and economically necessary projects. While some of this new provincial spending would likely have the character of short-run consumption, some would be directed toward capital projects (e.g., building roads and schools) that would pay off over a longer time horizon. In this latter sense, a portion of the pension funds accumulated by Ottawa would help to finance subnational policy investments in other sectors. Yet the core intertemporal bargain that German and U.S. policymakers had perceived in actuarial funding – higher pension taxes today for lower taxes and a more financially secure program tomorrow – emerged in Canada as a mere byproduct of an *intergovernmental* bargain over the current distribution of fiscal resources. In this dynamic, the Canadian case suggests a distinctive causal pathway to policy investment – one driven less by its long-term returns than by the short-term incidental effects of its mechanism of intertemporal transfer. I consider the logic of "investment for the short run" in more general terms in the concluding chapter.

It is also important to note that Canada's moderate-sized policy investment was enacted despite the opposition of major interest groups to funded public pensions. Once Ottawa and Quebec had struck their investment-based deal, what lent the Pearson government the capacity to enact it over the objection of well-organized groups? Consistent with the argument in Chapter 2, political institutions that dispersed authority enhanced ministers' capacity to invest by limiting the menu of options confronting other actors. Specifically, low insulation of the federal executive – in particular, the decentralization of power across levels of government – structured policy trade-offs for both interest groups and subnational governments in ways that made partial funding more attractive to these actors than the feasible alternatives.

It is worth spelling out this menu-shaping dynamic more explicitly. As will be recalled, labor wanted enhanced public investment but opposed financing it through funded pensions for distributive reasons: as compared to general tax-financing, financing via funded pensions would impose the costs of new public projects disproportionately on lower-paid workers. The CLC in the mid-1960s also enjoyed unusual leverage over Pearson's minority government in Ottawa, which relied on the votes of labor's NDP allies to enact much of its legislative program. Yet low insulation of the policymaking process – the multiple access points provided by intergovernmental bargaining – structured the menu of options in a way that made it difficult for labor to reject the final outcome of partial funding. Just as Pearson's hands were tied by the dynamics of Canada's highly decentralized form of federalism, so too were labor's. A public contributory pension plan and enhanced public investment were both central policy objectives for unions and the social democratic left. Labor may not have liked the idea of extracting funds for public investment via a regressive tax, but its first choice of financing methods was unlikely to win enactment within this decentralized institutional context. The provinces would not agree to a PAYGO pension scheme, and Ottawa was unlikely to simply hand the provinces billions of additional dollars of federal general revenues for their own use. The status quo – with no CPP at all and tight subnational budgetary constraints – was far worse for labor than the *achievable,* second-best outcome of partially funded public pensions supporting expanded provincial fiscal capacities.

For its part, business opposed funded public pensions because it did not believe that governments could credibly promise to keep their hands off of accumulated assets. Business favored instead a system of funded, private occupational schemes. With close allies in power in Ontario, business also enjoyed privileged access to a key provincial government and an important avenue of influence over the process. Yet business influence was muted by the dominance of left-leaning forces at other key institutional locations – particularly, Liberal progressives and labor-aligned New Democrats at the federal level and a statist government in Quebec. The strong agenda-setting capacity of these actors allowed them to confront Ontario with an offer that was difficult for the Robarts government to refuse. In part, business won an important concession in the strong safeguards against future expansion that were built into the final plan. Yet Ottawa and Quebec also tilted the Ontario Tories' calculation steeply in favor of agreement by attaching large financial rewards to participation; and they made rejection unappealing by isolating the province as the sole potential obstacle to a popular social initiative and constitutionally momentous accord. If the Ontario government had acted alone, it would never have chosen a partially funded public pension plan. But in a context of widely diffused authority, it made more political and fiscal sense for the Robarts government to compromise than to pursue a maximalist version of its group allies' demands.

PART III

PROGRAMMATIC CHANGE:

INTERTEMPORAL CHOICE IN
PENSION REFORM

Introduction

By the 1970s and 1980s, policy investments in German, U.S., and Canadian public pension financing had unraveled. While policy investment in the U.S. quickly proved defenseless against political attack, the German financing regime buckled after three decades under the combined strain of economic distress and political temptation. Canadian policy investment in pensions, on the other hand, was allowed to die of benign neglect as provincial and federal policy makers left contribution rates untouched as expenses rose. Though the timing varied, each of these three countries eventually converged with Britain on a pay-as-you-go (PAYGO) path.

In the decades of rapid wage and population growth following World War II, PAYGO financing could support a comfortable political and social equilibrium. As contributory pension programs matured,[1] expenditures automatically rose, but so too did the flow of revenues from an expanding and increasingly affluent workforce. Governments could even raise benefit and payroll tax rates without undue impact on workers' take-home pay. And in an era of relatively easy fiscal choices, political conflict over the basic principles of retirement security was supplanted by a broad consensus in support of existing programs – even, in some instances, with competition between parties of right and left to promise the elderly ever-more-generous pensions.

This fiscal and political dynamic, however, relied on a transient set of economic and demographic conditions.[2] Payroll tax rates in a PAYGO

---

[1] Program maturation refers to a process that typically unfolds over the first few decades of operation of a contributory pension system: after a program begins operation, each successive cohort of retirees will collect higher benefits because it has paid into the system for a longer period of time. A system with a strict relationship between contribution record and benefits will take approximately 45 years to mature; programs that offer older workers more generous terms will mature more quickly.

[2] For more detailed accounts of the complex economic, demographic, and programmatic dynamics summarized here, I refer the reader to Barr (2000), Economic Policy Committee (2001), Pierson and Myles (2001), Iversen and Wren (1998), Swank (2002), and Huber and Stephens (2001b).

scheme depend heavily on trends in aggregate real wages, and by the mid-1970s aggregate wages would suffer a double blow. First, supply-side oil shocks raised unemployment and stalled wage growth across Europe and North America. Though the deep recessions they induced were temporary, most advanced economies now seemed locked into permanently lower levels of employment and slower productivity growth. It also became apparent by the middle of the decade that the "baby bust" in most OECD countries marked a secular fall in fertility rates in the industrialized world that would reduce the relative size of future labor forces. And by the 1980s and 1990s, many governments came to believe that, in a world of liberalized international product and capital markets, their options for raising new revenues through payroll or other taxes affecting business were severely constrained.

These pressures on the revenue side coincided with greater spending demands in addition to program maturation. Some of the slowed employment growth took the form of early retirement on state pensions, shifting middle-aged workers from the contributing population into the beneficiary group. With increasing longevity, new cohorts of retirees would also collect benefits for a longer period than had their parents. Finally, and somewhat ironically, in many countries these adverse changes followed on the heels of major benefit expansions premised on the continuation of favorable background conditions.

To those with an ideological or self-interested objection to state provision, these objective pressures represented an opportunity. In most OECD countries, conservative politicians and liberal economists – along with a financial-service sector interested in an expanded market for its products – increasingly questioned the long-term sustainability of public PAYGO arrangements. What was once a buoyant, overlapping intergenerational exchange could now be persuasively portrayed as a "Ponzi scheme" that was, over time, bound to collapse. Yet it did not take a free-market ideologue to realize that the era of easy pension choices was now over. While public pension systems' moral logic and political support were still intact, they now looked like much less appealing – and less secure – fiscal propositions. Governments would have to run just to stand still: merely meeting existing commitments would require them to deliver pain to some segment of society.

Though the field of pension reform has been well tilled by scholars of welfare state retrenchment, the chapters in Part III examine reform through a distinctive lens. As noted in Chapter 1, most recent studies have conceptualized governments' responses to economic, demographic, and ideological pressures on the welfare state as the *imposition of losses,* through means such as benefit cuts or increases in contribution and tax burdens. In conceptualizing reform as a process of loss-imposition, these analyses have zeroed in on the cross-sectional tradeoff between those who pay for and those who receive social benefits and services. Yet in deciding how to allocate the pain of pension reform, all governments have faced stark tradeoffs over time as well as distributive choices. Moreover, reforms with similar distributive profiles of loss-imposition have varied widely in their intertemporal effects.

In conceptualizing these choices, it is useful to return to the two-dimensional policy space depicted in Figure 1.5. As in Part II, the primary outcome to be explained is the north-south position of policy choices within this space – that is, their intertemporal profile. In the top half of this space are policy investments that, typically, take the form of a *shift* in the basis of pension financing from PAYGO to funding. Governments making a shift to funding must impose higher costs in the near term than immediately necessary to keep the system in balance – via short-term benefit cuts and/or short-term tax increases – in order to accumulate a fund that will be dedicated to helping pay future benefit claims. In the reform period, it became increasingly common for such funds to be invested not just in government bonds but also *outside* the public sector in portfolios of stocks and corporate debt. If funds and investment earnings accumulate as actuarially planned, the long-term result should, in principle, be an expansion of long-term fiscal capacities: future taxpayers and contributors will face lower burdens than they would under the status quo, or governments will be able to sustain current benefits without raising tax or contribution rates. In other words, as populations age, pension systems will face less financial strain and their participants will face less painful adjustments. In the interim, the accumulating fund may also represent an enlargement of national savings and the pool of available capital. To the extent that fund purchases of equity or debt help finance the creation of new physical or human capital – whether by governments or by firms – funding may also increase society's long-term productivity and the future stock of real economic resources.

At or below the x-axis lie a range of policy options that leave future aggregate resources unchanged or deplete them, respectively. For instance, governments might enact legislation today that schedules benefit cuts to take effect at a future point in time when demographic shifts are expected to generate operating deficits in the system. Relative to a status quo in which those deficits would have to be met by future tax increases, such a reform would shift resources from tomorrow's beneficiaries to tomorrow's taxpayers; but it would do nothing to change the aggregate consumption possibilities of tomorrow's citizens. In the language of Chapter 2, this reform would constitute a policy of *long-term redistribution* and (with beneficiaries and taxpayers coded as Groups A and B, respectively) would be located along the right hand side of the x-axis, around Option 5 in the figure. Though unusual in the reform period under study, Option 2, below the x-axis, would represent a policy of depletion – for instance, a reduction in current contribution burdens that aggravates long-run financial strains on the program.

As Figure 1.5 also helps illustrate, policies with very different distributive effects may look similar in intertemporal perspective. On the one hand, a government might decide to accumulate a fund within the existing public pension scheme by imposing, say, a payroll tax increase on both workers and employers. Such a reform would be located somewhere around Option 1: by preserving the basic mode of retirement provision, it would maintain the same distributive allocation of costs and benefits across groups, but it would transfer consumption possibilities from present to future.

Alternatively, a government might choose to replace part of the PAYGO *public* pension system with funded *private* provision. For instance, it might scale back future state benefit promises to current workers and require them to contribute to their own individual retirement-savings vehicles. Assuming that promised benefits are still to be paid to today's retirees, today's contributors in this scenario also face a higher total short-run cost burden since they will have to continue to pay for current state pensions while building up funds in their own personal accounts. As with a shift to funding within the state system, the buildup and investment of individual private funds represents a mechanism of intertemporal transfer from present to future. Yet the move from public to private provision will typically also have major cross-sectional implications – for instance, shifting costs from employers to workers or reducing the degree of redistribution (a common feature of public schemes, but absent in private ones) from higher to lower earners. In the figure, we would thus locate this privatization initiative around Option 4.

Likewise, reforms that look similar in *distributive* terms may involve disparate intertemporal tradeoffs. In our examples, Options 4 and 5, for instance, both impose losses on workers, but one enacts a policy investment while the other effects a long-term redistribution. Option 4 asks workers to pay more now to finance a mechanism of intertemporal transfer that is directed toward the provision of future income (the accumulation of private pension funds). Option 5, in contrast, postpones and redirects the pain: it cuts those same workers' pensions once they are in retirement and, in turn, relieves burdens on future taxpayers.

To be clear, there is no need to assume that options above the x-axis will yield better long-run social outcomes than those on the x-axis – that pension reforms that promote funding will work out better than those that retain PAYGO financing. As emphasized in Part I – and noted by many actors involved in the initial design of pension programs – policy investments can *fail* to deliver future net benefits. Rather, the key distinguishing feature of funding as a policy investment is structural: its imposition of net short-run social costs and the activation of one or more mechanisms of intertemporal transfer toward the future (accumulation and, depending on asset-management, the creation of productive capital).

Of course, the distributive and intertemporal dimensions of pension reform both represent important policy choices with major social consequences. For the sake of analytical clarity, however, Part III maintains our focus on explaining *intertemporal* variation in outcomes. The case studies nonetheless pay close attention to the distributive features of politicians' decisions. In fact, as implied by our theoretical framework, political actors should to some extent view the two dimensions of choice as *alternative* strategies for managing long-run problems: they can respond to future strains on pension programs by investing in future financial capacities (policy investment) *or* by reallocating the future impact of the problem from one social group to another (long-term redistribution). Because the two dimensions of choice are causally connected, explaining the intertemporal features of reform will typically require attention to its distributive qualities – and vice-versa.

To preview the specific outcomes to be explained: the United States (in two episodes) and Canada reduced long-term deficits in their pension systems in large part through strategies of policy investment via a shift to partial funding of the public plan. By imposing higher contribution rates on workers and employers and reducing benefits in the short term, they began to amass large programmatic surpluses that were invested in interest-bearing assets and dedicated to the payment of future pension benefits. Germany (in two episodes) and Britain, on the other hand, chose largely long-term distributive strategies: they mitigated future contribution burdens through a scheduled reduction in future benefit levels – far more dramatically in Britain – all the while keeping their public systems on a PAYGO basis. Paired with this redistributive strategy, these two governments also sought to encourage an expansion of private funded pensions to partially replace shrinking state benefits. But their investments in private provision were limited, relying on voluntary incentives rather than the imposition of mandatory short-term burdens and yielding a modest intertemporal transfer.

These governments' varying intertemporal choices would later generate divergent social and political consequences potentially just as significant as the distributive tradeoffs to which analysts have typically been attuned. Though their full ramifications will only play out in coming decades, the Canadian and U.S. reforms, through their early payroll tax increases, have already imposed far higher costs on workers – especially those on low and moderate incomes – than the British and German strategies of delayed pain. In coming decades, however, the U.S. and Canadian programs are expected to have resources on hand to deliver benefits – only modestly reduced from pre-reform levels – with limited need for further hikes in contributions (Board of Trustees 2006; Office of the Chief Actuary 2007). As a result, both countries are also likely to see relatively muted intergenerational conflict over the distribution of the burdens of demographic change. With their public retirement systems flush with cash, contentious reform proposals are unlikely to gain much traction in either context for some time. Already in the United States, mounting trust fund surpluses amidst stable contribution rates have helped to blunt the force of repeated conservative attacks on the Social Security program through the 1990s and 2000s.

Meanwhile, Germany and Britain are likely to face decades of continued and prolonged political conflict over retirement security as demographic conditions deteriorate. In Germany, in the absence of a substantial buildup in public or private retirement assets, rapid population aging will have painful consequences for both seniors and contributors. Pensioners in coming years will feel the squeeze of deepening cuts in state pensions without, in most cases, enjoying a compensating expansion of private provision. At the same time, German employers will likely continue a pitched battle to rein in the system's outlays as contribution rates resume their climb about a decade from now (Sailer 2004). In Britain, radical long-term benefit cuts will largely insulate tomorrow's taxpayers against the costs of demographic change, and young workers are unlikely to wage intergenerational warfare. In contrast, Britain faces a looming crisis of inadequate pensions and old-age poverty. In coming decades, the United Kingdom is projected to rank near the bottom of advanced democracies in the level of state spending on pensions as a share of GDP. Private provision, meanwhile, is shrinking, rather than growing to offset the withdrawal of public benefits (Pensions Commission 2004).

Facing a broadly similar long-term problem, why did some elected governments impose near-term costs on constituents to invest in long-run retirement incomes and fiscal capacities while others chose to delay and merely redistribute the pain of adjustment?

CHAPTER 7

Investment as Last Resort

Reforming U.S. Pensions, 1977 and 1983[1]

In 1977, the U.S. Congress and President Carter enacted the largest peace-time tax increase in American history in order to rescue Social Security from both immediate and long-term insolvency. A few years later, amidst continued economic malaise, Social Security found itself again on the brink of trust fund exhaustion. In 1983, Congress and the White House stepped in once more to restore system balances for the short and long term, this time combining substantial benefit cuts with an acceleration of the existing tax schedule.

Strikingly, both of these acts of loss-imposition were enacted during periods of historically high unemployment levels and, in the case of 1977, high inflation rates – seemingly inauspicious conditions for raising labor costs or cutting into workers' take-home pay. Moreover, in both cases politicians rejected an easier option. Rather than carrying the system through bad times with a relatively painless infusion of general revenues – as President Carter initially proposed in 1977 – Congress chose both times to rescue the program through visible contribution increases and benefit cuts. Nor was the pain eased much by delay: workers would see the effects of the December 1977 reform on their January 1979 pay slips while the 1983 increases would start to pinch in 1984.

While the 1983 reforms have received far more attention in both academic and public discussions, the 1977 law was arguably the more important reform in intertemporal terms: it closed a much larger long-term financing deficit and scheduled the short-run tax increases that the 1983 amendments merely accelerated. Moreover, the 1977 reform is, at least at first glance, more puzzling in electoral terms. While the 1983 law was designed by a bipartisan and quasi-corporatist commission that allowed for the diffusion of blame for short-term losses, the 1977 changes were enacted by a Democratic White House and Democratic Congress over the nay-votes of most Republicans, who promised to turn the tax increase into an electoral issue.

[1] Parts of this chapter draw on Jacobs (2008) and Jacobs (2009b).

Equally surprisingly, politicians imposed major short-run losses on constituents despite what, in hindsight, could be viewed as weak mechanisms for committing the accumulating funds to their stated long-term objective. Together, the two reforms would lead to the buildup of reserves that would top $1 trillion by the year 2001 – equivalent to nearly three times annual benefit payments, or about 10 percent of GDP.[2] By 2009, the fund would climb to nearly 4 times annual outlays and over 16 percent of GDP (Board of Trustees 2010). Yet, in making this massive policy investment, policymakers took no action to make sure that this surplus was any more credibly committed to its actuarial purpose than it had been in the 1930s. Like the far smaller reserves of the 1960s and 1970s, the prodigious fund of the 21st century was to be invested in government bonds and counted as part of the overall federal budget. As Eric Patashnik (2000) has written,

> For all the trust fund's exceptional strengths as a mechanism for locking-in spending promises … it is an intrinsically weak instrument for prefunding the system's liabilities. The main reason for this weakness is the lack of a credible mechanism to prevent the trust fund's reserves from becoming a captive market of the Treasury (82).

While many funding advocates argue that Social Security surpluses are in a meaningful sense being saved, one striking fact about the 1977 and 1983 reforms remains: policymakers imposed tremendous visible short-term losses on constituents without building robust structures for binding the resulting surpluses to their long-term purpose. How, under these conditions, did policy investment emerge? We address this question for each reform process in turn.

A FOCUSING SIGNAL (1977)

Since the early 1940s, Social Security's Board of Trustees had been legally obligated to provide annual reports to Congress, prepared by the program's actuaries, on the short- and long-term status of the program's trust funds (both the old-age and survivors insurance [OASI] fund and the disability insurance [DI] fund, created in the 1950s). Starting in 1973, those reports predicted a small long-term imbalance in the funds' finances. By 1976, high unemployment and high inflation – together with a significant flaw in the benefit indexation formula – had dramatically darkened the program's financial prospects. The Trustees were now forecasting both the exhaustion of the funds within a few years – by 1979 for the DI fund and 1983 for the OASI fund – and a long-range actuarial deficit (Board of Trustees 1976, 1975, 1974, 1973). The long-range deficit was gaping – equivalent to an immediate and permanent 8-percentage-point hike in the payroll tax.

---

[2] The figures here refer to the Old-Age and Survivors Insurance Fund, and thus exclude Disability Insurance (Office of Management and Budget 2002; Congressional Budget Office January 2002; Board of Trustees 1976).

The structure of the Social Security program and the routine of annual actuarial reports combined to generate remarkably clear public signals of long-term policy consequences (Patashnik 2000). Through the Trustees' reports, subtle and often slow changes – in demographic or economic expectations, in tax and benefit formulae, or in the behavior of the insured – were distilled into relatively unambiguous indicators of both impending and distant financial developments. The program's structure – its lack of a general-revenue subsidy or cushion – greatly enhanced the clarity of these signals. As a social program completely dependent on its contribution revenues, the program could be declared either solvent or insolvent – or, more evocatively, "bankrupt" – over the forecasting period. In a sense, these notions of actuarial balance were an accounting fiction: a government, after all, can always infuse additional funds into a public program if it chooses. With the program reliant on a single source of tax financing, however, the concept of insolvency was a highly *plausible* fiction as well as a powerful *simplifying* device. It allowed both actuaries and politicians to frame the program's capacity to keep its promises as a seemingly technical matter of resource availability – of whether or not projected contributions were sufficient to meet projected outlays. Further dramatizing the signal in this instance was the fact that, in the mid-1970s, the funds faced not just a long-run imbalance but the prospect of *imminent* exhaustion.

The trustees' forecasts served as a dramatic and negative focusing event: echoed and amplified by the news media, these projections of program insolvency drew voters' attention to both the immediate and long-term losses that the status quo would impose on them. As one poll in the middle of 1977 reported, 82 percent of respondents were either "very" or "somewhat" concerned that the Social Security system might not be able to pay all promised benefits.[3] Another showed nearly two-thirds responding that they sometimes worried that there would not be sufficient funds in the system to pay them benefits.[4] Responding to widespread public concern, both major-party candidates in the 1976 Presidential election proposed reform plans for correcting the fund's short- and long-term financial imbalances. In stoking fears of default, the trustees' reports thus had an action-forcing effect, confronting politicians with the prospect of electoral punishment if they did *not* act to solve the problem.

INSTITUTIONAL PROCESSES OF ELIMINATION (1977)

Public concern about Social Security's finances, however, did not tell politicians *how* to respond. About half of the long-term deficit was a result of an inadvertent feature of the formula, adopted in 1972, that indexed benefits to inflation. A

[3] Cambridge Reports/Research International, July 1977, Accession Number: 0364458, Question ID USCAMREP.77JUL, R293, Roper Center for Public Opinion Research, LexisNexis™ Academic, http://www.lexis-nexis.com (last accessed May 15, 2004).
[4] Yankelovich, Skelly and White, May 23, 1977 (conducted 5/19 – 5/23/1977), Accession Number: 0131933, Question ID USYANK.777610, Q10H, Roper Center for Public Opinion Research, LexisNexis™ Academic, http://www.lexis-nexis.com (last accessed May 15, 2004).

subtle "kink" in the formula meant that, in periods of unusually high inflation, benefit levels would rise faster than wages, an outcome unintended by those who designed the mechanism. Under some assumptions, the algorithm would eventually lead to retirement benefits that were *higher* than preretirement wages for low-income workers (Derthick 1979). Across the two main political parties, there was widespread consensus that the formula should be corrected, thus closing a substantial portion of the long-range gap.

Beyond this technical fix, however, politicians' favored responses to the crisis tended to reflect the distributive interests of their respective electoral and interest-group support bases. Organized groups and party leaders sought to solve Social Security's financing problem by shifting the costs of adjustment onto groups *outside* their own political coalitions. Within the Republican Administration of Gerald Ford, the Treasury Department and the Council of Economic Advisors (CEA) had advocated a solution that relied on reducing benefits well below their projected levels. Social Security benefits initially payable at retirement had always been indexed to earnings, rising over time as wages rose; since 1975, that initial benefit at retirement was then automatically indexed to prices for subsequent years. Going well beyond a mere correction to the indexation formula, the Treasury-CEA plan would have converted *all* benefits – both *at* and *during* retirement – to pure price-indexation, eliminating the link to earnings. Future retirees' benefits would thus have the same real value as today's, but as average earnings rose over time, those benefits would replace a progressively smaller percentage of wages. So dramatic was this cutback that it would have eliminated the program's entire long-range deficit (Derthick 1979). Pure price indexing was also the favored solution of two of the most powerful business lobbies, the U.S. Chamber of Commerce and the National Association of Manufacturers (NAM).[5]

If Republicans and employers sought to place the burden of adjustment on beneficiaries' shoulders, the left preferred to ask more of companies and higher earners. In 1977, the new Democratic President Jimmy Carter proposed to keep the system solvent over the long term through three primary measures, in addition to fixing the indexation formula. First, Carter would eliminate the wage ceiling on employers' contributions, requiring firms to pay Social Security taxes on their entire payroll (while workers' share would be paid only on wages up to the ceiling). Second, the President's plan would move forward a payroll tax rate increase scheduled for 2011 to a pair of increases in 1985 and 1990. Finally, and most significantly, Carter proposed the establishment of a counter-cyclical mechanism that – for the first time ever – would infuse the program with general revenues whenever the unemployment rate topped 6 percent (Congressional Quarterly 1978). Together, these measures would close the Social Security deficit beyond the end of the century. Liberal Democrats in Congress, including House Speaker Thomas P. O'Neill and House Social

[5] David Koitz (Controller's office of the Department of Health, Education, and Welfare during reform), interview with author, Washington, D.C., May 1, 2002.

Security subcommittee chairman James A. Burke, supported an even more radical proposal – a massive, permanent infusion of general revenues (Cowan 1977). Since general revenues came from sources more progressive than the payroll tax, these proposals would have placed the costs of the program's rescue squarely on the shoulders of affluent taxpayers and business, while protecting the material interests of key members of the Democratic Party's traditional support base – labor unions and senior citizens.

In each set of proposals, Social Security's financial problems would be solved through long-term redistributive *rather* than intertemporal means. Each coalition sought to address the strain on program finances by externalizing its impact, imposing an increasing burden over time on another segment of society. Rather than inflicting short-term pain to invest in reducing the overall size of the long-run problem, each plan would simply redirect the future costs of that problem.

However, a minimally insulated policymaking process, generated by the decentralized structure of U.S. political institutions, left each coalition with only a modest ability to reallocate burdens cross-sectionally. As hypothesized in Chapter 2, the institutional dispersion of political authority restricted the menu of feasible options by impeding long-term redistributive solutions. With Democrats in control of both the White House and both chambers of Congress, groups on the left were well positioned to prevent the significant cuts in Social Security benefits proposed by the right. And at the same time, despite unified Democratic government, the left itself faced insurmountable obstacles to its own ideal distributive outcome. Low party discipline, combined with deep regional and ideological fissures within the Democratic Party, left the President with weak claims on the loyalty of his nominal copartisans in the legislature. Standing committees and their chairmen also wielded formidable gatekeeping powers to prevent bills of which they disapproved from ever reaching a floor vote. Among the most formidable was the House Committee on Ways and Means, through which any Social Security reform legislation would have to pass. By dispersing veto authority so widely, U.S. institutions thus offered numerous access points to those who stood to lose from any redistributive policy change.

Predictably, Carter's plan drew a howl of protest from those who would pay its costs. Organized business objected, in part, to the proposed one-sided increase in the employer's portion of the payroll tax. With equal vehemence, however, employers also opposed introducing any element of general-revenue financing into the program. Their concern was less with the immediate effects of such a mechanism than with its longer-term implications for the politics of redistribution. As they had for decades (see Chapter 5), U.S. capitalists continued to view democratic electoral competition as tending toward populist largesse and fiscal irresponsibility. Business leaders viewed strict payroll tax financing of public pensions as the only defense against the endless growth of a popular social program: every time Congress wanted to raise benefits, it also had to raise taxes on workers. Employers were worried that a break with the self-supporting principle would open the doors to easy finance, fueling a dangerous political dynamic of expansion. As a spokesperson for the NAM put it, "To draw money from general revenues and impose Social Security taxes on the entire payroll [as suggested in the Carter plan] constitutes a rather dangerous tinkering with the historic characteristics of the program" (Jensen 1977, D1). Another business executive explained, "I've got some real reservations about using general funds to pay part of Social Security costs.... It's a precedent that would be too easy for future Administrations to follow" (Jensen 1977, D7).

In Congress, a powerful alliance of conservative Democrats and Republicans on the tax-writing committees echoed business concerns, warning of the precedent that general-revenue infusions would set. Party leaders tended to appoint legislators with fiscally moderate views to the chambers' finance committees, allowing these panels to act as budgetary guardians that helped protect Congress from itself (Zelizer 1998). Since the 1950s, these committees had rigidly enforced the principle of self-support – that Social Security spending should be financed strictly by Social Security taxes – as a way of imposing discipline on the politics of the program, much as Roosevelt had sought to do in 1935 (Cowan 1976). At the same time, strict contributory financing made it far easier politically for the finance committees to collect necessary revenues for the program, both by enhancing the program's perceived legitimacy and reinforcing the credibility of its benefit promises. A sole reliance on payroll taxes undergirded the continued, widespread understanding of the program as an *insurance* scheme, a reciprocal arrangement in which receipt of benefits depended on past contributions. Contributory financing thus allowed policymakers to clearly distinguish the program from welfare and connect it to widely held individualist values. Notionally separating the program's finances from the general budget, moreover, made it easier for legislators to argue that all revenues collected in Social Security's name would indeed be spent on this popular benefit – and not on something else (Patashnik 2000; Zelizer 1998). Excluding general revenues from Social Security had thus strengthened the hand of Congress's fiscal guardians both by allowing them to contain social spending and by helping them to justify any payroll tax increases by reference to credible long-term benefit promises.

Now, members of Ways and Means and the Senate's Finance Committee from both parties argued that Carter's proposal would set a dangerous new precedent, undermining the stable contributory politics of the program. First, they repeatedly argued that a move to general revenues would gut the moral logic at the heart of the program (Eccles 1977a, 1977c; Singer 1977a). As Al Ullman, chairman of Ways and Means, worried, the Carter plan "violates the general principle of having a contributory system and makes it easy to move into a broad welfare concept" (Russell and Chapman 1977, A2). Like employers, fiscal guardians in Congress also warned that allowing general revenues to infiltrate the program would set a dangerous example and make it all too painless for future legislative majorities to enact benefit increases (Derthick 1979; Eccles 1977a, 1977c;

Singer 1977a).[6] The Carter plan was essentially dead on arrival on Capitol Hill.

With opponents positioned at critical bottlenecks in the legislative process, the left's redistributive strategy had no hope of enactment. At the same time, labor and senior citizens' organizations had sufficient backing from Democrats in Congress and the White House to block attempts to redistribute future resources away from them. Dispersion of veto power, in other words, created a distributive stalemate in which neither business and conservatives nor the program's clientele groups could simply externalize the costs of solving Social Security's long-term problems.

The final reform package thus emerged through an institutionally structured process of elimination. Facing an imperative to act, but with both benefit cuts and general revenues removed from the menu of alternatives, Congress's finance committees adopted the only remaining option for balancing the program's books: an increase in contribution revenues. While the House and Senate panels proposed somewhat differing remedies, the bill that emerged from conference committee would impose a quick, sharp hike in payroll taxes on both workers and employers starting in 1979. Under preexisting law, the contribution rate was already scheduled to rise gradually between 1979 and 1986, from 5.85 percent to 6.45 percent. Under the reform bill, they would jump faster and farther, reaching 7.65 percent by 1990.[7] Equally importantly, the earnings ceiling below which the tax was levied would leap between 1979 and 1982 from $17,700 to $31,800 (Congressional Quarterly 1978). As enacted by Congress and signed by the President, the law imposed the largest peacetime tax increase in the country's history.

Because it would impose so much pain so early, the reform would generate a massive policy investment: an intertemporal transfer from current workers and employers to future retirees and contributors. In the short run, the tax hike would generate the revenues required to avoid immediate insolvency. As the economy revived and the immediate cash crunch subsided, however, the system would start taking in greater revenues than it needed to pay benefits, generating a large fund that would later help finance a growing pension burden without further tax hikes.[8] Together with the fix to the indexation formula, this near-term tax hike was projected to resolve both the short- and long-term financing troubles that the system faced, eliminating the deficit for the next 50 years.

---

[6] The Ford Administration had, before leaving office, rejected a general-revenue solution on just these grounds, arguing that such easy financing "would lead to an enlargement of the program's cost commitments" (Secretary of Health, Education and Welfare David Matthews, quoted in Cowan (1976, E3)).

[7] They would jump to 6.13 percent in 1979, 6.65 percent in 1981, 6.7 percent in 1982, 7.05 percent in 1985, 7.15 percent in 1986, and 7.65 percent in 1990.

[8] Confirmed by David Koitz (at the Controller's office of the Department of Health, Education, and Welfare during the reform period), telephone interview with the author, July 16, 2002; and in a telephone interview with a former staff member of the Senate Finance Committee who worked on both the 1977 and 1983 reforms, May 2, 2002.

THE ELECTORAL CALCULUS (1977)

The reform would inflict substantial short-run pain on both workers and employers. Yet the inability of either group to simply shift the burden of adjustment had structured the menu in a manner favorable to policy investment. The removal of redistributive options from the menu forced each group to *internalize* the costs of doing nothing; and for all groups the status quo risked the worst possible outcome. For current and future beneficiaries, doing nothing would leave the program unable to pay promised pensions. For conservatives and employers, a failure to act now would – by leaving the system with insufficient funds of its own – risk precisely the kind of general-revenue bailout that they most wanted to avoid. Not only was the bill written by fiscal conservatives on Ways and Means and Senate Finance, but the NAM and the U.S. Chamber of Commerce also came out in favor of this immediate hike in payroll taxes as the only *politically feasible* solution that was acceptable to them (Jensen 1977; Singer 1977a).

For elected officials, voting for such visible and immediate loss-imposition might still have posed considerable risk of losing office. The bill passed largely on the votes of members of the Democratic majority, with the bulk of Republicans in the House of Representatives voting against it (Solomon 1986; Congressional Quarterly 1978). There was, therefore, no cross-party consensus to shield those Democrats who supported the bill, and many Republicans were perfectly poised to turn the Democrats' tax hike into an electoral liability in the midterm congressional campaigns of 1978.[9] Indeed, in an *unconstrained* vote-maximizing choice, Democrats' initial proposals – to infuse general revenues into the fund as and when the system ran short of cash, rather than to invest – would clearly have been preferable, both in delaying most of the pain and in diffusing it across the federal budget.

However, the gatekeeping authority wielded by fiscal conservatives on the tax committees left the White House and other Democratic legislators with a tightly constrained electoral calculation. Either they could accept the tax writers' plan, or they could let the Social Security system run out of money within a few years. In the event, Democratic incumbents did face attack by challengers at the next election for raising taxes, especially as a broad-based "tax revolt" was gathering steam across the country.[10] Adopting *no* rescue package, however, would have

---

[9] For instance, by the spring of 1978, Democratic Representative Jim Mattox faced a Republican opponent who was attacking him for his vote for the tax increase (Havemann 1978).

[10] In fact, legislators would later interpret the revolt in 1978 partly as an outcry against the payroll tax increases, and many would propose repealing the rises in the 1977 reform package. Importantly, this position did not reflect the view that *no* rescue would have been politically safer than the enacted reforms. Rather, it reflected an electoral preference for a rescue with less conspicuous costs, financed via general revenues – an option that, as discussed, was institutionally precluded. As in 1977, the tax writers in 1978 would firmly resist further attempts to alter the program's financial basis and protected the original policy investment against repeal (Havemann 1978; Conte 1979; "Social Security Rollback Gains Momentum in House" 1978).

been a straightforward act of electoral suicide, as it would have seriously threatened the benefits of over 30 million voters who formed a critical part of the Democrats' electoral base.

Moreover, politicians were operating in an informational environment that offered them an unusual opportunity to justify short-term pain to constituents as necessary to avoid even *greater* losses in the future. As discussed earlier, the trustees' annual reports had sent clear, dramatic signals to voters about both the negative short- and long-term consequences of inaction. Indeed, the program actuaries' unchallenged technical authority generated broad consensus about the fact that the program was about to run out of money, and that it would remain in trouble for decades to come if nothing were done. Further, the program's contributory and trust-fund financing structure created a direct connection between the pain of tax increases and a widely valued benefit. This informational environment constituted a powerful rhetorical resource for supporters of the reform. On the floor of the House, Democratic Speaker Tip O'Neill urged his colleagues to support the measure by framing the issue as a matter of loss-avoidance, ensuring the survival of a highly popular federal program (Eccles 1977b). The actuaries' authoritative projections similarly allowed President Carter to persuasively declare upon signing the bill that "[t] his legislation will guarantee that from 1980 to the year 2030, the social security funds will be sound."[11] Indeed, public opinion polls conducted shortly after the reform's enactment suggests that relatively few voters planned to punish their representatives for the tax hike. One survey, informing voters that "Social Security taxes increased substantially in order to improve the financial health of the Social Security system," found that 56 percent favored the measure, with just over a third opposing it.[12] Another pair of polls informing people that "Social Security taxes have just been increased so that the Social Security fund will not run out" found an almost identical level of support.[13]

UNCERTAINTY OVERLOOKED (1977)

As a result of the reform measure, Social Security's actuaries projected in 1978 that by 2010 the old-age and survivors program would accumulate a reserve equivalent to 3 years' expenditures. In accordance with preexisting rules on the management of program assets, Social Security would invest these accumulating

---

[11] Quoted in Light (1995, 85).

[12] Cambridge Reports/Research International, January 1978, Question ID USCAMREP.78JAN, R032, Roper Center for Public Opinion Research, LexisNexis™ Academic, http://www.lexis-nexis.com.

[13] In one, the result was 57 percent in favor to 38 percent against. NBC News, January 13, 1978, (conducted 1/10 – 1/11/1978), Accession Number: 0083648, Question ID USNBC.26A, R22, Roper Center for Public Opinion Research, LexisNexis™ Academic, http://www.lexis-nexis.com. In the second, it was 56 to 38. NBC News, March 23, 1978, (conducted 3/21 – 3/23/1978), Accession Number: 0083943, Question ID USNBCAP.28A, R26, Roper Center for Public Opinion Research, LexisNexis™ Academic, http://www.lexis-nexis.com.

surpluses in federal Treasury bonds. The reform's long-term benefits depended entirely on how safely those reserves were committed to the payment of future Social Security benefits; it hinged, that is, on the capacity of future legislative majorities to avoid spending the mounting fund for other purposes. What is striking, however, is how little legislators did to address potential causal sequences – noted later by politicians and policy analysts – through which this intertemporal effort might fail.

Social Security's accumulating assets would generate a successful intertemporal transfer to the extent that the program was increasing *net* savings: that is, to the extent that the program's fund would be purchasing federal bonds that would *otherwise* have been issued to the public. Under this assumption, Social Security's reserves would improve the government's overall long-term fiscal capacities: once the bonds came due, the Treasury would then be channeling resources back to Social Security that it would otherwise have owed to private bondholders. A key vulnerability of this mechanism lay in established procedures of federal fiscal accounting: since the 1960s, Social Security's annual balance had been counted as part of the overall government budget, and the 1977 law did nothing to change this. Keeping Social Security "on budget" meant that the program's future surpluses would make the federal government's total fiscal position look better than otherwise. One risk was that mounting Social Security surpluses would allow or encourage future Congresses and Presidents to run higher deficits in the rest of the budget – and, thus, issue more bonds to the public – than otherwise would have been politically acceptable. Every additional dollar that policymakers ended up spending elsewhere (or every dollar by which other tax burdens were reduced) as a result of Social Security's fund would simply offset the savings effect of the reform. The consequence would not be an enhancement of the government's overall capacity to pay future benefits but merely a shift of the future burden from those who pay Social Security taxes to those who pay the general taxes out of which federal bonds are serviced.

In other words, policymakers in 1977 imposed large visible costs on constituents without taking seemingly simple steps – such as removing Social Security from the general budget – to better ensure that the accumulating resources were securely committed to their long-term purpose. Indeed, the critique just presented would be commonly voiced in Congressional and academic circles as soon as the larger surpluses began to materialize in the late 1980s.[14] How can we explain politicians' willingness to adopt a policy investment so weakly insulated against political predation over the long term?

Though prominent in hindsight, the risks of future political manipulation were in fact but one of myriad possible causal sequences that might have arisen from policymakers' choices. The evidence suggests that, amidst enormous policy

---

[14] For an account of the debate on the issue in Congress in the late 1980s, see Patashnik (2000, 88–90). For academic critiques of the commitment mechanism, see for instance the following contributions from an edited volume: Buchanan (1990), Kotlikoff (1990), or Leonard (1990). For a more recent version, see Schieber and Shoven (1999).

complexity, actors allocated cognitive resources *selectively* across the causal possibilities that they confronted. There are multiple indications that legislators did not pay attention to facts that became salient in retrospect, including (a) that the tax committees' plans would produce a reserve buildup and (b) that the plan's long-term benefits depended on how those funds were managed. According to the independent accounts of three policy actors closely involved in the legislative process, members of Congress paid little notice to the size of the program's trust fund beyond the first few years after the reform, when the program was to be rescued from imminent insolvency. Not only did legislators express no intention to accumulate a fund, but they appear to have been *unaware* of how their choices would affect medium and long-term trust fund balances.[15] Nor did the surpluses attract the attention of even sophisticated analysts and journalists outside government. Derthick's (1979) account of the reform process in her definitive monograph on Social Security politics never mentions the projected reserve buildup; nor did detailed, inside-the-beltway reporting on the reform process by *Congressional Quarterly* and the *National Journal* (Congressional Quarterly 1978; Eccles 1977a, 1977b, 1977c, 1977d, 1977e, 1977f; Gottron 1977a, 1977b; "Social Security Plan Faces Tough Fight" 1977; Singer 1977a, 1977b; "Panel Votes to Raise Social Security Taxes" 1977; "Congress Moves on Social Security Legislation" 1977; Samuelson 1977; "Social Security Bill Passes, Stripped of Student Tax Credit" 1977).

Two principal forces directed policymakers' attention away from the causal dynamics of fund accumulation. First, decision makers allocated scarce attention most intensively toward those implications of their decisions that they were most motivated to address. Electoral and interest-group pressures generated a set of urgent political imperatives for incumbents: most importantly, ensuring that the trust fund would both remain solvent in the short term and be able to pay future pensions promised to current workers. Moreover, policymakers had to achieve these goals while keeping the program's financing on a strictly contributory basis and without being seen to reduce benefits. Merely meeting these most pressing objectives was itself a daunting task of optimization under constraints, involving complex trade-offs across contribution rates, contribution ceilings, inter-trust-fund borrowing, and the timing of cost-imposition. Problems of managing and

---

[15] The account here is derived from Lawrence Thompson (staff economist at the Department of Health, Education and Welfare when 1977 reform was developing), interview with the author, Washington, D.C., October 16, 2001; David Koitz, (at the Planning and Evaluation office of the Department of Health, Education and Welfare as the 1977 reform was developed), interview with the author, Washington, D.C., May 1, 2002; Bert Seidman (Social Security specialist at the labor umbrella organization, the AFL-CIO), interview with the author, Washington, D.C., May 2, 2002. Alicia H. Munnell confirms that the reform package was not viewed as an act of savings. "Projected Trust Fund Buildup: Social Security Issues," presented to the Public Trustees' Policy Symposium, September 16, 1988, Washington, D.C. She writes, "No one involved in the process ever considered the advantages or disadvantages of trying to increase our national saving rate through the Social Security program. If they had, I trust they would never have devised the plan of building up reserves and then drawing them back down."

accounting for funds to be accumulated decades hence were, by contrast, of little immediate import.

The information that Congress received from the Social Security Administration's actuaries was, in turn, tailored to politicians' most urgent imperatives. For each proposal that legislators considered, the actuaries produced tables showing its effects on program balances for the first few years, indicating whether the plan would rescue the trust fund from the immediate threat of exhaustion. In expressing a plan's long-term effects, however, the actuaries reported the size of the resulting *average* program deficit over the next several decades, but not year-by-year trust fund balances. As long as the program was in balance on average over the period, and the trust fund always remained in the black, the size of future *annual* balances were actuarially irrelevant to the goal of long-term solvency.[16] Members of Congress were thus informed of the scale of the tax increases that the reform package would impose and that it would eliminate the program's average deficit for the next 50 years: they knew, that is, about the sizes of the short-term pain and of the long-term gain. But these bottom-line figures did not highlight for legislators the precise *intertemporal mechanism* through which this goal would be achieved: that those tax hikes would eventually generate a large fund that would need to be saved for a long stretch of time and then drawn down to help pay benefits decades later.

Second, the ideational lens through which U.S. policymakers viewed Social Security supported this allocation of attention, obscuring the political risks of fund accumulation. Most members of the Social Security policy-making community largely understood the program as an *insurance* arrangement (Derthick 1979). Since President Roosevelt's choice to model the program on this commercial analog, Social Security's administrators and the leadership of the tax-writing committees in Congress had carefully culti-vated and defended this understanding through both structural and linguistic choices. Since the shift to PAYGO financing in the 1940s, the insurance analogy had been somewhat loosened and redefined, such that it no longer necessarily implied funding (Jacobs 2009b). Yet administrators and Congressional leaders had assiduously reinforced the definitional import-ance of contributory financing, routinely distinguishing this self-supporting "insurance" program from "welfare," and judging proposed contribution and benefit rates according to their "actuarial soundness" (Zelizer 1998). Moreover, until the present crisis, this model and the decision-making rou-tines that followed from it had delivered decades of fiscally and politically successful outcomes.

Facing immense policy complexity and limited time, policymakers in 1977 again leaned heavily on this model in interpreting the policy challenge. This means that they focused on the technical problem of actuarial balance central to

---

[16] Author interview with Thompson.

the administration of an insurance policy: whether projected revenues are expected to cover projected outlays. At the same time, the private-insurance model – drawn from a domain of enforceable contracts and secure property rights – drew no attention to the uniquely *political* risks that might bedevil long-range financial management in the *public* sector. Concentrating decision makers' minds on the importance of financial balance, it encouraged little consideration of the specific institutional conditions or policy mechanisms that would be required for safe investment in a state program. In Congressional debates over the 1977 reform package, within committee and on the floor, there was no discussion of the challenge of committing future Social Security reserves to their intended purpose. The reform was framed as a simple trade-off of sacrifice today for the avoidance of greater losses tomorrow, without complicating considerations of the mechanism that lay between.

REFORM REDUX (1983)

As it turned out, the most immediate vulnerability of the 1977 reform was its overly optimistic economic assumptions. Two recessions and renewed high inflation pushed the program back to the brink of bankruptcy by the early 1980s. As in 1977, this short-run insolvency crisis created an immediate need for reform while also widening the long-term deficit, both of which drew public attention. By 1983, Congress and Ronald Reagan's White House had negotiated a new package of reform that shored up the program's short-term finances and the long-term policy investment of 1977. Because this reform process has been well documented elsewhere, and in its intertemporal outlines largely mirror the 1977 episode, I point out just a few instructive features here.[17]

As in 1977, incumbents had to balance the electoral risks of imposing short-term pain through reform against the electoral risks of inaction. In the absence of legislative change, the program would immediately become unable to pay benefits to tens of millions of seniors. Short-term crisis also drew public attention to the actuaries' longer-term projections of financial trouble, casting doubt on the program's promises to current workers. Unlike the 1977 package, however, the 1983 reform plan was drawn up within a decision-making venue unusual in American politics: a bipartisan, quasi-corporatist national commission, featuring representatives of both major political parties, business, and labor. This bargaining arrangement in part mirrored the even greater diffusion of authority across policymaking institutions, with Republicans now in control of the executive and the Senate and Democrats holding a majority in the House of Representatives; neither party could hope to enact reform without the assent of the other. In part, the commission process also reflected all incumbents'

---

[17] For the outlines of the 1983 reform process, unless otherwise noted, I rely on the detailed account in Light (1995). In the essentials that I draw on here, Light's narrative agrees with the independently researched account in Tynes (1996).

interest in spreading blame for the painful near-term measures that any fix would require.

While the prospect of immediate bankruptcy generated the imperative to act, the character of the policy response itself was strongly shaped by the logic of low institutional insulation deriving from dispersed veto power. Had either liberals or conservatives been able to act alone, pursuing their own allies' distributive interests, each would have devised a solution that relied solely on burden-shifting, without recourse to investment. Shortly after taking office, President Reagan had already made a major distributive push away from Social Security's beneficiaries, proposing significant cuts in pension outlays to be followed by a freeze in payroll tax rates. And, as they had in 1977, labor groups and liberals in Congress responded to the new crisis by pushing *their* favored redistributive solution of revenue transfers from outside the program, with modest payroll tax increases scheduled only as needed in future years (Pierson 1994). Neither coalition's preferred solution would have entailed an additional accumulation of resources in the trust fund or an intertemporal transfer.

In an institutional context that widely dispersed veto power, however, neither distributive coalition could entirely get its way. Unable to simply shift burdens onto others, each side was forced to internalize the long-term costs of inaction: for labor and the left, the possible collapse of the system; for business and the right, the ultimate erosion of the wall between Social Security and the general budget. Enjoying a somewhat stronger bargaining position than they had in 1977, Republicans were this time able to ensure that the final package balanced tax increases with benefit cuts. Cutting the benefits previously promised to *current* pensioners was, of course, by far the most electorally dangerous solution. Thus, the reform's near-term costs mostly took the form of payroll tax increases, including the acceleration of the 1977 schedule of tax hikes and an increase in the contribution rate paid by the self-employed.[18] Near-term losses on the benefit side were designed to be modest, hard-to-detect, and focused on those most able to afford them (Pierson 1994): a one-time six-month delay in inflation adjustment would keep *nominal* benefits untouched while a new income tax on benefits would apply only to higher-income retirees. These near-term measures not only resolved the immediate cash crunch but also began generating massive surpluses that would reduce the system's 75-year deficit by two-thirds (Board of Trustees 1983).

The package was not pure investment: among the major elements of long-term redistribution was a gradual increase in the retirement age scheduled to begin in 2000. The urgency of repairing the trust fund, combined with a set of restrictive rules adopted by congressional leaders, gave business groups and their

---

[18] The Commission and Congress did end up engaging in small amounts of indirect general revenue transfer for tightly circumscribed purposes in order to help square the short-term financing circle. But conservatives and business in both arenas stood firm in opposing any significant breach in the wall between the contributory program and the federal budget: outright emergency infusions of Treasury dollars to get the system through to 1990 were out of the question (Patashnik 2000).

legislative allies just enough leverage to push these benefit-reductions through potential veto points. Even under emergency conditions, however, the scope for distributive change in the United States was sharply limited by the fragmentation of political authority. The institutional restriction of the menu of feasible options again forced a resort to major investment to solve the bulk of the problem.

Further echoing 1977, policymakers in 1983 set in motion a massive accumulation of resources without making provision for their credible commitment to the program. Though they did remove Social Security from the unified federal budget for definitional purposes, future official budgetary projections would continue to report a bottom-line federal-deficit figure that included the program's activities.[19] As in 1977, a lack of attention to the *mechanism* of policy investment explains why even fiscal conservatives favored the reform despite the absence of strong commitment structures. According to nearly all accounts of the national commission's work, its members had no explicit intention of building up a large reserve or of partially funding the Social Security system (Patashnik 2000).[20] Members of Congress seem to have been equally unconcerned with the trust fund's annual medium-term balances.[21] As a Social Security specialist in Congress's research service and close observer of the reform process explains:

When deliberating on the 1983 amendments, Congress gave little attention to how the new provisions would affect the system's financial flows year by year or decade by decade after 1990. The focus was almost exclusively on assuring the system could meet its commitments over the next 10 years and *on average* over the next 75. The fact that the average 75-year imbalance was remedied by having surpluses in the early decades followed by large deficits later went largely unnoticed (Koitz 2001, 28)[22].

[19] The Gramm-Rudman-Hollings deficit reduction package of 1985, for instance, included Social Security in the size of the deficit.

[20] Patashnik draws on published lectures by Commission member Robert Ball and by Commission executive director Robert Myers – individuals who disagreed about many of the substantive issues in Social Security policy but agreed on this historical point. See Myers (1991) and Ball (1990). In my own interview with him, Ball also stated that "there was no deliberate, talked-out move to partial funding" and no discussion of the dangers of a trust-fund buildup. He said that Commission chairman Alan Greenspan paid little attention to the fund buildup and that he never heard fund accumulation mentioned by White House staff. Nancy Altman, Greenspan's staff assistant, told me in our interview that, although the Commission members were briefed on the fund buildup, most were focused on "the bottom line" and were relatively unconcerned with *how* they achieved their short- and long-term goals. Ball, interview with the author, Alexandria, VA, October 10, 2001; Altman, interview with the author, Bethesda, MD, October 16, 2001.

[21] In an interview with the author, May 2, 2002, a Senate Finance staffer from the reform period stated that neither the Finance Committee nor Congress as a whole ever discussed the future surpluses. Light's (1995) detailed account, based on his own close observation of the process, makes no mention of any consideration given on the Commission or in Congress to the surpluses their decisions would generate.

[22] Emphasis in original. Koitz sat through both the Ways and Means and Finance Committees' markup sessions. Koitz also writes in endnote 43, "Congress had no perception of the system's financial flows after the first 10 years, and with respect to the long run, only 'average' 75-year estimates were prepared for committee deliberations. There was no discussion of 'advance

As in 1977, legislators focused their attention on actuarial forecasts of the bottom-line outcomes that they were most motivated to solve, not on the details of the causal processes that might generate these outcomes. Although members of Congress knew that the reform would have short-run costs and was projected to eliminate its long-term deficit, they did not intentionally choose the policy mechanism of fund accumulation and did not think through the conditions required to sustain it. Legislators' continued reliance on an insurance model and actuarial frame in understanding the long-term problem was an indispensable simplifying device amidst vast policy complexity. It meant that actors' limited attention was focused on the fiscal problem of *insufficient* reserves rather than on the problem of protecting large reserves. And it reduced a potentially multidimensional problem of devising and securing policy investments to a single dimension of choice: a choice between short-term sacrifice and much larger long-term losses. As compared to plausible alternative understandings of the problem, this was a choice-definition relatively favorable to investment. Once again, the passage of policy investment was unimpeded by a form of political uncertainty to which policymakers never attended.

CONCLUSION

In both the 1977 and 1983 cases, it is unlikely that U.S. policymakers would have made long-term investments in Social Security without the focusing event of near-term insolvency. In each case, voter attention to Social Security's problems depended on a clear signal of *imminent* danger from the system's actuaries. And with public attention focused on the program's ability to continue paying benefits in the near term, incumbents' electoral calculation strongly favored action over inaction. Moreover, once Social Security's short- and long-term financing troubles had become salient public issues, politicians enjoyed a rare opportunity to adopt a credible loss-avoidance frame: to *justify* any pain of reform as the avoidance of the even greater costs of doing nothing, for both current and future beneficiaries.

Electoral safety deriving from impending crisis, however, was a necessary but not a sufficient condition for policy investment. Politicians could theoretically have dealt with the program's financing difficulties through strategies of redistribution – like general-revenue financing or benefit cuts – that would have involved little or no intertemporal transfer. Indeed, the favored strategy of each distributive coalition was to close the financing gap by making some *other* set of actors – whether affluent taxpayers (labor's first choice) or pensioners (business's first choice) – pay the costs of adjustment. Such solutions would largely impose their costs gradually over time – raising income taxes or, alternatively, reducing benefits as and when Social Security faced financial difficulties. While some of this pain would have to be inflicted immediately in

funding' the system's commitments, and little or no appreciation for the fact that an early build up of reserves would occur."

order to resolve the program's current cash crunch, the costs of easing Social Security's *future* financial strains would, in either distributive strategy, be long delayed.

As predicted in Chapter 2, however, a minimally insulated policymaking process – defined by a wide dispersion of veto power – made it impossible for either redistributive strategy to succeed; the losers from a shift in either direction had ample opportunity to block it. With substantial burden-shifting removed from the menu, Congress was limited to responses that would minimally alter the program's existing cross-sectional allocation of costs and benefits – i.e., that would maintain payroll tax financing and keep pension replacement rates from falling too far from currently projected levels. In both episodes, these strictures forced complete (1977) or substantial (1983) reliance on near-term increases in the payroll tax. While these tax hikes (and, in 1983, modest benefit cuts) were chosen primarily for the extra revenues they would generate in the near term at moments of economic difficulty, these higher tax levels (and slightly lower benefit levels) would still be in place once the economy rebounded. The result, over the long run, would be a policy investment: the accumulation of vast surpluses that could be dedicated to paying benefits in the next century.

From the perspective of organized labor and business, these two investments were vertical ones: while extracting resources from each in the short run, they would deliver benefits of even greater value to each – saving the program from financial collapse while preventing a shift to general-revenue financing – over the long run. And the decentralization of authority enhanced groups' willingness to accept the costs of vertical investment by limiting the range of feasible alternatives. With their preferred redistributive solutions institutionally impeded, powerful interests faced a trade-off structured in policy investment's favor: a choice between the short-term costs of investment and the more disastrous consequences of doing nothing.

In each episode, politicians' time horizons were remarkably extended, a result in part of an informational environment that brought distant but highly consequential outcomes into sharp relief. Legislators knew that their reform measures were projected to substantially enhance Social Security's long-term fiscal capacities, and they publicly justified their actions in part in these terms. Yet their thinking about the long run was also selective in nature, their perception of threats and solutions shaped by the prevailing mental model of the policy domain. If the policy problem – as framed by the insurance model and by the actuaries to whom that model granted expert authority – was that the program lacked sufficient resources to meet its liabilities, then the appropriate solution seemed to lie in adjusting that model's key "moving parts" – tax and benefit provisions – to balance income with outlays. And with the dilemma defined by actuarial logic, a profitable intertemporal trade-off – cost-imposition today for greater loss-avoidance tomorrow – appeared eminently achievable.

The informational and technical complexity of the issue, combined with the urgency of action, did not leave policymakers with a great deal of cognitive slack for thinking outside that model or questioning its premises. Once informed that their package of measures would achieve actuarial balance over the next 50 or 75 years, legislators inquired neither into the specific financial mechanism through which balance would be achieved nor into the possible unintended consequences or vulnerabilities of such a method. And the dominant, nearly apolitical understanding of the program as an "insurance" scheme did not encourage decision makers to consider the political dangers of accumulating large reserves. Policy investment in Social Security was not a consequence of comprehensively rational foresight. It depended critically on policymakers' *selective* cognizance of the future: *inattention* to some potential long-term outcomes alongside attention to others.

CHAPTER 8

Shifting the Long-Run Burden
Reforming British Pensions, 1986[1]

Margaret Thatcher came to power in 1979 determined to control the growth of public expenditure, cut government deficits, and scale back the role of the state. As soaring unemployment placed upward pressure on social spending, however, the size of government increased rapidly during her first administration.[2] When Nigel Lawson took office as Chancellor of the Exchequer in 1983, he sought both to reverse this disappointing trend in the near term and to hold down the long-term trajectory of government spending. While immediate cuts to programs such as defense and education helped the Chancellor pursue near-term fiscal discipline, pension reform would play a central role in his longer-term strategy. Old-age pensions were, on the one hand, a spending category in which quick savings were hard to achieve because current beneficiaries had come to depend on past benefit promises. At the same time, it was an area of expenditure that was scheduled to grow automatically over the next several decades as the ranks of retirees swelled.

Accounts of the British pension reforms of the 1980s – especially those that set it in cross-national perspective – typically emphasize their relative radicalism (Huber and Stephens 2001a; Bonoli 2000). Thatcher's success in dismantling Britain's public retirement programs is usually considered dramatic by comparison, for instance, with Ronald Reagan's modest cutbacks to Social Security (Pierson 1994). This conventional view of the British reform outcome, however, occludes two important features of the case. First, our characterization of the outcome depends critically on whether we think about change cross-sectionally or over time. While Thatcher's reforms to the British pension system wrought an unusually large long-term *distributive* shift, they enacted only a modest *intertemporal* one. Her initiative would bring about an enormous transfer of resources from future retirees to future taxpayers, but it engineered a far less dramatic

---

[1] Parts of this chapter draw on Jacobs (2008).
[2] Total managed public expenditures grew between 1978–79 and 1984–85 by 14 percent in real terms. Data available on the UK Treasury website at www.hm-treasury.gov.uk/mediastore/otherfiles/pubfinance_april02.xls (last accessed May 15, 2004).

investment than did either of the U.S. reforms (or, as we shall see, those adopted in Canada).

Second, the distributive outcome that typically marks the British reform as a neo-liberal triumph – the massive reallocation of incomes away from future pensioners – was *not* in fact Thatcher's first choice. Thatcher and the responsible minister originally aimed not to reduce the incomes of future retirees but to invest in a long-term shift in the *source* of that income, from collective to individualized pension arrangements. As we will observe, the outcome in the British case did *not* represent the striking fulfillment of conservative ambitions but, rather, a sharp strategic adjustment in the face of organized opposition. The central puzzle of British reform is not how Thatcher's government achieved so much, but why policy change mostly took the form of long-term redistribution rather than of the large policy investment that ministers had initially planned. And, more specifically, why – by comparison to U.S. and Canadian politicians – were the British Conservatives so intertemporally cautious despite the advantages of highly centralized authority and a divided electoral opposition? The chapter's concluding section also considers the ultimate failure of Britain's modest policy investment, and what the source of this policy mistake reveals about elite preference-formation under uncertainty.

PLANNING INVESTMENT

The Thatcher government's first significant foray into the field of pension reform was a little-noticed but consequential adjustment to the flat-rate, general-revenue financed Basic State Pension. In 1980, the government shifted the basis for annual uprating of this benefit from the higher of either prices or earnings to pure price indexation – a subtle long-term redistributive move that would save several billion pounds in the course of the next decade (Pierson 1994). Ministers' more ambitious efforts, however, centered around a transformation of second-tier, earnings-related pensions. As of the mid-1980s, all workers were members of one of two types of earnings-related scheme. By default, all workers covered by the National Insurance program were enrolled in the State Earnings-Related Pension Scheme (SERPS), into which they and their employers paid payroll contributions. Employers who ran qualifying occupational pension plans, however, could choose to "opt out" of SERPS; to offset contributions paid into the occupational scheme, these firms and their workers would receive a rebate on part of their National Insurance premiums.

Through the early 1980s, a series of government reports on public expenditure – by the Treasury, the prime minister's policy review staff, and the Government Actuary – warned of a steep upward trajectory in state pension outlays starting early in the next century, largely attributable to SERPS. Since the scheme had been operating only since 1978, current retirees were currently eligible to collect only modest benefits, but spending was set to rise sharply in coming decades as successive cohorts of workers retired with progressively longer contribution records. To ministers intent on *shrinking* the role of the state, this pre-programmed growth in public largesse was a sobering prospect.

Against this backdrop of long-term fiscal anxiety within government, Norman Fowler, Secretary of State for Social Services, formulated a plan to dramatically recast earnings-related pension provision. In Fowler's view, the trouble with Britain's existing retirement arrangements related less to their fiscal costs than to the rigidities and inequities that they generated in an era of high labor mobility. An "early leavers problem" commonly arose as workers who lost or changed jobs in mid-career forfeited rights to occupational pensions that they had earned with their former employer. Fowler was thus drawn to individualized savings vehicles as a means of making pension rights portable and insulating retirement incomes from the vagaries of employment trajectories (Nesbitt 1995; Fowler 1991). Meanwhile, prominent Conservative Party thinkers based at New Right think tanks were advocating personal pensions for a different set of reasons: as a way of extending property ownership and fashioning a "people's capitalism." While requiring individuals to take greater responsibility for their own welfare in retirement, investment in equity markets through personal pensions would also lend them a greater stake in the country's economic prosperity than could collective forms of provision – whether public or employer-operated. In the most ambitious form of this vision, the lines of class conflict would eventually blur as Britain's workers began to think – and vote – like the capitalists they had become (Araki 2000; Lewis 1996).

Ministers' interest in reducing public social expenditure and – especially in Fowler's case – in moving toward personal pensions was underwritten not just by their individualist value orientation but also by a set of specific causal understandings. According to the market-liberal ideas to which many of Thatcher's officials subscribed, generous public provision sapped individual initiative, rendered labor markets less flexible, and dampened economic productivity, while government borrowing was understood to foster inflation and to displace more productive private-sector investment. A liberal model of economic activity also highlighted two key causal logics through which private, individualized savings vehicles would generate substantial long-term social benefits. First, the model was founded on a belief in the formidable capacity of individuals, given the right information, to make prudent choices in their own interests. Second, the model predicted a general tendency of vigorous competition among providers to generate products that maximize consumer preferences and yield optimal value for money. Applied to private pensions, these twin market logics implied that individual savers would choose investment vehicles suited to their retirement needs and that financial-service providers would compete to keep fees low and returns high.

Like all mental mappings of complex dynamics, ministers' conceptualization of financial consumer-product markets considerably simplified the causal possibilities. The model's assumptions about consumer decision making especially discouraged reasoning about the sources of potential market failure: in particular, about the possibility that inexperienced individual investors choosing among complex and unfamiliar financial products might make foolhardy long-term choices.[3] This incomplete causal map, however, powerfully shaped executive officials' preferences. Viewed through the ideational lens at hand, private personal pensions appeared to offer the prospect of generating a bundle of long-run social outcomes – fiscal, moral, political, and economic – valued highly by free-market conservatives.

Both the legacy of existing public provision and the actuarial logic of private schemes meant that any transition from current modes of provision toward personal pensions would require a substantial policy investment. One source of the intertemporal trade-off would derive from the "double-payment" problem inherent in a switch from public pay-as-you-go (PAYGO) to private pensions. As workers had already contributed for several years to the existing earnings-related scheme, they were already entitled to some SERPS payout upon retirement. Under the PAYGO rules governing the British National Insurance system, however, those revenues had been spent on meeting current benefit obligations, rather than being set aside to cover future liabilities. If workers were now permitted to leave SERPS for a private alternative, a financing gap would open up: as contributions formerly flowing to the program were rechannelled into personal schemes, the state would have to find new resources to cover those pension entitlements that had already been earned. In addition, because contributions to private pensions enjoyed tax preferences, the state would have to subsidize the transition costs by exempting the additional private contributions from taxation. While the transition would have substantial short-run costs, its full benefits would only emerge over the long run. The outlays avoided by eliminating earnings-related state pensions would *eventually* amount to a massive £26 billion a year (at 1985 prices) but would approach that level only gradually (Secretary of State for Social Services 1985). At the same time, because they would be financed out of accumulated savings, personal pensions would only be able to play a major role in providing retirement incomes after decades of individual contributions.

In 1985, Fowler brought this intertemporal proposition to Cabinet, proposing to phase out SERPS and replace it with a regime of compulsory private pensions. Under the Fowler plan, all men under 50 and women under 45 would stop paying into the public scheme, and SERPS benefits would be completely eliminated for those retiring after 2010. In lieu of payments to the public scheme, current workers under the age threshold would be required to make tax-exempt contributions to either a private occupational scheme or a portable personal pension. Moreover, all employees of firms that offered occupational pensions would now be free to opt out of those collective arrangements and into their own personal pension. While those retiring after 2010 would no longer receive SERPS benefits, benefits owed to past SERPS contributors would be honored and paid for out of future National Insurance contributions.

---

[3] As discussed later in this chapter, these assumptions would prove to be woefully unfounded with respect to the system of personal pensions ultimately adopted in 1986.

Senior Cabinet members shared a common understanding of the basic structure of the intertemporal bargain: Fowler's plan would imply short-run social and fiscal costs in exchange for far greater long-run fiscal savings and tax reductions and a dramatic long-term shift in retirement provision toward private and individualized arrangements. Yet ministers weighed the elements of this trade-off differently. Chancellor Lawson, particularly focused on the near-term commitments that he had made to fiscal consolidation and tax cuts, objected to the proposal's hefty short-run price tag for the Exchequer. While Lawson was willing to countenance some short-term expense in exchange for long-term savings, Fowler's proposal would in his view have squeezed too much from government coffers too quickly, jeopardizing other urgent fiscal imperatives.[4] Lawson's judgment, however, did not win the day. The prime minister found Fowler's vision of institutional transformation highly persuasive and, in her view, the pursuit of this long-run achievement was worth the necessary near-term fiscal and economic losses. Thatcher overruled the Chancellor's objection, and the proposal was published as an official Green Paper (Nesbitt 1995).

RETREAT FROM INVESTMENT

As we will see, Cabinet would soon revisit and revise the basic elements of Fowler's plan. Why did Thatcher's government ultimately reject this massive investment? The near-term costs that investment would impose on the average voter did *not* constitute one of the primary obstacles. The British electorate in the mid-1980s does not appear to have had much appetite for welfare-state retrenchment: opinion polls suggested that a majority of the public favored increases rather than reductions in social expenditures and cared far more about public services than about tax cuts (McKie 1986; Prowse 1986; Hencke 1985). As one commentator observed, "Contrary to the Government's expectations, the public apparently, still does not feel excessively overtaxed, nor does it regard a 'roll back' of the state as a priority" (Prowse 1986). Indeed, Labour Party leaders promised to make the government's pension cutbacks a theme of their next general-election campaign.

Yet the government's ultimate failure to invest was not a consequence of either public myopia or the difficulty of imposing near-term costs on the median voter. In fact, the feature of the plan to which voters were most hostile was not its short-term cost but the *long-term* "benefit" that it sought to achieve. To the extent that the initiative risked voter backlash, the problem was an *inversion* of the conventional view of the electoral dangers of investment. The Green Paper's short-run costs would all fall on the revenue side, in the form of increased

---

[4] As former senior Treasury economist Norman Glass explained, the Treasury accepted that it might be worth paying a price now for savings in the long term, "but the question was how much." Interview with the author, London, August 16, 2001.

National Insurance contribution rates for some workers[5] and possible income-tax cuts foregone. With the British public in the mid-1980s relatively uncon-cerned about tax burdens, these near-term costs were unlikely to be a key mobilizing issue for the left. By far, the most salient and least popular aspect of the plan – and the object of Labour attacks – was the replacement of public with private provision, an outcome that would take decades to emerge. What was potentially risky about the plan, then, was not that voters might *ignore* its long-term effects but that they would *notice* them – that the plan would invest in a gradual institutional transformation that, to many British citizens, would look more like a social bad than a social good. To the extent that Thatcher's govern-ment needed to take voters' policy attitudes into account, those attitudes would have militated against *any* significant rollback of state provision rather than against policy investment itself. And as we will see, the reform ultimately adopted would itself deal a devastating blow to social protection for the aged, doing far *more* long-term damage to seniors' incomes than the Green Paper plan would have.

Equally significantly, however, the Conservative government enjoyed a rare degree of electoral insulation – far more so than reforming politicians in the U.S. cases. For one thing, the British economy – one important predictor of incum-bents' electoral fortunes – was robust in the leadup to reform (National Science Board 2000). More importantly, the British left had fractured into two major political parties in the early 1980s: the Labour Party and the breakaway Social Democratic Party, operating in electoral alliance with the Liberals. Under first-past-the-post electoral rules, a divided left would be operating at a substantial strategic disadvantage against the unified right (Garrett 1993). While the Thatcher administration was not freed from all electoral moorings, the opposi-tion's capacity to threaten the Tories' grip on power was unusually limited.[6]

Beyond the reactions of the mass public, however, the plan faced fierce opposition from those organized interests who would bear its costs. As could have been expected, trade unions and welfare advocates criticized the disman-tling of solidaristic public provision. Yet, Britain's highly insulated policymaking process – generated by institutions that concentrated authority in the leadership of a single-party parliamentary majority – offered few access points to groups that were not allied with the ruling party. Labor and other interest groups on the left enjoyed virtually no leverage over the policy initiatives of a hardline Conservative government wielding a massive majority.

More consequential was opposition from groups upon whom the governing party depended. Unexpectedly, the financial services industry itself reacted coolly to the idea of compulsory private pensions. Most financial service pro-viders were unconvinced that there was much profit to be reaped in managing

---

[5] Those currently in occupational pension schemes.

[6] Other secondary accounts of this reform episode, in fact, make little or no mention of voters' preferences as a factor driving the government's subsequent retreat from the Green Paper proposal. See, e.g., Nesbitt (1995), Pierson (1994), or Bonoli (2000).

millions of small funds since the administrative costs would eat up a large share of the assets. If it wanted to create a market for individualized retirement provision, the government would have to find a way of making market entry more appealing to potential providers (Jacobs and Teles 2007).

What gave ministers greatest pause, however, was opposition from employers, who balked at the short-term costs that the plan would impose on them (Schulze and Moran 2006; Prowse 1985a; Short 1985b). As explained earlier, the shift from public PAYGO pensions to private funded arrangements would generate substantial transition costs in the form of a "double payment" burden. A large share of this transition burden would be borne by firms that currently operated their own occupational pension plans *in lieu* of SERPS membership, and were thus receiving a National Insurance rebate. As all SERPS contributions were eliminated, while the program's existing obligations continued to be honored, the "opt out" rebate would be withdrawn, immediately adding 3 percentage points to the payroll tax burden of those firms running their own occupational plans (Nesbitt 1995).

The powerful Confederation of British Industry (CBI) led business's assault against the Fowler plan,[7] objecting first and foremost – as an internal CBI memo revealed – to the transition costs of a shift to private pensions (Short 1985a).[8] It was not that this shift out of public provision did not offer employers major long-term gains. From their perspective, Fowler's plan implied a clear vertical investment, imposing costs on them in the short run but delivering to them much larger benefits over the long run. Without investment, SERPS' contribution burden would rise from only 2 percent of earnings in 1991 to 6.2 percent by 2011 and 10.6 percent in 2033.[9] By paying 3 percent more now, British firms could eliminate the program entirely, thus escaping far greater costs in coming decades. Why would employers reject an opportunity to so dramatically reduce their long-term tax burdens?

The main obstacle to policy investment in Britain was that, for business, an even more advantageous alternative was readily available: a cross-sectional *redistribution* of the long-run costs of retirement. The Green Paper's short-term transition costs derived from its attempt to construct a wholly new pillar of funded retirement provision to take the place of the public earnings-related program. Retirement incomes on the whole were not meant to fall; their source would simply shift. Rather than investing in the creation of a private alternative, however, employers could also see their long-term tax burdens fall dramatically if future state benefit levels were simply *reduced* rather than

---

[7] The Engineering Employers Federation joined the attack, with the smaller Institute of Directors the only significant employer group to support the original proposal.

[8] Among other concerns, employers also objected to allowing individuals in occupational schemes to opt out of them. Since many of these schemes were partially financed on a PAYGO basis, an exodus of members would destabilize their finances. On this point, however, employers' views did not prevail as the final reform still gave workers the right to leave their employers' plans for a personal pension.

[9] Calculation by Institute for Fiscal Studies, cited in Prowse (1985b).

comprehensively *replaced* (Nesbitt 1995; Short 1986). While Fowler's policy investment would have acted intertemporally – imposing costs on current producers to relieve future taxpayers – cutting pension rates would act *cross-sectionally* at a future point in time: it would enact a long-term redistribution of resources away from tomorrow's retirees and toward tomorrow's producers, *without* the short-term transition costs of building up private pension funds.

Employers' preference for a redistributive over an intertemporal solution was not itself unusual or a definitive bar to investment. As our other reform cases illustrate, organized groups' first choice is typically to shift their long-term burdens onto others, not to invest in reducing those burdens in the aggregate. Yet a crucial distinguishing feature of the present case was the institutional and strategic *context* within which British employers were pursuing their preferences. Less-insulated policy making processes in the United States (and, as we shall see, in Canada) sufficiently dispersed veto power to enable labor and beneficiary groups to block major benefit cuts. With large-scale burden-shifting impossible, U.S. and Canadian employers saw investment at short-term cost as preferable to skyrocketing future burdens, and both accepted quick increases in premiums comparable to those that the CBI was now rejecting.

In contrast, the institutional setting within which British business was operating – a context of high insulation of the executive, in the terms of Chapter 2 – made a burden-shifting strategy eminently feasible. With political authority almost completely centralized in the hands of a pro-market conservative ruling party, the losers from such a redistribution of resources – labor and welfare groups – would be practically powerless to prevent a reduction in benefit rates. In other words, with employers' allies in executive office, the concentration of authority within the British polity militated against policy investment by facilitating business-friendly redistributive alternatives. British firms had little reason to accept the costs of policy investment because they knew that they could likely achieve comparable long-term gains by externalizing the future burden of retirement provision.

If the government enjoyed some insulation from public opinion and could safely ignore lobbies on the left, Conservative leaders could ill afford to dismiss the objections of strategic allies in the business community. As will be recalled, the Green Paper had emerged from Cabinet deliberations in which the Chancellor had objected to the plan's near-term costs. When Cabinet reconvened to consider the form of the government's formal legislative proposal, business opposition now greatly strengthened the Treasury's hand. According to the reports of participants, employers' demands were critical in tipping the scales in favor of the Chancellor's view, pushing the final outcome away from policy investment.[10] The Chancellor won fundamental revisions that would

---

[10] See the minister's own account in Fowler (1991). A senior civil servant closely involved with the reform, who wished to remain anonymous, confirmed Fowler's account in an interview with the author, London, 3 August 2001.

impose far less short-term pain while still radically shrinking long-term public spending on pensions.

Now, consistent with business preferences, the state contributory program would be deeply slashed rather than eliminated, with most of the cutbacks long delayed. Starting with those retiring after 2010, SERPS benefits would be reduced from 25 to 20 percent of earnings, would accrue more slowly, and would be based on lifetime average earnings rather than the recipient's 20 highest-earning years; benefits for surviving spouses would also be slashed deeply. Overall, these cutbacks would roughly halve government spending on earnings-related pensions by 2033, holding National Insurance taxes 4 percentage points lower than they would have otherwise been (Pierson 1994).

Personal pensions remained an element of the plan but only as a voluntary option for those who wanted to leave SERPS or their employer's scheme. At Fowler's insistence, the White Paper also included a state subsidy to personal pensions equal to 2 percent of earnings for the first 5 years in order to make this alternative more attractive to both workers and pension providers.[11] All in, however, the short-term costs of the new plan were expected to reach only £750 million over the first 5 years (as compared with £1 billion in the first year alone under the original reform blueprint) with no increase in contribution rates required (Secretary of State for Social Services 1985). The Government Actuary estimated that the new voluntary option would draw a mere 500,000 individuals out of occupational schemes and SERPS into new personal pension arrangements – a shadow of the initial plan for universal private provision (Bonoli 2000).[12] In turn, this modest investment was itself projected to contribute little to the reform's overall long-term benefits for taxpayers, relieving contributors 40 years hence of a mere 0.1 percentage point in payroll tax.[13] The lion's share of the long-term savings would come from future benefit cuts – i.e., from the plan's long-term redistributive elements. Given its institutional advantages, the government had little trouble converting this revised proposal into the Social Security Act of 1986.

CONCLUSION AND CODA

While Thatcher's Cabinet encompassed a range of ideological views, the reform process was dominated by senior ministers with strong commitments to a reduced state role in society and market liberalism. Their combination of normative goals and causal understandings drove them to seek a massive shift away

---

[11] During parliamentary deliberations, the government also acceded to employers' demands to make conditions for the 2 percent bonus more restrictive for those who had the option of joining an employer scheme.

[12] As a result of the "misselling scandal," discussed later in this chapter, this estimate proved to be far too low.

[13] Annual net new savings arising from personal pensions have been estimated at 0.1% of GDP in 1989, rising to 0.2% a decade later (Disney, Emmerson, and Wakefield 2001).

from public and toward private pensions. In turn, the policy logic of this transformational project required that it take the form of an investment, with resources committed in the near term for benefits decades away. In pursuing radical change, not only did Conservative leaders enjoy the electoral luxuries of a divided opposition and a strong economy, but they also wielded a massive and disciplined parliamentary majority within one of the most centralized polities in the democratic world. In this highly insulated policymaking process, opponents on the left would have virtually no institutional opportunities to block adverse policy change.

However, centralized authority did not imply high capacity to invest. In the language of Chapter 2's theoretical framework, the policy process in Britain displayed *high* – but not hyper- – insulation from societal pressure: parties had to win elections to gain office but, once in office, faced few veto points in enacting policy change. Highly insulated governments can, by virtue of their concentrated authority, ignore demands from *some* organized interests. But as organizations that must win votes to achieve power, parties in such a polity must still nurture strategic relationships with well-resourced interest groups aligned with their broad policy orientation. Such ties allow politicians to draw on a set of electoral goods that organized interests can generate, but require the party, in turn, to attend to these groups' core policy demands.

A key strategic ally of the ruling Conservatives, British employers, opposed policy investment for reasons predicted in Chapter 2: they preferred to externalize the long-term costs of population aging rather investing at short-run expense in an aggregate long-term reduction in those costs. At the same time, precisely because their partisan allies wielded concentrated policymaking authority (given an absence of veto points outside the executive), business leaders knew that major distributive shifts in their favor were readily achievable. Put another way, employers had little reason to accept the costs of investment in an institutional setting that made it so easy, instead, to shift long-term burdens onto groups outside the governing coalition. Unlike U.S. capitalists in 1977 and 1983, that is, U.K. employers did not face an institutionally *constrained* choice between policy investment and the higher long-term losses implied by the status quo. Rather, British business had the luxury of choosing between investment and a long-term redistribution of resources in their favor, and they naturally opted for the latter. Conservative leaders, for their part, may have had little need to negotiate with the parliamentary opposition, but they had strong incentives to attend closely to the policy demands of a critical organizational and electoral ally.

In its most significant component – the gradual but devastating cuts in SERPS benefits – the resulting reform engineered a massive, long-run redistribution of resources from future pensioners toward future taxpayers. With its modest investment in additional private accounts, its net long-term effect would be a large reduction in future pensioners' incomes. In comparative terms, the British Social Security Act of 1986 is widely regarded as a rare triumph of neoliberal reform ambition. What is often obscured in existing accounts, however, is that this redistributive outcome was *not* Thatcher's first choice. She and Fowler had in fact preferred a large policy investment that would have reduced state spending while maintaining pensioners' incomes. The final outcome reflected not Thatcherite ideological vision but strategic adjustment to the demands of her own party's key constituencies.

As in our other cases, choice-definitions had a powerful effect on actors' policy positions and on the outcome. As we have also observed elsewhere – perhaps most strikingly in the creation of the U.S. Social Security system – actors at different locations within the political system defined the relevant trade-off in starkly differing terms. In the U.S. episode of 1935, Administration officials and American capitalists understood funding in two contrasting ways – respectively, as a credible intertemporal trade-off for society or as a redistributive trade-off to the disadvantage of firms – because of their divergent causal perceptions, deriving in large part from differing underlying mental models of democratic politics. Thatcher's officials and important segments of British industry also confronted the choice over investment in highly contrasting terms. But the difference in this case owed less to actors' causal understandings than to the differing *goal*-orientations of officeholders and organized interests.

Tory ministers were focused on a set of aggregate social outcomes valued by conservatives – including greater individual self-reliance, labor-market flexibility, and reduced public spending – which they hoped to pursue while preserving retirement incomes. From this *societal* perspective, investment in personal pensions implied an increase in short-run fiscal and taxation burdens in exchange for a set of greater long-run social and fiscal gains. To Thatcher and Fowler, a simple cutback in state pension benefits – i.e., long-term redistribution – was not as attractive a societal proposition because it would do much less to *replace* collective forms of provision with individualized forms of savings (and, in turn, would likely lead to a large long-term fall in seniors' incomes).

For business groups oriented toward their own *members'* interests, however, this comparison of societal consequences did not describe the relevant payoff structure. While long-term redistribution offered lower net societal benefits, employers themselves would capture a tremendous *share* of those gains while paying minimal costs. Many of the gains of investment, by contrast, would not be captured directly by business and would come with a hefty short-term price tag for firms. Employers, that is, had little quarrel with the basic causal premises of the government's reform plans and, for that matter, shared many of the government's market-oriented policy goals; firm owners also had an important stake in the political success of the Tory Party. But the particular interests of business are not identical with the policy goals of their conservative allies in office: while the former will sometimes be drawn to investment in projects of market-oriented societal and institutional transformation, the latter will often prefer a strategy of cross-sectional redistribution toward capital.[14]

While the reform legislation took only modest steps toward the creation of a personal pensions market, it is nonetheless worth noting how this small investment turned out. In particular, the disastrous consequences of this investment are illuminating for what they suggest about the cognitive influences on long-term preference-formation. In designing their personal-pensions scheme, ministers did strikingly little to ensure that even the limited resources to be invested would be safely channeled toward their long-term purpose. Officials embedded the new pensions market within a remarkably lax financial oversight regime (governed by the new Financial Services Act, or FSA), based largely on self-regulation by the industry. The FSA imposed a set of general obligations on those selling personal pensions, including responsibilities to obtain enough information about and provide enough information to customers to permit a reasoned choice (Black and Nobles 1998).

What the government did not regulate in detail, however, was the actual character of the product sold. In particular, ministers left completely to market forces perhaps the most important feature of a pension transaction: the administrative fees charged by providers. In the event, consumer choice and competition proved wholly inadequate to the task of keeping these fees within reason. In fact, over a 25-year period, management fees reduced the value of many pension portfolios by as much as *30 percent* (Lewis 1996). And, for the most part, these fees represented a straight transfer from the Exchequer (via the National Insurance rebate) to the financial services industry, a diversion of invested resources that would add nothing to the stock of retirement savings.

At the same time, individuals proved unable to resist aggressive sales tactics and make well-informed long-run choices among pension arrangements, and millions of individual sales interactions proved nearly impossible for the authorities to monitor. As would later emerge, hundreds of thousands of workers who had left occupational schemes for personal pensions had done so unwisely in actuarial terms, in response to bad advice from overzealous sales agents. (Indeed, the personal pensions market would, as a result, grow much larger than the government had ever intended.) Meanwhile, ministers imposed no requirement that holders of personal pensions actually contribute their own money, beyond the National Insurance rebate. And, in the event, with providers' fees front-loaded, an estimated 35 to 40 percent of subscribers never contributed enough to their personal pensions to recover the principal initially deposited, running a grave risk of inadequate payouts in retirement (Liu 1999).

By the mid-1990s, it would become clear that the personal pensions regime had produced one of the greatest policy debacles in recent British history, often termed the "misselling scandal" (Blake 2002; Budden 1999). These disastrous

---

[14] This argument resembles an observation common in the literature on regulatory politics that the particular interests of current market incumbents are not identical to the interests of an industry or the economy as a whole (e.g., Stigler 1971, Derthick and Quirk 1985; see also Vogel 1981).

outcomes, however, did not derive from wholly unforeseeable causal dynamics or a mere fluke of misfortune. In fact, the major elements of the misselling scandal were publicly predicted by prominent actors – including opposition members of parliament and senior civil servants – *during* the decision-making process, forecast as consequences of the structure of the new market and of the light-touch regulatory regime. Why then did the government not build stronger safeguards against the risks of imaginable market failures – failures that undid ministers' own social and economic objectives?

As Steven Teles and I have detailed elsewhere (Jacobs and Teles 2007), ministers' reasoning and information-processing appear to have been powerfully guided by the market-liberal model of economic behavior described earlier – a causal framework that Thatcher's officials routinely applied to issues of social and economic policy. This is the model that led them to understand investment in private funded pensions as a profitable intertemporal trade-off. And this ideational lens simultaneously obscured from them particular risks of serious failure. The model rested on a set of crucial simplifying premises: among the most important, that individuals, given the right information, would make prudent decisions in their own interests and that vigorous competition among providers would yield good value-for-money. Viewed through a market-liberal lens, price controls and other constraints on the content of products sold were not only unnecessary but counterproductive.

This causal framework appears to have acted as a strong confirmatory filter, directing ministers' attention disproportionately to supportive arguments and data. When Fowler convened an inquiry to consider pension reform in 1983, for instance, he specifically instructed the committee to devise plans for personal pensions – a process better suited to uncovering evidence *for* this arrangement than to scrutinizing its feasibility or weighing it against alternatives (Nesbitt 1995). Later, when queried in Parliament about particular market risks to the new regime, Fowler responded either with incredulity that such risks would emerge or with the vaguest of indications of the protective measures to be taken against these dangers (for details, see Jacobs and Teles 2007). Nor did these responses merely represent face-saving defiance in the face of public opposition attack: ministers were equally unwilling to adjust their plans in response to bureaucratic experts' private warnings about risks to the new market.[15]

In other words, in weighing investment's merits, Thatcherite officials appear to have paid far greater attention to those causal dynamics about which their mental model of economic behavior facilitated reasoning. In turn, they placed far less cognitive weight on available information and logics of causation that this framework simplified away. To be clear, it is not that Thatcher's government ignored *obvious* signs of probable policy catastrophe. The novelty and intricacy of the reform enterprise invited myriad lines of causal reasoning and generated substantial ambiguity around signals of danger. Yet policy

---

[15] Guy Fiegehen (senior civil servant, Department of Work and Pensions), interview with the author, London, June 18, 2001.

makers' *interpretation* of this uncertainty appears to have been distinctly tilted against the identification of those risks that could not be derived from the premises of their pre-existing causal framework. In short, it was not enough that the possibility of investment failure was imaginable and relevant information available, or even that ministers had strong incentives to get the policy right. Effortful information-processing by motivated decision makers was still subject to the constraints of bounded attention and structured by powerful cognitive biases toward confirmation. Amidst high complexity and ambiguity, the logical *possibility* of investment risk was no cognitive match for a deeply entrenched mental model that predicted high returns.

CHAPTER 9

Committing to Investment

Reforming Canadian Pensions, 1998

For most of its first three decades in operation, the Canada Pension Plan (CPP) was a model of stability (Béland and Myles 2005; Banting 1987). For 20 years, premiums remained frozen at their initial rate of 3.6 percent, even as workers accumulated longer contribution records and growing entitlements to benefits. Organized labor, women's groups, and social-welfare lobbies were also unsuccessful in attempts to substantially enhance the program's relatively modest payouts. An incremental reform in 1987 – instituting a 25-year schedule of contribution rates, to be adjusted every 5 years – was expected to keep the system in balance as the program matured.

In the early 1990s, however, economic recession and a rise in the disability caseload put severe strains on the program's long-run financial balance. Actuarial projections were showing sharp increases in expenditures over the next four decades, requiring as much as a *tripling* of contribution rates to keep the system solvent. As the pension scheme's financial picture darkened, officials within the federal Finance Department spearheaded a complex reform effort – involving extensive public and federal-provincial consultations – that resulted in a massive policy investment in the CPP's long-term sustainability, with parallel reforms to the Quebec Pension Plan (QPP) enacted simultaneously. In combination with modest benefit cuts, the programs' contribution rates would be nearly doubled to 9.9 percent by 2003, far higher than the required PAYGO rate for many years. As annual surpluses built up a fund, a professional investment board would seek the highest returns for those assets in a portfolio of equities and bonds.[1] Over time, the investment income generated would increasingly relieve the contributory burden on future workers and employers. Whereas PAYGO financing would have required a contribution rate of 14.2 percent as soon as 2030, partial funding with equity investment was projected to keep the rate steady at 9.9 percent until the end of the next century.

---

[1] The reserves of the Quebec Pension Plan had in fact always been invested in a mixture of bonds and equities by the Caisse de Dépôt et Placement. The reform would, however, greatly increase the size of the QPP's fund.

Among all of the reform episodes considered in this book, the Canadian case is perhaps the most dramatic instance of policy investment. Not only did an elected government choose to impose large and immediate visible costs on constituents to solve a problem still decades away. It did so without a near-term financing shortfall – akin to the impending insolvency of the U.S. Social Security system in 1977 and 1983 – to force painful action. Moreover, the Canadian case is striking for the degree to which policymakers consciously sought to accumulate massive resources within state hands. As we will see, the buildup of an enormous reserve fund was not (as in the United States) an inadvertent byproduct of other measures: in Canada, fund accumulation was the central strategy of reform. It was, explicitly, by hoarding and investing today's tax dollars for decades that politicians sought to convert short-term pain into long-term gain.

Furthermore, Canada's investment stands out for the degree to which its designers crafted policy mechanisms to address the *uncertainty* surrounding the long-run consequences of their endeavor. Canadian officials were acutely sensitive to the fact that, in enacting their investment, they would be bequeathing a massive pool of resources to future incumbents whose preferences might diverge from their own. Instead of backing away from investment, however, Canada's policymakers chose to *design* it to be difficult to derail, encasing it within institutional structures that would hobble future attempts to divert or manipulate the fund. Among the cases of investment examined in this study, it is in the Canadian reform that we find by far the most elaborate, intentionally designed mechanisms of long-term resource-commitment. We observe here the striking combination of both a broadly perceived *problem* of political promise-keeping and an institutional *solution* broadly perceived as credible. This chapter thus examines the conditions that made it possible for the Canadian government to impose visible near term costs on constituents in order to invest in distant benefits that were widely understood to be vulnerable to the uncertainty of the long run.

SHAPING THE LONG-TERM AGENDA

In 1995, the CPP Chief Actuary's 15th biennial report portrayed a dire financial future for the program. Previous reports had predicted some need for adjustment, and it was well known that the program's expenditures would rise as the "baby boom" cohort entered retirement. Yet a recession in the early 1990s now combined with a skyrocketing disability caseload to produce a far more ominous fiscal outlook. According to the 1995 actuarial forecast, under the current schedule of gradual contribution rate increases, the CPP fund would be depleted and unable to pay promised benefits by 2015. Moreover, in order to keep pace with rising expenditures, contribution rates would have to rise from their current level of 5.4 percent to 14.2 percent by 2030 – a near-tripling of the pension tax in the space of just 35 years (Office of the Chief Actuary 1995).

The forecasts in this 1995 report placed the long-term challenge of financing the CPP squarely onto the agenda of senior officials within the federal

Department of Finance. It was, in particular, the prospect of a vertiginous spike in premiums that most concerned senior bureaucrats. As one federal Finance official put it, "The 15th Actuarial Report was a shock." According to another, "The projected pay-go rate of 14% freaked people out."² As one official recalled, referring to the likelihood that future workers and employers would be willing to pay a 14.2 percent rate, "We sat there and said, 'They're not going to do it.'" Like their counterparts in many industrialized countries, civil servants in the Canadian Finance Department were trained to think systematically about public programs in terms of their implications for state fiscal capacities over time (Savoie 1999). To these guardians of the public purse, the CPP looked like a fundamentally unsustainable state commitment, an insupportable burden on future payrolls that would only get harder to relieve the longer action was delayed.³

With top bureaucrats convinced of the need for reform, two factors made it likely that Finance Minister Paul Martin would take the issue seriously. First, while Martin had not entered office as a fiscal hawk, the broader economic environment of the early 1990s starkly dramatized for him the dangers of fiscal laxity. The federal budget deficit had mushroomed under the Progressive Conservative governments of the previous decade, bequeathing to the Liberals a gathering fiscal storm. When Martin initially responded with modest spending cuts in his 1994 budget, the reaction from the international financial community was quick and severe. Against the unsettling backdrop of the collapse of the Mexican peso, the *Wall Street Journal* deemed Canada "an honorary member of the Third World in the unmanageability of its debt problem," warning of the prospect of an IMF bailout and labeling the Canadian dollar a "basket-case currency" (Sesit and McGee 1995). As a run on the loonie brought Canada's currency to its lowest point against the greenback in over 8 years, the Bank of Canada responded with a rare 100-basis-point hike in interest rates. Rising interest rates, in turn, drove the government's debt charges ever higher, further increasing the size of the tax hikes and spending cuts that would ultimately be needed to restore fiscal balance. As a believer in the social good that an active state could do, Martin was dismayed to watch mounting interest payments crowd out program expenditures and became increasingly focused on the task of fiscal consolidation (Lewis 2003; Greenspon and Wilson-Smith 1996).

---

² First quotation from author's interview with a civil servant in the Department of Finance, Ottawa, January 31, 2002, under condition of anonymity. The second quotation comes from a former official at Human Resources Development Canada (HRDC) closely involved in the initial stages of reform: Alan Puttee, unpublished email, December 14, 1998. This account was confirmed by Don Drummond, (former Assistant Deputy Minister of Finance), interview with the author, Toronto, January 21, 2002; David Walker, (former Liberal MP who led the public consultation process on reform), interview with the author, Ottawa, January 25, 2002; in an interview with a second former official at HRDC who requested anonymity, Ottawa, January 31, 2002; and in the author's interview with two civil servants in the Ontario Ministry of Finance who also requested anonymity, Toronto, January 21, 2002.

³ This account derives from two sources within the Finance Department, a source within HRDC, and a senior Ontario source.

Second, the Finance Department was an institutional setting in which civil servants had an unusually high degree of influence over the agendas of their ministers. In mastering a brief that encompasses the entire range of government activity, finance ministers depend heavily on the experience and knowledge of career bureaucrats in identifying the issues to which they need to attend. As Donald Savoie has estimated, Canadian finance ministers spend between eight and thirty hours a week being briefed by officials, far more than their counterparts in spending departments (Savoie 1999). This relationship of informational dependence made the department an environment particularly conducive to the upward flow of ideas and agenda items from civil servant to minister.[4]

On matters of broad fiscal strategy, Martin's senior officials operated with an ideational economic framework that both made sense of Canada's crisis of market confidence and suggested a solution. In step with an intellectual trend throughout OECD bureaucracies, Canadian Finance officials had by the mid-1990s largely abandoned postwar Keynesian thinking in favor of more orthodox fiscal precepts inspired by monetarist and rational-expectations theories of economic behavior. According to the dominant outlook within the department, budget deficits would always exert a drag on economic growth because any demand stimulation would merely fuel inflation and trigger a painful rise in interest rates. In this mental model, economic recovery would depend on credible fiscal control. During the Liberals' first year in office, finance officials conveyed these causal understandings to their minister, schooling Martin intensively in the logic of conservative public economics.

The counsel of top advisors, reinforced by harrowing market developments, appears to have substantially reshaped Martin's perception of the fiscal dilemmas he confronted and reordered his policy priorities. By most accounts, the finance minister had by late 1994 undergone a dramatic conversion to the orthodoxy of fiscal discipline (Lewis 2003; Greenspon and Wilson-Smith 1996). His landmark 1995 budget would begin a stunning reversal of Canada's fiscal position over the course of the next decade, turning 20 years of deficits into a string of surpluses and a rapid pay-down of the federal debt. Restoring the confidence of financial markets, however, meant not only addressing Ottawa's current budget gap but also confronting *long-term* spending commitments that might threaten the state's fiscal capacities. Bond-rating agencies, as they revised downward their ratings and trend outlooks on Canada's federal debt, often cited the CPP's future troubles as a major cause for concern (Little 1995). As one Toronto credit analyst pointedly warned in 1995, "What I'm concerned about is that the government still has significant steps to take to control the cost of the OAS [Old Age Security] and Canada Pension [Plan], and there hasn't yet been any movement on those programs."[5]

---

[4] On the unusual status of Finance officials as compared with civil servants in other departments, see also Savoie (1990).

[5] Brian Miron, senior financial analyst at Dominion Bond Rating Service, quoted in Ferguson (1995).

DISTRIBUTIVE CONSTRAINT, INTERTEMPORAL OPPORTUNITY

Eager to reverse Canada's fiscal fortunes, Martin was receptive to his officials' arguments for addressing the CPP's long-range financing gap, and he authorized them to explore options for reform. One of the department's first steps was to begin consultations with those actors who would have to agree to any solution: provincial finance ministries. While power *within* Ottawa was highly centralized – Westminster institutions tended to grant the federal executive enormous leverage over parliament – the federal government's room for maneuver was often constrained by an unusually decentralized form of federalism. In the case of the CPP, the program's highly restrictive amendment rules, adopted in 1965, required the agreement of Ottawa and the governments of two-thirds of the provinces representing two-thirds of the country's population for any changes to take effect. This rule not only gave an effective veto to any four provinces; it also gave Ontario (the most populous) by itself, or Quebec (the second-most-populous) plus one additional province, the power to block change. Moreover, although Quebec operated its own provincial pension plan outside the CPP, the two schemes could not easily go their separate ways. In order to maintain labor mobility across the country, federal policymakers needed to ensure that the Canada and Quebec Pension Plans retained closely equivalent tax and benefit provision. Aside from the amendment rules, this policy logic thus gave Quebec politicians an effective veto over changes to the CPP.

As negotiations began, provincial finance ministers did not seriously contest the need to close the financing gap.[6] They diverged, however, in their preferences over a possible solution. Intergovernmental negotiation did not simply provide an opportunity for the assertion of geographically specific demands: it also furnished a key avenue of access for social interests with a stake in the reform outcome. In bargaining with Ottawa, the government of each province sought not just to voice regional concerns but also to protect the welfare of the particular economic interests to which the party in power was most closely allied. At the provincial level, each government enjoyed high institutional insulation in the form of centralized policymaking authority. Each government was thus relatively free to represent the interests of those social groups to which the ruling party was most closely linked. The result was the presentation, by the two largest provinces, of starkly opposing long-term redistributive demands, reflecting the differing coalitions and distributive goals to which the two governing parties were committed.

Ontario's ruling Progressive Conservatives (PC) had come to power on a platform of drastic provincial tax cuts and spending reductions designed to boost job creation and economic growth. The party had especially strong, long-standing ties to Canada's business and financial-services community, which were heavily concentrated in the province (Heinzl 1996; Papp 1994). In line with these

---

[6] Senior Ontario government source, interview with author (Toronto, January 21, 2002).

coalitional commitments, the PC government now sought to defend the prospective interests of employers and the private-pension industry. As the province's business leaders had made clear, their favored approach to CPP reform would largely involve reductions in benefits by, for instance, raising the retirement age and slowing the indexation of benefits (Cohen 1993). Put differently, they favored a long-term redistributive solution that would place the burden of demographic change onto the backs of future pensioners. In its negotiations with Ottawa, the Ontario government likewise advocated solutions to the CPP's financial troubles based largely on shrinking long-run expenditures and limiting new revenues. Critically, Ontario Treasurer Ernie Eves drew a line in the sand on tax increases, insisting that the ultimate CPP contribution rate go no higher than 10 percent (Freeman 1996; Greenspon 1996b).[7]

In Quebec, on the other hand, the governing Parti Québécois (PQ) took a position consistent with its own, very different organizational and ideological commitments. Since its founding, this francophone-nationalist party had espoused a broadly social democratic philosophy, had crafted its appeals to the province's blue-collar workers, and enjoyed strong ties to the labor movement (Banting 1985). Though the party moved rightward in the face of fiscal pressures in the 1990s, it continued to link its fight for secession with collectivist values and to draw strong working-class support (Gagnon and Lachapelle 1996; Freeman 1995). As lower-income workers were among those most dependent on the public program's benefits, the PQ's stance on reform reflected the future distributive interests of a key segment of its partisan coalition. Moreover, the QPP (along with the investment funds that it generated) was a proud nationalist achievement and a symbol of French-Canadian economic independence. Consistent with this broad ideological orientation and organizational base, the Quebec government rejected proposals that would have raised the pension eligibility age or significantly scaled back benefits, favoring instead a hike in contribution rates.[8]

That the two veto-wielding provinces took such divergent and uncompromising distributive positions created a substantial hurdle to Ottawa's reform goals, greatly limiting the menu of feasible options. To be clear, these governments' positions did not simply constrain the reform possibilities in the short term. Each governing party sought to protect the *long-term* interests of the groups to which it was most closely allied: Ontario demanded that the payroll tax rate not exceed 10 percent for the entire actuarial projection period, and Quebec objected to substantial cuts in benefits even over the long run. To

---

[7] Ontario's negotiating position confirmed by David Walker, Liberal MP closely involved with reform, interview with author, Ottawa, January 25, 2002; and by a former HRDC official, interview with author, Ottawa, January 31, 2002.

[8] A former Quebec Finance official, requesting anonymity, explained the position taken by the Quebec government in an interview with the author, Quebec City, February 2, 2002. Quebec's position can also be followed through news reports during the negotiations, including Freeman (1995, 1996), and Séguin (1996). Its opposition to benefit cuts can be further inferred through a comparison of the Quebec government's consultation document with the *Information Paper* released by Ottawa and the other provinces.

satisfy both of these governments, the long-term payroll tax rate would have to be kept nearly a third below the level projected to be necessary to finance the current benefit schedule, but at the same time significant spending reductions were off the table. Viewed as a problem of distribution – of how to allocate the costs of reform between beneficiaries and contributors – the arithmetic of CPP reform was not promising.

What allowed Ottawa to thread this intergovernmental needle was the possibility of making trade-offs not just cross-sectionally but also *over time*. In seeking to minimize the pain of reform, Canada's policymakers enjoyed a significant advantage in acting on a problem that still lay some distance in the future. This time lag provided an opportunity to capitalize on the logic of compound interest, turning a given amount of short-run pain into a greater measure of long-run gain. Contribution increases or benefit cuts imposed in the near term – *before* the CPP actually ran out of money – would generate surpluses within the program that could then be invested in interest-bearing assets; as those returns compounded over time, they would then provide an additional source of revenue to help pay benefits as the baby boomers retired and the program's costs exploded. Put in other terms, a policy investment would allow policymakers to escape the budget constraint of a pure zero-sum distributive choice, generating a social profit that could be used to minimize the total costs that had to be imposed on beneficiaries and contributors over the long run.

Moreover, unlike legislators engaged in the U.S. reforms of the Carter and Reagan years, Canadian officials in 1995 thought explicitly about advance funding as a reform strategy. Indeed, Canada's reformers were acting in a very different intellectual environment than had policymakers in the United States in the late 1970s and early 1980s. While controversy over PAYGO financing and funding had been ongoing in economic journals since the mid-1970s,[9] arguments over the choice of financing method took time to filter into broader policymaking communities. As early-movers on pension reform, U.S. policymakers did not yet possess the conceptual tools to explicitly define the complex of measures that they adopted as a distinct financing mechanism. By the middle of the 1990s, however, influential organizations like the World Bank were aggressively promoting the merits of a deliberate transition to funded pensions, citing the potential benefits for government budgets, national savings rates, and economic productivity (e.g., World Bank 1994). As one IMF economist described the ideational shift:

During the 1980s, relatively little attention was paid to the possibility of changing the way in which public pensions were financed, and specifically to switching from PAYG[O] to funding. Move on to the mid-1990s and all the talk is about a switch to funding (Hemming 1999, 4).

---

[9] The seminal article challenging the wisdom of PAYGO arrangements was Feldstein (1974).

Finance officials in Ottawa saw a promising investment opportunity in a transition to greater funding. As a 1995 paper by Finance Department economists argued (James et al. 1995),[10] current rates of return to capital now made funding a particularly attractive option. When the CPP was first introduced, real wage growth surpassed real long-term interest rates by a wide margin. However, starting in the 1980s, as real wage growth slowed and real interest rates climbed, the relationship was reversed and PAYGO seemed increasingly unprofitable.[11] A switch to full funding of the CPP, the report argued, would require a sacrifice of 0.7 percent in present consumption, but over the next 50 years would boost national savings by 9.05 percent and GNP by 3.75 percent. While *full* funding might have been politically impractical, some measure of fund accumulation and investment in interest-bearing assets seemed to Finance officials a promising way to mitigate the dilemma framed by the Actuary's reports.[12]

In principle, a policy investment in funding could have taken place either through immediate cuts in benefit outlays or through a quick increase in CPP premiums. Significant short-term benefit reductions were politically impractical, however, since they would have meant defaulting on explicit commitments to millions of lifelong contributors already in retirement. Indeed, as the CPP debate was unfolding, Canadian seniors' organizations were flexing their political muscles by forcing Martin into embarrassing retreat over a planned overhaul of the country's other, general-revenue-financed pension programs, OAS and the Guaranteed Income Supplement (Weaver 2003; Greenspon and Wilson-Smith 1996). Not even Margaret Thatcher had considered sharply cutting benefits for the elderly in the near term. Any realistic move to funding would thus have to rely largely on a short-run hike in the pension *tax*, raising contribution revenues above the level needed to pay benefits for the next couple of decades.

Fortunately, Ontario's 10-percent line in the sand on contribution rates still allowed substantial scope for maneuver – room above the current 5.6 percent PAYGO rate. As actuarial calculations indicated, however, it would only be possible to close the CPP's financing gap without either large benefit cuts or a breach of the 10-percent tax ceiling if two conditions were met. First, contribution rates would have to be raised to this cap *quickly:* in the logic of compound interest, a crucial parameter is the length of time over which returns are earned, placing a premium on early savings. Second, the CPP's current investment practice – lending to the provinces at below-market interest rates – would have to change. Rather than placing pension funds in provincial bonds, Ottawa would have to seek maximal returns – on a par with those achieved by private pension funds – by investing the program's assets on open financial markets.

[10] The report was produced by the Department's Economic Studies and Policy Analysis Division.

[11] For the seminal formulation of this argument, see Aaron (1966)

[12] Author interviews with two federal Finance officials (requesting anonymity) in Ottawa, January 31, 2002.

The prospect of reaping these returns over time nonetheless suggested an important opportunity. Chosen from a limited menu of options, this strategy would not correspond to any government or social group's first choice, and would inflict substantial short-run pain on both workers and business. Yet it allowed Ottawa to present provincial governments and their interest-group allies with a long-term improvement over the status quo: a reform that would keep short-run costs within each coalition's zone of acceptability while averting much larger losses for each over the long run.

JUSTIFYING THE PAIN

Even if policy investment could protect the long-term interests of politically influential groups, it might still have run short-term electoral risks for the incumbents who enacted it. An intertemporal solution that threaded the Ontario-Quebec needle would require imposing quick and substantial costs on large numbers of voters. And, since the program was generally viewed by the public as a federal responsibility, the electorate would most likely attribute any pain associated with reform to Ottawa, not to the provinces; it was thus the federal Liberals who potentially ran the greatest political risk in adopting a costly investment.

A number of factors, however, helped to protect incumbents against the prospect of voter backlash. For one thing, the federal Liberals enjoyed a substantial electoral cushion. They had won a large majority in the 1993 election and held an impressive lead in the polls as the CPP reform was being formulated. More significantly, the conservative camp had split into two federal parties at the last election, and were running candidates against one another within districts; under Canada's first-past-the-post electoral rules, this division on the right would give the center-left Liberals a built-in advantage.[13]

This is not to say that the Liberals could completely ignore the electoral costs of their policy choices. The last vote, in 1993, had been an "earthquake" election that fundamentally destabilized the existing party system – generating not only a rupture on the right, but the emergence of a formidable federal sovereigntist party in Quebec. Notwithstanding its opponents' past failures of coordination, the Liberals could not be too certain how voters would coalesce around parties in this still-fluid environment at the next election. Economic conditions also suggested potential trouble: the unemployment rate, though declining, remained high, hovering above 9.5 percent, and per capita disposable income was falling (Nevitte 1999). The policy investment that the government would ultimately adopt would itself reduce disposable incomes substantially, nearly doubling the pension taxes that workers and employers would pay within the space of 6 years.

---

[13] Despite a popular vote total equal to the Liberals' in 1997, the two conservative parties together won only half as many seats. The Liberals faced their own challenge on their left flank from the social democratic NDP. But it was this much smaller party that paid the costs of division, winning only 7 percent of seats with 11 percent of the popular vote.

Given these large near-term costs, federal politicians took elaborate measures to justify policy investment to the public. From April to June of 1996, the federal Finance Department held a series of 33 public meetings across Canada to which it invited representatives of a wide range of affected groups – seniors, youth, business, taxpayers, women, and labor – along with private pension professionals and social policy experts. The forums, carefully orchestrated by Martin's parliamentary secretary, provided an opportunity for the government to raise the salience of the CPP's long-term problems, to get key stakeholders on the record acknowledging these challenges, and to frame the key dilemmas for citizens.

In this endeavor, the Finance Department enjoyed a crucial advantage in the informational environment within which it was operating – in particular, in the availability of clear, dramatic, and undisputed information about the long-term consequences of policy alternatives. In broad terms, public discourse in Canada in the mid-1990s was already saturated with concern about the long-run sustainability of the country's fiscal arrangements. Substantial public attention to the size of the federal budget deficit was, in fact, a new and rare development. As recently as the summer of 1994, fewer than one in five Canadians had told pollsters that the deficit was the problem that should receive the most attention from government. But by February of 1995 – for the first time ever – Angus Reid reported that the deficit had jumped to first place, with half of respondents mentioning it as the problem most in need of a solution (Greenspon and Wilson-Smith 1996).

While the problem itself had not changed much in the intervening months, the *signals* that voters were receiving from the media and political elites had (Lewis 2003; Savoie 1999). Though few voters closely tracked levels of government debt, they were led to focus on the problem by the behavior of *other* actors – especially, international investors and central bankers – who had strong incentives to pay careful attention to the sustainability of state finances. The *Wall Street Journal*'s dark prognosis – reprinted in major Canadian papers – and adverse market shocks set off a flurry of domestic media debate about the federal debt and deficit.[14] Partisan competition then served to amplify the bad news as the opposition found it useful to highlight the threat of economic collapse: the leader of the right-wing Reform Party, for instance, followed the *Journal*'s lead, calling Canada "a banana republic without the bananas."[15]

Thus, as federal and provincial finance officials were weighing a major policy investment in the CPP, Canadian voters witnessed a string of focusing events that dramatized the dire consequences of fiscal irresponsibility. This

---

[14] As just one measure of the public prominence of this event, an electronic search revealed 31 separate articles in 8 of Canada's largest urban English-language daily newspapers that referred directly to the *Wall Street Journal* article, including several reprints of the article, between January 11 and 31. Search for words "Wall Street Journal" AND "dollar." The search did not include the *Financial Post* or the *National Post*. Conducted online through Micromedia Proquest's *Globe and Mail* archives and through Proquest Historical Newspapers.

[15] Reform Party leader Preston Manning cited in Campbell and Boras (1995).

informational environment made it far easier for incumbents to justify the pain of fiscal consolidation: heightened awareness of Canada's precarious circumstances lent plausibility to the claim that financial pain today could prevent economic disaster tomorrow.

Moreover, the particular structure of the CPP made it much easier for governments to credibly link policy investment in the program to the avoidance of a specific set of negative consequences. Like Social Security in the United States – and unlike the British and German pension schemes – the CPP lived completely off of its own contribution revenues, with no subsidy from the general budget. It was thus a program that could technically run out of money if its own, dedicated flow of resources failed to keep pace with its spending commitments. It was, of course, impossible for a public program to literally go bankrupt, but the conceit of self-financing helped crystallize an enormous amount of policy complexity into simple messages about long-run consequences. It enabled the CPP Chief Actuary's reports to transmit authoritative signals about future outcomes that were inherently meaningful to voters – indicating, for instance, whether the program would have sufficient funds to pay future benefits, or the size of future tax burdens that would be required to pay those benefits.

Precise information about long-term outcomes greatly boosted politicians' capacities to frame the reform in loss-avoiding terms: as short-term sacrifice in exchange for the avoidance of even greater long-term pain. A glance at the content of the governments' public consultations suggests how such information enabled reform advocates to structure the debate. For one thing, actuarial authority and the logic of self-financing allowed reformers to state with apparent certainty a set of clear and meaningful long-term consequences of doing nothing. As the Information Paper issued by Ottawa and the provinces to guide public discussion formulated the problem:

- CPP contribution rates are already legislated to increase in the years ahead, and will have to be increased even more. If nothing is done, rates will reach 14.2 percent by 2030.
- How high can the rates go before they become unaffordable? beyond the limits of fairness? (Federal, Provincial, and Territorial Governments of Canada 1996, 46)

Wielding a credible and specific measure of future financial loss, reformers could pose the central issues in a way that took this long-term outcome for granted. The question was not what would happen if governments failed to act; the simplifying lens of actuarial projection allowed politicians to narrow debate to whether the negative consequence of inaction was *acceptable* as a matter of affordability and fairness.

More broadly, the structure of the CPP, and the insurance logic that it reinforced, helped to frame the policy problem in ways favorable to an investment in funding. In principle, the challenge of state pension financing in the context of an aging population could be understood in a diverse range of ways. For instance, demographic change could be treated as a fundamental problem of resource scarcity, with the number of producers projected to fall relative to the number of nonproducing consumers. Alternatively, policymakers might define the problem as one of inadequate rates of national savings and thus insufficient levels of investment in future productive capacities. Or the difficulty could be understood primarily in distributive terms as a challenge of mounting tax burdens.

The CPP's strict contributory financing regime, however, and its widely accepted status as an "insurance" program, strongly encouraged a distinctive and far narrower understanding of the policy challenge – as the need to eliminate a long-run imbalance between a program's revenues and its expenditures. This actuarial view of the problem, in turn, dramatically simplified debate about the long-term effects of a policy investment in funding. What might be the long-run consequences of an immediate increase in contribution rates to generate higher levels of funding within the CPP? In the full complexity of economic reality, the distant consequences of funding a public pension program would depend on an intricate web of economic and social interactions. The relevant ramifications would include the effects of the current tax increase and of public fund accumulation and asset investment itself on (among other things) levels of private savings, rates of return to capital, levels of real domestic investment, labor productivity, and governments' taxing and spending decisions elsewhere in the budget.[16] The direction and magnitude of each of these causal relationships was, of course, imperfectly understood, and a full assessment of the economic and social effects of funding would have been shot through with uncertainty.

The actuarial logic of contributory insurance, in contrast, allowed the federal and provincial governments to reduce a highly complicated choice problem to a relatively tidy intertemporal trade-off. If the broad economic effects of funding were ambiguous, its implications for the finances of the pension scheme itself were far more easily represented. As the public consultation document framed the choice, Canadians had to decide how they wanted to distribute the program's financing burden over time:

If pay-as-you-go financing is left in place, future generations of Canadians will be paying 14.2 percent of contributory earnings for their CPP benefits – much more than the 5.6 percent that today's workers are paying. The advantage of pay-as-you-go financing would be that the increase to 14.2 percent could be gradual – taking place over many years. However, it fails to deal with the fundamental challenge of whether it is either reasonable or fair to expect younger generations to pay such high contribution rates. . . . The financing of the CPP can be strengthened by ensuring that today's working Canadians pay a fairer share of CPP costs. Raising contributions more quickly now would ease some of the contribution burden that will otherwise be passed on to future generations of workers. This would not only be fairer across generations – it would also make the CPP more sustainable for future participants (Federal, Provincial, and Territorial Governments of Canada 1996, 26–27).

---

[16] For a review of the economic debate on the complex effects of pension funding, see Barr (2000).

Moreover, the choice was not just pain now versus pain later; rather, as the paper argued, the costs of adjustment would be *lower* the earlier they were paid. In the actuarial logic of compound interest, any surpluses generated within the program today could be invested to produce even greater returns for the program over time. With the problem framed narrowly as one of balancing a program account at minimal expense, officials found it far easier to focus public attention on a strikingly simple – and relatively attractive – intertemporal proposition: as the discussion paper put it, "increasing contributions now to avoid even higher contributions later" (46). Indeed, throughout the reform process, public discussion of the broader economic effects of a move toward funding was extremely limited, with debate focused narrowly on its effects on program taxes and benefits (Pesando 2001).

Politicians typically seek to frame their preferred policy options in ways calculated to generate public support or disarm opposition, but not all potential frames are equally plausible in every policy context. In Canada in the mid-1990s, the information available to the public, partly structured by the character of the CPP itself, made persuasive a framing of the pension problem that was highly favorable to policy investment: a framing in which pain today would, with a high degree of certainty, avoid even greater pain tomorrow. The terms on which the CPP debate had taken place would later allow Martin credibly to claim, as he introduced the bill in the Commons, "The proposed changes will ensure the plan's financial sustainability and make it fairer and more affordable for future generations of Canadians" (McCarthy 1997b). Polls taken before and after reform suggest that the government's strategy of persuasion worked. One pair showed a large jump in the proportion of Canadians who were confident that they would receive their CPP benefits, from 44 percent six months before the passage of legislation to 67 percent five months after.[17] It is, of course, never easy for elected officials to impose visible new costs on constituents in the near term. But for Canada's governing Liberals, the informational context of reform – together with the strategic advantage of a divided right – made the electoral risks of policy investment relatively modest.

To summarize the account so far, a policy investment based mostly on quick increases in the contribution rate would allow the Liberal government to reform the CPP without imposing unacceptable losses on workers, employers, or current senior citizens. In an institutional context in which no group could unilaterally achieve its first-choice option – by redistributing the full burden of adjustment onto others – a transition to greater funding promised to protect each group against the likelihood of devastating long-term loss at acceptable

---

[17] The results refer to two similar polls conducted by Gallup for the Investors Group (Mabell 1998). Polling conducted for Canada Imperial Bank of Commerce showed a decline in the numbers who thought the CPP would *not* be there for them, from 45 percent in fall 1997 (pre-reform) to 36 percent in January 1999 (post-reform). These two pairs of figures are particularly telling, coming as they do from an industry with a large incentive to highlight the uncertainties surrounding the CPP's benefit promises (Marron 1998).

near-term expense. Indeed, the most influential business organizations and the Canadian Labour Congress expressed broad support for the idea of a quick increase in payroll taxes to stabilize the burden and secure the program's finances over the long run (Federal/Provincial/Territorial CPP Consultations Secretariat 1996). From the view of elected incumbents, it also appeared possible to implement such an investment without a backlash at the polls.

INVESTING AT ARMS-LENGTH

Yet the case for policy investment was still potentially vulnerable on another front: groups' intertemporal calculations depended on their taking as credible the policy investment's promise of long-term benefits. Though investment could *in principle* ease the actuarial arithmetic of CPP financing, its long-term benefits would depend on how safely the massive reserves to be accumulated would be dedicated to their long-term purpose. If today's employers and workers paid the costs of investment today, what was to prevent future governments from using the resulting fund for other programmatic purposes? And what would keep tomorrow's politicians from wielding this vast pool of public capital as an instrument of social or economic policy as they invested it on Canada's financial markets?

A striking feature of the debate over CPP reform is that interest-group and political leaders did *not* prominently voice concerns that the future fund might be spent on purposes other than those for which it was intended – either diverted toward other programs or used in unplanned ways to raise pension benefits or cut pension taxes. In the public consultations, in newspaper reports and editorials, and in my own interviews a few years following the enactment of reform, no participant in the reform process raised the specter of a misappropriation of the invested resources.

Why, as they considered amassing an enormous fund over the course of several decades, did actors express so little concern about how future governments might spend the money? A glance at the politics of another social insurance program suggests that the *overall* credibility of government promises was not especially high. In the mid-1990s, as Canada's Unemployment Insurance (UI) program was running large surpluses, this buildup of programmatic resources aroused deep suspicion. While the Finance Minister argued that such surpluses were necessary to cushion the program against economic fluctuations, employers, labor unions, provincial governments, and opposition politicians routinely argued that Martin was maintaining unnecessarily large reserves merely to make the government's overall fiscal position look better and ease spending elsewhere (Greenspon 1996a, 1996c).

The proposal to amass enormous surpluses within the CPP, however, provoked no comparable criticism by key policy actors, no charges of potential budgetary gimickry or diversion. One important difference lay in the nature of the two programs' financing structures. Both insurance schemes were financed through earmarked taxes funneled directly into program accounts. But unlike the CPP fund, the UI fund was a part of the government's consolidated budget. This conflation of accounts gave federal politicians, seeking to reduce public borrowing or raise spending on other priorities, both motive and opportunity to raise UI premiums or cut UI benefits for reasons that had nothing to do with the program's stated purposes. By contrast, not only was the CPP off-budget – never counted as part of the federal government's overall fiscal position – but the 1998 reform was explicitly designed to remove the CPP's fund even further from political control than it had been for its first 30 years in operation. As discussed in Chapter 6, prior to 1998 all CPP surpluses were lent to the provinces at below-market rates, a practice occasionally criticized as a hidden subsidy of provincial budgets. If invested on open capital markets, however – as federal and provincial Finance officials were now planning – the fund would be structurally unavailable for use in financing other state activities. Moreover, the CPP's longstanding amendment rules – requiring a special supermajority of the provinces to change policy – made the program exceptionally difficult to change (Banting 1987). For future politicians to spend the accumulated fund on benefit enhancements or premium reductions would require them to achieve unusually broad consensus across federal and provincial governments, including rightward-leaning Ontario and leftward-leaning Quebec.

Historical experience of pension politics within the Canadian federation also lent these commitment structures substantial credibility. The original 1965 law had placed the program on a partially funded basis, and those funds had never been reappropriated toward other programmatic purposes. And despite substantial social and political pressures for expansion, the CPP's benefit formula and scope had remained largely unchanged since 1965. The so-called "Great Pension Debate" of the late 1970s and early 1980s – which saw the release of more than fifteen reports by major public bodies on reform of old-age programs, many pressing for expansion – resulted in no change in the CPP until 1987, and then only a modest increase in disability and early retirement benefits and an urgently needed revision of the contribution rate schedule. As a result of the program's obduracy, federal parties did not even bother to campaign on promises of boosting CPP benefits, in sharp contrast to the competitive strategies of U.S., British, and German politicians. In other words, both the structure of the CPP and cognitively available historical experience would have dampened any fears among Canadian actors that funds accumulated within the CPP might be diverted or misspent.

Yet recent, domestic policy history did make salient a somewhat different risk of the planned policy investment: the possibility that the fund might be *invested* for purposes other than the pure maximization of returns. What Canadian business groups and conservatives feared most was not that governments would drain the fund, but rather that they would wield it on financial markets for political or social purposes (Pesando 2001). As Ottawa and the provinces made clear that they were seriously considering partial funding and investment in equities, opposition politicians and pundits warned of this danger. As one *Globe and Mail* commentator put the problem, "Do we really want some $200-billion government-run pension fund running amok in the nation's capital markets" (Coyne 1996)? Much of the concern about public asset-investment derived from the experience of the CPP's Quebec counterpart, the QPP, which had long invested its own funds on private markets. Indeed, the promotion of a francophone industrial base had originally been one of the Quebec government's primary reasons for partially funding the QPP (see Chapter 6). For Lesage's Quiet Revolutionaries, funding was less an instrument of prudent pension financing than a means of creating a large pool of capital that could be used for public province-building purposes. Unsurprisingly, many on the right had routinely critiqued the Caisse de Dépôt et placement du Québec – the QPP's investment arm – arguing that its choices of assets were often made on the basis of social or political goals rather than maximization of returns for contributors.

When governments in the mid-1990s proposed allowing the CPP to invest on private markets, many drew the obvious parallel. As one Progressive Conservative parliamentarian warned:

The potential for abuse is enormous. The president of the [CPP] investment board will have powers that are almost equal to the Prime Minister's. We saw how a pension plan could abuse today or down the road, its powers two years ago, when the Caisse de Dépôt et placement du Québec went to the market and propped up the Canadian dollar to the tune of $5 billion or $6 billion.[18]

Another declared his "concerns with any potential government interference with the management and investment practices of a fund which will, in a very few years, accumulate over $100-billion in assets."[19] One of the right-wing Reform Party's chief lines of attack was to argue that the CPP reserve would quickly become an economic development fund wielded for partisan purposes (Greenspon 1997b).

Importantly, the response of business groups to emerging reform plans suggested that they had no fundamental objection to the reform's core intertemporal proposition or to market investment of the fund. Indeed, most employer organizations welcomed the federal-provincial proposal as a way of stabilizing long-run contribution burdens (Gibb-Clark 1997; Little 1996). Rather, industry was specifically concerned about the robustness of the mechanisms that would tie future governments' hands and called for ironclad institutional safeguards that would minimize the risk of political interference.[20] As one banker told the *Globe and Mail,* he was concerned about public ownership of private stock, but, "If I could be assured that it was totally independent and that there was no input from the government at all, then I think I might at least be talked into partial use of the money [for private investment]" (Carrick 1997).

---

[18] Jim Jones, Progressive Conservative MP, House of Commons, Standing Committee on Finance, 36th Parliament, 1st Session, Meeting 33, October 29, 1997. For similar critiques, see also Coyne (1996), Frum (1997), or Nankivell (1997).

[19] Senator Michael Meighen quoted in Feschuk (1997).

[20] See also Federal/Provincial/Territorial CPP Consultations Secretariat (1996) and Chamber of Commerce testimony in House of Commons, Standing Committee on Finance, 36th Parliament, 1st Session, Meeting 44, October 29, 1997.

Federal officials thus went to great lengths to address fears of political interference through their design of the new CPP Investment Board (CPPIB). An important part of this design process was a series of public and private consultations with the investment and pension communities about how to create robust governance structures that would protect the interests of beneficiaries in maximizing returns. The accounts of participants suggest that Finance officials listened carefully to financial experts' advice in crafting the CPPIB structure and writing its rules and amended early drafts in response to criticism from the investment community.[21]

Among the most important mechanisms by which the federal government bound the hands of future incumbents were the following provisions:

1. The broad investment policy of the board was to be set by an independent Board of Directors. The nomination process for the twelve Board members contained several checks on political manipulation. First, the selection process was to be staggered, with only three Board members named in a given year, each serving a three-year term. Second, the selection of members was to be mediated by a nominating committee, appointed by the provincial finance ministers (naming one member each) and the federal finance minister (appointing the chair). This committee would draw up a list of board candidates from which the Finance Minister could choose three names. As a further check on manipulation by Ottawa, these three choices would then have to be approved by the provincial finance ministers.

2. According to the Act, Board members had to have sufficient business, financial, or economic experience to carry out their duties, signaling that the Board was to be a professional, rather than a representative, body.

3. Management of the fund was then separated from the Board. The Board would appoint a President who would hire the management team, which would make specific investment decisions in line with Board policies. Managers were to be compensated according to their performance.

4. The Board was to be subject to the same investment and conflict-of-interest rules and definitions of directors' fiduciary responsibilities that legally govern Canadian occupational pension funds. This included a "prudent person" standard and a requirement to invest solely for the purpose of maximizing returns and in the "best interests" of contributors and beneficiaries.

---

[21] For instance, when investment experts warned that an early text gave too much power to ministers to direct the Board's investment decisions, Finance officials tightened the rules, eliminating the power of the finance minister and provinces to issue specific investment directives. On this revision, see McCarthy (1997a). The influence of the financial and pension interests' advice in shaping the CPPIB's legislation and regulations was confirmed by Larry Weatherley (chief of the Government Finance Section in the Financial Markets Division of the federal Finance Department), interview with the author, Ottawa, January 31, 2002; Drummond, interview with the author; and Keith Ambachtsheer (pension consultant), interview with the author, Toronto, January 30, 2002.

5. For its first few years, the Board would be required to invest the CPP fund passively, tracking the composition of a broad market index of shares.
6. Amendments to the above rules, like amendments to the CPP Act, would require the consent of two-thirds of the provinces representing two-thirds of the population.

In part, these rules represented a set of Madisonian checks and balances, dispersing power according to a logic familiar to students of constitutional design. And in doing so, it built upon the existing constitutional dispersion of authority in the Canadian federation. More than that, however, the fiduciary framework explicitly emulated a private-sector model of governance that was considered legitimate and credible to industry and financial actors. Not only was the language of the Act written to mirror those governing private pensions, but the rules were designed to ensure that the professional profile of the directors and managers who were making CPP investment decisions would resemble those of the management of most occupational pension funds. These were structures, that is, designed to look especially robust when viewed through the conceptual lens of private-sector finance and investment.

By structurally removing the investment board so far from political control, the federal Liberals greatly reduced the political costs of policy investment. Had corporate and financial interests been alarmed by the proposed new investment policy, they would likely have supported conservative attacks on the fund. A concerted opposition and business attack would likely have threatened the support of the Ontario government, undermined public confidence in the reform, and raised the electoral risks of pursuing it. In the end, rather than assailing its vulnerabilities, business groups lauded the structure of the new investment regime. The Canadian Chamber of Commerce told the House of Commons' Finance Committee that it "welcome[d] the proposed establishment of an arm's length investment strategy,"[22] and the business-dominated Conference Board of Canada would later give the CPPIB its 2002 award for governance structures in a public body.

CONCLUSION

As adopted by the federal parliament and a supermajority of the provinces in 1998 – and as enacted in parallel for the QPP by the government of Quebec – Canada's reform represents one of the most ambitious investments in pension sustainability made by any government in the OECD in the last 30 years. The package was notable, in part, for the size of the short-term costs that it would impose on citizens. On the contribution side, the 1998 Act would raise the payroll tax rate to just below Ontario's limit – from 5.6 to 9.9 percent – in the

---

[22] Don McIver, representing Sun Life Insurance Company Canada and the Canadian Chamber of Commerce (House of Commons 1997, 1850).

space of just 6 years (Office of the Chief Actuary 1997).[23] This quick hike in revenues – equivalent to about half a percent of GDP over this period – would generate sufficient surpluses to close the vast majority of the scheme's long-term financing gap. The remainder of the savings would come from a package of modest, gradual benefit cuts that would reduce expenditures by 9.3 percent in 2030, bringing down the long-term contribution rate by 1.1 percentage points. By far the largest cut was a change in the formula by which benefits would be calculated for new pensioners, basing them on an average of pensionable earnings over the five years before retirement, instead of the previous three years.[24]

The 1998 package was also impressive for the magnitude of the long-term benefits that it was projected to confer on future generations of workers and retirees. As a result of the near-term austerity measures, annual CPP contribution revenues were projected to exceed expenditures until 2022, allowing a fund equal to five times annual outlays – and topping C$1 trillion by 2040 – to accumulate. Assuming that these assets could be invested at a 4 percent average real rate of return, the plan's Chief Actuary projected that the fund would generate sufficient earnings to allow the contribution rate to remain stable at 9.9 percent for a *century* – through 2100 – while benefit rates were maintained only marginally below their 1998 level.[25]

Achieving these long-run benefits depended, in turn, on a third feature of the reform that was unusual in cross-national perspective: its placement of the assets of a public pension program on private financial markets in order to maximize returns. Under the auspices of the new CPPIB, ordinary payroll tax revenues would now be invested by professional fund managers in a portfolio of stocks and bonds, just like the assets of any private or public-sector-employee pension plan. Indeed, the fact that the program's assets would now be placed on financial markets, rather than being lent to provincial governments, contributed substantially to the perceived security of the investment's long-term returns.

---

[23] The package also included a stealthy increase in revenues: the Year's Basic Exemption, the earnings level below which no contributions are paid, would be frozen in nominal terms, eventually wiping out its value. A description of the agreed changes and their impact can be found in Office of the Chief Actuary (1997).

[24] Because most workers retire at their peak wage level, extending this calculation period backwards by two years would slightly reduce their entitlements.

[25] The final deal worked out by the federal and provincial governments also involved a change to the Unemployment Insurance program. Ontario's Eves had demanded that Martin cut UI premiums to help offset higher pension payroll taxes, and Martin obliged with a token 0.1 percentage point reduction in the UI tax, at a cost of $700 million (Greenspon 1997a). The left-wing New Democratic Party governments of British Columbia and Saskatchewan, elected in the course of the reforms, did not officially sign on to the package. Late in the negotiation process, they put forward a plan that would have raised the wage base on which contributions were calculated instead of cutting benefits. This proposal was extremely unpopular among the other provinces because of its effect on middle- and upper-income earners. In the end, though the two provinces went on record with votes against the package (which did not jeopardize the required super-majority support), they kept their criticisms of the deal restrained out of a recognition that the CPP urgently needed adjustment.

Unlike the surpluses produced by the reforms to the U.S. Social Security program, the buildup of the CPP fund would occur completely off-budget and, thus, would not mask or facilitate higher levels of spending or borrowing elsewhere in the state sector. The reform would thus plausibly set in motion an intertemporal transfer of welfare via the mechanism of capital-creation – as it made new savings available for investment, by both private and public actors, in future productive capacities.

What allowed Canadian politicians to achieve such a substantial intertemporal transfer was a favorable combination of ideational, institutional, and informational conditions that enhanced expectations of long-term returns, eliminated the scope for redistributive alternatives, and minimized electoral risk. Put differently, dominant causal ideas, political institutions, and salient information structured the policy trade-off for officeholders, interests, and voters in the terms most favorable to policy investment: as a clear and relatively certain choice between losses today and far greater losses tomorrow.

Crucial in shaping officeholders' beliefs in the long-run benefits of investment were a set of causal understandings dominant within the lead government ministry. The longstanding view of the CPP as an "insurance" plan governed by actuarial principles lent credibility to the notion that the program faced "insolvency" and to a solution based on the accumulation of reserves. At the same time, orthodox fiscal ideas and a World Bank-inspired mental model of pension financing emphasized both the dangers of massive state liabilities and the long-run economic advantages of fund accumulation. The short-run pain of pension tax increases, in all of these views, could be reliably converted into greater long-term fiscal and economic gain.

Meanwhile, Canada's decentralized political institutions created a policy-making process with relatively low insulation from societal interests. The dispersion of effective veto power across a broad range of groups then structured the policy trade-off for organized actors in ways that favored an intertemporal over a redistributive solution. Like the U.S. reforms, the Canadian episode illustrates how a diffusion of policymaking authority can force social groups to internalize long-term policy consequences by preventing them from shifting the burden of future problems onto others. What Canada's business leaders (and their allies in Ontario's government) would have most preferred was a solution that imposed the costs of demographic change on future beneficiaries through gradual reductions in pension entitlements; labor and beneficiary groups (and their allies in Quebec's government), in contrast, favored a strategy that kept benefits intact while allowing payroll taxes to rise over time. Had a single party of either the right or the left wielded concentrated authority over the outcome – as in Thatcher's Britain – the resulting reform would likely have effected a long-term, cross-sectional redistribution of burdens in favor of that party's group allies.

With institutional influence spread widely, however, the major stakeholders in the field each enjoyed the capacity to block change and, thus, none wielded sufficient influence to unilaterally impose it. As in the U.S. cases, the wide dispersion of veto power meant that no group could achieve its long-term goals through purely redistributive means. The only politically feasible alternative in this context of distributive stalemate was a reform that spread the pain widely. And, for either labor or business, simply blocking change would have meant paying very high costs in the long run as the CPP hit the financial wall – forcing some combination of skyrocketing tax burdens or devastating future cuts in benefits. With each group forced to internalize a large share of the costs and benefits of the policy output, a vertical policy investment looked like an attractive trade-off in *relative* terms: while it meant higher short-run losses for capital and labor than the status quo, the reform would capitalize on the logic of compound interest to avoid the far greater long-term losses that these groups could expect to face under current policy.

Meanwhile, the structure of the CPP itself supplied powerful informational tools for federal politicians eager to remain in office. When Canadian politicians sought to justify the pain of reform, they were aided by a financing structure that was highly *inelastic:* one that generated a relatively clear and precise relationship between current policy choices and future outcomes that were inherently meaningful to most citizens. Most importantly, as a scheme fed by a single dedicated revenue source, the CPP could in principle run out of money to pay benefits – a possibility that opened up a powerful persuasive option for Canadian politicians. The "negativity bias" characterizing voters' judgments and information-processing makes it perilous for politicians to seek to impose visible losses on constituents even while delivering offsetting policy benefits (Pierson 1994; Vonk 1993; Weaver 1986; Lau 1985). The prospect of insolvency, however, evened the cognitive scales: with actuarial projections of program bankruptcy in hand, Canadian ministers could credibly frame their investment as an exercise in loss-avoidance – as the imposition of modest costs today to avoid policy disaster tomorrow.

We might further observe that the Canadian reform episode suggests an important role for institutional structure – in addition to ideas – in shaping perceptions of long-term uncertainty. The structure of the CPP as a completely off-budget vehicle lent credibility to arguments that its accumulated fund would remain untouched. The decentralization of authority within the Canadian federation also helped considerably to dampen fears of political manipulation of the new fund. While business organizations and conservatives worried about placing so much capital in public hands, Canada's fragmented constitutional arrangements provided the structural ingredients for a solution. Two of the most important mechanisms of hand-binding built into the reform – the multistage, arms-length appointment process for Investment Board members and the super-majoritarian amendment procedure – were made possible by the decentralized federal context within which the reform was enacted. Had policymakers in Britain sought to similarly limit a public investment authority, they would have lacked constitutional *terra firma* in which to anchor their constraints: in a unitary, Westminster context, tomorrow's central-government majority could ultimately revise any arrangement chosen today. Canada's reformers, however, were able to leverage that country's unwieldy multilevel governance structure, with its formidable obstacles to coordination, into a diffusion of investment authority and an entrenchment of investment rules. While the availability of institutional tools was structurally determined, however, the *credibility* of these hand-binding mechanisms rested on important ideational foundations: in their plausibility, the rules constraining the investment board piggybacked on the perceived credibility of the private-sector arrangements on which it was modeled. Actors' perceptions of long-term policy consequences thus seem to have depended on an interplay between dominant ideas and structural context – a causal dynamic that I consider further in the book's concluding chapter.

CHAPTER 10

Constrained by Uncertainty

Reforming German Pensions, 1989 and 2001[1]

In few countries have the objective pressures for pension reform been as strong as in Germany. On one level, demographic change is expected to hit Germany earlier and harder than most other industrialized countries. At the same time, the 1990s brought unusually high and sustained levels of unemployment, especially in the former East, combined with high rates of early retirement. Together, demographic and economic forces have pushed total social-insurance tax rates – contributions for pensions as well as health care and unemployment insurance – to unprecedented levels: by the end of the 20th century, they would add 40 percent to employers' total wage bill. Moreover, with the pension program financed partly out of general revenues, the scheme's financial difficulties began to place mounting demands on the federal budget just as Economic and Monetary Union was placing tight limits on European Union member states' deficit levels. As Germany's economic woes deepened, the country's ideological climate also began to shift, with the postwar social-market consensus giving way to conflict over the fundaments of social policy. With increasing persistence and persuasive effect, German business organizations, economic institutes, and reformist politicians insisted that the country could no longer compete on world markets or generate jobs unless it scaled back its generous, status-preserving welfare state.

As a result of these combined strains, the domestic policy agenda in West and unified Germany has, since the mid-1980s, been increasingly dominated by efforts to reform the welfare state. In this chapter, we will consider the two most significant reforms of the pension system from this period: one adopted in 1989 by the center-right government of Helmut Kohl, the other enacted in 2001 by the center-left government of Gerhard Schröder.

From a certain perspective, the political conditions for policy investment would seem to have been especially propitious in these cases. In particular, Germany's

---

[1] Archival records cited here are found in the Bundesarchiv-Koblenz (BArch). For German-language sources quoted here in English, all translations are mine. Parts of this chapter draw on Jacobs (2009a).

traditional social policymaking structures should have been an ideal setting for the formulation of farsighted policies. Traditions of cross-party coopera- tion and neo-corporatist policymaking – including routine consultation and collaboration with employer and trade-union umbrella organizations – should have allowed German governments to achieve broad consensus on the wisdom of trading short-term pain for long-term gain. The central role of experts in these relatively closed-door deliberative processes ought to have favored the consideration of important but temporally distant problems. And the tradi- tional role of the social partners in administering Germany's social insurance funds ought to have enhanced the credibility of any investment that relied on the accumulation of capital within the system: those who paid the costs of investment would be able to play a direct role in safeguarding its implementation.

Yet policy investment has played only a modest role in German pension reform over the last two decades. The reformers of 1989 responded to long- term financing problems with pure distributive adjustment, relieving some of the burden on future contributors by reducing long-term benefit levels. The changes imposed minimal costs in the near term and would involve no fund accumulation within the pension program. The Schröder government's reform in 2001 included a modest dose of policy investment, a state subsidy of voluntary contributions to supplemental, private retirement accounts. But far more ambi- tious ministerial plans for the creation of a new funded pillar of compulsory private pensions were shelved, and the reform included substantial long-term benefit cuts.

Though both reforms favored redistributive over intertemporal solutions, I will argue that the causal forces constraining investment in 2001 were very different from those that impeded investment in 1989. In the 1980s, while policymakers enjoyed the electoral and institutional preconditions for an inter- temporal trade-off, the dominant causal model of pension financing emphasized the dangers to which policy investment would be subject and minimized its potential advantages. In the second episode, although the intellectual environ- ment had now shifted in favor of funded pensions, a new polarization of social politics left ministers with little electoral room for maneuver and modest institu- tional capacity to impose the short-term costs that policy investment required. We turn first to the landmark reform of 1989.

ELITE-DRIVEN DELIBERATIONS (1989)

In the mid-1980s, actuaries were projecting that the state pension system faced a spectacular deterioration in its finances over the following four decades: by 2030, either contribution rates would have to double from 18 to 36 percent, or benefit levels would have to be cut in half (Hinrichs 2003). Indeed, the system would come under serious strain well within the lifetime of a large share of West German voters. Yet, if the actuaries' message was a dire one, it took a form that was unlikely to attract the attention of the average citizen in the near future.

In the short term, with employment levels rising and demographic ratios temporarily improving, contribution rates were expected to remain stable, and current pension promises were not threatened (Jochem 1999).

Furthermore, the structure of the German pension program itself dampened the salience of the available information about future financial conditions. Because the scheme received a regular infusion of general revenues – a buffer between contribution intake and outlays – it was not subject to the same iron logic of financial balance and solvency that governed the U.S. and Canadian retirement programs. Since the program could be subsidized via the federal budget, West German actuaries could not refer to a date by which the pension fund would be exhausted in the absence of reform. While indicators of financial difficulty were available, the information did not take a form likely to draw citizens' notice – such as a forecast of financial incapacity to pay pension entitlements. Indeed, surveys from the period indicate little public attention to retirement issues on the whole: the percentage of Politbarometer respondents listing pensions or old age as the country's most or second-most important policy problem never rose above 18.5 percent between 1986 and 1988, always substantially outranked by unemployment and environmental problems (both represented by much more vivid information including, for the latter, the Chernobyl nuclear disaster).[2]

The policymaking process leading to the 1989 reform (embodied in the 1992 Pension Act) was triggered not by public demands or electoral pressure but by elite concern about the long-term financial strains on the system. In a quintessential instance of top-down agenda setting, pension experts within the main stakeholder interest organizations, the main political parties, and the Labor Ministry initiated the reform process and chose its direction. The social partners played an especially important role in driving deliberations forward. Policymaking and administration in the field of pensions had traditionally displayed a strongly neo-corporatist character, with representatives of employer and trade union associations granted a central role in overseeing the system's finances and evaluating policy options. In the mid-1980s, leaders of both capital and labor agreed that the pension scheme was on an unsustainable course. For Germany's large export-oriented manufacturing sector, contribution rates projected to climb past 30 percent represented a mounting nonwage labor cost that would threaten their ability to compete on world markets. From labor's perspective, a crushing payroll-tax burden would likely threaten job growth, diminish take-home wages, and undermine the political foundations of the scheme's basic intergenerational bargain.

Starting in 1985, the reform initiative moved through a series of consultative arenas largely shielded from public view. First, a working group of employer, trade union, and Labor Ministry representatives began to contemplate ways of

---

[2] Forschungsgruppe Wahlen (Mannheim), "Politbarometer West [Germany], Partial Accumulation, 1977–1998," 2nd ICPSR version (Köln, Germany: Zentralarchiv fuer Empirische Sozialforschung [producer], Köln, Germany: Zentralarchiv fuer Empirische Sozialforschung/Ann Arbor, MI: Interuniversity Consortium for Political and Social Research [distributors], 2000).

moderating the long-term rise in pension contribution rates, expected to double within the next 40 years. From this working group, proposals moved to a reform commission within the Federation of German Pension Insurance Institutes, a neo-corporatist umbrella organization representing all of the country's *Land*-level pension insurance bodies. In 1988, deliberations then shifted into the state arena, with the formation of a committee representing the members of the governing coalition – the Christian Democratic Union, Christian Social Union, and Free Democratic Party. Finally, the government engaged in consultations with the Social Democratic opposition, who agreed to co-sponsor the bill in the lower house of parliament (Jochem 1999). The law that emerged was thus the product of what Karl Hinrichs (1998) has called a "double grand coalition," reflecting consensus both across interest organizations and across the largest political parties (Nullmeier and Rüb 1993).

In many respects, the stage would seem to have been set for a substantial policy investment in the sustainability of the pension program's finances. For one thing, the process was dominated by actors with unusually long time horizons. In the absence of any immediate crisis, interest-group, ministry, and party leaders were devoting scarce time and organizational resources to addressing a problem that was still many years away. Moreover, given relatively low insulation of the policymaking process – the institutionalized access of a broad range of interests – neither labor nor business groups could have unilaterally redistributed and externalized the long-run costs of demographic change. Within prevailing neo-corporatist, consensual patterns of social policymaking, employers could not have won a sufficiently deep cut in benefits to stabilize contribution rates; nor could labor have achieved the massive payroll tax increases required to sustain benefits at current levels. The major stakeholders would have to share the pain of any solution. Furthermore, for actors interested in long-run outcomes, policy investment ought in principle to have been an appealing option: because of the logic of compound interest, the sooner the costs of reform were paid, the smaller they would need to be. In electoral terms, moreover, the breadth of the reform coalition would have offered ideal conditions for blame-avoidance. With labor, capital, and the chief opposition party signed up to the pact, pension reform had effectively been removed from the arena of electoral competition (Schulze and Jochem 2006).

In sum, forward-looking interests had good reason to carefully consider the possible long-term payoffs of investment while elected incumbents enjoyed substantial insulation against short-run repercussions at the ballot box. Why, then, did policy investment fail to emerge?

THE UNCERTAINTY OF THE LONG RUN (1989)

For German interest-group and party pension experts in the 1980s, the problem with policy investment in pensions was not its short-term political consequences but the risk of *long-term* policy failure. Like policymakers in all of our cases, these actors confronted enormous causal and informational complexity as they sought to predict the long-run consequences of their choices; like decision makers elsewhere, they also drew heavily on available conceptual frameworks to simplify causal relationships and interpret causal ambiguities. Yet the particular mental model with which postwar German pension experts operated – shaped, in part, by the country's dramatic historical experience with past policy investments – focused their attention far more sharply on the economic and political risks of asset accumulation and persuaded them that the long-run benefits of funding were unlikely to outweigh its short-term costs.

As discussed in Chapter 3, the original architects of the world's first public contributory pension scheme understood the enterprise as a form of *insurance,* drawing their principal concepts and causal understandings from this private-sector analog. Among other effects, the insurance model directed Reich officials' attention toward the risk of insolvency and the long-term advantages of asset accumulation. At the same time, this imported causal framework obscured the unique political and economic risks that fund accumulation within a *public* social program might face, such as the danger of manipulation by governments and threats to the real value of the accumulated assets. Indeed, the analogy occluded critical differences between the two types of arrangement and their logics. In a private insurance scheme, accumulated assets are generally protected by judicially enforceable contractual obligations and property rights; in a public program, in contrast, the current government's resource commitments may have little binding effect on future incumbents. And while the benefits promised by a private insurance policy are typically expressed in nominal terms, officials managing *public* programs will usually care most about the distribution of *real* economic resources. Thus, for instance, if inflation has little effect on a private insurer's ability to meet its obligations, a devaluation of the currency can wipe out the capacity of a government to use accumulated assets to meet citizens' social needs.

While the policy investment of 1889 unfolded smoothly for almost three decades, the pension fund met with disaster in the late 1910s – a result of causal dynamics not captured by the insurance model and not attended to in the 1880s. During World War I, over half of the assets accumulated in the pension scheme were invested in Reich war bonds (Manow 2000). Meanwhile, the government took the inflationary steps of leaving the gold standard and financing the war largely through borrowing (Craig 1981). Together, these choices constituted a raid on all Reichmark-denominated savings to finance the war. Exacerbated by the terms of defeat, inflation was followed by hyperinflation that wiped out the entire real value of the pension scheme's assets, built up over 30 years. Benefit promises, denominated in nominal units, were similarly rendered worthless in real terms. With its assets gone and the economy fragile, the program was left on a *de facto* PAYGO basis throughout most of the Weimar period. Then in the 1930s, the National Socialist regime pushed the pension system back onto a basis of full funding (Geyer 1987). This second experience with funding, however, ended as badly as the first. Decreeing in the late 1930s that the social insurers had to invest 75 percent of their assets in state bonds, the Nazi regime used these resources to finance Germany's rearmament and war effort (Teppe 1977). After World War II, defeat and inflation once again destroyed the pension reserves.

After the Second World War, these twin policy debacles helped to uproot the prewar conceptualization of pension policy.[3] As I detail elsewhere (Jacobs 2009a), the insurance model had in fact proved remarkably resilient during the interwar years. In the decades since the pension scheme's creation, the insurance concept and actuarial norms had become deeply institutionalized within the information-gathering and administrative apparatus of the German state. Despite the seemingly disconfirming experience of hyperinflation after World War I, most policymakers in the 1920s continued to understand the scheme as an insurance plan and to support funding as the only appropriate method for financing it. During interwar debates, experts engaged in strongly confirmatory processing of available data: they continued to devote surprisingly little attention to the dangers of inflation and political manipulation – risks signaled by recent experience but difficult to square with actuarial logic. And, in a self-validating interpretation of causal ambiguity, they blamed the recent loss of the pension reserves on a set of extraordinary economic *circumstances*, rather than on the policy of funding itself (for details, see Jacobs 2009a; Manow 2000; Geyer 1987).

If the insurance analogy could survive one spectacular failure, however, the second sequence of fund manipulation, rapid inflation, and fund devastation left the model deeply discredited after World War II. If the first episode could be discounted as exceptional, confirmatory cognitive mechanisms were unable to withstand the *repetition* of such clear and dramatic evidence of policy failure. Once actors finally turned concentrated attention to this evidence, the private-insurance model simply could not make sense of the data – of the processes of political promise-breaking and currency devaluation through which the scheme had twice been devastated. To policymakers who now understood political and monetary instability as characteristic features of their environment, the task of pension financing no longer looked like an *actuarial* problem of balancing assets and liabilities.

Meanwhile, German economists and social policy experts in the late 1940s and early 1950s were developing an alternative understanding of the logic of social protection that was a far better fit with policy experience. The most prominent new conception, grounded in contemporary theories of the macro-economy, modeled social welfare policies as *redistributive* mechanisms, rather than as methods of insurance. The redistributive logic was most famously formulated by economist Gerhard Mackenroth: "All social spending," he wrote, "must always be paid for out of the national income of the period in which it occurs" (Mackenroth 1952, 41). In the Mackenrothian view, societies are fundamentally different from firms or individuals: there is in fact no way for a society to save for the future by accumulating funds. No matter how public

---

[3] See Manow's (2000) superb account of changing German conceptions of public pension financing since Bismarck.

pensions are financed – whether from current tax revenues or accumulated assets – they always represent a reallocation of current production from non-beneficiaries to beneficiaries. Just as PAYGO financing extracted resources through the mechanism of taxation, a funded scheme collected interest, dividends, and the proceeds from asset sales, transferring those resources from borrowers, firms, and other investors to pension claimants. Put another way, whether future pension outlays were financed out of the earnings on accumulated assets or future payroll contributions, the payment of benefits would still grant tomorrow's pensioners a claim on a share of the *real* goods and services currently available in the economy – a share that would, in consequence, be unavailable to nonpensioners. In this view, funding affected only the mechanism of transfer from one group to another; it could not affect the long-run cost of spending on pensions.

As the German economy recovered from the devastation of World War II, Konrad Adenauer's center-right government turned in the mid-1950s to the task of rebuilding and reforming the state pension scheme. By this point, the redistributive model had achieved wide acceptance in elite social policy circles (Hockerts 1980), and participants in reform debates brought it explicitly and repeatedly to bear in discussing methods of financing the state pension plan.[4] In one of the most influential formulations, top Adenauer advisor and Bonn economist Wilfrid Schreiber described the public-pension program as a "contract of solidarity between generations" – in which the young, supported by their elders in the past, now transferred resources to them in retirement (Schreiber 1955, 18; Hockerts 1980). Minutes and memoranda from internal government deliberations reveal a wide range of participants echoing this understanding of the program, as a mechanism of redistribution between age groups.[5] For the first time, moreover, records of internal government pension-policy deliberations during this period reveal numerous experts and state officials taking pains to draw a sharp *distinction* between public retirement benefits and private insurance.[6]

---

[4] See comments by Auerbach [Labor Ministry State Secretary], Liebing [Director, Association of German Pension Insurers], and Liefmann-Keil [Freiburg University economist], in "Niederschrift über die 13. Sitzung"; comments by Hensen [Kiel economist] at "Niederschrift über die 14. Sitzung des Arbeitsausschusses für Grundsatzfragen [Minutes of the 14th Meeting of the Working Group on Basic Principles]," April 25 and 26, 1955, B149/414, BArch; the contribution by Schmölders of the Finanzwissenschaftliches Forschungsinstitut at Köln University, "Die Pläne für eine Neuordnung der sozialen Leistungen im Lichte der Finanz- und Währungspolitik [The Plans for Reforming Social Benefits in Light of Fiscal and Monetary Policy]" [no date], B126/13804, BArch; and comments by Bundesbank President Wilhelm Vocke before the Bundestag's Social Policy Committee September 15, 1956, B126/13807, BArch.

[5] See the comments of multiple committee members in "Niederschrift über die 13. Sitzung" and of Imhof in "Niederschrift über die 14. Sitzung."

[6] See discussion in the lead Labor Ministry committee on pension reform, the General Secretariat for Social Reform, in "Niederschrift über die 2. Sitzung des Arbeitsausschusses für Fragen der Rentenversicherung [Minutes of the 2nd Meeting of the Working Group on Pension Issues]," June 11, 1954, B149/422, BArch; "Niederschrift über die 3. Sitzung des Arbeitsausschusses für Fragen der Rentenversicherung [Minutes of the 3rd Meeting of the Working Group on Pension

This new causal model and the "lessons" of salient policy disasters were thus mutually reinforcing: while past failures of fund-accumulation lent the redistributive view greater credibility as an account of pension financing, the new mental model also channeled actors' attention toward historical experiences of which it could make sense. Like the insurance model that preceded it, the model of pension policy as a mechanism of redistribution of real resources captured some causal dynamics while simplifying others away. In particular, the new model was well suited to reasoning about the kinds of economic and political threats that could confront fund accumulation within a state scheme. In representing the problem of pension financing as a matter of *real* economic value, the model could, for instance, aid reasoning about inflation. Accumulated money, in this model, has no value aside from the real resources that it represents; from this perspective, a devaluation of the currency thus stands out as a serious threat to any attempt to stockpile funds over time. Moreover, in characterizing the scheme as a distinctly *political* arrangement – a pact over time between social groups – the redistributive framework lent itself far more easily than the insurance metaphor to reasoning about political threats to previously established bargains.

In a stark redirection of policy reasoning, participants in postwar pension debates now showered cognitive resources on these two dangers to the long-term commitment of pension funds. In committee meetings and internal correspondence, decision makers made continual references to the twin financing disasters of the past, citing them as evidence of the grave risk that inflation posed to funding.[7] Policymakers and experts repeatedly expressed broad and deep concern about the stability of the currency and its impact on long-term fund accumulation.[8] Even civil servants in the Finance Ministry – proponents of

Issues]," June 24, 1954, B149/422, BArch; in minutes of subsequent sessions in same file group; and in "Niederschrift über die 13. Sitzung des Arbeitsausschusses für Grundsatzfragen [Minutes of the 13th Meeting of the Working Group on Basic Principles]," March 28 and 29, 1955, B149/414, BArch.

7 See the references to past disaster in Haensel's [Senate President, Munich, member of Advisory Board for Reorganization of Social Benefits] and Lepinski's [member, Working Group for Pension Insurance Issues] remarks in "Niederschrift über die 13. Sitzung des Arbeitsausschusses für Grundsatzfragen," March 28–29, 1955, B 149/414, BArch; Lepinski's and Stock's [former premier of Hessen; member, Advisory Council] comments in "Niederschrift über die Sitzung des Beirats für die Neuordnung der sozialen Leistungen [Minutes of the Meeting of the Advisory Council for the Reform of Social Benefits]," June 2–4, 1955, B149/410, BArch; see also the characterization of PAYGO arguments in Gesellschaft für Versicherungswissenschaft und –gestaltung, "Vorschläge für eine Neuordnung der sozialen Rentenversicherung," September 11, 1954, B 149/424, BArch. Adenauer made prominent reference to experiences of inflation in Cabinet (Hockerts 1980, 347).

8 See comments by Tietz [Division Director, Labor Ministry] and Auerbach in "Niederschrift über die 24. Sitzung des Arbeitsausschusses für Grundsatzfragen [Minutes of the 24th Meeting of the Working Group on Basic Principles]," March 22, 1956, B149/423, BArch; and by Hofmann, Professor Dr. Noack [member, Working Group on Pension Insurance Issues], and others in "Niederschrift über die 4. Sitzung des Arbeitsausschusses für Fragen der Rentenversicherung [Minutes of the 4th Meeting of the Working Group on Pension Issues]," July 21, 1954, B149/422, BArch.

funding before and between the wars – advised their minister against full funding of pensions on the same historical grounds: "The past has proved that the accumulation of a large capital stock corresponding to actuarial calculations is not possible," a Finance bureaucrat memoed his minister. "Twice, the loss of insurance reserves through inflation. ..."[9] Similarly, in sharp contrast to interwar discussions, records of postwar debate reveal widespread anxiety about *political* threats to a pension fund. Large pension surpluses, officials and advisors argued, would inevitably lead to demands for benefit increases, and elected officials would never fail to resist the temptation to expand a popular program.[10] Alternatively, social insurance assets could end up being diverted to nonsocial policy purposes, helping the Finance Minister meet general budgetary needs.[11]

In objective terms, these threats to the commitment of pension assets were no greater now than they had been in the 1880s; indeed, they were arguably lower. With the emergence of an increasingly independent and hawkish Bundesbank, inflation was far less likely to spiral out of control (Berger 1997). Bonn institutions, moreover, were arguably better designed to bind governments' hands, with greater authority vested in the legislature and well-developed neo-corporatist structures that gave workers and employers a central role in the scheme's administration. Institutional logic, however, mattered less than cognitive availability. More important than the objective magnitude of such risks was how the dominant ideational framework and salient policy experience directed actors' attention across causal possibilities.

Equally important were the ways in which the redistributive model *suppressed* lines of causal reasoning about potential long-term *benefits* of policy investment. In particular, this new model did not capture causal sequences – foremost in the minds of Reich policymakers – through which funding might ease the financial burden of rising pension outlays. Policymakers and advisors on key deliberative committees in the mid-1950s rarely referred to the tendency of PAYGO financing toward increasing contribution costs over the long run or to the ability of funding to smooth contribution rates over time even as spending levels climbed (Hockerts 1980).[12] This is not surprising: as a model of real resource flows, Mackenroth's framework blurred any distinction between the long-term costs of PAYGO financing and those of funding – between one method's reliance

---

[9] Draft of memo from Unterabteilung IIC, MR. Dr. Elsholz [Division Director, Finance Ministry] to the Minister of Finance, December 10, 1955, B126/13804, BArch.

[10] Der Generalsekretär für die Neuordnung der sozialen Sicherung, "Betr. Nächste Sitzung des Interministeriellen Ausschusses [Re: The Next Meeting of the Interministerial Committee]," November 30, 1955, B149/408; [Generalsekretär], "Die Gestaltung," December 12, 1955, B149/480, BArch.

[11] Lepinski and Stock in "Niederschrift über die Sitzung des Beirats"; Lepinski in "Niederschrift," March 28/29, 1955, B149/414, BArch; Auerbach in "Niederschrift über die 24. Sitzung" and in "Niederscrhift über die 14. Sitzung."

[12] Aside from file groups just cited, sources reviewed include Labor Ministry groups B149/412, 413, 425, 3316, 3764, 16832 and Finance Ministry groups B126/13804 and 13807, all at BArch.

on taxes and the other's reliance on asset yields. In the old actuarial view, a shift to funding represented an intertemporal trade-off: by amassing a fund today, a program could in future earn income on its assets and could thus operate at a lower long-term contribution rate than would be possible under PAYGO. In the current redistributive view, in contrast, the earnings on a fund and contribution revenues are modeled as identical dynamics: both, a reallocation of real resources from producers to retirees.

The redistributive model undoubtedly captured an important macroeconomic reality that had been lost on earlier generations of policymakers. At the same time, the elegant notion that all social spending must be paid for out of the national income also *obscured* potentially important causal relationships. For instance, while the two modes of revenue-extraction are similar in the broadest distributive terms, taxing labor and drawing on asset earnings could have widely divergent microeconomic implications, affecting (among other things) the demand for labor. The framework also provided no tools for thinking about the effect that pension capital accumulation might have on other macroeconomic variables, such as levels of national savings and investment and, in turn, the future productivity of the economy.

The landmark pension reforms of 1957 established the postwar system on a PAYGO basis. And over the next several decades, the Mackenrothian view of pensions as a method of redistribution between generations, and the accompanying historical lessons, became deeply entrenched within West Germany's cross-party and neo-corporatist community of pension policy experts (Nullmeier and Rüb 1993). The unusually small, stable, and tightly networked character of this community allowed the metaphor of a "generational contract" and the suspicion of government promises to remain well preserved and relatively unchallenged for decades. In 1987, for instance, as a top actuary at the pension insurers' federation sought to explain the financing of the system, he did so by reference to the same economic precepts and policy record that had motivated decision makers 40 years earlier: "The most important reason for the pay-as-you-go system," he told a crowd of assembled journalists, "that has been used since 1957 lies in an economic principle that was recognized as correct in light of the inflation of 1923 and the world economic crisis of 1930."[13] Through the late 1990s and early 2000s, key policy actors remained similarly attuned to the political risks of public fund-accumulation. When members of the Social Democratic Party's Old-Age Security Commission considered a shift to funding in the mid-1990s, they rejected the option partly because "it cannot be ensured that a future government would not misappropriate the funds indirectly through shifting funds between social programs."[14] As one commission member later

[13] "Das 'Finanzierungssystem der gesetzlichen Rentenversicherung,'" transcript of speech delivered at Pressefachseminar, *Finanzierungssystem der GRV*, Verband Deutscher Rentenversicherungsträger, Bad Nauheim, March 25 and 26, 1987, p. 8.
[14] SPD Alterssicherungskommission, "Strukturreform statt Leistungskürzungen: Vorschläge der Alterssicherungskommission der SPD," 1996, Bonn, pp. 21–24.

recalled, "We didn't even trust ourselves."[15] Interviewed in 2002, the head of the German Trade Union Federation's social-policy division similarly cautioned, "Whenever there are reserves [in the public pension system], the state grabs them."[16] And a senior Labor Ministry official, in the early 2000s, criticized contemporary proposals for fund-accumulation in the state pension scheme on identical grounds: "This would be too big a temptation, especially during a crisis or for improvements in the pension system."[17]

Theoretically, policy investment might have offered the reformers of the late 1980s an attractive bargain: more long-term financial relief for less overall pain. But those negotiating the reform package did not view funding's intertemporal promise as credible. West German union, employer, and bureaucratic actors viewed the system through an ideational lens, carved by historical experience, that both diminished the perceived advantages of funding and magnified its potential risks. While a few neo-liberal and business voices at the time called for a transition to partial funding, core members of the pension policy community – even those, like business and labor representatives, with competing material interests – shared a firm commitment to the redistributive model and PAYGO financing. Despite long time horizons and the electoral freedom to maneuver, that is, politicians and the social partners did not *define* funding as a profitable intertemporal tradeoff: in their view, resources extracted today would simply be diverted or demolished tomorrow.

Thus, instead of seeking to trade pain now for gain later, organized interests and party leaders sought to moderate the long-term rise in pension costs by rebalancing of the *future* distribution of benefits and burdens across groups. The resulting legislation would shift resources away from future beneficiaries (and, in part, general taxpayers) and toward future contributors. Enacted in 1989, the Pension Reform Act of 1992 (named after the year in which it would take effect) imposed a small penalty for early retirement, boosted general-revenue infusions into the program, and – most significantly – changed the formula by which benefit levels would be adjusted for inflation. Instead of rising with average gross wages in the economy, benefits would rise with after-tax wages, which were expected to grow more slowly in coming years as payroll tax rates climbed. As a result of these changes in total, pension contribution rates were projected to rise far more slowly over time: rather than hitting 36 percent by 2030, premiums were expected to remain below 27 percent for the next 40 years (Jochem 1999; Schmähl 1998; Hinrichs 1998). These long-run savings would not represent an

---

[15] Jörg Deml (SPD parliamentary party pension expert), interview with the author, Berlin, November 5, 2001.

[16] Ruth Palik (Social Policy Division Head, Deutscher Gewerkschaftsbund), interview with the author, Berlin, November 12, 2001.

[17] Official requested anonymity. Interview with the author, Berlin, November 12, 2001. The conservative commitment of policy community members to PAYGO financing was confirmed by Wolfgang Rombach (a Ministry of Labor and Social Affairs official), interview with the author, Berlin, April 17, 2001. See also Schulze-Cleven (Unpublished Manuscript) and Hinrichs (1998).

intertemporal transfer from the present but an intergroup transfer from tomorrow's retirees to tomorrow's contributors: lower future contribution rates made possible by lower future pensions.

END OF THE POSTWAR CONSENSUS (2001)

After a few years of optimism following the 1989 reform, Germany's broad postwar consensus on the virtues of the "social market" economy soon began to show signs of strain. By the middle of the 1990s, economic and policy conditions had shifted in ways that sharpened the lines of distributive conflict. By far, the most dramatic of these developments was the unification of East and West Germany. With the collapse of eastern Germany's main export market in the Soviet Union and the dismantling of its command economy, unemployment in the "new" states skyrocketed, placing an enormous burden on the now-unified social-insurance system. Meanwhile, as western German industry faced stiffer competition on world export markets and began to shift production abroad, unemployment in the old states also moved upwards (Vitols 2005). Falling payroll revenues and rising benefit outlays combined to push total contribution rates to the social-insurance system – unemployment and health insurance as well as the pension program – above 40 percent of wages (Verband Deutscher Rentenversicherungsträger 2005). Projections, meanwhile, showed that an aging population would continue to drive pension contribution rates up another 25 percent over the next 30 years ("Entwurf eines Gesetzes zur Reform der gesetzlichen Rentenversicherung (Gesetzentwurf der Fraktionen der CDU/CSU und F.D.P.)" 1997).

What followed was another major shift in the economic ideas shaping pension policymaking. This ideational transformation was driven by a combination of factors. On the one hand, clear, dramatic, and sustained policy failure made the old "intergenerational contract" conception vulnerable to replacement. More importantly, however, a change in the locus of decision making authority moved debate away from venues dominated by the redistributive, Mackenrothian view and gave greater influence to actors with alternative ideational commitments (as well as a particular set of distributive interests). As economic crisis deepened, Germany's business community, conservatives, and top economic institutes began to articulate a specific diagnosis of the country's economic ills, based on a distinctive understanding of the political economy. Within international policy circles, the 1990s saw the intellectual and institutional ascendancy of what we might term a *microeconomic* model of labor markets. In the microeconomic view – which took strong hold within the OECD, the International Monetary Fund, and the European Commission[18] – employment outcomes were understood to be largely a function of the ways in which labor-market institutions shape incentives

---

[18] For reviews of this thesis and its advocacy, see Krueger and Pischke (1997) and Howell and Huebler (2005).

for workers and employers. Structures such as employment protection rules, generous unemployment benefits, and high social-insurance taxes were all argued to depress employment, either by making hiring more expensive or riskier for employers or by raising workers' reservation wages. In a globalized economic context, the costs of labor-market rigidity were held to be especially high since capital is increasingly free to exit in pursuit of lower-cost sources of labor abroad. In this model, the welfare state was not simply a Mackenrothian engine of redistribution, without effect on the real economy. Viewed through a microeconomic lens, the growing cost of social insurance had real consequences for economic activity by choking off employment growth (Hering 2001a; Hinrichs 2000).

As unemployment rates continued to climb through the 1990s, this alternative causal framework found an increasingly receptive audience within the Kohl government, and market liberals in cabinet gained enhanced leverage to pursue new welfare-retrenchment initiatives. In 1996 and 1997, the government pursued new long-term pension cutbacks and – in a landmark break with postwar patterns – enacted this retrenchment outside the long-standing neo-corporatist pension network. This departure from traditional routines of policy bargaining reflected an emerging polarization of policy preferences, with German business leaders increasingly drifting away from the central principles of the social-market consensus. Enhanced capital mobility, sustained high unemployment, and continually rising social insurance costs collectively drove a wedge between the perceived interests of capital and those of labor, and business leaders lost patience with traditional patterns of societal compromise (Hering 2001a; Hinrichs 2000; Jochem 1999).

Unilateral reform, however, had its costs. After 15 years of center-right rule, the Social Democratic Party (SPD) defeated the Christian Democrats in the federal election of 1998, in large part by campaigning against the pension cuts (Traynor 1998). Yet when Gerhard Schröder entered office, in coalition with the Green Party, he in turn faced a dilemma. On the one hand, his party had pledged during the election battle to reverse the most significant of the center-right's reform initiatives – the introduction of a "demographic factor" that would, in coming decades, gradually lower benefits as the population aged. The logic of electoral accountability compelled him to follow through on this promise and suspend the demographic factor within months of taking office (Hering 2001b).

On the other hand, Schröder himself largely subscribed to the new, microeconomic understanding of Germany's economic troubles. Consistent with a trend sweeping mainstream parties of the European left, a new generation of "modernizers" at the helm of the SPD sought to move the party toward the ideological center, loosening its commitment to traditional collectivist principles and reconciling its agenda with new market imperatives. Shortly after assuming office, Schröder outlined his guiding philosophy in a paper jointly written with Britain's New Labour prime minister Tony Blair. The "Neue Mitte," as the

Chancellor termed his own "Third Way," was – in the authors' words – a "supply-side agenda for the left." The agenda amounted to an endorsement of a staggering range of neo-liberal aims, including commitments to tax cuts for corporations and workers, fiscal discipline, and deregulation of labor markets. In the Neue Mitte's redefinition of social-democratic politics, priority should be accorded to markets over state intervention and to individuals over collectivities (Blair and Schröder 1999). In the field of social insurance, the SPD's modernizers were convinced that success in Germany's long-running battle against unemployment would depend on reducing nonwage labor costs. Since the pension system received a substantial and growing subsidy from general revenues, controlling the program's outlays would also constitute a crucial step toward reducing Germany's public-sector deficits, which were running up against the Maastricht criteria for membership in Europe's single currency zone.

Thus, if electoral pressures compelled Schröder's ministers to reverse the previous government's benefit cuts, their own causal understanding of Germany's economic problems pushed them to seek spending reductions of their own. The new government had to find a way to replicate the fiscal *effects* of the center-right's reforms through alternative *means*. Meanwhile, a second intellectual development – specific to the field of pensions – suggested a potential strategy for squaring this policy circle. As discussed in Chapter 9, actors within the international social-policy community – most prominently, economists at the World Bank – had begun to make an aggressive case for shifting national pension systems away from PAYGO financing and toward funding (Hemming 1999). According to advocates, since funded benefits were paid for out of the returns to accumulated assets rather than payroll taxes, funding would allow governments to detach long-term contribution rates from adverse demographic developments (World Bank 1994).

Of course, German pension policymakers in the postwar era had tended to discount precisely this potential advantage of funding – its capacity to moderate long-term tax burdens. In a Mackenrothian framework, financing benefits with current payroll contributions was economically equivalent to financing them out of the returns to capital; both methods necessarily represented a transfer of resources from producers to retirees. Following the Kohl government's example, however, Schröder's Labor Ministry drew up reform plans largely outside the traditional pension policy community in which postwar mental models had been so deeply entrenched. Turning instead to a handpicked group of outside economic advisors,[19] the SPD modernizers substantially loosened the grip of the Mackenrothian, redistributive framework on pension-policy deliberations.

Moreover, the newly ascendant pension paradigm furnished policymakers with fresh lines of causal reasoning that departed from the older model in

---

[19] The Federal Labor Ministry formed its own advisory committee, dubbed Pension Reform 2000. Its members were Bert Rürup (who had designed the Kohl government's "demographic factor"), Winfried Schmähl, Barbara Riedmüller, Frank Nullmeier, Hans-Jürgen Krupp, Richard Hauser, and Gerd Bäcker (Forster 1999).

important respects. Mackenroth's apparent truism – that all current social spending derives from current national income – hinged critically on a set of simplifying assumptions: most importantly, (1) that society's productive potential was exogenously given and (2) that the national economy was a closed system. Advocates of funding in the 1990s, in contrast, drew attention to the ways in which economic productivity might, over the long run, be influenced by pension policy choices themselves and to the globalized character of contemporary capital markets. By accumulating assets, a funded pension program could boost levels of national savings available for investment. If invested domestically, those assets would contribute to local capital formation, thus enhancing long-term productivity growth in the economy. And if invested abroad, especially in emerging markets with more favorable demographic profiles, retirement funds would capture returns from economies in which labor was more plentiful – effectively importing younger workers. In either case, funding was now understood in international policymaking circles not merely as an alternative method of redistributing shares of a fixed economic pie; it now appeared to be an opportunity to invest, over the long run, in expanding the pie itself (Feldstein 1997; Edwards 1996; Corsetti and Schmidt-Hebbel 1995; World Bank 1994).

At the same time, the pension debates of the late 1990s suggested a broader menu of policy tools than that from which earlier generations of policymakers had chosen. German reformers in the 1980s were largely making choices about the structure of the public program; for them, a shift to funding would have meant fund accumulation *within* the state retirement system. A decade later, however, reform discussions within domestic and international policy communities were often structured around the merits of a "multi-pillar" system – one that assigned distinct roles to different sectors. While the state could most effectively carry out the redistributive functions of a pension regime, private occupational and individual retirement vehicles were widely considered better suited to the tasks of encouraging savings and capital formation (World Bank 1994).

Thus, as Schröder's Labor Minister, Walter Riester, began to formulate a reform blueprint, prominent among the options before him were proposals to expand the role of *private* funded pensions. This broadening of the policy menu could potentially reshape the reform debate in important ways. Whereas the center-right's "demographic factor" represented the simple withdrawal of public benefits, occupational and individualized options opened up the possibility of *replacing* state payments with private sources of retirement income. A shift from public toward private arrangements, rather than mere retrenchment, would help the new government distinguish its policy approach from the previous government's pure cost-cutting efforts, reducing the fiscal burden without reducing the standard of living of tomorrow's seniors.

Equally important, the availability of private savings instruments might enhance the *credibility* of any proposed policy investment in funding. While funding within the public pension system would leave the accumulated capital within easy reach of state officials, assets amassed within employer schemes or individual accounts were fairly well insulated against political interference.

Though governments could nibble at the margins of private pensions – for instance, through changes in their tax treatment – individuals and firms enjoyed a robust set of institutional protections, including a well-established regime of enforceable property rights, against any substantial diversion of private savings toward other purposes.

A partial transition from PAYGO public benefits toward private funded pensions thus offered Schröder's Social Democrats a potential method of reconciling apparently conflicting objectives, moderating the future social burden of pension provision while protecting future retirees against substantial losses. Whereas the reforms of the 1980s and 1990s had merely reallocated resources cross-sectionally – from future beneficiaries to future taxpayers – funding represented an intertemporal strategy that could make both groups better off over the long run. The long-term benefits of funding, however, could only be won at short-run cost. In order to amass pension assets for the future while continuing to pay benefits to existing pensioners, the government would have to increase the total flow of resources to the pension system in the near term. It was on the allocation of these short-term costs that plans for substantial policy investment would ultimately falter.

LIMITS TO LOSS-IMPOSITION (2001)

While Labor Minister Riester formulated his plans largely outside the traditional neo-corporatist policy network, his options were still considerably constrained by the preferences of Germany's well-organized producer groups. In part, organized labor's leverage derived from its ability to generate mass protest. At key moments during the reform process, more radical branches of the labor movement – particularly, the metalworkers' and white-collar organizations – threatened public demonstrations against proposed pension reductions (Schmitz 2000b; "Einsam auf dem Rentengipfel" 1999). With the threat of mass mobilization looming, the more moderate Federation of German Trade Unions could wield considerable influence as a "good cop" pushing the government to adjust its planned cutbacks (Thelen 2001). Trade unionists also enjoyed strong links to the left wing of the Social Democratic Party, which threatened to buck the party leadership over the government's welfare reform agenda; the government's slim Bundestag majority gave potential defectors particular leverage.[20] Despite the presence of a center-left government, employers also enjoyed an important institutional access point within postwar Germany's decentralized political system. Under Germany's constitutional rules, any grants or tax subsidies directed toward private pensions would require the assent of the Bundesrat, the upper legislative chamber, where the

---

[20] See Hering (2001b) for a discussion of the role of the SPD parliamentary grouping Democratic Left Forum 21, and backbench dissent more broadly, in shaping the final reform outcome.

CDU held a majority. Winning opposition agreement would thus be far easier if the CDU's business allies backed the reform.[21]

Aside from shaping the institutional feasibility of enactment, the positions taken by these groups and their partisan allies would also heavily influence the *electoral risks* of reform. If trade unions could be kept off the streets and leftwing critics in parliament appeased, then public attention was less likely to focus on the reform's less-appealing features. And if business's allies in the main opposition party could be persuaded to vote for reform in the Bundesrat, then the SPD-Green coalition would enjoy substantial insulation against electoral attack. Through both institutional access points and opinion-shaping opportunities, both labor and capital thus enjoyed substantial capacity to obstruct proposals that threatened their interests.

The scales of influence, however, were far from balanced. Economic and ideational conditions in Germany in the late 1990s and early 2000s allowed business to press its own claims from a substantially stronger position than labor's. In essence, German employers at this moment enjoyed an enhanced form of the structural leverage that business often wields in a market economy (Lindblom 1982). As discussed, in the microeconomic model accepted by many in the senior ranks of Schröder's SPD, Germany's economic woes stemmed from an excessive social and regulatory burden on firms. This causal understanding lent particularly strong credibility to employers' claims that their costs of business needed to go *down,* not up. Economic stagnation, climbing tax rates, and a global trend toward enhanced capital mobility had sparked broad public debate over the issue of *"Standort Deutschland"* – Germany's relative attractiveness as an investment location – raising widespread fears of German production moving offshore (Vitols 2005; Jochem 1999; Tüselmann 1998; Hinrichs 1998; Casper and Vitols 1997). While the extent of actual firm relocation was frequently exaggerated, mass joblessness intensely concentrated policymakers' minds on the impact of their choices on firms' investment and hiring decisions. To put the point another way, economic crisis and widespread causal beliefs encouraged, to an exceptional degree, an equation between business's own distributive interests and the general interests of society.

Employers' chief reform aim was to place a ceiling on their own pension-contribution burden, capping the premium for the next 30 years at a level only marginally higher than the rate in 2000. In the context of an aging population, limiting pension tax rates would, of course, require reductions in state benefit levels. Employers also called for a shift in the basis of old-age income from public to private sources.[22] In looking to private arrangements, however, employers

---

[21] In fact, in the final stages of reform, business exercised considerable influence through this back channel by urging the Christian Democrats to end their blocking tactics and let the bill pass, which they did. Jana Liebscher, personal communication, Social Security division of Federation of German Employers' Associations, Nov. 13, 2002, Berlin. Confirmed in Schwennicke (2001).

[22] Liebscher, personal communication; Volker Hansen, personal communication, Social Security section of Federal Association of German Employers, November 13, 2001, Berlin. See also Hinrichs (2000).

specifically had in mind schemes that would operate *outside* the joint-financing principles of social insurance – plans, that is, into which only *workers* would pay. While German business saw a shift to funded pensions as a useful mechanism for moderating future costs, employers were not willing to help pay for this investment themselves. Because they believed that the social burden on firms was *already* too high, and a threat to their short-run survival, business leaders were uninterested in an intertemporal trade-off of greater sacrifice today for cost-savings tomorrow. Moreover, in their relatively strong political position, employers had good reason to believe that the final reform outcome would, in any case, include a substantial long-term redistribution in their favor in the form of future benefit cuts. They thus had little reason to signal a willingness to pay the short-run costs of investment. To win business approval, in short, any shift to funded pensions would have to be financed by someone else.

While trade-union opinion was divided on some social-welfare issues, most labor leaders were determined to safeguard the core distributional features of the state pension insurance scheme. For one thing, the unions were intent on preserving the century-old principle of parity financing, whereby employers shared the costs of social insurance equally with workers (Schulze and Jochem 2006). Labor leaders had watched nervously in recent years as business groups had repeatedly proposed measures that would extract firms from financial responsibility for social protection. Even more important to labor was the preservation of the public pension program's function as a guarantor of living standards (*Lebensstandardsicherung*). As of the late 1990s, the state pension amounted to approximately 70 percent of earnings for a retiree with a full employment record at average wages. Any major reduction in the level of state benefits threatened to hollow out the scheme's capacity to replace earnings as individuals made the transition from work into retirement.

Further, even if public benefits were to be notionally replaced by private, trade unionists did not view the two types of arrangements as functionally interchangeable. While the public scheme offered "defined benefits" – guaranteeing a stipulated schedule of payouts – most private options under discussion were "defined contribution," leaving retirement incomes dependent on the performance of pension assets. A shift from public to private thus meant swapping the security of a statutory promise for market risk. Finally, many labor leaders did not share employers' or SPD modernizers' causal assumptions, having never fully bought into the ascendant microeconomic model. They looked with considerable skepticism on employers' dire warnings about the job-killing effects of social contributions, countering that pension premiums in excess of 25 percent would still be economically sustainable (Hering 2005; Anderson and Meyer 2003; Hinrichs 2000; Deckstein 1999).[23]

---

[23] Confirmed by Palik, interview with the author; same expression of unions' policy preferences conveyed in interview with another trade-union social policy specialist, on condition of anonymity, November 6, 2001.

Importantly, most of organized labor was not in principle opposed to an expansion of funded, private provision. Union leaders were even willing to see a short-run increase in the contribution burden on workers – if matched by their employers – in return for more generous private pensions over the long run. That is, the *intertemporal* trade-off implied by a move toward funding was acceptable to labor. What concerned trade unionists were the *distributive* implications of a *replacement* of defined-benefit pensions by defined-contribution pensions – with benefits dependent on market conditions – that were financed *only* by workers. On balance, most labor leaders would have preferred no investment over an investment that weakened labor's distributive position. From labor's perspective, the prospect of a rising contribution burden over the next 30 years was far less worrisome than a departure from the solid-aristic financing principles and income-replacement goals at the core of the postwar welfare-state.

Riester's initial reform proposal largely reflected the microeconomic diagnosis of Germany's economic troubles and business demands for a moderation of the social burden. Initially presented in June of 1999, the reform strategy ran along two tracks. First, benefit levels in the state pension program would be reduced in order to stabilize contribution rates. Riester's proposal would suspend the annual indexation of benefits to net wages in 2000 and 2001, allowing benefits to rise only in line with prices for those two years. By itself, this pause in wage-indexation was expected to reduce the scheme's earnings-replacement rate from 70 to 67 percent, and it was expected to hold contribution rates (now 19.5 percent) under 20 percent until 2020. The second element of Riester's blueprint was a new compulsory private pension scheme to compensate for cutbacks to the public program. This private pillar would be financed on a funded basis by mandatory contributions, from employees only, of 2.5 percent of wages (MAJ 1999b),[24] applying to all workers who did not yet have company pensions or life insurance policies. Yet, according to Labor Ministry projections, these new private benefits would hold senior citizens harmless against loss of income, bringing total pension payments to an earnings-replacement level above 70 percent (MAJ 1999a). As a whole, the plan would thus shift resources along two dimensions, pairing a substantial investment with a reallocation of financing burdens in favor of employers.

Predictably, the trade unions' reaction to this plan was swift and scathing. The association for white collar workers argued that the proposal would reduce state pension levels by nearly as much as the Kohl government's "demographic factor" (MAJ 1999a). The chief of the metalworkers' union, IG Metall, condemned the plan as a "gigantic redistributive machine to the benefit of employers,"[25] a reform "unworthy of a social-democratic led government" (CSK, KK and MAJ 1999). The labor peak association's social-policy department criticized

---

[24] These contributions would be exempted from income tax but not from social-insurance contributions.

[25] IG Metall head Klaus Zwickel quoted in Hank (1999).

the scheme in particular for placing its heaviest burden on low earners, who were least likely to have private arrangements currently and who could least afford the additional contribution burden (Kieselbach 1999). Though mostly supportive of an investment in compulsory private pensions, unions insisted that the distribution of its short-term costs mirror the parity financing of the public system (Hank 1999).[26]

The plan also met with censure from across the political spectrum in parliament. The Christian Democrats accused the SPD of "the greatest election fraud in the history of the Federal Republic" for enacting cuts similar to those that it had campaigned against. In opposition, the party now positioned itself as champion of the interests of pensioners and low-income workers, attacking the benefit cutbacks and the dismantling of solidaristic provision.[27] Most ominously, the package – especially the move toward worker-financed compulsory private pensions – faced attack from the SPD's own backbench, with the party's leading social-policy expert, Rudolf Dressler, rebuking the government for a "paradigm change in pension policy" that departed from the party's own 1998 manifesto commitments (Quoted in Hering 2005, 260). MPs from the Green Party, the SPD's junior coalition partner, also objected to the compulsory nature of the new worker-financed private pensions, assailing Riester's proposal as a socially unjust "savings orgy," rather than meaningful structural reform (MAJ 1999a). The package as a whole appeared to lack a majority even within the governing coalition.

The two elements of Riester's reform plan met with differing fates. Partly through artful sequencing of fiscal decisions – and in an important win for business interests – the Chancellor managed to maneuver his party into acceptance of the pause in wage-indexation. Shortly before the unveiling of the pension reform plan, Schröder had won agreement from his parliamentary group to a DM 30 billion, 2-year target for deficit reduction. With transfers to the pension program comprising about one third of federal expenditures, this goal could only be met with slowed growth in retirement outlays, and the SPD parliamentary faction reluctantly approved the indexation measures as a component of the agreed fiscal tightening (Hering 2001b). Within and beyond the SPD backbench, however, opposition to compulsory private pensions financed only by employees was so intense that Riester was forced to rework this component of the package.

In a second round of reform initiated in 2000, the government sought to revisit its plans for private, funded retirement vehicles. Yet its capacity to invest in them remained tightly limited by the competing distributive demands of business and labor. If the government imposed the costs of an investment in

---

[26] Interestingly, in several interviews with trade-union officials, I heard no mention of the view, common among labor economists, that the employer's share of a tax on labor is paid by the worker in the form of a lower wage. Subjects spoke as though the direct incidence of the pension payroll tax was its final incidence.

[27] Horst Seehofer in CSK, KK and MAJ (1999).

private pensions on both employers and workers, it might appease unions and the left of the SPD, but employers would mount fierce opposition in public and through their veto-wielding CDU allies in the Bundesrat. A plan that imposed those costs only on workers, however, would court vocal protest and the risk of parliamentary defeat from the left.

Against these unpromising odds, the Labor Minister chose to abandon his plans for large-scale investment by discarding the principle of compulsion. In mid-2000, he announced the creation of a *voluntary* scheme of private funded pension provision, in which workers would be free to contribute up to 4 percent of gross wages into a range of approved retirement vehicles. The contributions of lower-income workers and recipients of unemployment insurance and sick pay would be generously subsidized. By making the payment of private contributions voluntary, the revised blueprint avoided imposing near-term losses on workers, partly assuaging the concerns of trade unionists and the social democratic left. Riester won further support from the SPD left and the CDU by making the tax treatment and subsidies to private accounts even more generous, especially for low-income workers (Schmitz 2000a; SM 2000a, 2000c; Hauschild 2000a, 2000b).

Having given up on a major investment, however, Riester needed to push for a vast long-term redistribution – in the form of major future benefit cuts – if he was to achieve his goal of long-run cost-control. He proposed radically reducing replacement rates in the public scheme over the next several decades, in proportion to the length of time that retiring workers would have had to contribute to their subsidized private accounts. By allowing state benefits to fall to 54 percent of average earnings by 2050, these cutbacks were projected to keep contribution rates in the public program below 22 percent until 2030 (Hering 2005).

Predictably, trade unions fiercely attacked this threat to their members' long-term welfare (Schmitz 2000e), underlining their demands with the threat of public demonstrations. Labor also received critical support from the left of the SPD parliamentary party (SM 2000b, 2000d; Schmitz 2000c; HB 2000). In the end, while the left was unable to avoid significant cutbacks, it did have sufficient leverage to avoid the worst. Under pressure from his own backbenches, Riester agreed to a benefit floor of 64 percent of earnings and to reinstating the wage-indexation of benefits for 2001 (Schmitz 2000c). As a final concession to union leaders, the government offered them an important organizational resource: union-negotiated *occupational* private pensions would take precedence over individual pension arrangements and would receive more generous tax treatment (Schmitz 2000d).

This revised package, as finally enacted into law in 2001, would require some commitment of state resources in the short term to finance a range of tax incentives and subsidies. But, as compared with Riester's original plan (and with the U.S. and Canadian reforms), the legislation represented a modest intertemporal trade-off. The policy investment in private pensions would only be as extensive as the voluntary uptake of the new savings options (Schulze and Jochem

2006). And several years after implementation, it appeared that the scheme had done little to generate new asset-accumulation: though 10 million individuals had taken out "Riester-Renten" by 2007, nearly all of this activity appears to represent the substitution of subsidized retirement vehicles for savings that individuals would have undertaken anyway (Corneo, Keese, and Schröder 2007).

A more significant investment would have required the government to impose substantial short-term costs on society by making private pensions compulsory. But the competing distributive demands of the most powerful organized interests had removed potential avenues of financing this investment from the realm of political feasibility. Despite initially ambitious intertemporal aims, the Schröder government's landmark reform would largely achieve its long-run goal of stabilizing contribution burdens by substantially curbing the growth of payments to future pensioners. The final outcome represented a significant *long-term redistributive* win for business, reflecting a balance of group power that favored capital over labor, even with a nominally center-left government in office.

CONCLUSION

Neither 1989 nor 2001 saw major policy investment in the financing of German pensions, but the chief obstacles to intertemporal reform differed between the cases. The reform process of 1989 was almost entirely driven by the policy preferences of politicians, bureaucrats, and interest-group leaders worried about the long-term trajectory of the social-insurance burden. By placing much of the policy process within neo-corporatist bargaining arenas and forging a consensus with the opposition, the government largely removed pension policy from the sphere of electoral competition. Thus, if German voters were relatively unconcerned about the pension system's distant troubles, the government was also relatively cushioned against electoral punishment for any pain that reform might inflict. Moreover, with a rough balance of power between the main organized stakeholders – capital and labor – neither could expect to solve its own long-run problems by unilaterally reallocating future burdens. In several key respects, then, political conditions in the 1980s favored policy investment.

Policymakers chose a strategy of long-term redistribution in 1989, however, because they did not expect that funding would deliver positive social returns. Crucial in shaping policymakers' causal beliefs was the ideational toolkit long employed by members of Germany's small and stable pension policy community. Embedded within this network was a shared mental model of pension policy forged by two massive failures of investment. Viewed through this frame, pension programs were mechanisms of intergenerational redistribution, not savings vehicles or insurance policies. State retirement schemes were inherently *political*, not actuarial, constructs and were hence subject to the vagaries of politics – including, critically, the tendency of governments to prey on accumulated funds. Hence, while the Kohl government enjoyed the electoral safety and institutional capacity to impose the short-term pain of investment, key decision makers simply did not perceive a credible and profitable long-term intertemporal trade-off to be available in this domain.

As in 1989, policymakers at the turn of the century thought hard about long-term consequences; and unlike in the prior episode, key decision makers now believed that successful policy investment was possible. By the late 1990s, dominant understandings of welfare-state financing within advanced industrialized democracies had shifted markedly, and Germany's long-standing corporatist pension policy network had been sidelined. The most influential models of pension financing now suggested multiple causal logics through which funding could generate long-run gains for aging societies. Moreover, the commonly presumed locus for funding had now shifted from the public to the private sector, further from the meddling hands of government. Prevailing ideas within the executive thus now supported a favorable understanding of policy investment, as a credible exchange of sacrifice today for the avoidance of far greater economic pain tomorrow.

But for the particular organized interests who would face investment's short-term costs – and who, to varying degrees, had the capacity to block policy change – the policy trade-off was structured in ways *un*favorable to investment. Thus, if policy investment now looked like a better idea to state officials, configurations of interest-group power and preferences made it impossible for the government to impose the necessary near-term costs. To a great degree, the specific redistributive outcome derived from the fact that business wielded substantially greater capacity than labor to shape policy in this period. That balance, moreover, depended on more than just constitutional structures. Despite a *formal* decentralization of authority that offered both labor and business substantial access to the policymaking process, dire economic conditions and dominant understandings of their sources gave German business associations the upper hand in the late 1990s and early 2000s. In fact, German employer groups in that period likely had the leverage to block almost any proposal that would substantially increase current costs for their members. Labor groups, for their part, had sufficient influence to resist the imposition of large one-sided short-run costs on their members, as Riester's initial proposed investment would have implied, and they were able to veto the most ambitious proposals of long-term benefit cuts. But relative to industry groups, trade unions were not strong enough to fend off demands for a significant long-run reduction in pension outlays.

As emphasized in Chapter 2, the *capacity* to veto does not necessarily imply a *willingness* to veto. Both business and labor might well have reaped long-run gains, relative to the status quo, from a policy investment in funded private pensions that was financed by both groups. Such an investment would have meant higher contribution costs in the near term, but it might have reduced financial burdens over the long term while maintaining overall retirement incomes. And, as our other cases indicate, organized producer groups are sometimes willing to accept precisely this kind of bargain.

Yet this intertemporal group calculus hinges critically on groups' being forced to *internalize* the costs of a long-term problem – on the absence, that is, of opportunities to escape or offload adverse long-run consequences. And in Germany in the late 1990s, the conditions for the calculus of cost-internalization were lacking. In particular, employers knew that current ideological and economic developments – the increasingly broad acceptance of the neo-liberal diagnosis, the ascendance of the Neue Mitte faction within the SPD, and a stubbornly weak labor market – would facilitate a substantial *redistribution* of benefits and burdens in their favor. Enjoying a privileged position, that is, German business leaders knew that they could likely achieve most of their aims by purely cross-sectional means – through long-run cutbacks in public provision – without paying the short-term costs of investment in private pension alternatives. Meanwhile, though business was far from perfectly mobile (see, e.g., Hall and Soskice 2001a), globalization had expanded capital's long-run exit options from the German political economy, opening an additional route of escape from long-term policy burdens. The logic of cost-internalization on the side of business was further undermined by current threats to firms' very survival. Whatever the future benefits of funded pensions, German employers saw *current* nonwage labor costs as a crushing burden that imperiled their capacity to compete on world markets. Long-run cost control would be worth little to companies that were pushed out of business (or out of Germany) by higher social contributions in the short run.

Employers' position then structured the trade-off faced by labor. If business was unwilling to share in the costs of investment, then labor had little reason to shoulder them on its own through compulsory worker-financed private savings vehicles. It would be of minimal value to workers if long-term pension contribution costs were tamed but a greater *share* of the social burden fell on labor, while private provision subject to market risk replaced guaranteed solidaristic benefits. To trade unionists, it was not worth upsetting the longstanding and highly beneficial *distributive* arrangement of jointly financed state social protection for an *aggregate* intertemporal gain.

As in Britain, a government that set out to reduce state pension costs – and preferred to do so through a major policy investment – found its capacity to invest greatly constrained by the unwillingness of powerful groups to pay short-term costs. And in both cases, a key factor was business's preference for long-term redistribution and its privileged capacity to achieve it. The chief difference, of course, was the far stronger organizational and institutional position of labor in the German case. If German unions were not powerful enough to fully maintain their members' welfare, they were sufficiently influential both to avert an asymmetrically financed investment and to limit the scale of their long-run losses. Thus, though major investment was removed from the menu of options in both cases, the German outcome was a much less radical long-term redistribution of resources than the British, reflecting a less lopsided distribution of group influence.

PART IV

CONCLUSION

CHAPTER II

Understanding the Politics of the Long Term

The politics of public policy is at once a struggle over who gets what and a struggle over when. In designing state action, governments face choices not just about the cross-sectional incidence of gains and losses, but also about how the benefits and burdens of policy should be allocated over time. In arenas ranging from environmental protection to economic reform to the management of scarce natural resources, the impact of public policy on citizens and societies may depend as much on the intertemporal character of governments' decisions as on their distributive profile. Moreover, as the preceding chapters have sought to demonstrate, explaining policy trade-offs over time requires a theoretical apparatus attuned to the distinctive cognitive and strategic features of intertemporal decision making.

The present chapter seeks first to summarize the evidence from the case studies in light of the book's theoretical framework. Then, expanding outward from specific causal hypotheses, I consider a set of general implications of the analysis for the study of public policymaking more broadly. In particular, the book's findings shed light on the relationship between distributive and intertemporal policy choice, on the nature of politicians' goals, on politicians' opportunities for electoral blame-avoidance, and on the role of ideas in policymaking. Finally, we will return to the exceptional Canadian episode of program design and consider the distinctive political logic of investment for the short term. Because the book's empirical investigation unfolded within a single policy field, the chapter also pays particular attention to the ways in which policy-making dynamics are likely to *vary* across issue areas.

TESTING THE THEORETICAL FRAMEWORK: A SUMMARY OF THE EVIDENCE

Governments have typically established contributory pension schemes to serve a distributive purpose: to provide a measure of income security to the aged. But the design and maintenance of these programs have repeatedly confronted policymakers with major intertemporal choices. At root, these dilemmas have derived from the projected growth of financial burdens on the programs over time – flowing initially from the inherent logic of contributory entitlement and, decades later, from the aging of populations. At the level of policy structure, pay-as-you-go financing and actuarial funding struck widely divergent balances between present and future. On the one hand, policymakers could choose to let future burdens fall where they may: collecting just enough tax revenues today to meet today's pension obligations, while deferring tomorrow's liabilities until tomorrow. Alternatively, governments could seek to moderate the future fiscal costs of social provision by smoothing them over time: by imposing higher payroll taxes and paying lower pensions in the short run, they could set in motion mechanisms of intertemporal transfer – the accumulation and investment of a fund – that might minimize tax burdens and enhance programs' capacities to pay benefits over the long run.

In the ten cases examined in this book, program designers and reformers responded to this dilemma in starkly differing ways. In crafting new retirement schemes, British officials chose the purely redistributive arrangement of PAYGO financing, and Canadian governments built up a modest fund, while politicians in the United States and Germany made massive investments in the full and nearly full funding, respectively, of future pension obligations. Similarly, reformers decades later would choose to allocate the pain of long-run demographic change in widely varying ways: from Canada's and the United States' (two) major policy investments in long-term fiscal capacities, to British and (two) German reforms that largely delayed the costs of adjustment and imposed them on tomorrow's pensioners.

Tables 11.1 and 11.2 summarize these outcomes together with the causal explanations presented in the empirical chapters. Structured by the theory spelled out in Chapter 2, the tables indicate for each case the degree of policy investment (High, Moderate, Low, or None), the strength of presence of each hypothesized necessary condition (High or Low), and the observable determinants that most powerfully influenced the strength of each condition. With the exception of the 1965 Canadian episode – considered separately later in the chapter – the cases lend strong support to the book's theoretical framework. Let us consider the evidence relevant to each condition in turn.

Electoral Safety

First, no government enacted a significant investment without some form of protection from the risk of electoral punishment for imposing its near-term costs on voters. In some cases – notably, Canada in 1998, the United States in 1935, and (though a case of low investment) Britain in 1986 – electoral safety derived in part from competitive conditions: a divided or enfeebled opposition meant that incumbents could afford to lose votes without great risk of losing office. And in Bismarck's Germany, institutional arrangements protected the incumbent government from short-term competitive threats. In a related dynamic, politicians in certain contexts enjoyed a competitive cushion deriving from cross-party *consensus* on reform. The U.S. reforms of 1983, for instance, were negotiated by a bipartisan commission. And, though they rejected investment for other

TABLE 11.1 *Summary of Outcomes and Explanations: Program Creation*

	Necessary Conditions *Observable determinants in italics*			Outcome
	Electoral safety	Expected long-term social returns	Institutional capacity	Degree of policy investment
Germany (1889)	**High:** Unelected executive means *low* short-term *competitive pressure*	**High:** *Dominant "insurance" mental model* emphasizes actuarial benefits, obscures political and economic risk	**High:** *Hyper-insulated institutions* minimize group access	**High**
Britain (1925)	**Low:** *Tight party competition;* investment *costs more salient than benefits*	**Low:** *Dominant Treasury mental model* emphasizes political uncertainty of investment	**Low:** *High institutional insulation* gives privileged access to organized allies of governing party, who prefer to avoid costs of investment	**None**
United States (1935)	**High:** *Weak opposition;* investment paired with *salient short-term benefits* and *costs* made *less salient* by delay	**High:** *Dominant "insurance" mental model* emphasizes actuarial benefits, obscures political and economic risk	**High:** Economic and electoral conditions temporarily concentrate authority, generating *hyper-insulated policymaking,* minimizing group influence	**High**
Canada (1965)	**High:** Investment a concession to provinces necessary for federal government to keep electoral pension promise	**Low:** But investment enacted for its *short-run benefits,* diminishing the relevance of unfavorable beliefs about long-term consequences generated by *redistributive and Keynesian models*	**High:** *Low insulation,* caused by decentralized federalism, reduces business influence and constrains labor's alternatives in ways favorable to investment; investment designed to pay off provincial veto players	**Moderate**

TABLE 11.2 *Summary of Outcomes and Explanations: Program Reform*

	Necessary Conditions *Observable determinants in italics*			Outcome
	Electoral safety	Expected long-term social returns	Institutional capacity	Degree of policy investment
United States (1977)	**High:** *Focusing event* of trust fund crisis raises salience of benefits and allows framing of investment as loss-avoidance	**High:** *Dominant "insurance" mental model* emphasizes actuarial benefits, obscures political and economic risk	**High:** *Low insulation* grants broad group access, precludes redistributive solutions, encouraging group acceptance of investment's costs	High
United States (1983)	**High:** *Focusing event* of trust fund crisis raises salience of benefits and allows framing of investment as loss-avoidance; plus *shared bipartisan responsibility* diffuses responsibility	**High:** *Dominant "insurance" mental model* emphasizes actuarial benefits, obscures political and economic risk	**High:** *Low insulation* grants broad group access, precludes redistributive solutions, encouraging group acceptance of investment's costs	High
Britain (1986)	**High:** *Divided* opposition *reduces electoral competition;* plus redistribution away from pensioners is as unpopular as investment	**High:** *Dominant market-liberal mental model* of economic behavior emphasizes benefits of individualized provision, obscures market risks	**Low:** *High insulation* gives disproportionate influence to group allies of governing party, making long-term redistribution a feasible alternative to policy investment	Low
Canada (1998)	**High:** *Focusing events* of current fiscal and economic crisis and clear projections of future trust-fund insolvency allow	**High:** *Dominant orthodox fiscal theory and World Bank model* emphasize economic dangers of debt	**High:** *Low insulation* grants broad group access, precludes redistributive solutions, encouraging group acceptance of investment's costs	High

TABLE 11.2 (*cont.*)

	Necessary Conditions *Observable determinants in italics*			Outcome
	Electoral safety	Expected long-term social returns	Institutional capacity	Degree of policy investment
	persuasive framing of investment as loss-avoiding trade-off; divided opposition *weakens electoral competition*	and benefits of funding; plus decentralized institutions allow policy design that dampens political uncertainty		
Germany (1989)	High: *Consensual institutions* allow bipartisan and neo-corporatist sharing of responsibility	Low: *Dominant redistributive mental model* emphasizes political and economic risks, obscures potential benefits of investment	High: *Low insulation* grants broad group access, precludes redistributive solutions to widely acknowledged long-term problem	None
Germany (2001)	Contingent: *Stiff electoral competition,* but reduced risk if organized groups and opposition party (in upper chamber) agree to reform	High: *Dominant World Bank and microeconomic models* emphasize economic benefits; private investment mechanism removes political risk	Low: Despite multiple veto points, economic crisis, dominant economic ideas, and exit options give employers privileged influence, approximating the power imbalance of *high insulation*; capable of achieving long-term redistribution, business is unwilling to accept short-term costs of equally financed investment; labor opposes distributive effects of remaining investment options	Low

reasons, German ministers in 1989 enjoyed the protection of highly cooperative neo-corporatist and cross-party bargaining institutions that removed the
issue of pension reform from the electoral arena.

To the extent that governments were exposed to potential attack by a credible
opposition, however, the cases confirm the predicted importance of the salience
of *information* about policy investment's consequences: informational conditions shaped politicians' capacity to effectively frame investment for voters in
favorable terms. In 1935 (despite a degree of competitive slack), the Roosevelt
Administration adopted tactics of policy design – familiar from the literature on
blame-avoidance – to minimize public attention to the *near-term costs* of the
Social Security Act and to enhance awareness of its compensating benefits: paying
immediate means-tested pensions to the aged poor and delaying the collection of
the first payroll taxes until just after the next election. This obfuscation of the Act's
full consequences allowed the Administration to define its proposal for voters as
an appealing combination of immediate relief *and* long-term security.

More striking is the role that clear and vivid information about policy investment's *long-term benefits* played in expanding politicians' rhetorical options
and shielding them from voter backlash. In the two U.S. reform cases the impending
bankruptcy of the program focused public attention on the danger of financial
imbalances, while in Canada a debt and currency crisis dramatized the risks of fiscal
profligacy. These focusing events allowed politicians to justify investment as a
project of loss-avoidance – sacrifice today to avert greater losses tomorrow – a
choice-definition particularly favorable to investment for a negatively biased electorate. Moreover, in both countries the strength of this frame was amplified by the
structure of the program itself – specifically, its strict reliance on a dedicated payroll
tax. Since only a program with a discrete revenue source could run out of money,
this financial arrangement made actuarial projections of "insolvency" plausible.
And the insulation of the program from the general budget clarified flows of
resources and, thus, greatly enhanced the credibility of politicians' claims that additional payroll taxes collected today would in fact be used to pay benefits tomorrow.

Competitive slack, favorable informational conditions, or a combination of
both was present in every case of major investment, suggesting an important
role for electoral calculations in governments' intertemporal policy choices. At
the same time, in some contrast to common intuitions about the electoral perils
of farsighted governance, these cases suggest a considerable range of mechanisms that can plausibly shield politicians from punishment for the costs of
investment. It is also striking that in not a single case were electoral considerations *decisive*: that is, there was no episode in which the other two necessary
conditions were met, but investment was rejected because of concerns about
voters' judgments. We cannot, of course, draw generalizations from our modest-
sized sample about the relative frequency of particular configurations of conditions in the full "population" of intertemporal policy choices. But the analysis
suggests, at a minimum, that intertemporal choice is not all about elections: that
we will frequently need to look beyond the dynamics of public support to
explain governments' intertemporal policy choices.

Expected Long-Term Social Returns

Our second condition proved at least as important a constraint on investment in the cases analyzed. As with electoral safety, no government (apart from the noted exception of Canada's in 1965) invested unless top officials believed that the long-term consequences of investment would be net-beneficial to society. Crucially, investing ministers did not merely justify their choices in *public* as socially beneficial. The available data indicate that, in privately debating and designing financing arrangements, politicians and bureaucrats paid sustained attention to the long-term social profit that they expected funding to yield. Bismarck's officials, for instance, focused heavily on the benefits of funding for the long-term trajectory of contribution rates and for the financial stability of the program, Roosevelt and Morgenthau on its capacity to restrain spending and protect the federal Treasury, and Canada's Paul Martin on its enhancement of the state's overall fiscal position.

Two of our cases of *non*-investment provide especially compelling evidence of the necessity of elite expectations of positive long-run social consequences. In Germany in 1989, reformers operating within the longstanding neo-corporatist pension-policy network enjoyed ideal institutional conditions for the forging of a cross-party and cross-group consensus on the imposition of losses – losses that all agreed were unavoidable, and that no social group could hope to unilaterally redistribute and externalize. In short, the electoral dangers of reform were low, and institutional capacity to impose costs on stakeholding interests was high. Investment failed to emerge, however, because members of the policy network believed that an accumulated fund was too vulnerable to the dangers of inflation and political manipulation. To these policy actors, funding appeared to mean certain and substantial costs today in exchange for the highly uncertain prospect of social benefits tomorrow. In Britain in 1925, investment faced multiple potential hurdles, including tight electoral competition, ministerial concerns about the effects of new pension taxes on the Tory vote, and hostility to new social burdens among business leaders influential within the governing party. Yet investment was removed from the menu of options *before* it could even be subject to these considerations: top civil servants vetting pension options rejected a funded plan because they believed that state reserves amassed for a specific long-term purpose would end up being spent by governments on other things in the short term.

Further, the case studies provide strong evidence that, in thinking through the consequences of their choices, policymakers drew on pre-existing and well-established ideational frameworks: mental models of the policy domain, often grounded in analogies to related spheres of activity, or of the political economy writ large. Decision makers in our cases conceptualized retirement schemes, variously, as insurance policies operating largely in isolation from politics and the real economy (Germany 1889; U.S. 1935, 1977, 1983); as mechanisms for redistributing real economic resources (Canada 1965; Germany 1989); as micro-economic incentive structures (Germany 2001); or, akin to private pensions, as engines of savings and investment (Canada 1998). Each conceptualization isolated a particular set of "moving parts" in the system and facilitated reasoning about the causal relationships among them.

In some cases, the most decisive causal beliefs derived not from actors' theories of public policy *per se,* but rather from their mental models of democratic *politics.* Particularly important was the degree to which actors conceived of democratic governance as bedeviled by an intrinsic and irresolvable tragedy of public choice – in which political leaders' motives are wholly defined by their electoral incentives and stand in inherent and constant tension with the demands of fiscal prudence, sound economic management, and long-range planning. This pessimistic model of democratic politics not only characterized the "Treasury view" dominant in the British bureaucracy of the 1920s but also the reasoning of British business leaders at the time and of capitalists in the United States in 1935 and in Canada in 1965. Roosevelt Administration officials in 1935 and policymakers and business groups in Canada in 1998 also perceived electoral politics as posing serious challenges of commitment. But, crucially, their causal model was a more differentiated one in which the myopic pressures on politicians were *variable,* rather than intrinsic, and could be *moderated* by well-designed program structures.

Because elites typically devoted substantial cognitive resources to the choice, their own causal understandings tended to be far more sophisticated than the frames that they used to publicly justify their choices. Policymakers' mental models were nonetheless *simplifications*: each model isolated a limited set of key parameters in the system, captured a subset of the relevant causal relations among them, and stripped away others – thus rendering a complex choice problem tractable. Actors' causal mappings powerfully shaped their perceptions of long-term consequences by filling in "unknowns" and by directing their attention toward particular long-term causal logics and – equally importantly – *away* from others. Thus, in those cases in which actors understood state pensions as insurance, we saw deliberations focused heavily on the actuarial dynamics that affect *private* arrangements. Actors' reasoning focused on the relations among a scheme's current contribution rates, its long-term financial balance, and its long-run contribution burden – key moving parts in an actuarial model. In turn, we observed these actors devoting scant attention to the political dynamics that might specifically surround the financing of a *public* program.

In contrast, where retirement programs were understood as politically derived mechanisms for distributing real economic resources – characterized by a different configuration of adjustable levers – policymakers gave serious consideration to political threats to the accumulation of public funds and to monetary threats to a fund's real asset values. At the same time, actors working with this redistributive model attended little or not at all to plausible causal dynamics that their mental model simplified away – including the effects of fund-accumulation on national savings and investment and the microeconomic effects of long-run contribution burdens on labor markets.

Similarly, a model of democratic politics as an unavoidable tragedy of governance encouraged reasoning about the dangers of expanding state fiscal capacities and about the impossibility of shielding funds from government predation. A model of politicians' behavior as *dependent* on structural context, on the other hand, generated reasoning about how the details of program design might amplify or constrain future political opportunism. It led actors to reason about the ways in which actuarial principles might bind future politicians' hands and in which investment rules could shield assets from manipulation.

The particular combination of causal relationships that a given mental model captured thus exerted a powerful effect on the weightings that boundedly rational decision makers ascribed to possible outcomes. In doing so, actors' prior causal ideas helped *define the structure* of the policy dilemma before them. In particular, policymakers' causal maps determined whether they understood policy invest-ment as a credible trade-off between short-term social costs and long-term social gain, a costly gamble, or a mere redistribution of resources. Indeed, actors' mental models helped them identify which social trade-offs were *available* to be made through pension program design, and which were unachievable. Thus, politicians were not merely *suppliers* of choice structures to voters: elites' own policy prefe-rences also depended heavily on their *own* definitions of the decision.

In Germany in 1889 and 2001, the U.S. in all episodes, Britain in 1986, and Canada in 1998 – cases in which actuarial or neoliberal mental models emphasized funding's advantages – policymakers conceived of investment as an exchange of economic sacrifice today for relatively certain and greater fiscal or economic benefits tomorrow. This was a trade-off that ministers were eager to make, if it could be achieved within electoral and institutional constrains. Under alternative ideational conditions, however, decision makers perceived funding's national long-term savings to be illusory. In the Canadian (1965) and German (1989) redistributive views, policy investment would, at best, mean inflicting short-term pain to change the source of pension financing (from tax revenues to asset-earnings), while leaving the overall long-run burden on producers unchanged. The dominant British (1925) and German (1989) models also foresaw worse: that the extracted resources might be redistributed right away (as politicians diverted surpluses toward their favored immediate spending goals) or lost altogether over the long run (to inflation). In each of these causal understandings, it was impossible to reliably store real value in a pension fund over time. To policymakers in these cases, the choice of financing mechanism thus did not imply an intertemporal trade-off at all: the only trade-off they perceived to be *available* was the cross-sectional allocation of burdens and benefits at a given moment in time. With the choice defined in these terms, PAYGO appeared the more advantageous option over both the short run *and* the long.

Institutional Capacity

Finally, where ministers saw investment as electorally safe and socially benefi-cial, their capacity to enact it hinged in large measure on the structure of political institutions: most importantly, on the ways in which institutions structured opportunities and trade-offs for the well-organized groups that would bear investment's costs. Institutional effects depended, first, on how cost-bearing groups understood the profile of investment's expected consequences: as a horizontal redistribution of resources away from them, or as a vertical trade-off that would impose costs on them today but deliver greater benefits to them tomorrow. In some instances – as in the case of German trade unions in 2001, considering a shift to private pensions paid for only by workers – groups perceived a proposed investment as an adverse horizontal redistribution because of easily understood, objective distributional features of the investment's structure. In many cases, however, interest group leaders – like policymakers inside the state – made use of longstanding cognitive models of policy and politics to draw inferences about investment's longer-term consequences. As noted, for instance, capitalists in several contexts drew on understandings of democratic politics as inescapably biased against fiscal restraint and policy stability. When politicians promised firms long-term gain in exchange for short-run pain, these business leaders simply did not find the promise credible. Rather, they expected that this intertemporal bargain would merely result in a redistributive loss, as resources extracted from them today were in fact spent on someone else tomorrow.

Where cost-bearing groups perceived policy investment as an adverse horizontal redistribution of resources, they believed that it would make them strictly worse off than the status quo. And political institutions, under these circumstances, affected governments' policymaking capacity in ways familiar from studies of distributive politics: the centralization of policymaking authority tended to enhance ministers' capacity to invest by locking out the groups that would pay its costs. Thus, in the United States in 1935, it was critical that employers – who perceived investment as fraught with political uncertainty and redistributive danger – were excluded from influence by a high (and temporary) concentration of authority in the hands of the President. And the failure of investment in Germany in 2001 owed much to the fact that incomplete party discipline within the governing party afforded a well-organized labor movement substantial influence within the Bundestag.

Yet when the cost-bearers perceived investment as a plausible *vertical* trade-off – credibly promising them long-term benefits that exceeded their short-run losses – institutions operated differently on ministerial capacities. Crucially, investment was no group's *first* choice. Even where they perceived investment as a long-term improvement over the status quo – as in the U.S., British, and Canadian reform episodes – business and labor groups still preferred a favorable *long-term redistribution* of resources over an intertemporal trade-off with short-run costs. Under these conditions, institutional effects displayed the curvilinear pattern predicted for vertical investments in Chapter 2. On the one hand, ministers could enact vertical investments, in spite of groups' preference-orderings, where institutions effected a *hyper-insulation* of policymaking – a lack of veto points *combined* with insulation from electoral competition – that largely excluded the cost-bearers from influence. Such was the case in Bismarck's Germany, where the outcome was largely dictated by the preferences of an unelected and dominant executive. At this end of the institutional spectrum, it was the *veto-opportunity* effect of institutions that determined ministers' capacity to invest.

On the other hand, ministers could also enact vertical investments where institutions effected a *minimal* insulation of policymaking such that group influence was widely dispersed. Where veto power was relatively evenly distributed, ministerial capacity derived from an institutional structuring of influential groups' *menus of options*: where organized interests found themselves institutionally constrained from achieving their first choice of long-term redistribution, they were willing to accept vertical investment as a "second best" alternative (again, as long as they perceived investment as making them better off than the status quo). In the decentralized Canadian and U.S. contexts, interest groups with strong influence over the policy process ultimately supported investment-based reforms that, while costly to them in the near term, would likely protect them against greater losses over the long run.

The institutional conditions *least* conducive to investment capacity were those that generated high (but not hyper-) insulation by concentrating authority in the hands of an elected executive. What made high insulation unfavorable to investment was its tendency to generate a large imbalance in interest-group influence: privileging groups that enjoyed a strategic alliance with the governing party – which depended on group resources to win elections – while locking out other social interests. In light of standard distributive theories of institutional effects, the fate of Thatcher's pension reform was perhaps the most surprising outcome examined: ministers with unrivalled policymaking authority abandoned an investment that would fulfill one of their chief long-term ideological objectives at relatively modest electoral risk. The problem, in essence, was that ministers wielded *enough* authority to redistribute and, thus, *too much* authority to impose an intertemporal trade-off on their group allies. While complete SERPS privatization offered employers massive long-term cost-savings, it would do so at considerable short-term cost. By contrast, a mere cutback in SERPS benefits would effect a long-term redistribution in business's favor *without* near-term sacrifice. With labor and welfare groups institutionally excluded from the policymaking process, business's first-best redistributive option was eminently achievable. So this is what employers demanded of – and secured from – their friends in office. A similar dynamic drove employers' influential demands during the 2001 reforms in Germany. While German institutions provided a measure of access to both labor and capital, the playing field was tilted considerably in capital's favor by economic crisis, enhanced exit options, and widely held causal understandings of the economy. Here, too, business leaders believed (correctly) that they could achieve a favorable reallocation of long-run resources and therefore used their influence to reject any investment option that would impose costs on firms in the short run.

Importantly, where groups opposed vertical intertemporal trade-offs that would be profitable for them over the long run, it was *not* because they took a short-sighted view. Where they were *forced* to choose between short-term sacrifice and even greater long-term losses, groups generally opted for the former. Critically, however, that was not always the structure of the trade-off that organized interests confronted. Where interest groups rejected profitable vertical investments, it was typically because the menu of feasible options included even more effective means of advancing their long-run interests.

The cases thus indicate that the institutional logic of investment differs markedly from that of cross-sectional redistribution. For policies that simply reallocate across groups (or are perceived as doing so), the losers' policy demands will be independent of strategic context: because those who bear the policy's costs will be left worse off than under the status quo, they will use any veto opportunity to block policy change. Policymaking capacity, for a purely cross-sectional trade-off, thus depends critically on the minimization of veto opportunities. But where policies offer interest groups their own internalized trade-offs – making them *better* off relative to the status quo but at some initial cost – their policy position will depend on the range of feasible alternatives. In particular, a group's stance on investment will hinge on whether it can achieve similar long-term gains through less-costly redistributive means. The broad institutional inclusion of societal interests can thus render intertemporal trade-offs more acceptable to their cost-bearers – and, in turn, more politically achievable – by removing more-appealing options from the menu.

Stepping back to look across the three conditions, the strength of each depended heavily on the policy preferences of a major class of political actor: of voters (electoral safety), of elected officials (expected long-term returns), and of organized groups (institutional capacity).[1] To underline a central theme of the study, these actors' policy preferences over investment turned in large part on how the trade-off was defined for them. Because of the vast causal and informational complexity of assessing long-run consequences, choice definition was partly a matter of *cognition* – as informational salience shaped politicians' rhetorical options vis-à-vis voters and as causal ideas guided elites' own reasoning about costs and benefits. Once actors had conceptualized the policy dilemma, institutions then lent *strategic* structure to the choice by configuring the menu of alternatives. On the whole, investment was far more likely to emerge where both cognitive understandings and structural constraints confined actors to a trade-off between a measure of short-run welfare and a greater measure of long-run welfare.

This dynamic has a powerful – if perhaps counterintuitive – implication: in the cases we examined, the greatest hurdle to investment was *not* that actors might not care enough about the future. Rather, it was the possibility that actors either might not *perceive* or could *escape* the intertemporal social dilemmas that their policy choices implied. The conclusion to be drawn is not that the conditions permitting policy investment are particularly common: democratic politics abounds with ideational and structural forces that can bias choice-definitions away from investment. And, as the necessary-conditions framework implies, many things have to go right – policy dilemmas have to be favorably aligned across multiple classes of actor – for investment to emerge. But where they do confront ineluctable trade-offs between pain today and greater pain

---

[1] As should be clear, however, the conditions did not depend *solely* on these actors' preferences. Where electoral competition was weak, voters' preferences were irrelevant; and where institutions hyper-insulated the policy process, group preferences could be ignored.

tomorrow, voters, politicians, and organized interests will be much more willing to accept costly policy investment as the least-bad option before them.

BROADER IMPLICATIONS

Beyond its bearing on the specific hypotheses derived in Chapter 2, the analysis also has more general implications for our understanding of public policy. In the succeeding subsections, I consider what the study's findings tell us about four central features of the politics of policymaking: the relationship between distributive and intertemporal policy choice; the nature of politicians' goals; the relative influence of ideational and material forces on policy; and the role of policy benefits in shaping politicians' electoral constraints. Finally, I return to the exceptional Canadian case of program creation to speculate on the distinctive political logic of investing for the short, rather than for the long, term.

Politics as Distributive and Intertemporal Choice

While the study has analytically distinguished between distributive and intertemporal conceptualizations of what governments do, it would be a mistake to view these as competing ways of thinking about public policy. In fact, a central implication of this book's arguments is that these two dimensions of policy choice – who gets what, and when – must be considered *simultaneously* if we are to arrive at valid explanations. For one thing, the analysis indicates that a temporal lens can help us account for some of the purely distributive choices governments make. When long-range problems are on the agenda, we gain substantial leverage in explaining distributive change by identifying the factors that make intertemporal solutions more difficult. In the British case of reform, for instance, the dramatic losses that Thatcher imposed on future pensioners make sense only by reference to the conditions that impeded the investment that she had hoped to achieve in the first place.[2]

Equally, we cannot understand why governments choose investment over short-run maximizing without examining the politics of distribution. As I have argued, a chief obstacle to policy investment in a democracy is that actors may understand or confront long-term policy choices in redistributive *rather* than intertemporal terms. In this important sense, opportunities to pursue a politics of zero-sum redistribution *get in the way* of a positive-sum politics of intertemporal choice. In addition, we have observed – as in the hostile response of German trade unions to proposals for worker-financed funded pensions – that groups' willingness to accept investments will depend on the cross-sectional distribution of those investments' consequences (on this dependence, see also King 1993).

---

[2] King (1993) also points out that the intensity of short-run distributive conflict may depend on the intertemporal posture of policy: where groups expect policy to generate a long-run expansion of the pie, they will fight less fiercely, King argues, over the allocation of short-term resources.

Explaining governments' intertemporal policy choices thus requires examining the opportunities for and constraints on cross-sectional redistribution. The central logic of this argument, building on Olson (1982), is that of the *internalization* of outcomes: groups are more willing to invest to the extent that they must internalize the long-term social consequences of governments' policy choices. I have focused in this study on one major determinant of groups' capacity to externalize consequences: the structure of political institutions. But the same logic implies that other conditions that inhibit redistribution or otherwise force cost-internalization should likewise make policy investment more likely. One likely candidate is the original focus of Olson's internalization argument: the degree of encompassing-ness of group organization. As Olson argues, the larger the share of society that an organized group represents, the more it is forced to internalize the aggregate-welfare effects of redistributive measures. A strand of more recent work on the economic effects of neo-corporatism also suggests that highly encompassing and centralized producer organizations are, under the right conditions, willing to forego distributive gains for bargains that expand the social pie as a whole (e.g., Garrett 1998; Calmfors and Driffill 1988). Because more encompassing groups have less scope to shift the impact of long-term social problems away from their members, they should have greater incentives to invest in aggregate solutions.

Similarly, the *technical* feasibility of shifting a long-run problem across groups should matter. In purely practical terms, it is easier to craft policy mechanisms that can redirect the costs of some social problems than of others. For instance, problems that impose localized physical damage (e.g., natural disasters) or that diminish the availability of scarce, non-substitutable resources (e.g., clean air) may be less amenable to redistribution than are problems involving highly fungible (e.g., financial) resources. The varying technical difficulty of reallocating different types of social outcomes cross-sectionally should be an important source of varia-tion in the politics of the long term: across issue areas, the prospects for investment should vary inversely with the technical opportunities for redistribution.

Finally, we need to analyze policy along both axes of choice because of the prominent role of *uncertainty* in intertemporal decision making. In the politics of the long term, uncertainty often means ambiguity about the *dimension* of choice along which a policy trade-off lies. As we have observed, governments may present organized interests with nominally intertemporal policy propositions: pay costs today in exchange for greater gains tomorrow. But where groups believe that the risk is high that governments will renege or that policy investments will otherwise fail, they tend to understand investment as a redistributive *rather* than an inter-temporal proposition: as the extraction of resources from them today and the diversion of those resources elsewhere tomorrow. Organized interests are likely to reject investment where they view the state as incapable of *implementing* intertem-poral bargains and avoiding redistributive temptation. Such groups might favor public investment *in principle*, but believe that the best they can hope to get out of politics *in practice* is distributional gain. We have to think jointly about "who gets what" and "when" in part because, in democratic decision making, much of story lies in how actors define the question that public policies are supposed to answer.

Politicians' Goals

Evidence from our ten case studies suggests that we may need to rethink some of the more common conceptions of elected officials' motives – especially, the notion of politicians as "single-minded reelection seekers" (Mayhew 1974, 17). This assumption has the advantages of analytical parsimony and a capacity to generate crisp predictions under many circumstances. The empirical analysis in this book also supports the general view that politicians in a democracy value political survival and, moreover, that they reject policy alternatives that pose a *substantial risk* of losing them the next election. We saw no sign that officeholders were willing to commit electoral suicide in order to invest in the long run. Moreover, detailed evidence drawn from internal policy deliberations indicated that politicians in almost every case were keenly sensitive to the electoral implications of their choices. In some cases, this meant thinking hard about the potential reaction of the average voter; in others, it meant responding to the demands of well-organized interests who wielded political resources that could bear on incumbents' reelection prospects.

At the same time, politicians were not consistent *maximizers* of public approval or votes in their intertemporal decision making. Consider the instances across our cases in which elected officials chose a policy option with more rather than less electoral risk than the alternatives. Most strikingly, in the creation of the U.S. pension program, Roosevelt chose an option that – compared to PAYGO financing – imposed far greater losses on and delivered far smaller benefits to citizens in the near term. The Canadian Liberals in 1998 chose to double payroll taxes within the space of six years in the absence of a short-term trust-fund crisis to force their hands, in order to help solve a financial problem to which few voters were paying attention. Even the Thatcher government's long-term redistributive reforms – slashing future pension payouts – were far from vote-maximizing choices. Given powerful public attachments to old-age pension benefits and the absence of any short-term imperative to act, the most popular policy by far would have been to do nothing at all. Nor is there evidence in any of these cases that governments reaped rewards in the form of enhanced interest-group support that offset the risks of a popular backlash. In all of these instances, the impetus for investment or reform came from within the state, not from organized interests.

Electoral considerations operated as a *constraint* on choice as politicians in our cases sought to avoid options that would court serious risk of electoral defeat – hence the necessity of some form of electoral protection for investment to emerge. But the electoral risk of policy action did not have to be zero for politicians to proceed. While Roosevelt, the Canadian Liberals, and Thatcher acted from positions of competitive strength, all faced volatile electoral environments (amplified in the latter two cases by first-past-the-post electoral rules), and reelection was a sure thing for none of them. Rather than strictly maximizing their chances of remaining in power, officeholders seemed willing to make *trade-offs* between policy goals and votes when the terms of trade were favorable. Not infrequently, politicians appeared willing to purchase highly valued outcomes – from fiscal discipline and economic growth to the moral advantages of contributory insurance over welfare – at some potential cost in votes. They acted not as though they valued office above all else, but as though office was a means to the ultimate end of shaping social conditions. As a result, politicians' own policy goals – and their causal beliefs about how to achieve them – played a critical role in shaping governments' choices.

Moreover, as politicians weighed the social costs and benefits of policy alternatives, it is striking how far into the future their time horizons extended. As the tracing of policy deliberations within the cases revealed, elected officials routinely devoted serious consideration to consequences still decades away. At moments of program creation, Roosevelt, Chamberlain and Churchill, and Canadian cabinet officials thought carefully about a range of temporally distant social effects of alternative financing methods. Likewise, the case studies of reform indicated that Canadian, British, and German ministers were strongly motivated by concern about the long-run development of tax and contribution rates and the state's fiscal position. Even where politicians opted for long-term redistribution over policy investment, this choice often reflected intense concern with shaping distant allocations of benefits and burdens.

It is important to emphasize that there is nothing *inherently* "long term" about pension policymaking. While the design of a pension scheme *has* long-run ramifications, ministers could have easily compared financing options solely in terms of their massive near-term consequences for the elderly, workers, employers, and public budgets. Only rarely, however, did the urgency of the immediate appear to crowd out the impact of longer-run concerns on policy deliberations. Put another way, when governments chose *not* to invest, it was not because they did not attend enough to or care enough about the long run. For the most part, it was because they – or their group allies – did not view investment as the best available means to their long-term goals.

There is certainly good reason to assume that politicians will accord *less* weight to more temporally distant consequences – outcomes that are less certain, require less urgent action, and will have a less immediate impact on their career prospects – and that policymaking in a competitive democracy will, as a result, display a bias toward the near term. Moreover, it is crucial to bear in mind that policy investment is only one way in which political actors can respond with foresight to long-term social problems. We should expect a great deal of far-sighted policy-seeking to take redistributive rather than intertemporal form: a reallocation of future resources in favor of a *particular* social group that makes no investment in greater *aggregate* social welfare. But the cases analyzed here suggest a need to reconsider and complicate the conventional understanding of decision making in democratic politics as dominated by short-run and electoral considerations. To explain governments' choices, we will often have to devote as much attention to politicians' own beliefs and goals as to the preferences of their constituents. And we will frequently need to conceive of their programmatic agendas as long-range endeavors. When they are pursuing policy goals, political leaders will rarely aspire to fleeting achievements; much more commonly, they will seek to leave an enduring mark on society.

Ideas and Rationality

The last two decades have witnessed an "ideational turn" in comparative politics (Blyth 2003). Scholars studying phenomena as varied as race politics (Bleich 2003), economic policymaking (Hall 1993; Derthick and Quirk 1985), and party programs (Berman 1998) have accorded a central role to ideas in shaping actors' policy and institutional preferences. At the same time, few analysts have argued that political decision making is a *purely* ideational process. Most scholars, even when emphasizing the effect of ideas, have retained a core understanding of elite behavior as largely purposive (i.e., goal-seeking) and, in some cases, strategic. Even in ideationally focused accounts of policymaking, political elites appear to be highly motivated to get their choices right, and to deliberately gather and analyze information about objective conditions that bear on the consequences of alternative options. Political decision making, in most ideational analyses, appears to be driven by an admixture of rationality and material circumstances, on the one hand, and cognition and construction, on the other.

This hybrid understanding of elite political choice is almost certainly more accurate than either a purely constructivist or a purely rationalist view. Yet the dual nature of elite decision making also raises important questions about how to integrate ideational and strategic insights with one another. In particular, it calls for a better understanding of the *conditions* under which ideas have greatest causal importance relative to objective factors, of the ways in which material and ideational structures *interact* with one another to generate actor preferences, and of the circumstances under which new material facts may yield ideational *change*. This study's findings suggest the outlines of a model of elite political decision making that may help to resolve important outstanding issues of theoretical integration.

On the one hand, the case studies presented here point to important limits to rationalist accounts – and, specifically, to rationalist accounts of how political actors manage *uncertainty*. The political problem of uncertainty has, of course, been a central theme in rationalist arguments, lying at the center of models of phenomena such as bargaining and delegation (e.g., McNollgast 1999; North 1993; Moe 1990). Rationalist theories typically treat uncertainty as an objective feature of a choice situation and as a strategic problem to which there is a single best response. Legislators delegating to executive-branch bureaucracies that they cannot directly control, for instance, face an objective problem of "agency drift" and, as a rational response, will choose to constrain agency discretion by adopting hand-binding mechanisms, such as the drafting of highly detailed statutes (Huber and Shipan 2002). Actors contemplating nonsimultaneous exchanges will be deterred by the (again, objective) risk of time inconsistency unless credible mechanisms exist or can be crafted to hold parties to their promises (Weingast and Marshall 1988). Rationalist scholars have tended to place special emphasis on the role of *institutions* – e.g., structures that bind actors' hands, deter reneging, or insulate decision making from political pressures – in resolving such problems of commitment (e.g., North 1990; see also Hall and Taylor 1996). And, in general, actors facing uncertainty – about, for instance, payoffs or other actors' responses – are held to engage in expected-utility calculations based on the probability of alternative possibilities.[3] In the rationalist view of uncertainty, in sum, actors tend to have optimal strategies that can be derived from objective features of the strategic context, payoff structure, and probabilities that they confront.

A comparison across our cases, however, is difficult to reconcile with an objectivist and institutionally focused understanding of preference-formation under uncertainty. Consider the two cases of Britain in 1925 and Germany in 1989. In both episodes, policymakers viewed fund-accumulation as extremely risky because of the danger that governments might break long-term promises and raid pension assets in the short term. This similarity in uncertainty-assessments, however, emerged from vastly differing institutional conditions: while authority in Britain was centralized within a single-party cabinet at the national level, power in Germany was spread across parties in a governing coalition and between federal and state governments. Perhaps most importantly, Germany's pension funds were administered jointly by representatives of the key stakeholders – trade unions, employers, and the state. If Britain's institutions facilitated unilateral executive action, Germany's seemed (and, in some sense, *were*) designed specifically to bind governments' hands and hold them accountable to the social interests to whom they had made commitments.

Consider also the creation of the German pension scheme and the design and two reforms of the U.S. Social Security program. In none of these four cases did policymakers within the executive display significant concern about the perils of fund-diversion or inflation *despite the objective presence of these risks*. Indeed, one or both of these threats materialized well within the time horizon over which each of these investments was intended to pay off. In Germany, inflation and political manipulation would together wipe out a massive accumulated fund within 30 years of the program's establishment. Following the enactment of the U.S. pension plan, it would take Congress just three years to begin a decade-long process of drawing down the program's trust fund by enriching benefits and delaying payroll-tax increases scheduled into the original 1935 law. And, following the 1977 and 1983 reforms, as assets again accumulated within the system, legislators would count program surpluses as part of the government's overall fiscal balance, effectively using dedicated payroll taxes to legitimize spending elsewhere in the federal budget. As we have noted, in 1977 and 1983 policymakers did not even take basic structural measures – such as meaningfully separating Social Security from general budgetary accounting – to insulate their investments from manipulation. It is not just that politicians did not seek to bind their *own* hands, but that hand-binding measures were not demanded by organized interests deeply involved in the policymaking processes – the very groups from whom short-term

---

[3] In his largely rationalist analysis of intertemporal policy choice in U.S. tax policy, King (1993) also emphasizes the structural and material determinants of actors' uncertainty about and expectations of long-run policy benefits, including the institutional locus of decision making, the structure of policy instruments, and the market rate of return to capital.

costs were being extracted and to whom long-term promises were being made. In principle, it might have been the case that actors in Germany and the United States seriously *considered* the monetary and political risks of investment but determined that they were modest – and thus weighted them, consistent with expected-utility theory, according to an assessment of their probabilities of occurring. It is also conceivable that actors might have pondered stronger institutional safeguards but decided that such measures would have short-term fiscal or political costs that outweighed their long-run benefits. But extensive searches of archival records, contemporaneous news reports, vast secondary literatures, and participant accounts in interviews and memoirs yielded virtually no indication that such considerations were even *raised* during policy deliberations in any of these cases.

To put the overall point differently, having the "right" institutions was neither necessary nor sufficient for overcoming problems of political uncertainty and making commitments credible. In the U.S. reform processes, policymakers and interest groups found the intertemporal bargain credible *despite* major structural vulnerabilities of the investment to future manipulation; and in Germany in 1989, a seemingly ideal set of institutions did little to reassure actors that pension assets could be safely committed.

These cases pose serious challenges to rational-institutionalist accounts of decision making under uncertainty. At the same time, the book's argument suggests an analytical strategy for integrating rationalist and ideational approaches – an approach grounded in cognitive mechanisms of information-processing. Somewhat surprisingly, cognition has not yet been a major focus in the literature on the role of ideas in public policy. In contrast to students of mass opinion, analysts of ideas in *elites'* policy choices have tended to leave weakly specified how – at the level of mental process – ideational frameworks shape choices.[4] I have argued, in particular, that a focus on the cognitive problem of *attention* offers an especially fruitful analytical path. While scholarship on agenda-setting has long demonstrated the importance of attention in the selection of problems for decision (Jones and Baumgartner 2005; Baumgartner and Jones 1993; Kingdon 1984), the findings of the present study suggest that attentional dynamics have broader implications for the formation of elites' beliefs and preferences.

In particular, a focus on attention allows us to model political decision makers as instrumental and motivated seekers of information, on the one hand, and as agents with bounded processing capacities, on the other. Evidence from our empirical cases indicates that elite actors gathered extensive data and reasoned intensively about objective features of their choice situation, such as the fiscal and actuarial implications, the economic impact, and the electoral ramifications of the alternatives. But in the face of massive causal complexity, they could not – and, as we observed, *did* not – attend to all potentially relevant features of their decisions. Which causal possibilities actors thought about – and which they ignored – was highly consequential in shaping their preferences.

---

[4] I refer here to the literature on domestic public policy. Work in international relations has been far more attentive to cognitive processes and biases (e.g., Jervis 1976; Johnston 1996).

The dangers of political predation, for instance, were in some measure objectively present in all of the episodes that we examined. If institutional arrangements could *dampen* the risk of promise-breaking, it is nearly impossible for one democratic government to completely bind the hands of the next. Even under the best of institutional rules, funding would be potentially vulnerable to future manipulation by sufficiently shrewd and motivated politicians. Thus, in principle, pension policymakers might have worried about the problem of political uncertainty in each of our cases. And, at the same time, political uncertainty represented only a small *subset* of the range of long-run causal dynamics that might arise from the choice of a financing method and to which policymakers might have attended. Variation in policymakers' belief sets was thus determined as much by *whether* they reasoned about the risk of manipulation as by the institutional factors that might objectively affect the magnitude of that risk. That allocation of attention, in turn, was driven at least as strongly by actors' cognitive mappings of the choice problem as by objective features of the environment.

I am thus suggesting that we can best understand political elites as engaging in processes of motivated and instrumental calculation that are *structured* by prior ideational expectations. For instance, whether institutions matter – whether they shape actors' perceptions of the credibility of commitments – depends on whether actors' prior cognitive frameworks induce them to attend to relevant institutional features. For British decision makers who took the "Treasury view" of public finance, founded on skepticism of governments' capacities for self-restraint, the high institutional concentration of authority in Britain would have been a highly salient and diagnostic fact about the environment – in large part *because* it confirmed their preexisting beliefs. Bismarckian officials and U.S. reformers, on the other hand, who understood pension financing as an actuarial problem akin to managing a private insurance plan, devoted little attention to the risk of future political manipulation and thus failed to reason carefully about the objective structure of institutional commitment mechanisms in their environments. In the Canadian reform process, actors were conditioned to think about problems of political interference by Quebec's long experience with fund management. As a result, both policymakers and business groups closely scrutinized the rules by which the investment board would be composed and operate. With their attention ideationally focused on the problem of commitment, objective features of the macro-institutional environment and of program rules – particularly the leveraging of Canada's federal structure to dilute the influence of any one government over the investment board – then played a key role in shaping actors' credibility perceptions.

In sum, in the synthesis that I am proposing, we would want to consider political institutions an important potential influence on causal beliefs, preferences, and choices in the face of uncertainty. But we would understand institutional effects to be highly *conditioned* by the ideational lens through which decision makers interpret choice problems: whether a given institutional fact matters will depend on whether actors are cognitively predisposed to reason through the very problem which that institutional structure might aggravate or solve.

Understanding attention as a key computational constraint can also shed light on the conditions under which ideational constructs, *as opposed to* objective circumstances, should yield greatest explanatory leverage. In particular, the importance of ideas should rise with the complexity and ambiguity of the causal relationships bearing on actors' goals. Where the relevant causal connections are interpretable and relatively few in number, it should be easy for actors to survey them fully and to connect policy choices to knowable consequences. For instance, when a policy's largest costs or benefits are inscribed transparently into statute – in the form, for instance, of a change in tax or benefit rates – and will arrive relatively soon, their assessment will present no particular cognitive challenge. In such situations, we can likely explain preferences as a straightforward response to the knowable distribution of a set of material policy spoils.

Ideas and their attentional effects should have the greatest impact, however, when options and actors' utilities are connected by dense webs of causation that are imperfectly understood: when actors face more potential causal logics, more potential outcomes, and more information than they can systematically and comprehensively assess. Attempts to use public policy to shape social conditions decades into the future are among the choice problems likely to bear these qualities. But so too are a range of common political endeavors that depend for their success on steering or restructuring complex social systems. An attentional approach would thus predict an especially important role for ideas in ambitious undertakings such as the management of the macroeconomy, the promotion of economic development, the design of constitutions, and the mitigation of ethnic conflict.

Finally, if my argument suggests that ideas condition the effect of material circumstances, a focus on attention can also help us think about how and when objective facts can reshape cognitive structures. If preexisting mental models bias attention in confirmatory ways, then we should expect ideas to be quite resilient, even in the face of seemingly discordant information. Our cases suggest that, once widely accepted, ideational frameworks – whether broad political-economic models or specific understandings of pensions – can remain dominant for decades within state bureaucracies, neo-corporatist policy communities, and legislative committees, enduring major changes in the political balance of power and in exogenous conditions. Most striking in this respect is the German experience during Weimar, when the insurance model and bureaucratic preferences for funding survived the disastrous loss of pension assets to political manipulation and inflation after World War I.

If powerful confirmatory biases tend to hold dominant ideas in place, however, cognitive patterns can also make sense of the emergence of ideational *change*. Indeed, psychological research indicates that the confirmation bias is not absolute. Disconfirmatory information is more likely to attract extra processing and to weaken pre-existing expectations when that information takes a particular form: when the discrepancy between beliefs and data is transparent (Anderson and Kellam 1992); when the divergence from expectations is large (Fiske and Taylor 1991); and when the unexpected outcomes are repeated across multiple contexts, making them less susceptible to discounting as exceptional

(Hewstone et al. 2000). We would thus expect to observe a pattern of punctuated equilibria in ideas over time (Jones and Baumgartner 2005). Most of the time, an actor's preexisting ideas should act as relatively exogenous and stable drivers of information-processing and causal inference. On rare occasion, however, multiple large and clear empirical divergences from the model should draw extra attention, generating rapid learning that leads to the model's replacement by an alternative framework more consistent with the newly salient data (see also Hall 1993).

The rare instances of major ideational change considered in this book yield suggestive support for these propositions. If Germany presents the most dramatic illustration of ideational resilience in the face of disaster, it also yields the most striking examples of conceptual replacement. As we observed, following the loss of the German pension fund in the early 1920s, state officials and pension experts adopted confirmatory interpretations of the event, directing their attention to the exceptional exogenous conditions of war and hyperinflation, rather than to choices of program design. When the insurance model finally gave way, it was only after a recurrence of the very same calamity – the misuse of pension funds by the Third Reich and their obliteration by postwar inflation. As actors sought to understand this second debacle, the evidence of *policy* failure – the risks inherent in treating a public pension plan as an actuarial arrangement involving the long-term accumulation of assets – was now too transparent to ignore. Not only was there a vast divergence between model and outcome, but its repetition under two different regimes made it too difficult to explain away as a stroke of misfortune. With the insurance analogy deeply discredited, confirmatory mechanisms could no longer hold ideational alternatives at bay. Postwar social policy experts and economists found a receptive audience when they advanced a rival understanding of a public retirement scheme – as a vehicle of redistribution – that was better able to make sense of the facts. This redistributive model survived for decades, guiding actors through the major reforms of 1989. And when an alternative, microeconomic framework became influential in the late 1990s, this shift also followed political rupture and enormous, repeated policy failure: the reconstitution of the state through reunification followed by an unemployment crisis that proved stubbornly unresponsive to massive federal intervention. As economic malaise persisted and social-contribution rates climbed, existing redistributive principles appeared increasingly untenable. Meanwhile, a microeconomic view of labor markets – as depressed precisely *because* of an excessive social burden – offered a plausible causal interpretation of the problem and a persuasive explanation of past policy failure.

Ideational change in politics will rarely be a purely cognitive process. Ideational dynamics themselves will often have important institutional, organizational, and power-based components (Hall 1993; Weir 1989; see also Baumgartner and Jones 1993). In both cases of change in Germany, for instance, once-dominant understandings were left far more vulnerable by a major shift in the locus of authority – through the mass replacement of public officials (1940s) or the sidelining of longstanding policy networks (1990s). As Hugh Heclo (1974) famously observed, there is no contradiction in understanding politics as driven by both "powering" and "puzzling" – as a struggle among purposive actors with bounded capacities to make sense of their environment. Indeed, I am contending that understanding how actors' conceptualize their choices is *essential* to good instrumentalist explanation. However, I am also arguing that ideational explanations must take seriously political elites' incentives – in particular, their strong motivation to gather diagnostic information, reason intensively, and get choices right. A theory of ideas should also be able to tell us when actors will lean on existing mental maps and when they take into account new information and update prior understandings. There are multiple possible ways to integrate rationalist and ideational insights, but I would suggest that any well-articulated synthesis is likely to be firmly grounded in what we know about patterns of information processing and the structure of human cognition.

The Electoral Relevance of Policy Benefits

As discussed in Chapter 2, policy investment might fit poorly with mass attitudes for at least two reasons. First, longer-term outcomes are less likely to be salient to minimally attentive voters than are shorter-term outcomes; hence, investment's near-term costs will on average receive more attention than its delayed benefits. Second, a negativity bias built into human cognition will tend to make policy losses more salient than policy gains, regardless of the relative timing of these consequences. Standard arguments about blame-avoidance strategies have often focused on this second bias and have generally implied that voters are, as a consequence, uninterested in *trade-offs* between pain and gain: if a policy imposes noticeable sacrifice on citizens, the fact that it may also offer them offsetting gains will do little to diminish the risk of electoral punishment (Pierson 1994; Arnold 1990; Weaver 1986). Politicians, in this view, are much better advised to avoid responsibility for a costly policy than to try to claim credit for its benefits. This logic also implies that variation in governments' willingness to impose losses derives largely from the degree to which politicians can escape *accountability* for those costs. The U.S. reform episode of 1983, in which bipartisan consensus on a package of pain helped insulate incumbents against the risk of electoral retribution, lends support to what we might call the "accountability view" of blame-avoidance.

The logic of accountability surely supplies an important piece of the puzzle of investment under electoral constraint. Yet the book's findings also suggest that the logic of accountability yields too narrow a view of the blame-avoidance strategies available to politicians and of their scope for imposing losses. In particular, U.S. Democrats in 1977 and Canadian Liberals in 1998 enacted massive, broad tax hikes that citizens undoubtedly noticed; and they did so over the objections of a political opposition that stood ready to attack this policy record at the next election. In both cases, that is, incumbents took *responsibility* for costly policy measures. As I have argued, what allowed politicians to make these investments at modest electoral risk was a capacity to persuasively connect this pain to offsetting gain. A key informational precondition, in both cases, was the presence of clear and dramatic signals of future *negative* outcomes that policy action could plausibly address. The pension program's financial operations (in the U.S.) and market developments (in Canada) provided the public with vivid, easy-to-interpret indicators of looming disaster, allowing incumbents to credibly *frame* policy investment as an exercise in loss-prevention – a trade-off of costs today for the avoidance of far greater costs tomorrow.

A full understanding of the effectiveness of such strategies will have to await micro-level studies of how citizens form intertemporal policy attitudes, an issue that has received little attention to date (though see Jacobs and Matthews 2008). Yet the logic of my argument – a logic of rhetorical effects conditioned by informational context – is consistent with what we already know about the sources and structure of mass policy preferences. Analysts have repeatedly found that citizens' attitudes and voting behavior on most issues are only weakly determined by a policy's true material costs and benefits to them (Lewis-Beck and Stegmaier 2000; Sears 1993; Sears and Funk 1991). Mass policy opinion instead seems to be heavily conditioned by elite cues and by the precise ways in which policy trade-offs are framed (Sniderman and Bullock 2004; Brewer 2003; Sniderman 2000; Nelson and Oxley 1999; Kinder and Sanders 1996; Zaller 1992). At the same time, political rhetoric is not a free-for-all: there appear to be important constraints on the framing strategies that elites can persuasively employ, including limits imposed by the broader informational setting within which arguments are made (Chong and Druckman 2007a; Druckman 2001; Lupia and McCubbins 1998). In other words, rather than revealing citizens to be uniformly focused on the costs of policy change, the literature on public opinion describes an electorate that pays varying degrees of attention to alternative policy considerations and the relations among them, depending in part on the information and lines of reasoning made available. Together with the evidence presented in this book, these studies suggest an expanded account of governments' capacities for blame avoidance: they imply some opportunity, given the right informational conditions, for politicians to rhetorically *justify* the pain that they inflict on their constituents. And, crucially, they imply that voters may sometimes be willing to make trade-offs across offsetting policy consequences, where the link between pain and gain can be made sufficiently clear and credible.

A further implication of this logic is that politicians' electoral opportunities to invest should vary systematically across *types of policy problem*. Not all long-term problems are equally well endowed with a capacity to generate clear, vivid signals that prefigure future harms – an informational environment supportive of a loss-avoidance framing. For one thing, policy problems vary in the degree to which they are associated with periodic emergencies or aggregated losses that are likely to serve as focusing events (Kingdon 1984). Severe storm activity or unusually warm temperatures, for instance, systematically boost public concern about climate change (Krosnick et al. 2006; Oppenheimer and Todorov 2006). Similarly, decaying public infrastructure generates transportation disasters, diminishing energy supplies can lead to speculative spikes in the price of gasoline, and environmentally hazardous industrial processes generate occasional toxic spills that tend to raise the salience of these issues.

But the temporal structure of the danger signals is crucial. For focusing events to facilitate policy investment, they must *foreshadow* future losses: they must occur well *before* the long-term problem has imposed its full costs on society, while there remains time to invest in a solution. Many long-run challenges – such as vanishing forests and future skill shortages – impose their mounting costs gradually and quietly over time, without vivid punctuation along the way. Others – like the need to invest in flood or earthquake protection – only become apparent in a single "big bang" after it is too late to act. In the absence of early-warning events, such problems are unlikely to draw public attention in advance, and governments will be far more constrained in their capacity to justify costly investment in a solution.

Second, long-term problems vary in the degree to which their consequences can be made *specific* and *concrete* for citizens, and thus rendered easy to imagine or interpret (Tversky and Kahneman 1974). The capacity of pension actuaries to express future harms in terms of specific financial costs makes it easy for individuals to imagine such outcomes, and to weigh the benefits of an investment (the avoidance of these losses) against its current costs. Similarly, voters likely have relatively little trouble giving concrete meaning to the long-term costs of crumbling roads or rail lines that lie in their vicinity and on which they regularly depend. In contrast, the range of unfamiliar, complex, and spatially dispersed economic, health, and environmental consequences of pollution or climate change are far more difficult for most citizens to concretely imagine and are thus likely to play a more modest role in their policy evaluations.

Third, it is easier to identify the losers from some long-term problems – and, in turn, the prospective beneficiaries of investment – than from others. In the case of pensions, contributors and future beneficiaries more-or-less know who they are. Similarly, residents of low-lying coastal regions know that they will face the most severe consequences of global warming, just as adult voters know whether they have children who stand to benefit over the long term from increased investment in education. It is much harder, however, to say who would benefit from public debt reduction, structural reform of the economy, or tougher regulation of forestry practices. At the individual level, this should make a framing of investment as pain-today-for-gain-tomorrow a much tougher sell.

Fourth – and related to identifiability and concreteness – future losses against a *current baseline* ought to be more salient than losses against uncertain future circumstances (Tversky and Kahneman 1991). Negatively biased voters should pay greatest attention to warnings of the withdrawal of goods and services that they already enjoy or rely on, such as threats to their current homes, jobs, or social benefits, or to future benefit entitlements on which they know they will depend. By contrast, predictions of increases in taxes or prices a decade or more away ask citizens to imagine losses relative to an unknown baseline income and are, therefore, likely to be felt as less threatening. All else equal, we should thus be more likely to see elected governments making costly investments in solving long-term problems that imperil particular current endowments than in addressing the potential loss of hypothetical future consumption possibilities.

In sum, we may gain important insight into cross-issue variation in intertemporal policy choices by considering the nature of the information that different types of social problems generate. In many policy fields, the distant gains from policy investment will be difficult for voters to comprehend or imagine or will fail to draw their attention. But in spheres in which citizens face specific threats to their present position, from future perils foreshadowed by current crises, governments should enjoy enhanced rhetorical options for favorably framing painful policy change. And in such situations, even incumbents in competitive electoral environments may be willing to take responsibility for the conspicuous costs of investment.

Investing for the Short Term

As we have noted, the case of the creation of the Canada and Quebec Pension Plans suggests a logic of policy investment that is not fully captured by the theoretical framework proposed in Chapter 2. That framework is based on the assumption that the potential appeal of investment to voters, politicians, and groups lies in its capacity to convert short-term pain into greater long-term gain. As will be recalled from Chapter 6, however, Ottawa and the Canadian provinces did not set up the CPP/QPP on a partially funded basis because of a concern about long-run outcomes. Indeed, they believed that funding offered no real long-term fiscal or economic advantage over PAYGO financing. Rather, they chose partial funding because this investment would generate a stock of assets that could be used, *in the short-to-medium term*, to finance enhancements in public services and infrastructure.

This logic of policy investment is worth pausing to ponder. Within and beyond the field of pensions, it may not be uncommon for investment to yield politically relevant short-run benefits. As observers of legislative appropriations know well, one social planner's investment may be someone else's "pork-barrel" benefit. Indeed, endeavors that generate social profit over the long term will often yield gains today that have little to do with the project's stated future goal. A chief reason is that investment in a long-term good usually relies on a mechanism of intertemporal transfer that begins operating in the near term. This will sometimes mean that policy investment will generate *current* income for those citizens who are paid to develop, maintain, and manage the human, natural, and financial resources being extracted and invested. Some policy investments may emerge, then, not because voters or interest groups value their long-term benefits, but because a group of short-term "winners" values the investments' immediate payoffs. The long-term returns will sometimes be merely a positive side effect of a policy enacted for other reasons – like a bridge that just happens to convey traffic across a river, decades after its construction provided well-paying jobs for local residents.

Policy investments will likely vary in the degree to which they activate a politics of short-term gains. A critical determinant should be the particular mechanism of intertemporal transfer on which the investment relies – specifically, whether that mechanism delivers concentrated short-run benefits to a well-organized group. So, for instance, policy investments that rely on the direct creation of new capital – such as physical infrastructure or skills – will generate a substantial short-term gain concentrated on workers and owners of firms in the capital-good-producing sector. Where production is highly localized – as in processes of physical construction – these short-term rents are likely to be all the more visible and politically relevant. Investments that rely on processes of financial investment may also generate well-organized winners in the near term if the management of these assets is contracted out to private financial-services firms that stand to earn considerable transaction and administrative fees.

On the other hand, not all policy investments will be championed by well-organized short-term winners. For instance, investments relying on the accumulation of scarce natural resources – such as state-imposed limits on the exploitation of fisheries or forests – will not usually require a greatly expanded workforce or generate near-term rents for private actors. Resource-preservation typically requires occasional monitoring and enforcement by existing (or incrementally expanded) regulatory agencies, and its positive employment effects rarely generate influential lobbying in its favor. Likewise, investment in the reduction of public debt does not rely on a concentrated group of producers to generate its long-run fiscal benefits.

In a similar vein, the temporal structure of the visibility of investment's *long-term* benefits may also affect its politics. Like any private investment, many policy investments deliver their gains in a *stream* of payoffs, rather than a lump sum, and become profitable only after an extended period of time. And policy investments vary widely in how soon that stream of benefits starts or otherwise becomes visible to constituents. Because of the slowness of the natural processes at work, the environmental benefits of a carbon tax may take decades to begin to materialize; even then, it will be difficult for voters to perceive those damages that, thanks to the investment, never occurred. In contrast, investments in physical infrastructure – schools, roads, bridges – often generate visible signs of future benefits as soon as the builders break ground. The stream of actual benefits, moreover, will typically commence quite quickly, once construction is finished. Thus, even if such projects become profitable in social-accounting terms only after many years of use, local citizens will have salient evidence of policy gains much sooner.

In explaining a policy investment that partakes of a logic of politically salient short-term gains, we would need to adapt this book's explanatory strategy in a couple of ways. Enacting politicians will still require some form of protection from the risk of retribution by those voters who would pay the investment's short-run costs; but that insulation could derive from the visibility of the policy's *immediate* payoffs – not just from the salience of its long-term benefits or the obfuscation of short-run losses. Where those costs fall on organized interests, governments' capacities to invest will still be higher when the same groups will also reap the policy's long-term benefits and where institutions inhibit redistributive alternatives. But even where cost-paying groups stand opposed, politicians may confront offsetting demands *for* investment by the organized constituencies that stand to capture rents in the short run. What is most distinctive about investment for the short run, however, is its possible independence from the long-run causal beliefs of policymakers. The prospect of generating visible, short-term gains for key constituencies may make the expectation of long-run social returns unnecessary: ministers need not believe that investment will improve social welfare tomorrow if they know that it will generate powerful winners today.

This study has outlined a broad analytical framework for explaining elected governments' choices for the long term and sought to demonstrate its utility within the largest sphere of state activity in advanced industrialized democracies. It is likely, however, that a productive research agenda into intertemporal politics will require careful disaggregation. As we seek causal patterns across space, time, and policy field, we are unlikely to uncover a single political logic of intertemporal choice. As with the study of who gets what, progress in understanding the politics of timing will depend on the careful development of middle-range arguments sensitive to the context and content of policy choice. Moreover, studying the politics of "when" by no means requires us to leave behind our longstanding interest in, and accumulated knowledge about, the politics of who gets what. As I have argued, the two dimensions of choice – cross-sectional and intertemporal – are inseparable whenever political actors deliberate or fight over the long-run allocation of burdens and benefits.

Conceiving of policy choice as a decision about timing can only enhance the relevance of political analysis to real-world policy problems. A striking range of the most serious policy challenges facing industrialized democracies today take the form of foreseeable crises mounting steadily over time. Though their full impact may lie decades away, these problems ultimately threaten the very sustainability of modern societies. And while these challenges raise important distributive trade-offs, some of the most excruciating dilemmas that they pose are intertemporal: they force us to choose between inflicting substantial pain now to mitigate future harms and maximizing present consumption at the risk of future devastation. Whether governments make significant investments today – in livable environments, sustainable technologies, and productive workforces – will largely determine how nasty and brutish the distributive battles of tomorrow will be.

Public discourse about democracy is frequently suffused with deep skepticism about the capacity of representative institutions to grapple with long-term policy challenges. Taken together, this book's findings suggest reason for somewhat greater optimism about the compatibility of democratic rule and prudent governance. They suggest that both politicians and organized interests frequently assess policies based on the long-run social outcomes that they will generate. They imply that citizens, under the right conditions, can be persuaded of the merits of trading present sacrifice for the avoidance of future loss. And they suggest that political institutions – especially those that constrain government action – can impose useful limits on actors' attempts to make long-term perils someone else's problem. Democracy may well produce a substantial policy tilt toward the short run, but democratic politics will not always be hostile terrain for those seeking to invest in the long run.

Bibliography

VI. Kommission des Reichstages. 1889. "Bericht der VI. Kommission über derselben zur Vorberathung überwiesenen Entwurf eines Gesetzes, betreffend die Alters- und Invaliditätsversicherung." *Stenographische Berichte über die Verhandlungen des Reichstags.* 2. Anlageband. 7. Legislaturperiode, IV. Session (Drucksache Nr. 141).

Aaron, Henry. 1966. "The Social Insurance Paradox." *Canadian Journal of Economics and Political Science* 32 (3):371–4.

Achenbaum, W. Andrew. 1986. *Social Security: Visions and Revisions.* New York: Cambridge University Press.

Addison, Paul. 1992. *Churchill on the Home Front: 1900–1955.* London: Jonathan Cape.

Ainsworth, Cameron, and Rashid Sumaila. 2007. Personal communication based on unpublished analysis. Vancouver, B.C., September 16.

Aldcroft, Derek Howard. 1970. *The Inter-war Economy: Britain, 1919–1939.* London: Batsford.

Alesina, Alberto, and Nouriel Roubini. 1992. "Political Cycles in OECD Economies." *The Review of Economic Studies* 59: 663–88.

Alt, James E., and K. Alec Chrystal. 1983. *Political Economics.* Berkeley: University of California Press.

Amenta, Edwin. 1992. "A Hero for the Aged? The Townsend Movement, the Political Mediation Model, and U.S. Old-Age Policy, 1934–1950." *American Journal of Sociology* 98 (2):308–39.

Anderson, Craig A., and Kathryn L. Kellam. 1992. "Belief Perseverance, Biased Assimilation, and Covariation Detection: The Effects of Hypothetical Social Theories and New Data." *Personality and Social Psychology Bulletin* 18 (5):555–65.

Anderson, Karen M., and Traute Meyer. 2003. "Social Democracy, Unions, and Pension Politics in Germany and Sweden." *Journal of Public Policy* 23 (1):23–54.

Araki, Hiroshi. 2000. "Ideas and Welfare: The Conservative Transformation of the British Pension Regime." *Journal of Social Policy* 29 (4):599–621.

Arnold, R. Douglas. 1990. *The Logic of Congressional Action.* New Haven: Yale University Press.

Bailey, Ian, and Susanne Rupp. 2004. "Politics, Industry and the Regulation of Industrial Greenhouse-Gas Emissions in the UK and Germany." *European Environment* 14: 235–50.

Balcer, Yves, and Izzet Sahin. 1984. "Dynamics of Pension Reform: The Case of Ontario." *The Journal of Risk and Insurance* 51 (4):652–86.

Baldwin, Peter. 1990. *The Politics of Social Solidarity: Class Bases of the European Welfare State 1875–1975*. Cambridge: Cambridge University Press.

Ball, Robert M. 1990. "Panel on Formulating a Deficit Reduction Package: What Is the Role of Social Security? First Presentation." In *Social Security and the Budget: Proceedings of the First Conference of the National Academy of Social Insurance*, ed. Henry J. Aaron. New York: University Press of America.

Bank of England. 2010. *Monetary and Financial Statistics*. Accessed July 14, 2010 at http://www.bankofengland.co.uk/mfsd/iadb/NewIntermed.asp.

Banting, Keith G. 1985. "Institutional Conservatism: Federalism and Pension Reform." In *Canadian Social Welfare Policy: Federal and Provincial Dimensions*, ed. Jacqueline. S. Ismael. Kingston and Montreal: McGill-Queen's University Press.

———1987. *The Welfare State and Canadian Federalism, 2nd Edition*. Montreal: McGill-Queen's University Press.

Barr, Nicholas. 2000. "Reforming Pensions: Myths, Truths, and Policy Choices." Washington, D.C.: International Monetary Fund.

Barro, Robert J. 1990. "Government Spending in a Simple Model of Endogeneous Growth" *Journal of Political Economy* 89 (5, Part 2):S103–S25.

Baumgartner, Frank R., and Bryan D. Jones. 1993. *Agendas and Instability in American Politics*. Chicago: University of Chicago Press.

Bawn, Kathleen. 1998. "Congressional Party Leadership: Utilitarian versus Majoritarian Incentives." *Legislative Studies Quarterly* 23 (2):219–43.

Becker, Gary S. and Robert J. Barro. 1988. "A Reformulation of the Economic Theory of Fertility." *Quarterly Journal of Economics* 103 (1):1–25.

Béland, Daniel, and John Myles. 2005. "Stasis Amidst Change: Canadian Pension Reform in an Age of Retrenchment." In *Ageing and Pension Reform around the World*, eds. Giuliano Bonoli and Toshimitsu Shinkawa. Cheltenham: Edward Elgar Publishing.

Berger, Helge. 1997. "The Bundesbank's Path to Independence: Evidence from the 1950s." *Public Choice* 93 (3):427–53.

Berkowitz, Edward. 1991. *America's Welfare State: From Roosevelt to Reagan*. Baltimore: The Johns Hopkins University Press.

Berman, Sheri. 1998. *The Social Democratic Moment: Ideas and Politics in the Making of Interwar Europe*. Cambridge, MA: Harvard University Press.

Black, Julia, and Richard Nobles. 1998. "Personal Pensions Misselling: The Causes and Lessons of Regulatory Failure." *Modern Law Review* 61 (6):789–820.

Blackbourn, David. 1998. *The Long Nineteenth Century: A History of Germany, 1780–1918*. New York: Oxford University Press.

Blair, Tony, and Gerhard Schröder. 1999. "Europe: The Third Way/Die Neue Mitte."

Blake, David. 2002. "The United Kingdom Pension System: Key Issues." Discussion Paper PI-0107. London: The Pensions Institute, Birkbeck College.

Bleich, Erik. 2002. "Integrating Ideas into Policy-Making Analysis: Frames and Race Policies in Britain and France." *Comparative Political Studies* 35 (9):1054–76.

———2003. *Race Politics in Britain and France: Ideas and Policymaking Since the 1960's*. New York: Cambridge University Press.

Blyth, Mark. 2002. *Great Transformations: Economic Ideas and Institutional Change in the Twentieth Century*. New York: Cambridge University Press.

———2003. "Structures Do Not Come with an Instruction Sheet: Interests, Ideas, and Progress in Political Science." *Perspectives on Politics* 1 (4):695–706.

Board of Trustees. 1973. "Annual Report of the Board of Trustees of the Federal Old-Age and Survivors Insurance and Disability Insurance Trust Funds." Washington, D.C.: U.S. Government Printing Office.

——1974. "Annual Report of the Board of Trustees of the Federal Old-Age and Survivors Insurance and Disability Insurance Trust Funds." Washington, D.C.: U.S. Government Printing Office.

——1975. "Annual Report of the Board of Trustees of the Federal Old-Age and Survivors Insurance and Disability Insurance Trust Funds." Washington, D.C.: U.S. Government Printing Office.

——1976. "Annual Report of the Board of Trustees of the Federal Old-Age and Survivors Insurance and Disability Insurance Trust Funds." Washington, D.C.: U.S. Government Printing Office.

——1983. "Annual Report of the Board of Trustees of the Federal Old-Age and Survivors Insurance and Disability Insurance Trust Funds." Washington, D.C.: U.S. Government Printing Office.

——2006. "Annual Report of the Board of Trustees of the Federal Old-Age and Survivors Insurance and Disability Insurance Trust Funds." Washington, D.C.: U.S. Government Printing Office.

——2010. "Annual Report of the Board of Trustees of the Federal Old-Age and Survivors Insurance and Disability Insurance Trust Funds." Washington, D.C.: U.S. Government Printing Office.

Bonoli, Giuliano. 1997. "Classifying Welfare States: A Two-Dimension Approach." *Journal of Social Policy* 26 (3):351–72.

——2000. *The Politics of Pension Reform: Institutions and Policy Change in Western Europe.* Cambridge: Cambridge University Press.

Borscheid, Peter. 1989. *Mit Sicherheit Leben: Die Geschichte der deutschen Lebensversicherungswirtschaft und der Provinzial-Lebensversicherungsanstalt von Westfalen.* Greven: Eggenkamp Verlag.

Bosse, Robert, and Erich von Woedtke. 1891. *Das Reichsgesetz betreffend die Invaliditäts- und Altersversicherung der Arbeiter vom 22. Juni 1889.* Leipzig: Verlag von Duncker & Humblot.

Bothwell, Robert, Ian M. Drummond, and John English. 1989. *Canada since 1945: Power, Politics, and Provincialism.* Buffalo: University of Toronto Press.

Boynton, G. R. 1990. "Ideas and Action: A Cognitive Model of the Senate Agriculture Committee." *Political Behavior* 12 (2):181–213.

Breger, Monika. 1982. *Die Haltung der industriellen Unternehmer zur staatlichen Sozialpolitik in den Jahren 1878–1891.* Frankfurt: Haag + Herchen Verlag.

——1994. "Der Anteil der deutschen Großindustriellen an der Konzeptualisierung der Bismarckschen Sozialgesetzgebung." In *Bismarcks Sozialstaat: Beiträge zur Geschichte der Sozialpolitik und zur sozialpolitische Geschichtsschreibung,* ed. Lothar Machtan. Frankfurt: Campus Verlag.

Brewer, Marilynn B. 1988. "A Dual Process Model of Impression Formation." In *Advances in Social Cognition, Volume 1,* eds. Robert S. Wyer and Thomas K. Srull. Hillsdale, NJ: Lawrence Erlbaum Associates, Inc.

Brewer, Paul R. 2003. "Values, Political Knowledge, and Public Opinion about Gay Rights: A Framing-Based Account." *Public Opinion Quarterly* 67 (2):173–201.

Brinkley, Alan. 1995. *The End of Reform: New Deal Liberalism in Recession and War.* New York: Knopf.

Bruner, Jerome S. 1973. *Going Beyond the Information Given.* New York: Norton.

Bryden, Kenneth. 1974. *Old Age Pensions and Policy-Making in Canada*. Montreal: McGill-Queen's University Press.

Bryden, P. E. 1997. *Planners and Politicians: Liberal Politics and Social Policy 1957–1968*. Buffalo: McGill-Queen's University Press.

Buchanan, James M. 1990. "The Budgetary Politics of Social Security." In *Social Security's Looming Surpluses: Prospects and Implications*, ed. Carolyn L. Weaver. Washington, D.C.: AEI Press.

Budden, Robert. 1999. "Trouble with Choice: The UK's Pensions Sales Abuses are Lessons for European Markets." *Financial Times*, October 5, 4.

Bueck, H. A., ed. 1887. *Verhandlungen, Mittheilungen and Berichte des Centralverbandes deutscher Industrieller*. No. 38. Berlin.

Burby, Raymond J., Peter J. May. 1997. *Making Governments Plan: State Experiments in Managing Land Use*. Baltimore: The Johns Hopkins University Press.

Buthe, Tim. 2002. "Taking Temporality Seriously: Modeling History and the Use of Narratives as Evidence." *American Political Science Review* 96 (3):481–93.

Butler, David, and Donald Stokes. 1969. *Political Change in Britain*. New York: St. Martin's Press.

Calmfors, Lars, and John Driffill. 1988. "Bargaining Structure, Corporatism and Macroeconomic Performance." *Economic Policy* 6 (April):13–61.

Cameron, David R. 1984. "Social Democracy, Corporatism, Labour Quiescence and the Representation of Economic Interest in Advanced Capitalist Society." In *Order and Conflict in Contemporary Capitalism*, ed. John H. Goldthorpe. Oxford: Oxford University Press.

Campbell, Donald, and Alan Boras. 1995. "National Debt Row Sparks New Call for Action." *Calgary Herald*, January 14, A1.

Caplan, Jane. 1989. *Government without Administration: State and Civil Service in Weimar and Nazi Germany*. Oxford: Clarendon Press.

Carrick, Rob. 1997. "Stocks to Bolster CPP: Bolder Strategy Sought for Canadians' Billions." *Globe and Mail*, February 15, B1.

Casper, Steven, and Sigurt Vitols. 1997. "The German Model in the 1990s: Problems and Prospects." *Industry and Innovation* 4 (1):1–13.

Chaiken, Shelly. 1980. "Heuristic versus Systematic Information Processing and the Use of Source versus Message Cues in Persuasion." *Journal of Personality and Social Psychology* 39 (5).

Chappell, Henry W., Jr., and William R. Keech. 1985. "A New View of Political Accountability for Economic Performance." *American Political Science Review* 79 (1):10–27.

Chong, Dennis, and James N. Druckman. 2007a. "Framing Public Opinion in Competitive Democracies." *American Political Science Review* 101 (4):637–55.

——2007b. "Framing Theory." *Annual Review of Political Science* 10: 103–26.

Cohen, Bruce. 1993. "Employers Push CPP Reform." *Financial Post*, September 23, 19.

Collier, David, Henry E. Brady, and Jason Seawright. 2004. "Toward an Alternative View of Methodology: Sources of Leverage in Causal Inference." In *Rethinking Social Inquiry: Diverse Tools, Shared Standards*, eds. Henry E. Brady and David Collier. Lanham, MD: Rowman and Littlefield.

Committee on Economic Security. 1935. *Report to the President of the Committee on Economic Security*. Washington, D.C.: U.S. Government Printing Office.

——1937. *Social Security in America: The Factual Background of the Social Security Act as Summarized from Staff Reports to the Committee on Economic Security.* Washington, D.C.: U.S. Government Printing Office.

"Congress Moves on Social Security Legislation." 1977. *National Journal,* November 5, 1737.

Congressional Budget Office. January 2002. "The Budget and Economic Outlook: Fiscal Years 2003–2012." Washington, D.C.: Government Printing Office.

Congressional Quarterly. 1978. *Congressional Quarterly Almanac, 95th Congress, 1st Session, 1977.* Vol. 33. Washington, D.C.: Congressional Quarterly, Inc.

Conte, Christopher R. 1979. "Economic Policy." In *Congressional Quarterly Almanac, 95th Congress, 2nd Session, 1978.* Vol. 34. Washington, D.C.: Congressional Quarterly, Inc.

Converse, Philip E. 1964. "The Nature of Belief Systems in Mass Publics." In *Ideology and Discontent,* ed. David E. Apter. New York: Free Press.

Corneo, Giacomo, Matthias Keese, and Carsten Schröder. 2007. "Erhöht die Riester-Förderung die Sparneigung von Geringverdienern?" Economics Working Paper No. 2007-30. Kiel: Christian-Albrechts-Universität zu Kiel.

Corsetti, Giancarlo, and Klaus Schmidt-Hebbel. 1995. "Pension Reform and Growth." Policy Research Working Paper No. 1471. Washington, D.C.: World Bank.

Cowan, Edward. 1976. "One Way or the Other, Social Security Will Need Help." *New York Times,* March 7, E3.

——1977. "Carter Asks Tax Rises, Funding Shift to Ease Social Security Drain." *New York Times,* May 10, 1, 55.

Coyne, Andrew. 1996. "Would You Buy a Used Car from This Pension Fund?" *Globe and Mail,* January 15, A12.

Craig, Gordon. 1981. *Germany 1866–1945.* New York: Oxford University Press.

CSK, KK, and MAJ. 1999. "Riester scheitert mit seinem Rentenplan." *Süddeutsche Zeitung,* June 18, 1.

Daunton, Martin. 2002. "Trusting Leviathan: The Politics of Taxation, 1815–1914." In *The Political Economy of British Historical Experience, 1688–1914,* eds. Donald Winch and Patrick Karl O'Brien. Oxford: Oxford University Press.

Deckstein, Dagmar. 1999. "Einsam auf dem Rentengipfel." *Süddeutsche Zeitung,* August 18, 1999, 1.

Delli Carpini, Michael X., and Scott Keeter. 1997. *What Americans Know About Politics and Why It Matters.* New Haven: Yale University Press.

Denzau, Arthur T., and Douglass C. North. 1994. "Shared Mental Models: Ideologies and Institutions." *Kyklos* 47 (1):3–31.

Derthick, Martha. 1979. *Policymaking for Social Security.* Washington, D.C.: The Brookings Institution.

Derthick, Martha, and Paul J. Quirk. 1985. *The Politics of Deregulation.* Washington, D.C.: Brookings Institution.

Deutscher Reichstag. 1888. *Stenographische Berichte über die Verhandlungen des Reichstages.* Band 112–113, 7. Legislaturperiode, II. Session, 1887/88. Berlin: Julian Sittenfeld.

——1889a. *Stenographische Berichte über die Verhandlungen des Reichstages.* Band 119–120, 7. Legislaturperiode, IV. Session, 1888/89. Berlin: Julian Sittenfeld.

——1889b. *Stenographische Berichte über die Verhandlungen des Reichstages.* Band 121, 7. Legislaturperiode IV. Session, 1888/89. Berlin: Julian Sittenfeld.

DiMaggio, Paul J. 1997. "Culture and Cognition." *Annual Review of Sociology* 23: 263–87.

Disney, Richard, Carl Emmerson, and Matthew Wakefield. 2001. "Pension Reform and Saving in Britain." *Oxford Review of Economic Policy* 17 (1):70–94.

Douglas, Paul Howard. 1939. *Social Security in the United States: An Analysis and Appraisal of the Federal Social Security Act.* New York: Whittlesey House, McGraw-Hill.

Downs, Anthony. 1957. *An Economic Theory of Democracy.* New York: Harper Collins.

Druckman, James N. 2001. "On the Limits of Framing Effects: Who Can Frame?" *Journal of Politics* 63 (4):1041–66.

——2004. "Political Preference Formation: Competition, Deliberation, and the (Ir)relevance of Framing Effects." *American Political Science Review* 98 (04):671–86.

Drummond, Michael F., Bernard J. O'Brien, Greg L. Stoddart, and George W. Torrance. 1997. *Methods for the Economic Evaluation of Health Care Programmes.* 2nd ed. New York: Oxford University Press.

Dynan, Karen E., Jonathan Skinner, and Stephen P. Zeldes. 2000. "Do the Rich Save More?" Working Paper 7906. Cambridge, MA: National Bureau of Economic Research.

Eccles, Mary Eisner. 1977a. "Carter Social Security Plan Greeted Coolly." *Congressional Quarterly Weekly Report,* May 14, 895–7.

——1977b. "Congress Clears Social Security Tax Increase." *Congressional Quarterly Weekly Report,* December 17, 2621–4.

——1977c. "Social Security Crisis: Committees to Weigh Financing Alternatives." *Congressional Quarterly Weekly Report,* September 3, 1874–7.

——1977d. "Social Security Financing Plans Emerging." *Congressional Quarterly Weekly Report,* September 24, 2005–6.

——1977e. "Social Security: House Votes Steep Tax Hike." *Congressional Quarterly Weekly Report,* October 8, 2291–3.

——1977f. "Ways and Means Approves Social Security Package." *Congressional Quarterly Weekly Report,* October 8, 2125.

Economic Policy Committee. 2001. "Budgetary Challenges Posed by Ageing Populations." Brussels: European Commission.

Edwards, Sebastian. 1996. "The Chilean Pension Reform: A Pioneering Program." Working Paper 5811. Cambridge, MA: National Bureau of Economic Research.

Eichengreen, Barry, and Torben Iversen. 1999. "Institutions and Economic Performance: Evidence from the Labour Market." *Oxford Review of Economic Policy* 15 (4):121–38.

Einhorn, Hillel J., and Robin M. Hogarth. 1988. "Behavioral Decision Theory: Processes of Judgment and Choice." In *Decision Making: Descriptive, Normative, and Prescriptive Interactions,* eds. David E. Bell, Howard Raiffa and Amos Tversky. New York: Cambridge University Press.

"Einsam auf dem Rentengipfel." 1999. *Süddeutschezeitung,* August 18, 1.

"Entwurf eines Gesetzes zur Reform der gesetzlichen Rentenversicherung (Gesetzentwurf der Fraktionen der CDU/CSU und F.D.P.)." 1997. Bundestagsdrucksache 13/8011. Deutscher Bundestag.

Erikson, Robert S., Michael B. MacKuen, and James A. Stimson. 2000. "Bankers or Peasants Revisited: Economic Expectations and Presidential Approval." *Electoral Studies* 19: 295–312.

Esping-Andersen, Gøsta. 1990. *The Three Worlds of Welfare Capitalism.* Princeton: Princeton University Press.

——1999. *Social Foundations of Postindustrial Economies.* New York: Oxford University Press.

Evans, Peter. 1992. "The State as Problem and Solution: Predation, Embedded Autonomy, and Structural Change." In *The Politics of Economic Adjustment: International*

Constraints, Distributive Conflicts, and the State, eds. Stephan Haggard, and Robert R. Kaufman. Princeton: Princeton University Press.

Federal, Provincial, and Territorial Governments of Canada. 1996. "An Information Paper for Consultations on the Canada Pension Plan." Ottawa: Department of Finance.

Federal/Provincial/Territorial CPP Consultations Secretariat. 1996. "Report on the Canada Pension Plan Consultations." Ottawa: Department of Finance.

Feldenkirchen, Wilfried. 1991. "Banking and Economic Growth: Banks and Industry in Germany in the Nineteenth Century and Their Changing Relationship During Industrialisation." In *German Industry and German Industrialization: Essays in German Economic and Business History in the Nineteenth and Twentieth Centuries*, ed. W. R. Lee. New York: Routledge.

Feldstein, Martin S. 1974. "Social Security, Induced Retirement, and Aggregate Capital Accumulation." *Journal of Political Economy* 82 (5):905–26.

——1997. "Transition to a Fully Funded Pension System: Five Economic Issues." Working Paper W6149. Cambridge, MA: National Bureau of Economic Research.

Ferguson, Jonathan. 1995. "Martin Aims Lower: Cut in Deficit Target May Not Be Enough: Cuts May Not Satisfy Nervous Markets, Some Analysts Warn." *Toronto Star*, December 7, B1.

Feschuk, Scott. 1997. "Tory Senators Stall Passage of CPP bill." *Globe and Mail*, December 12, A4.

Fiorina, Morris P. 1978. "Economic Retrospective Voting in American National Elections: A Micro-Analysis." *American Journal of Political Science* 22 (2):426–43.

Fishman, Paul A., Beth E. Ebel, Michelle M. Garrison, Dimitri A. Christakis, Sarah E. Wiehe, and Frederick P. Rivara. 2005. "Cigarette Tax Increase and Media Campaign: Cost of Reducing Smoking-Related Deaths." *American Journal of Preventive Medicine* 29 (1):19–26.

Fiske, Susan T., and Shelley E. Taylor. 1991. *Social Cognition*. New York: McGraw-Hill.

Fitzmaurice, John. 1985. *Québec and Canada: Past, Present and Future*. London: C. Hurst and Company.

Flemming, Jens. 2000. "Sozialpolitik, landwirtschaftliche Interessen und Mobilisierungsversuche. Agrarkonservative Positionen im Entstehungsprozeß der Rentenversicherung." In *Geschichte und Gegenwart der Rentenversicherung in Deutschland: Beiträge zur Entstehung, Entwicklung und vergleichenden Einordnung der Alterssicherung im Sozialstaat*, eds. Stefan Fisch and Ulrike Haerendel. Berlin: Duncker & Humblot.

Flora, Peter, and Arnold J. Heidenheimer, eds. 1981. *The Development of Welfare States in Europe and America*. New Brunswick, NJ: Transaction Books.

Forster, Jürgen. 1999. "Im Rentensystem wächst der Reformstau." *Süddeutsche Zeitung*, February 11, 22.

Fowler, Norman. 1991. *Ministers Decide: A Personal Memoir of the Thatcher Years*. London: Chapmans Publishers.

Franzese, Robert J., Jr. 2002. "The Positive Political Economy of Public Debt: An Empirical Examination of the OECD Postwar Experience." Available at SSRN: http://ssrn.com/abstract=1084130.

Frederick, Shane, George Loewenstein, and Ted O'Donoghue. 2002. "Time Discounting and Time Preference: A Critical Review." *Journal of Economic Literature* 40 (2):351–401.

Freeman, Alan. 1995. "Quebec Opposes CPP Age Rise to 67: Ministers to Meet on Future of Plan." *Globe and Mail*, December 12, A1.

——1996. "Canadians to Get Say on Pensions: Federal, Provincial Ministers Agree to Cross-Country Consultations on Plan's Future." *Globe and Mail*, February 9, A1.

Frieden, Jeffry. 1991. "Invested Interests: National Economic Policies in a World of Global Finance." *International Organization* 45 (4):425–52.

Friedman, Milton. 1953. "The Methodology of Positive Economics." In *Essays in Positive Economics*. Chicago: University of Chicago Press.

Frum, David. 1997. "Governments Are Not Fund Managers." *The Financial Post*, November 18, 29.

Gagnon, Alain-G., and Guy Lachapelle. 1996. "Québec Confronts Canada: Two Competing Social Projects Searching for Legitimacy." *Publius* 26 (3):177–91.

Garrett, Geoffrey. 1993. "The Politics of Structural Change: Swedish Social Democracy and Thatcherism in Comparative Perspective." *Comparative Political Studies* 25 (4):521–47.

——1998. *Partisan Politics in the Global Economy*. New York: Cambridge University Press.

Garside, W.R. 1990. *British Unemployment 1919–1939: A Study in Public Policy*. New York: Cambridge University Press.

Geddes, Barbara. 1994. *Politician's Dilemma: Building State Capacity in Latin America*. Berkeley, CA: University of California Press.

Gentner, Dedre. 2002. "Mental Models, Psychology of." In *International Encyclopedia of the Social and Behavioral Sciences*, eds. Neil J. Smelser and Paul B. Bates. Amsterdam: Elsevier Science.

Gentner, Dedre, and Alan Collins. 1987. "How People Construct Mental Models." In *Cultural Models in Language and Thought*, eds. Dorothy Holland and Naomi Quinn. New York: Cambridge University Press.

George, Alexander L., and Andrew Bennett. 2005. *Case Studies and Theory Development in the Social Sciences*. Cambridge, MA: MIT Press.

Gersen, Jacob E. 2001. *Strategy and Cognition: Regulating Catastrophic Risk*. Ph.D. Dissertation. Department of Political Science, University of Chicago, Chicago.

Geyer, Martin H. 1987. *Die Reichsknappschaft: Versicherungsreform und Sozialpolitik im Bergbau 1900–1945*. Munich: Verlag C.H. Beck.

Gibb-Clark, Margot. 1997. "Managing Benefits: CPP Changes Spark Differences." *Globe and Mail*, February 25, B18.

Gioia, Dennis A., and Peter P. Poole. 1984. "Scripts in Organizational Behavior." *The Academy of Management Review* 9 (3):449–59.

Goertz, Gary, and Harvey Starr, eds. 2003. *Necessary Conditions: Theory, Methodology, and Applications*. New York: Rowman & Littlefield.

Gold, Marthe R. 1996. *Cost-Effectiveness in Health and Medicine*. New York: Oxford University Press.

Goldstein, Judith. 1993. *Ideas, Interests, and American Trade Policy*. Ithaca: Cornell University Press.

Goldstein, Judith, and Robert O. Keohane. 1993. "Ideas and Foreign Policy: An Analytical Framework." In *Ideas and Foreign Policy: Beliefs, Institutions, and Political Change*, eds. Judith Goldstein and Robert O. Keohane. Ithaca: Cornell University Press.

Gottron, Martha V. 1977a. "Senate Rejects Delay on Social Security." *Congressional Quarterly Weekly Report*, November 5, 2349–50.

——1977b. "Social Security: Conference Action Delayed." *Congressional Quarterly Weekly Report*, November 12, 2407–11.

Graebner, William. 1980. *A History of Retirement: The Meaning and Function of an American Institution, 1885–1978.* New Haven: Yale University Press.

Greenspon, Edward. 1996a. "B.C. Proposes CPP Overhaul: Expand Program, Minister Suggests." *Globe and Mail,* September 23, A1.

——1996b. "Discord over GST on Agenda for Talks: Finance Ministers Not in Harmony." *Globe and Mail,* June 17, A1.

——1996c. "Liberals, Reform Courting Taxpayers." *Globe and Mail,* October 10, A1.

——1997a. "Martin Strikes CPP Deal: Ottawa Gives Ground to Ontario on UI Premiums to Get Province's Support." *Globe and Mail,* February 14, A1.

——1997b. "Reform Attacks Liberals on CPP: Pensions Seen as Election Issue." *Globe and Mail,* March 6, A4.

Greenspon, Edward, and Anthony Wilson-Smith. 1996. *Double Vision: The Inside Story of the Liberals in Power.* Toronto: McClelland-Bantam.

Hacker, Jacob S. 2000. *Boundary Wars: The Political Struggle over Public and Private Social Benefits in the United States.* Ph.D. Dissertation. Department of Political Science, Yale University, New Haven, CT.

——2002. *The Divided Welfare State: The Battle over Public and Private Social Benefits in the United States.* New York: Cambridge University Press.

——2004. "Privatizing Risk without Privatizing the Welfare State: The Hidden Politics of Social Policy Retrenchment in the United States." *American Political Science Review* 98 (2):243–60.

Hacker, Jacob S., and Paul Pierson. 2002. "Business Power and Social Policy: Employers and the Formation of the American Welfare State." *Politics and Society* 30 (2):277–326.

Haerendel, Ulrike. 2000. "Regierungen, Reichstag und Rentenversicherung. Der Gesetzgebungsprozeß zwischen 1887 und 1889." In *Geschichte und Gegenwart der Rentenversicherung in Deutschland: Beiträge zur Entstehung, Entwicklung und vergleichenden Einordnung der Alterssicherung im Sozialstaat,* eds. Stefan Fisch and Ulrike Haerendel. Berlin: Duncker & Humblot.

——2001. *Die Anfänge der gesetzlichen Rentenversicherung in Deutschland: Die Invaliditäts- und Altersversicherung von 1889 im Spannungsfeld von Reichsverwaltung, Bundesrat und Parlament.* Speyer: Forschungsinstitut für Öffentliche Verwaltung bei der Deutschen Hochschule für Verwaltungswissenschaften Speyer.

——ed. 2004. *Die gesetzliche Invaliditäts- und Altersversicherung und die Alternativen auf gewerkschaftlicher und betrieblicher Grundlage, Quellensammlung zur Geschichte der deutschen Sozialpolitik.* II. Abteilung, Band 6. Darmstadt: Wissenschaftliche Buchgesellschaft.

Hall, Peter A. 1993. "Policy Paradigms, Social Learning, and the State." *Comparative Politics* 25 (3):275–96.

——2003. "Aligning Ontology and Methodology in Comparative Politics." In *Comparative Historical Analysis in the Social Sciences,* eds. James Mahoney and Dietrich Rueschemeyer. New York: Cambridge University Press.

Hall, Peter A., and David W. Soskice. 2001a. "An Introduction to Varieties of Capitalism." In *Varieties of Capitalism: The Institutional Foundations of Comparative Advantage,* eds. Peter A. Hall and David W. Soskice. New York: Oxford University Press.

——eds. 2001b. *Varieties of Capitalism: The Institutional Foundations of Comparative Advantage.* New York: Oxford University Press.

Hall, Peter A., and Rosemary C. R. Taylor. 1996. "Political Science and the Three New Institutionalisms." *Political Studies* 44: 936–57.

Hammond, Thomas H. 1996. "Formal Theory and the Institutions of Governance." *Governance* 9 (2):107–85.

Hank, Rainer. 1999. "Walter Riester hält trotz Kritik an seinen Rentenplänen fest." *Frankfurter Allgemeine Zeitung*, June 19, 13.

Hanson, Stephen E. 1997. *Time and Revolution: Marxism and the Design of Soviet Institutions*. Chapel Hill: University of North Carolina Press.

Harrison, Kathryn. 1996. *Passing the Buck: Federalism and Canadian Environmental Policy*. Vancouver, B.C.: UBC Press.

Hauschild, Helmut. 2000a. "DGB will Abstriche beim Rentenniveau akzeptieren." *Handelsblatt*, September 4.

——2000b. "Rentenkonsens rückt näher." *Handelsblatt*, September 4.

Havemann, Joel. 1978. "The Taxpayers' Revolt, Part I – Second Thoughts on Social Security." *National Journal*, April 1, 504–8.

HB. 2000. "Weiter breiter Widerstand gegen Riesters Rentenpläne." *Handelsblatt*, June 19.

Healy, Andrew, and Neil Malhotra. 2009. "Myopic Voters and Natural Disaster Policy." *American Political Science Review* 103 (03):387–406.

Heclo, Hugh. 1974. *Modern Social Politics in Britain and Sweden: From Relief to Income Maintenance*. New Haven: Yale University Press.

Heinzl, Mark. 1996. "Ontario's 30% Tax-Cut Plan Gets Lukewarm Reception: Premier Hopes to Stimulate The Economy, but Voters Aren't Convinced." *Wall Street Journal*, March 12, A2.

Hemming, Richard. 1999. "Should Public Pensions Be Funded?" *International Social Security Review* 52 (2):3–29.

Hencke, David. 1985. "Concern on All Sides at Welfare Review." *The Guardian*, May 27.

Hennock, E. P. 1987. *British Social Reform and German Precedents*. Oxford: Clarendon Press.

Hennock, Peter. 2000. "Die Anfänge von staatlicher Alters- und Invaliditätsversicherung. Ein deutsch-englischer Vergleich." In *Geschichte und Gegenwart der Rentenversicherung in Deutschland: Beiträge zur Entstehung, Entwicklung und vergleichenden Einordnung der Alterssicherung im Sozialstaat*, eds. Stefan Fisch and Ulrike Haerendel. Berlin: Duncker & Humblot.

Hering, Martin. 2001a. Competitive Euro-liberalism and the Reform of the German Pension System. Paper presented at European Community Studies Association 7th Biennial Conference, May 31-June 2, at Madison, WI.

——2001b. The New Approach to Welfare State Reform in German Social Democracy. Paper read at Third Ways in Europe Workshop, European Consortium for Political Research Joint Sessions, April 6–11, at Grenoble, France.

——2005. *Rough Transition: Institutional Change in Germany's "Frozen" Welfare State*. Ph.D. Dissertation, Department of Political Science, The Johns Hopkins University, Baltimore, MD.

Hessing, Melody and Michael Howlett. 1997. *Canadian Natural Resource and Environmental Policy: Political Economy and Public Policy*. Vancouver, B.C.: UBC Press.

Hewstone, Miles, Manfred Hassebrauck, Andrea Wirth, and Michaela Waenke. 2000. "Pattern of Disconfirming Information and Processing Instructions as Determinants of Stereotype Change." *British Journal of Social Psychology* 39 (3):399–411.

Higgins, E. Tory, and John A. Bargh. 1987. "Social Cognition and Social Perception." *Annual Review of Psychology* 38: 369–425.

Hinrichs, Karl. 1998. "Reforming the Public Pension Scheme in Germany: The End of the Traditional Consensus?" ZeS-Arbeitspapier Nr. 11/98. Bremen: Zentrum für Sozialpolitik, Universität Bremen.

———2000. "Auf Dem Weg zur Alterssicherungspolitik – Reformperspektiven in der gesetzlichen Rentenversicherung." In *Perspektiven des deutschen Sozialstaats: Bilanzen, Reformen und Perspektiven*, eds. Stefan Leibfried and Uwe Wagschal. Frankfurt: Campus.

———2003. "The Politics of Pension Reform in Germany." Paper read at Conference on Pension Reform in Europe: Shared Problems, Sharing Solutions?, December 5, London School of Economics, Hellenic Observatory/The European Institute, London.

Hoberg, George. 1997. "Governing the Environment: Comparing Canada and the United States." In *Degrees of Freedom: Canada and the United States in a Changing World*, eds. Keith G. Banting, George Hoberg and Richard Simeon. Montreal & Kingston: McGill-Queen's University Press.

———2000. "How the Way We Make Policy Governs the Policy We Make." In *Sustaining the Forests of the Pacific Coast: Politics, Policy and the War in the Woods*, eds. Debra J. Salazar and Donald K. Alper. Vancouver, B.C.: UBC Press.

Hockerts, Hans Günter. 1980. *Sozialpolitische Entscheidungen im Nachkriegsdeutschland*. Stuttgart: Klett-Cotta.

Hope, Chris. 2006. "The Social Cost of Carbon Following the Stern Review." Judge Business School.

Horn, Murray J. 1995. *The Political Economy of Public Administration*. New York: Cambridge University Press.

House of Commons. 1997. Standing Committee on Finance. *Bill C-2, An Act to establish the Canada Pension Plan Investment Board and to amend the Canada Pension Plan and Old Age Security Act and to make consequential amendments to other Acts*. 36th Parliament, 1st Session, Meeting 44. November 4.

Hovi, Jon, Detlef F. Sprinz, and Arild Underdal. 2009. "Implementing Long-Term Climate Policy: Time Inconsistency, Domestic Politics, International Anarchy." *Global Environmental Politics* 9 (3):20–39.

Howell, David R., and Friedrich Huebler. 2005. "Wage Compression and the Unemployment Crisis: Labor Market Institutions, Skills, and Inequality-Unemployment Tradeoffs." In *Fighting Unemployment: The Limits of Free Market Orthodoxy*, ed. David R. Howell. Oxford: Oxford University Press.

Huber, Evelyne, and John D. Stephens. 2001a. *Development and Crisis of the Welfare State: Parties and Policies in Global Markets*. Chicago: University of Chicago Press.

———2001b. "Welfare State and Production Regimes in the Era of Retrenchment." In *The New Politics of the Welfare State*, ed. Paul Pierson. New York: Oxford University Press.

Huber, John D., and Charles R. Shipan. 2002. *Deliberate Discretion?: The Institutional Foundations of Bureaucratic Autonomy*. New York: Cambridge University Press.

Ikenberry, G. John, and Theda Skocpol. 1987. "Expanding Social Benefits: The Role of Social Security." *Political Science Quarterly* 102 (3):389–416.

Immergut, Ellen M. 1992a. *Health Politics: Interests and Institutions in Western Europe*. New York: Cambridge University Press.

————1992b. "The Rules of the Game: The Logic of Health Policy-Making in France, Switzerland, and Sweden." In *Structuring Politics: Historical Institutionalism in Comparative Analysis*, eds. Sven Steinmo, Kathleen Thelen and Frank Longstreth. New York: Cambridge University Press.

Immergut, Ellen M., and Karen M. Anderson. 2006. "Editors' Introduction: Dynamics of Pension Politics." In *The Handbook of West European Pension Politics*, eds. Ellen M. Immergut, Karen M. Anderson and Isabelle Schulze. New York: Oxford University Press.

International Monetary Fund. 1996. "Fiscal Challenges Facing Industrial Countries." In *World Economic Outlook*. Washington, D.C.: IMF.

Iversen, Torben, and Anne Wren. 1998. "Equality, Employment and Budgetary Restraint: The Trilemma of the Service Economy." *World Politics* 50 (4):507–46.

Iyengar, Shanto. 1990. "Shortcuts to Political Knowledge: The Role of Selective Attention and Accessibility." In *Information and Democratic Processes*, eds. John Ferejohn and James H. Kuklinski. Urbana: University of Illinois Press.

————1991. *Is Anyone Responsible?: How Television Frames Political Issues*. Chicago: University of Chicago Press.

Iyengar, Shanto, and Adam Simon. 1993. "News Coverage of the Gulf Crisis and Public Opinion: A Study of Agenda-Setting, Priming, and Framing." *Communication Research* 20 (3):365–83.

Jacobs, Alan M. 2008. "The Politics of When: Redistribution, Investment, and Policymaking for the Long Term." *British Journal of Political Science* 38 (2):193–220.

————2009a. "How Do Ideas Matter?: Mental Models and Attention in German Pension Politics." *Comparative Political Studies* 42 (2):252–79.

————2009b. "Policymaking as Political Constraint: Institutional Development in the U.S. Social Security Program." In *Explaining Institutional Change: Ambiguity, Agency, and Power*, eds. James Mahoney and Kathleen Thelen. New York: Cambridge University Press.

Jacobs, Alan M., and J. Scott Matthews. 2008. "Does Timing Matter? Intertemporal Policy Choice and the Mass Public." Paper presented at the Annual Meeting of the American Political Science Association, August 28–31, Boston, MA.

Jacobs, Alan M., and Steven Teles. 2007. "The Perils of Market-Making: The Case of British Pensions." In *Creating Competitive Markets: The Politics of Regulatory Reform*, eds. Marc K. Landy, Martin A. Levin and Martin Shapiro. Washington, D.C.: Brookings Institution Press.

James, Steven, Chris Matier, Humam Sakhnini, and Munir Sheikh. 1995. "The Economics of Canada Pension Plan Reforms." Ottawa: Department of Finance.

Jensen, Michael C. 1977. "Carter Payroll Tax Plan Is Opposed by Business." *New York Times*, May 11, D1 and D7.

Jervis, Robert. 1976. *Perception and Misperception in International Politics*. Princeton: Princeton University Press.

Jochem, Sven. 1999. "Sozialpolitik in der ära Kohl: Die Politik des Sozialversicherungsstaat-es." ZeS-Arbeitspapier Nr. 12/99. Bremen: Zentrum für Sozialpolitik, Universität Bremen.

Johnson-Laird, Philip N. 1983. *Mental Models: Towards a Cognitive Science of Language, Inference, and Consciousness*. Cambridge, MA: Harvard University Press.

Johnston, Alastair Iain. 1996. "Learning Versus Adaptation: Explaining Change in Chinese Arms Control Policy in the 1980s and 1990s." *The China Journal* (35):27–61.

Johnston, Louis D. and Samuel H. Williams. 2008. "The Annual Real and Nominal GDP for the United States, 1790-Present." http://www.measuringworth.com (last accessed February 27, 2008).

Jones, Bryan D. 2001. *Politics and the Architecture of Choice: Bounded Rationality and Governance*. Chicago: University of Chicago Press.

Jones, Bryan D., and Frank R. Baumgartner. 2005. *The Politics of Attention: How Government Prioritizes Problems*. Chicago: University of Chicago Press.

Kahneman, Daniel, Jack L. Knetsch, and Richard H. Thaler. 1991. "Anomalies: The Endowment Effect, Loss Aversion, and Status Quo Bias." *Journal of Economic Perspectives* 5 (1):193–206.

Kahneman, Daniel, and Amos Tversky. 1984. "Choices, Values, and Frames." *American Psychologist* 39 (4):341–50.

Kamieniecki, Sheldon. 2000. "Testing Alternative Theories of Agenda Setting: Forest Policy Change in British Columbia, Canada." *Policy Studies Journal* 28 (1):176–89.

Kates, Robert W. 1962. "Hazard and Choice Perception in Flood Plain Management." *Department of Geography Research Paper No. 78*. Chicago: University of Chicago.

Kelman, Steven. 1981. *Regulating America, Regulating Sweden: A Comparative Study of Occupational Safety and Health Policy*. Cambridge, MA: MIT Press.

Kennedy, David M. 1999. *Freedom from Fear: The American People in Depression and War, 1929–1945*. New York: Oxford University Press.

Kent, Tom. 1988. *A Public Purpose: An Experience of Liberal Opposition and Canadian Government*. Kingston and Montreal: McGill-Queen's University Press.

Kernell, S. 1977. "Presidential Popularity and Negative Voting: An Alternative Explanation of the Midterm Congressional Decline of the President's Party." *American Political Science Review* 71 (1):44–66.

Key, V. O., and Milton C. Cummings. 1966. *The Responsible Electorate; Rationality in Presidential Voting, 1936–1960*. Cambridge: Belknap Press of Harvard University Press.

Khong, Yuen Foong. 1992. *Analogies at War: Korea, Munich, Dien Bien Phu, and the Vietnam Decisions of 1965*. Princeton: Princeton University Press.

Kieselbach, Kurt. 1999. "Erbitterter Widerstand gegen Riesters Renten-Pläne." *Die Welt*, June 18.

Kinder, Donald R., and Lynn M. Sanders. 1996. *Divided by Color: Racial Politics and Democratic Ideals*. Chicago: University of Chicago Press.

King, Anthony. 1997. *Running Scared: Why America's Politicians Campaign Too Much and Govern Too Little*. New York: M. Kessler Books.

King, Ronald F. 1993. *Money, Time, and Politics: Investment Tax Subsidies and American Democracy*. New Haven: Yale University Press.

Kingdon, John W. 1984. *Agendas, Alternatives, and Public Policies*. New York: Harper/Collins.

Klein, Jill. 1991. "Negativity Effects in Impression Formation: A Test in the Political Arena." *Personality and Social Psychology Bulletin* 17 (4):412–8.

Knudsen, Eric I. 2007. "Fundamental Components of Attention." *Annual Review of Neuroscience* 30 (1):57–78.

Koitz, David. 2001. *Seeking Middle Ground on Social Security Reform*. Stanford, CA: Hoover Institution Press.

Kotlikoff, Laurence J. 1990. "The Social Security 'Surpluses' – New Clothes for the Emperor?" In *Social Security's Looming Surpluses: Prospects and Implications*, ed. Carolyn L. Weaver. Washington, D.C.: AEI Press.

Kramer, Gerald H. 1971. "Short-Term Fluctuations in U.S. Voting Behavior, 1896–1964." *American Political Science Review* 65 (1):131–43.

Krosnick, Jon, Allyson Holbrook, Laura Lowe, and Penny Visser. 2006. "The Origins and Consequences of Democratic Citizens' Policy Agendas: A Study of Popular Concern about Global Warming." *Climatic Change* 77 (1):7–43.

Krueger, Alan B., and Jörn-Steffen Pischke. 1997. "Observations and Conjectures on the U.S. Employment Miracle." Working Paper 6146. Cambridge, MA: National Bureau of Economic Research.

Kuklinski, James H., and Paul D. Quirk. 2001. "Conceptual Foundations of Citizen Competence." *Political Behavior* 23 (3):285–311.

Kuklinski, James H., Paul D. Quirk, Jennifer Jerit, David Schwieder, and Robert F. Rich. 2000. "Misinformation and the Currency of Democratic Citizenship." *Journal of Politics* 62 (3):790–816.

Landmann, Robert, and Karl Ralp. 1891. *Das Reichsgesetz über die Invaliditäts- und Altersversicherung der Arbeiter vom 22. Juni 1889*. Munich: C.H. Beck'sche Verlagsbuchhandlung.

Lange, Peter, and Geoffrey Garrett. 1985. "The Politics of Growth: Strategic Interaction and Economic Performance in the Advanced Industrial Democracies, 1974–1980." *Journal of Politics* 47 (3):792–827.

Lasswell, Harold D. 1936. *Politics: Who Gets What, When, How*. New York: Peter Smith.

Lau, R. Richard. 1985. "Two Explanations for Negativity Effects in Political Behavior." *American Journal of Political Science* 29 (1):119–38.

Leff, Mark H. 1978. *The New Deal and Taxation, 1933–1939: The Limits of Symbolic Reform*. Ph.D. Dissertation. Department of History, University of Chicago, Chicago.

——1988. "Speculating in Social Security Futures: The Perils of Payroll Tax Financing, 1939–1950." In *Social Security: The First Half-Century*, eds. Gerald D. Nash, Noel H. Pugach and Richard F. Tomasson. Albuquerque: University of New Mexico Press.

Leonard, Herman B. 1990. "In God We Trust – The Political Economy of the Social Security Reserves." In *Social Security's Looming Surpluses: Prospects and Implications*, ed. Carolyn L. Weaver. Washington, D.C.: AEI Press.

Leuchtenburg, William Edward. 1963. *Franklin D. Roosevelt and the New Deal, 1932–1940*. New York: Harper & Row.

Levi, Margaret. 1988. *Of Rule and Revenue*. Berkeley: University of California Press.

Levitt, Barbara, and James G. March. 1988. "Organizational Learning." *Annual Review of Sociology* 14: 319–40.

Lewis-Beck, Michael, and Mary Stegmaier. 2000. "Economic Determinants of Election Outcomes." *Annual Review of Political Science* 3: 183–219.

Lewis, Paul. 1996. "Consequences: Personal Pensions." January 23, BBC Radio 4.

Lewis, Timothy. 2003. *In the Long Run We're All Dead: The Canadian Turn to Fiscal Restraint*. Vancouver, B.C.: UBC Press.

Light, Paul. 1995. *Still Artful Work: The Continuing Politics of Social Security Reform*. New York: McGraw Hill.

Lindblom, Charles E. 1982. "The Market as Prison." *Journal of Politics* 44 (2):324–36.

Little, Bruce. 1995. "Canada's Debt Outlook Revised: Negative Trend Reflects Heavy Burden of Paying Interest, Dominion Bond Rating Agency Says." *Globe and Mail*, March 29, B6.

——1996. "Keep CPP Benefits, Panel Told: Business, Labour Say Cuts Would Disrupt Company Pensions." *Globe and Mail*, April 16, B1.

Liu, Lillian. 1999. "Retirement Income Security in the United Kingdom." *Social Security Bulletin* 62 (1):23–46.

Lochner, Lance, and Enrico Moretti. 2004. "The Effect of Education on Crime: Evidence from Prison Inmates, Arrests, and Self-Reports." *American Economic Review* 94 (1):155–89.

Lodge, Milton, and Ruth Hamill. 1986. "A Partisan Schema for Political Information Processing." *American Political Science Review* 80 (2):505–20.

Lodge, Milton, and Kathleen M. McGraw. 1991. "Where Is the Schema? Critiques." *American Political Science Review* 85 (4):1357–64.

Lupia, Arthur, and Mathew D. McCubbins. 1998. *The Democratic Dilemma: Can Citizens Learn What They Need to Know?* New York: Cambridge University Press.

Luskin, Robert C. 1987. "Measuring Political Sophistication." *American Journal of Political Science* 31 (4):856–99.

Lynch, Julia. 2006. *Age in the Welfare State: The Origins of Social Spending on Pensioners, Workers, and Children.* New York: Cambridge University Press.

Mabell, David. 1998. "Seniors Cheer Retreat on OAS: Martin to Keep Federal Benefits Programs as They Are." *Lethbridge Herald*, July 30.

Macdonald, Doug. 1991. *The Politics of Pollution.* Toronto: McClelland & Stewart.

Mackenroth, Gerhard. 1952. "Die Reform der Sozialpolitik durch einen deutschen Sozialplan." *Schriften des Vereins für Sozialpolitik NF 4.*

Macnicol, John. 1998. *The Politics of Retirement in Britain, 1878–1948.* Cambridge: Cambridge University Press.

Magnani, Corrado, Daniela Ferrante, Francesco Barone-Adesi, Marinella Bertolotti, Annalisa Todesco, Dario Mirabelli, and Benedetto Terracin. 2008. "Cancer Risk After Cessation of Asbestos Exposure: A Cohort Study of Italian Asbestos Cement Workers." *Occupational and Environmental Medicine* 65 (3):164–70.

MAJ. 1999a. "Grüne lehnen Riesters Rentenpläne ab." *Süddeutsche Zeitung*, June 17, 1.

——1999b. "Riester will Rentenerhöhung an Inflationsrate binden." *Süddeutsche Zeitung*, June 16, 7.

Mann, Golo. 1968. *The History of Germany Since 1789.* New York: Praeger.

Manow, Philip. 2000. "Kapitaldeckung oder Umlage: Zur Geschichte einer anhaltenden Debatte." In *Geschichte und Gegenwart der Rentenversicherung in Deutschland: Beiträge zur Entstehung, Entwicklung und vergleichenden Einordnung der Alterssicherung im Sozialstaat*, eds. Stefan Fisch and Ulrike Haerendel. Berlin: Duncker & Humblot.

March, James G., and Johan P. Olsen. 1989. *Rediscovering Institutions: The Organizational Basis of Politics.* New York: Free Press.

Marron, Kevin. 1998. "Surveys Paint Grim Picture of Future: Half of Us Don't Set Aside Retirement Funds because Daily Money Situation Is Too Precarious." *Globe and Mail*, February 23, R8.

Mayhew, David R. 1974. *Congress: The Electoral Connection.* New Haven: Yale University Press.

McCarthy, Shawn. 1997a. "Ottawa Drafts New CPP Law." *Globe and Mail*, July 5, B2.

——1997b. "Ottawa to Rule CPP Fortune: Pension Plan Changes Introduced Yesterday Would Give Federal Board $126-billion to Invest." *Globe and Mail*, September 26, B1.

McKie, David. 1986. "Tory Voters Say Boost Spending." *The Guardian*, June 23.

McNollgast. 1999. "The Political Origins of the Administrative Procedure Act." *Journal of Law, Economics, and Organization* 15 (1):180–217.

Mehra, Rajnish. 2003. "The Equity Premium: Why Is It a Puzzle?" *Financial Analysts Journal* 59 (1):54–69.

Mill, John Stuart. 1868. *A System of Logic*. London: Longmans.

Miller, George. 1956. "The Magic Number Seven, Plus or Minus Two: Some Limits on Our Capacity for Processing Information." *Psychological Review* 63: 81–97.

Mitchell, Broadus. 1947. *Depression Decade: From New Era through New Deal, 1929–1941*. Vol. 9. New York: Rinehart.

Mityakov, Sergey, and Christof Rühl. 2009. "The Stern Review on Climate Change: Inconvenient Sensitivities." *Energy and Environment* 20 (5):779–98.

Moe, Terry. 1989. "The Politics of Bureaucratic Structure." In *Can the Government Govern?*, eds. John E. Chubb and Paul E. Peterson. Washington, D.C.: The Brookings Institution.

———1990. "The Politics of Structural Choice: Toward a Theory of Public Bureaucracy." In *Organization Theory: From Chester Barnard to the Present and Beyond*, ed. Oliver Williamson. New York: Oxford University Press.

Mörschel, Richard. 1990. "Die Finanzierungsverfahren in der Geschichte der gesetzlichen Rentenversicherung." *Deutsche Rentenversicherung* 90 (9/10):619–61.

Müller, Wolfgang, and Kaare Strøm. 1999. *Policy, Office, or Votes?: How Political Parties in Western Europe Make Hard Decisions*. New York: Cambridge University Press.

Myers, Robert J. 1991. "Will Social Security Be There When the Baby Boomers Retire?" In *The 1991 E.J. Faulkner Lecture Series*. Lincoln: College of Business Administration, University of Nebraska.

Nankivell, Neville. 1997. "Senate Intervention Helps Widen Debate Over Retirement Systems." *The Financial Post*, December 20, 29.

National Science Board. 2000. "Science and Engineering Indicators, 2000." Arlington, VA: National Science Foundation.

Nelson, Joan M. 1992. "Poverty, Equity, and the Politics of Adjustment." In *The Politics of Economic Adjustment: International Constraints, Distributive Conflicts, and the State*, ed. Stephan Haggard and Robert R. Kaufman. Princeton: Princeton University Press.

Nelson, Thomas, Rosalee Clawson, and Zoe Oxley. 1997. "Media Framing of a Civil Liberties Conflict and Its Effect on Tolerance." *American Political Science Review* 91: 567–83.

Nelson, Thomas E., and Zoe M. Oxley. 1999. "Issue Framing Effects on Belief Importance and Opinion." *Journal of Politics* 61 (4):1040–67.

Nesbitt, Steven. 1995. *British Pensions Policy Making in the 1980s*. Brookfield: Avebury.

Nevitte, Neil. 1999. *Unsteady State: The 1997 Canadian Federal Election*. Don Mills, ON: Oxford University Press.

Nicholls, Robert J., and Jason A. Lowe. 2004. "Benefits of Mitigation of Climate Change for Coastal Areas." *Global Environmental Change* 14: 229–44.

Nickerson, Raymond S. 1998. "Confirmation Bias: A Ubiquitous Phenomenon in Many Guises." *Review of General Psychology* 2 (2):175–220.

Nordhaus, William D. 1975. "The Political Business Cycle." *The Review of Economic Studies* 42 (2):169–90.

———2008. *A Question of Balance: Weighing the Options on Global Warming Policies*. New Haven: Yale University Press.

Nores, Milagros, Clive R. Belfield, W. Steven Barnett, and Lawrence Schweinhart. 2005. "Updating the Economic Impacts of the High/Scope Perry Preschool Program." *Educational Evaluation and Policy Analysis* 27 (3):245–61.

North, Douglass C. 1990. *Institutions, Institutional Change, and Economic Performance.* New York: Cambridge University Press.

———1993. "Institutions and Credible Commitment." *Journal of Institutional and Theoretical Economics* 149 (1):11–23.

North, Douglass C., and Barry R. Weingast. 1989. "Constitutions and Commitment: The Evolution of Institutions Governing Public Choice in Seventeenth-Century England." *Journal of Economic History* 49 (4):803–32.

Nullmeier, Frank, and Friedbert W. Rüb. 1993. *Die Transformation der Sozialpolitik: vom Sozialstaat zum Sicherungsstaat.* New York: Campus Verlag.

OECD. 2007. *Social Expenditure Database (SOCX), 1980–2003.* Accessed July 3, 2008 at http://www.oecd.org/els/social/expenditure.

———2008a. *Education at a Glance: OECD Indicators.* Paris: OECD.

———2008b. *Environmental Data Compendium.* Paris: OECD.

———2008c. *Key Environmental Indicators.* Paris: OECD.

———2010. *OECD Economic Outlook: Statistics and Projections.* Accessed July 14, 2010 at http://www.oecdilibrary.org/.

Office of Management and Budget. 2002. "Fiscal Year 2003: Historical Tables: Budget of the United States Government." Washington, D.C.: Government Printing Office.

Office of the Chief Actuary. 1995. "Canada Pension Plan: Fifteenth Actuarial Report as at 31 December 1993."

———1997. "Canada Pension Plan: Sixteenth Actuarial Report."

———2007. "23rd Actuarial Report on the Canada Pension Plan as at 31 December 2006."

Olson, Mancur. 1971. *The Logic of Collective Action: Public Goods and the Theory of Groups.* Vol. 124. Cambridge, MA: Harvard University Press.

———1982. *The Rise and Decline of Nations: Economic Growth, Stagflation, and Social Rigidities.* New Haven: Yale University Press.

Olson, Robert A. 2003. "Legislative Politics and Seismic Safety: California's Early Years and the 'Field Act,' 1925–1933." *Earthquake Spectra* 19(1):111–31.

Oppenheimer, M., and A. Todorov. 2006. "Global Warming: The Psychology of Long Term Risk." *Climatic Change* 77 (1):1–6.

Orloff, Ann Shola. 1988. "The Political Origins of America's Belated Welfare State." In *The Politics of Social Policy in the United States,* eds. Margaret Weir, Ann Shola Orloff and Theda Skocpol. Princeton: Princeton University Press.

———1993a. "Gender and the Social Rights of Citizenship: The Comparative Analysis of Gender Relations and Welfare States." *American Sociological Review* 58 (3):303–28.

———1993b. *The Politics of Pensions: A Comparative Analysis of Britain, Canada, and the United States 1880–1940.* Madison: University of Wisconsin Press.

Pal, Leslie A., and R. Kent Weaver. 2003. "The Politics of Pain." In *The Government Taketh Away: The Politics of Pain in the United States and Canada,* eds. Leslie A. Pal and R. Kent Weaver. Washington, D.C.: Georgetown University Press.

"Panel Votes to Raise Social Security Taxes." 1977. *National Journal,* October 8, 1586.

Papp, Leslie. 1994. "Harris Gets 'Revolution' Rolling: Ontario Tories Launch $600,000 Recruiting Drive." *Toronto Star,* May 9, A1.

Patashnik, Eric. 2000. *Putting Trust in the U.S. Budget: Federal Trust Funds and the Politics of Commitment.* New York: Cambridge University Press.

Peden, G. C. 2000. *The Treasury and British Public Policy, 1906–1959.* New York: Oxford University Press.

——2002. "From Cheap Government to Efficient Government: The Political Economy of Public Expenditure in the United Kingdom, 1832–1914." In *The Political Economy of British Historical Experience*:1688–914, eds. Donald Winch and Patrick Karl O'Brien. Oxford: Oxford University Press.

Pensions Commission. 2004. "Pensions: Challenges and Choices." London: The Stationery Office.

Perkins, Frances. 1946. *The Roosevelt I Knew*. New York: The Viking Press.

Pesando, James E. 2001. "The Canada Pension Plan: Looking Back at the Recent Reforms." In *The State of Economics in Canada: Festschrift in Honour of David Slater*, eds. Patrick Grady and Andrew Sharpe. Montreal: McGill-Queen's University Press.

Petty, Richard E., and John T. Cacioppo. 1981. *Attitudes and Persuasion: Classic and Contemporary Approaches*. Dubuque, IA: W.C. Brown.

——1986. *Communication and Persuasion: Central and Peripheral Routes to Attitude Change*. New York: Springer-Verlag.

Pierson, Paul. 1994. *Dismantling the Welfare State? Reagan, Thatcher, and the Politics of Retrenchment*. New York: Cambridge University Press.

——2004. *Politics in Time: History, Institutions, and Social Analysis*. Princeton: Princeton University Press.

Pierson, Paul, and John Myles. 2001. "The Comparative Political Economy of Pension Reform." In *The New Politics of the Welfare State*, ed. Paul Pierson. Oxford: Oxford University Press.

Platt, Rutherford H., and Claire B. Rubin. 1999. "Stemming the Losses: The Quest for Hazard Mitigation." In *Disasters and Democracy: The Politics of Extreme Natural Events*, ed. Rutherford H. Platt. Washington, D.C.: Island Press.

Ponting, Clive. 1994. *Churchill*. London: Sinclair-Stevenson.

Powell, G. Bingham, and Guy D. Whitten. 1993. "A Cross-National Analysis of Economic Voting: Taking Account of the Political Context." *American Journal of Political Science* 37 (2):391–414.

Preußischer Volkswirtschaftsrat. 1887. *Protokolle über die Sitzungen des Preußischen Volkswirtschaftsraths*. Berlin: Preußischer Volkswirtschaftsrat.

Prowse, Michael. 1985a. "CBI President Criticises Pensions Phase-out Plan." *Financial Times*, June 22, 20.

——1985b. "Why 11m Pensions Are in the Balance." *Financial Times*, May 2, 24.

——1986. "The Tax Cuts Nobody Wants." *Financial Times*, July 1, 24.

Przeworski, Adam. 1991. *Democracy and the Market: Political and Economic Reforms in Eastern Europe and Latin America*. New York: Cambridge University Press.

Przeworski, Adam, and Henry Teune. 1970. *The Logic of Comparative Social Inquiry*. New York: Wiley-Interscience.

Przeworski, Adam, and Michael Wallerstein. 1982. "The Structure of Class Conflict in Democratic Capitalist Societies." *American Political Science Review* 76 (2):215–38.

Pugh, Martin. 1982. *The Making of Modern British Politics 1867–1939*. Oxford: Basil Blackwell.

Quadagno, Jill S. 1984. "Welfare Capitalism and the Social Security Act of 1935." *American Sociological Review* 49 (5):632–47.

Quirk, Paul D. 1990. "Deregulation and the Politics of Ideas in Congress." In *Beyond Self-Interest*, ed. Jane J. Mansbridge. Chicago: University of Chicago Press.

Ramsden, John. 1998. *An Appetite for Power: A History of the Conservative Party since 1830*. London: Harper Collins.

Renaud, Marc. 1987. "Quebec's New Middle Class in Search of Social Hegemony: Causes and Political Consequences." In *Quebec Since 1945: Selected Readings*, ed. Michael D. Behiels. Toronto: Copp Clark Pitman Ltd.

Riker, William H. 1986. *The Art of Political Manipulation*. New Haven: Yale University Press.

Ritter, Gerhard A. 1983. *Sozialversicherung in Deutschland und England: Entstehung und Grundzüge im Vergleich*. Munich: C.H. Beck.

Rivara, Frederick P., Beth E. Ebel, Michelle M. Garrison, Dimitri R. Christakis, Sarah E. Wiehe, and David T. Levy. 2004. "Prevention of Smoking-Related Deaths in the United States." *American Journal of Preventive Medicine* 27 (2):118–25.

Rodgers, Daniel T. 1998. *Atlantic Crossings: Social Politics in a Progressive Age*. Cambridge: Belknap Press of the Harvard University Press.

Rodgers, Terence. 1988. "Employers' Organizations, Unemployment and Social Politics in Britain during the Inter-War Period." *Social History* 13 (3):315–41.

Rogoff, Kenneth. 1990. "Equilibrium Political Budget Cycles." *American Economic Review* 80 (1):21–36.

Rogowski, Ronald. 1987. "Political Cleavages and Changing Exposure to Trade." *American Political Science Review* 81 (4):1121–37.

Romer, Paul. 1990. "Endogenous Technological Change." *Journal of Political Economy* 98 (5):S71–S102.

Roosevelt, Franklin D. 1938. *The Public Papers and Addresses of Franklin D. Roosevelt*. ed. Samuel I. Rosenman. New York: Random House.

Rosenstock, Günther. 1934. *Versicherungstechnische Probleme in der Geschichte der Bismark'schen Sozialgesetzgebung*. Köslin: C.G. Hendeß.

Rudloff, Wilfried. 2000. "Politikberater und opinion-leader? Der Einfluß von Staatswissenschaft und Versicherungsexperten auf die Entstehung der Invaliditäts- und Altersversicherung." In *Geschichte und Gegenwart der Rentenversicherung in Deutschland: Beiträge zur Entstehung, Entwicklung und vergleichenden Einordnung der Alterssicherung im Sozialstaat*, eds. Stefan Fisch and Ulrike Haerendel. Berlin: Duncker & Humblot.

Russell, Mary, and William Chapman. 1977. "Carter's Bailout Plan for Social Security Is Opposed on Hill." *Washington Post*, May 10, A2.

Sailer, Markus. 2004. "Pension Reform in Germany: An Assessment." In *Reforming Public Pensions: Sharing the Experiences of Transition and OECD Countries*. Paris: OECD.

Salant, Walter S. 1989. "The Spread of Keynesian Doctrines and Practices in the United States." In *The Political Power of Economic Ideas: Keynesianism Across Nations*, ed. Peter A. Hall. Princeton: Princeton University Press.

Salazar, Debra J. and Donald K. Alper, eds. 2000. *Sustaining the Forests of the Pacific Coast: Forging Truces in the War in the Woods*. Vancouver, B.C.: UBC Press.

Samuelson, Robert J. 1977. "Social Insecurity." *National Journal*, December 3, 1893.

Savage, Gail. 1996. *The Social Construction of Expertise: The English Civil Service and Its Influence, 1919–1939*. Pittsburgh: University of Pittsburgh Press.

Savage, Leonard Jimmie. 1954. *The Foundations of Statistics*. New York: Wiley.

Savoie, Donald J. 1990. *The Politics of Public Spending in Canada*. Buffalo: University of Toronto Press.

———1999. *Governing from the Centre: The Concentration of Power in Canadian Politics*. Buffalo: University of Toronto Press.

Schieber, Sylvester J., and John B. Shoven. 1999. *The Real Deal: The History and Future of Social Security*. New Haven: Yale University Press.

Schlabach, Theron F. 1969. *Edwin E. Witte: Cautious Reformer*. Madison: State Historical Society of Wisconsin.

Schlesinger, Arthur M., Jr. 1958. *The Coming of the New Deal*. Boston: Houghton Mifflin Company.

Schmähl, Wilfried. 1998. "Discussion of 'The Politics of Pensions: Lessons from Abroad' by R. Kent Weaver." In *Framing the Social Security Debate: Values, Politics, and Economics*, eds. R. Douglas Arnold, Michael J. Graetz and Alicia H. Munnell. Washington, D.C.: National Academy of Social Insurance.

Schmitz, Heinz. 2000a. "Der Weg zum Rentenkonsens führt über Finanzminister Eichel." *Handelsblatt*, June 2.

———2000b. "Gewerkschaften und Sozialverbände machen mobil gegen Rentenpläne." *Handelsblatt*, June 14.

———2000c. "Riester korrigiert sein Rentenkonzept." *Handelsblatt*, June 16.

———2000d. "Rot-Grün ändert Rentenplan." *Handelsblatt*, November 15.

———2000e. "Widerstand gegen Riesters Plan zur Absenkung der Sozialrenten." *Handelsblatt*, June 5.

Schreiber, Wilfrid. 1955. *Existenzsicherheit in der industriellen Gesellschaft: Vorschläge des Bundes Katholischer Unternehmer zur Reform der Sozialversicherung*. Köln: Verlag J.P. Bachem.

Schreurs, Miranda A. 2002. *Environmental politics in Japan, Germany, and the United States*. Cambridge: Cambridge University Press.

Schulze, Isabelle, and Sven Jochem. 2006. "Germany: Beyond Policy Gridlock." In *The Handbook of West European Pension Politics*, eds. Ellen M. Immergut, Karen M. Anderson and Isabelle Schulze. New York: Oxford University Press.

Schulze, Isabelle, and Michael Moran. 2006. "United Kingdom: Pension Politics in an Adversarial System." In *The Handbook of West European Pension Politics*, eds. Ellen M. Immergut, Karen M. Anderson and Isabelle Schulze. New York: Oxford University Press.

Schulze-Cleven, Tobias. Unpublished Manuscript. "A New Politics in the German Welfare State? Pension Policymaking in the 1990s."

Schwennicke, Christoph. 2001. "Union lehnt Rentenpläne der Regierung kategorisch ab." *Süddeutsche Zeitung*, April 2, 1.

Scruggs, Lyle A. 1999. "Institutions and Environmental Performance in Seventeen Western Democracies." *British Journal of Political Science* 29 (1):1–31.

Sears, David. 1993. "Symbolic Politics: A Socio-Psychological Theory." In *Explorations in Political Psychology*, eds. Shanto Iyengar and William J. McGuire. Durham: Duke University Press.

Sears, David, and Carolyn Funk. 1991. "The Role of Self-Interest in Social and Political Attitudes." *Advances in Experimental Social Psychology* 24: 1–91.

Secretary of State for Social Services. 1985. "Reform of Social Security: Programme for Action." London: HMSO.

Séguin, Rhéal. 1996. "Quebec May Double Pension Payments: Rapid Rise in Contribution Rates Proposed to Avoid Danger of Future Shortfalls in Fund." *Globe and Mail*, June 14, A5.

Seldon, Anthony. 1994. "Conservative Century." In *Conservative Century: The Conservative Party since 1900*, eds. Anthony Seldon and Stuart Ball. Oxford: Oxford University Press.

Self, Robert. 2000. *The Evolution of the British Party System 1885–1940*. Harlow: Longman.

Sesit, Michael R., and Suzanne McGee. 1995. "Long-Suffering Canadian Dollar Slips to 8 1/2-Year Low." *Wall Street Journal*, January 11, C1.

Sheingate, Adam D. 2001. *The Rise of the Agricultural Welfare State: Institutions and Interest Group Power in the United States, France, and Japan*. Princeton: Princeton University Press.

Shepsle, Kenneth A. 1979. "Institutional Arrangements and Equilibrium in Multi-Dimensional Voting Models." *American Journal of Political Science* 23 (1):27–59.

Short, Eric. 1985a. "CBI Chiefs Oppose Pensions Reform Plans." *Financial Times*, August 3, 4.

———1985b. "Employers Reject Pensions Reform." *Financial Times*, September 19, 6.

———1986. "CBI Condemns Plan For Pension Switch Bonus." *Financial Times*, April 21, 11.

Simon, Herbert A. 1971. "Designing Organizations for an Information-Rich World." In *Computers, Communication, and the Public Interest*, ed. Martin Greenberger. Baltimore: The Johns Hopkins University Press.

Singer, James W. 1977a. "Carter Is Trying to Make Social Security More Secure." *National Journal*, June 11, 893–5.

———1977b. "Help Is on the Way for the Sagging Social Security System." *National Journal*, October 1, 1535–6.

Siracusa, Joseph M., and David G. Coleman. 2002. *Depression to Cold War: A History of America from Herbert Hoover to Ronald Reagan*. Westport, CT: Praeger/Greenwood.

Skocpol, Theda. 1992. *Protecting Soldiers and Mothers: The Political Origins of Social Policy in the United States*. Cambridge, MA: Belknap Press of Harvard University Press.

Skocpol, Theda, and Edwin Amenta. 1985. "Did Capitalists Shape Social Security?" *American Sociological Review* 50 (4):572–5.

Skocpol, Theda, and Margaret Somers. 1980. "The Uses of Comparative History in Macrosocial Inquiry." *Comparative Studies in Society and History* 22: 174–97.

Skolnikoff, Eugene B. 1999. "The Role of Science in Policy: The Climate Change Debate in the United States." *Environment* 41 (5):16–20, 42–5.

SM. 2000a. "Entscheidung über Rentenkonsens vertagt." *Handelsblatt*, June 14.

———2000b. "Gewerkschaften und Sozialverbände machen mobil gegen Rentenpläne." *Handelsblatt*, June 14.

———2000c. "Kanzler soll Streit um Rentenreform schlichten." *Handelsblatt*, June 8.

———2000d. "SPD will Riesters Rentenkonzept nachbessern." *Handelsblatt*, June 15.

Smith, Eliot R. 1998. "Mental Representation and Memory." In *The Handbook of Social Psychology, Volume I, Fourth Edition*, eds. Daniel T. Gilbert, Susan T. Fiske and Gardner Lindzey. San Francisco: McGraw-Hill.

Smith, Eliot R., and Jamie DeCoster. 2000." Underlying Memory Systems Dual-Process Models in Social and Cognitive Psychology: Conceptual Integration and Links to Underlying Memory Systems." *Personality and Social Psychology Review* 4 (2):108–31.

Sniderman, Paul M. 2000. "Taking Sides: A Fixed Choice Theory of Political Reasoning." In *Elements of Reason: Cognition, Choice, and Bounds of Rationality*, eds. Arthur Lupia, Mathew D. McCubbins and Samuel L. Popkin. New York: Cambridge University Press.

Sniderman, Paul M., Richard A. Brody, and Philip Tetlock. 1991. *Reasoning and Choice: Explorations in Political Psychology*. New York: Cambridge University Press.

Sniderman, Paul M., and John G. Bullock. 2004. "A Consistency Theory of Public Opinion and Political Choice: The Hypothesis of Menu Dependence." In *Studies in Public Opinion: Attitudes, Nonattitudes, Measurement Error, and Change*, eds. Willem E. Saris and Paul M. Sniderman. Princeton: Princeton University Press.

Sniegs, Monika. 1996. "Die Gestaltungskraft der Prognose: Modellrechnungen in der Invaliditäts- und Altersversicherung 1891–1912." Sonderforschungsbereich 186, "Statuspassagen und Risiken im Lebensverlauf," Arbeitspapier des Teilprojekts D1, "Risikobiographie im historischen Wandel des Sozialversicherungssystems." Bremen: Universität Bremen.

"Social Security Bill Passes, Stripped of Student Tax Credit." 1977. *National Journal*, December 17, 1971.

Social Security Board. 1937. *Social Security in America: The Factual Background of the Social Security Act as Summarized from Staff Reports to the Committee on Economic Security.* Washington, D.C.

"Social Security Plan Faces Tough Fight." 1977. *National Journal*, May 14, 765.

"Social Security Rollback Gains Momentum in House." 1978. *National Journal*, April 8, 567.

Solomon, Carmen D. 1986. "Major Decisions in the House and Senate Chambers on Social Security: 1935–1985." Washington, D.C.: Congressional Research Service.

Soroka, Stuart N. 2006. "Good News and Bad News: Asymmetric Responses to Economic Information." *Journal of Politics* 68 (2):372–85.

Sprinz, Detlef F. 2009. "Long-Term Environmental Policy: Definition, Knowledge, Future Research." *Global Environmental Politics* 9 (3):1–8.

Steinmo, Sven. 1993. *Taxation and Democracy: Swedish, British, and American Approaches to Financing the Modern State.* New Haven: Yale University Press.

Steinmo, Sven, Kathleen Thelen, and Frank Longstreth, eds. 1992. *Structuring Politics: Historical Institutionalism in Comparative Analysis.* Cambridge: Cambridge University Press.

Stigler, George. 1971. "The Theory of Economic Regulation." *Bell Journal of Economics* 2 (1):3–21.

Stocks, Bonds, Bills and Inflation: Market Results for 1926–2000. 2000. Chicago: Ibbotson Associates.

Stokes, Susan C. 1996. "Public Opinion and Market Reforms: The Limits of Economic Voting." *Comparative Political Studies* 29 (5):499–519.

Stone, Randall W. 2009. "Sharing Risk in International Politics." *Global Environmental Politics* 9 (3):40–60.

Sumaila, Rashid, and Elizabeth Suatoni. 2005. *Fish Economics: The Benefits of Rebuilding U.S. Ocean Fish Populations.* Vancouver, B.C.: Fisheries Economics Research Unit, Fisheries Center, University of British Columbia.

Swank, Duane. 2002. *Global Capital, Political Institutions, and Policy Change in Developed Welfare States.* New York: Cambridge University Press.

Teles, Steven. 2009. "Transformative Bureaucracy: Reagan's Lawyers and the Dynamics of Political Investment." *Studies in American Political Development* 23 (1):61–83.

Tennstedt, Florian. 2002. "Einleitung." In *Altersversorgungs- und Invalidenkassen: Quellensammlung zur Geschichte der deutschen Sozialpolitik, 1867 bis 1914.* I. Abteilung, Band 6, eds. Florian Tennstedt and Heidi Winter. Darmstadt: Wissenschaftliche Buchgesellschaft.

Tennstedt, Florian, and Heidi Winter, eds. 2002. *Altersversorgungs- und Invalidenkassen: Quellensammlung zur Geschichte der deutschen Sozialpolitik, 1867 bis 1914.* I. Abteilung, Band 6. Darmstadt: Wissenschaftliche Buchgesellschaft.

Teppe, Karl. 1977. "Zur Sozialpolitik des Dritten Reiches am Beispiel der Sozialversicherung." *Archiv für Sozialgeschichte* 17: 195–250.

Thaler, Richard. 1991. *Quasi-Rational Economics*. New York: Russell Sage Foundation.

Thelen, Peter. 2001. "Rentenreform kurz vor dem Abschluss." *Handelsblatt*, January 15.

Traynor, Ian. 1998. "Germans Offered 100-day Rescue." *The Guardian*, August 21, 12.

Tsebelis, George. 1995. *Veto Players: How Political Institutions Work*. Princeton: Princeton University Press.

Tufte, Edward R. 1978. *Political Control of the Economy*. Princeton: Princeton University Press.

Tüselmann, Heinz-Josef. 1998. "Standort Deutschland: German Direct Foreign Investment – Exodus of German Industry and Export of Jobs?" *Journal of World Business* 33 (3):295–313.

Tversky, Amos, and Daniel Kahneman. 1973. "Availability: A Heuristic for Judging Frequency." *Cognitive Psychology* 5 (2):207–32.

——1974. "Judgment under Uncertainty: Heuristics and Biases." *Science* 185 (New Series) (4157):1124–31.

——1991. "Loss Aversion in Riskless Choice: A Reference-Dependent Model." *Quarterly Journal of Economics* 106 (4):1039–61.

Twigg, John. 2001. "Physician, Heal Thyself?: The Politics of Disaster Mitigation." Working Paper 1/2001. London: Benfield Greig Hazard Centre.

Tynes, Sheryl. 1996. *Turning Points in Social Security: From "Cruel Hoax" to "Sacred Entitlement."* Stanford, CA: Stanford University Press.

U.S. House of Representatives. 1935a. Committee on Ways and Means. *Economic Security Act (H.R. 4120)*. First Session, 74th Congress. January 21 to February 12.

——1935b. Committee on Ways and Means. *Social Security Bill (H.R. 7260)*. April 5.

U.S. Senate. 1935. Committee on Finance. *Economic Security Act (S. 1130)*. First Session, 74th Congress. January 22 to February 20.

Ullmann, Hans-Peter. 1979. "Industrielle Interessen und die Enstehung der deutschen Sozialversicherung, 1880–1889." *Historische Zeitschrift* 229: 574–610.

——1981. "German Industry and Bismarck's Social Security System." In *The Emergence of the Welfare State in Britain and Germany*, ed. Wolfgang J. Mommsen (in collaboration with Wolfgang Mock). London: Croom Helm.

Vaughn, Leigh Ann, and Gifford Weary. 2002. "Roles of the Availability of Explanations, Feelings of Ease, and Dysphoria in Judgments about the Future." *Journal of Social and Clinical Psychology* 21 (6):686–704.

Verband Deutscher Rentenversicherungsträger. 2005. *Rentenversicherung in Zahlen 2005*. Berlin: VDR.

Vitols, Sigurt. 2005. "Globalization and the Transformation of the German Model." In *Political Economy and the Changing Global Order*, eds. Richard Stubbs and Geoffrey R. D. Underhill. New York: Oxford University Press.

Vogel, David. 1981. "Why Businessmen Distrust Their State: The Political Consciousness of American Corporate Executives." *British Journal of Political Science* 8 (1):45–78.

——1986. *National Styles of Regulation*. Ithaca: Cornell University Press.

Vonk, R. 1993. "The Negativity Effect in Trait Ratings and in Open-Ended Descriptions of Persons." *Personality and Social Psychology Bulletin* 19 (3):269–78.

Waller, Robert. 1994. "Conservative Electoral Support and Social Class." In *Conservative Century: The Conservative Party since 1900*, eds. Anthony Seldon and Stuart Ball. Oxford: Oxford University Press.

Walley, John. 1972. *Social Security: Another British Failure?* London: Charles Knight & Co.

Walsh, James P., and Gerardo Rivera Ungson. 1991. "Organizational Memory." *The Academy of Management Review* 16 (1):57–91.

Waterbury, John. 1992. "The Heart of the Matter? Public Enterprise and the Adjustment Process." In *The Politics of Economic Adjustment: International Constraints, Distributive Conflicts, and the State*, eds. Stephan Haggard and Robert R. Kaufman. Princeton: Princeton University Press.

Weaver, R. Kent. 1986. "The Politics of Blame Avoidance." *Journal of Public Policy* 6 (4):371–98.

———2003. "Cutting Old-Age Pensions." In *The Government Taketh Away: The Politics of Pain in the United States and Canada*, eds. Leslie A. Pal and R. Kent Weaver. Washington, D.C.: Georgetown University Press.

Weaver, R. Kent, and Leslie A. Pal, eds. 2003. *The Government Taketh Away: The Politics of Pain in the United States and Canada*. Washington, D.C.: Georgetown University Press.

Weeks, Priscilla and Jane M. Packard. 1997. "Acceptance of Scientific Management by Natural Resource Dependent Communities." *Conservation Biology* 11 (1):236–45.

Weingast, Barry R., and William J. Marshall. 1988. "The Industrial Organization of Congress; or, Why Legislatures, Like Firms, Are Not Organized as Markets." *Journal of Political Economy* 96 (1):132–63.

Weingast, Barry R., Kenneth A. Shepsle, and Christopher Johnsen. 1981. "The Political Economy of Benefits and Costs: A Neoclassical Approach to Distributive Politics." *Journal of Political Economy* 89 (4):132–63.

Weir, Margaret. 1989. "Ideas and Politics: The Acceptance of Keynesianism in Britain and the United States." In *The Political Power of Economic Ideas: Keynesianism Across Nations*, ed. Peter A. Hall. Princeton: Princeton University Press.

Weyland, Kurt. 1998. "Swallowing the Bitter Pill: Sources of Popular Support for Neoliberal Reform in Latin America." *Comparative Political Studies* 31 (5):539–68.

Whitten, Guy D., and Harvey D. Palmer. 1999. "Cross-National Analyses of Economic Voting." *Electoral Studies* 18 (1):49–67.

"Widows,' Orphans', and Old Age Contributory Pensions Bill: Report by the Government Actuary on the Financial Provisions of the Bill." 1925. Cmd. 2406, Volume XXIII, 1924–5. London: HMSO.

Williams, Patricia Mary. 1970. *The Development of Old Age Pensions Policy in Great Britain, 1878–1925*. Ph.D. Dissertation. University of London, London.

Williamson, John. 1994. "In Search of a Manual for Technopols." In *The Political Economy of Policy Reform*, ed. John Williamson. Washington, D.C.: Institute for International Economics.

Wilson, Graham K. 1985. *The Politics of Safety and Health: Occupational Safety and Health in the United States and Britain*. New York: Oxford University Press.

Wilson, James Q. 1980. "The Politics of Regulation." In *The Politics of Regulation*, ed. James Q. Wilson. New York: Basic Books.

Witte, Edwin E. 1962. *The Development of the Social Security Act: A Memorandum on the History of the Committee on Economic Security and Drafting and Legislative History of the Social Security Act*. Madison: University of Wisconsin Press.

Wolff, Hertha. 1933. *Die Stellung der Sozialdemokratie zur deutschen Arbeiterversicherungsgesetzgebung von ihrer Entstehung an bis zur Reichsversicherungsordnung*. Thesis.

Rechts- und Staatswissenschaftlichen Fakultät, Albert-Ludwigs-Universität zu Freiburg, Freiburg.

Wood, Stewart. 2001. "Business, Government, and Patterns of Labor Market Policy in Britain and the Federal Republic of Germany." In *Varieties of Capitalism: The Institutional Foundations of Comparative Advantage*, eds. Peter A. Hall and David Soskice. New York: Oxford University Press.

World Bank. 1994. *Averting the Old Age Crisis: Policies to Protect the Old and Promote Growth*. New York: Oxford University Press.

Wright, Joseph. 2008. "To Invest or Insure?: How Authoritarian Time Horizons Impact Foreign Aid Effectiveness." *Comparative Political Studies* 41 (7):971–1000.

Yoshikawa, Hirokazu. 1994. "Prevention as Cumulative Protection: Effects of Early Family Support and Education on Chronic Delinquency and its Risks." *Psychological Bulletin* 115 (1):28–54.

Zaller, John. 1992. *The Nature and Origins of Mass Opinion*. New York: Cambridge University Press.

Zelizer, Julian E. 1998. *Taxing America: Wilbur D. Mills, Congress, and the State, 1945–1975*. New York: Cambridge University Press.

Index